Raising.Your
Business

A Canadian woman's guide
to entrepreneurship

D1417401

Raising Your
Business

A Canadian
woman's guide to
entrepreneurship

Joanne Thomas Yaccato
with Paula Jubinville

Prentice Hall Canada Inc., Scarborough, Ontario

Canadian Cataloguing in Publication Data

Thomas Yaccato, Joanne, 1957–
    Raising your business: a Canadian woman's guide to entrepreneurship

Includes index.
ISBN 0-13-673849-4

1. New business enterprises. 2. New business enterprises – Management.
3. Businesswomen. I. Jubinville, Paula. II. Title.

HD62.5.T46 1998   658.1'1'082   C98-932095-2

© 1998 Joanne Thomas Yaccato
Prentice Hall Canada Inc.
Scarborough, Ontario
A Division of Simon & Schuster/A Viacom Company

Prentice-Hall, Inc., Upper Saddle River, New Jersey
Prentice-Hall International (UK) Limited, London
Prentice-Hall of Australia, Pty. Limited, Sydney
Prentice-Hall Hispanoamericana, S.A., Mexico City
Prentice-Hall of India Private Limited, New Delhi
Prentice-Hall of Japan, Inc., Tokyo
Simon & Schuster Southeast Asia Private Limited, Singapore
Editora Prentice-Hall do Brasil, Ltda., Rio de Janeiro

ISBN 0-13-673849-4

Director, Trade Group: Robert Harris
Editor: Tanya Long
Copy Editor: Catharine Haggert
Assistant Editor: Joan Whitman
Production Coordinator: Shannon Potts
Cover and Interior Design: Mary Opper
Cover Image: Kirk McGregor
Page Layout: Zena Denchik/Joan Wilson

1 2 3 4 5 RRD 02 01 00 99 98

Printed and bound in the U.S.A.

Visit the Prentice Hall Canada Web site! Send us your comments, browse our
catalogues, and more. **www.phcanada.com**

To Michael and Kate
For giving me the space, the love,
and the reason to do this.

About the Authors

Joanne Thomas Yaccato is the president and founder of Women and Money Inc., a consulting firm that specializes in education and research in the area of women as consumers, investors, and entrepreneurs. She has been nominated twice for Ernst & Young's Entrepreneur of the Year Award. Joanne is the host of *Pocketbook,* a CTV News1 program. Her previous book, *Balancing Act: A Canadian Woman's Financial Success Guide,* was a national bestseller.

Paula Jubinville is a chartered accountant by trade, though not by nature. She is co-founder and president of AQUEOUS Advisory Group Inc., a firm that specializes in providing business advice and support to Canadian entrepreneurs and uniquely to women who are starting, running, and growing their own businesses.

Contents

1   Becoming the Woman I Am: The Creation of an Entrepreneur   1

Joanne's company grew so fast that she almost lost it a year after it started. This is an account of what not to do.

2   Conception   13

There are as many ways to come up with a business idea as there are people who have them. This chapter helps people recognize the creative process and guides them through it.

What Moves Us? **14** ▪ So, What Do You Want to Be When You Grow Up? **21** ▪ Am I an Entrepreneur Yet? **33**

3   Giving Birth   35

As painful as childbirth is, business birth can rival the experience. But with advanced planning and knowledge, it can be almost as exhilarating. What you need to begin thinking about: sales and marketing, technology, whether to be home-based or off-site, and on your own or with someone else.

Different Types of Business Births **38** ▪ Planning for a Healthy Business Birth **49** ▪ The Art of Planning Your Business **52** ▪ Stay in Touch With Your Goals **55** ▪ Test the Waters **59** ▪ Anticipate Life's Little Bumps **75** ▪ What Do You Need to Make Your Dream Happen? **78** ▪ Show Me the Money **86** ▪ Should You Move Away from Home? Pros and Cons of a Home Office **93** ▪ Incorporate? Sole Proprietor? Partnership? **97** ▪ Business, Government, and Tax Accounts **113** ▪ The Business Birth Experience **116** ▪ The Biological Birth Experience — Welcoming Kate **116**

4 The First Year   119

What you need to know about hiring, accounting, taxes, keeping sane, what technology to buy, how to sell, what happens after the first deal is closed, and how and where to get financing.

5 The Toddler Years   208

Years 2 to 4 and how to keep pace with growth. Sales and marketing, technology, human resources, financing — all the same topics, but as they pertain to the middle years.

Epilogue   298

Good Lord, you've made it. The fifth year in business is a pivotal one, with huge decisions to be made about future direction.

Acknowledgments

Writing *Raising Your Business* has clearly demonstrated to me why acknowledgments exist. When I wrote *Balancing Act*, I was a solo act. I had trouble getting a date, let alone thinking about being married or having a baby. I didn't have employees and my banker was any faceless teller machine.

How life has changed. I'm now a busy wife and mother, business owner, boss and writing partner. Finishing this book was no small task. Ask my publisher. Twelve minutes after signing the contract, I got pregnant. This book is two years late. Thank you Prentice Hall for so easily rolling with the punches.

And thank you from the most bottom place of my heart, Michael and darling Kate. Your extraordinary patience and humour were my lifeline. Our nanny, Marilyn (family member, really), went well beyond the call of duty to see that I stayed sane and balanced. She literally kicked Michael and I out of the house a least a couple of times a month to go out on a soul-restoring date.

My company would not exist if not for the skill and independent spirit of my general manager, Rosa. Can you imagine working for someone you don't even see for weeks on end? She took over everything for almost a year. Frankly, I'm just a tad miffed it turned out to be the best year we ever had.

My parents have always been front and centre in the cheering section, no matter what weirdness I embarked upon. This book was no exception.

I'm not kidding when I say this book would not be here if it weren't for Denise Araiche and Angus Hutchinson, my bankers. Concerned about how I was going to financially handle running a business and writing a book, they said, "Do what ever it takes, Joanne. We'll be here." No matter how high our operating line may have ballooned, the only calls I received were ones of encouragement. You two give bankers a very good name.

Paula and I would like to acknowledge our technical team for their sometimes brutal honesty and enthusiasm for this project. This book is a million percent better because of their involvement. However, any technical errors are solely Paula and mine's responsibility. Thank you Leslie Slater, Margaret Cusimano, Doug Gray, Andrina Lever, Barbara Caldwell, Mona Bandeen, Betty Wood, Anne Sutherland, Sherry Fotheringham, Audrey Vrooman, Sabine Schleese, Lou Martins, Ellen Roseman, Tasha Taklovich, Caroline Hamill-

Best, and Karen O'Bireck. Thank you Karen Bodirsky. You gave "slashing through the red tape" a whole new meaning. Also, a very special acknowledgment to the women who shared their stories with us. You have given this book soul.

Paula would also like to personally acknowledge the hundreds of business clients who have shared and entrusted their entrepreneurial dilemmas, solutions, frustrations, and victories with her over the years. She thanks both her business family, partner Debbie, Sandy and associates, and her immediate family, husband Aidan, brother Brent, mommy and dad, for their extra support, love, and encouragement while writing this book.

As for you Paula, I thank you, my friend. You have shown me what partnership and patience really mean.

Foreword
by Pamela Wallin

Serendipity, lack of alternatives, instinct, no fear of hard work — all are forces that lead women down the entrepreneurial path. But whether you're a reluctant recruit or a willing participant, learning to navigate the unpredictable waters of the marketplace will be an emotional and exhausting, but ultimately exhilarating, ride.

As Charles Darwin reminds us, it is not just the fit or the smart that survive, it is those who are the most adaptable to change. Or as the boys of business would say, you have to learn to roll with the punches. The marketplace is indeed an unpredictable world ruled by needs, by wants and whims, and by constant change. You will function creatively and thrive financially only if your antennae are well tuned. Fortunately, this comes naturally to many women.

I am President of a company, the Current Affairs Group, in which nearly all of the participants are women. People ask whether this was deliberate, was I making a political point or a sisterly statement. No, I simply set out to hire the best and the brightest. The women are smart, well read, thoughtful, and hard working. But there is something else in their attitude that defines a special and valuable work ethic. It's not only a willingness to put in long hours and stay till the task is done. It's their desire to make change, inform minds, and make a difference. And in the process, to treat consumers with respect and as if they are intelligent. This approach is crucial in both understanding the mission of the enterprise and those it is designed to serve. Perhaps it's no accident that most of the job-creating and successful new businesses in Canada are being conceived by women.

My business, as is the case in most entrepreneurial enterprises, is about people. And women have an intuitive sense about others. We are not afraid to ask questions and we actually listen to the answers. We hear more accurately. This is not some reverse sexist slander but facts found in the academic research of Dr. Deborah Tannen, one of the world's leading thinkers on communication and gender. She and others suggest that while men listen and talk about what's going on, women really listen and then talk about what's really going on. That sensitivity, intuition, and emotion can be huge benefits in business if they are harnessed for entrepreneurial ends.

May lightning strike, but women, it now appears, are capable of running car companies or steel mills, and not only beauty parlours or human resource departments. Though let me be quick to add that when my sister and I set out to open a hairdressing salon several years back, the bank refused our request for a measly five thousand dollar loan. The refusal was because my sister is married to a farmer, which conveniently ignored the more pertinent fact that between the two of us we had been more than 40 years in the work world, earning solid pay cheques larger than either of our spouses'. But live and learn. That setback only served as a challenge. We would, for our own satisfaction, prove their policies and their judgment wrong. This and other such constraints have convinced me that in fact many of the perceived disadvantages can be blessings in disguise, because they force you to think and work smarter.

I am, by nature, not risk-averse, but neither am I foolhardy. Debt is an anathema to me. I like to pay my bills and earn my own keep. So why then did I choose the frustrations, the tears, and the fears of a life lived with uncertainty, unpredictability, and unknowns? I, like millions of others, found myself at odds with a corporation and out on the street with nothing but my journalistic reputation and experience to sell. But my belief in the intelligence of viewers and their willingness to choose fair and respectful journalism was motivation enough. The hours have been long and the learning curve steep, but the rewards of building and running my own company have far exceeded my expectations. You can, I now know, choose to live and create in a world inhabited by doers and thinkers who pursue ideas and work, not just pay cheques and job security.

So whether it is the beauty parlour or the television production company, the goals are the same. See a need, fill a need. Have an idea? Create a customer. Hear a question, offer an answer. It's about trusting your own instinct and about being "an avid seeker and consumer of advice." And it's about being willing to ask questions and ask for help. Declare your head a testosterone-free zone. Embarking on a risky venture takes courage and confidence but not necessarily ego. It also takes hard work and understanding from those around you.

After reading Joanne's first book, *Balancing Act,* it seemed inevitable that chronicling the lessons learned as an entrepreneur would become her next project. She is a consummate storyteller with a remarkable gift for combining the sobering with the hilarious, while distilling invaluable information for the benefit of Canadian women with business in their blood.

Reading *Raising Your Business* is like déjà vu all over again. The confessions, stories, and insights that fill the pages that follow will amuse you, anger you, inspire you, and reinforce the belief that women are naturals despite the roadblocks, both institutional and cultural, that still exist. They are compelling stories because each of us who has tried, failed, or succeeded is by definition a role model. And if we want to leave the indelible imprint of a high heel on the business landscape, we will have to re-invent the rules chiselled on the walls of the business hall of fame. We will have to be impatient with mediocrity, both strive for and expect perfection, and cherish the short attention span that sparks creativity. And we will shed both tears and our fears in the process.

Pamela Wallin
Toronto

Introduction

I was in my favourite bookstore, leafing through a women's magazine, when the title of an article jumped out at me: "Women Business Owners—Canada's Exploding Trend." Always thrilled to be part of an "explosion," I approached with great interest the writer's description of the typical woman entrepreneur. As I began to read, I thought, not without a little sarcasm, "Wow, imagine being able to figure out what a typical woman entrepreneur is when women are a mere 52 percent of the population representing every age, race, religion, socio-economic class, and education level." Though I was one and had read tons of material on women entrepreneurs, I thought maybe the author knew something I didn't.

But this account was no different from the others: Women get into their own businesses so they can find time to balance their lives. Women tend to be conservative and risk-averse. Women are afraid of success. The vast majority of women-owned businesses grew from "hobbies," most of which are home-based or in the retail sector, yadda, yadda, yadda. Frustrated, I put the magazine back and thought, "Why don't I ever see myself in these stories?"

Of course, some businesses do, but *my* company did not evolve from a hobby. It evolved, as many do, from passion. The greatest area of growth for women entrepreneurs is agribusiness and financial services, not retail. I'm not exclusively home-based. I am not, nor ever have been, averse to risk. And afraid of success? I can't imagine a more ludicrous notion. And if it was more time I wanted in order to be balanced, why did I start my own business?

Staring at that magazine cover, the seed of an idea for a second book began to germinate. I scoured the bookshelves and saw two kinds of books that women entrepreneurs had to choose from. The first kind—purely technical reference books and usually American—was in abundance. The second kind was made up entirely of profiles, stories of fascinating women, but no "news you could use."

"Well, there it is," I thought to myself. "Wouldn't it be great to write a book that combines both worlds, the experiential and the technical; a 'how it is' book as well as a 'how to' book? How about a book about our lives that's actually useful to the 'just-thinking-about-it' women or women entrepreneurs within their first five years of business?"

Over the next few months I contemplated how I was going to have the time to write a book as comprehensive as I dreamed. A solution fell right into my lap in the form of Paula Jubinville. Paula is a business adviser/accountant who specializes in helping women start and grow their own businesses. I was convinced she would bring an amazing depth and breadth to this book. With her technical expertise and my experience, we decided to join forces to create a most unusual business book. I would provide the heart, she would provide the teeth.

Why is this book so unusual? Well, most women I know, including those who don't have children, often refer to their business as "my baby." And it was during my second year in business, at the tender age of 37, that I had my daughter Kate. I was profoundly struck by the similarities of the experience of conceiving, giving birth to, and raising both my biological and business babies. Biologically or in business, conception and the pregnancy phase, birth, the first year, and the toddler years are all very different from each other. You conceive the business idea and grow it to the point that it can be born strong and healthy. You take the first year to nurture the business, tenderly guiding it, looking after all of its most basic needs. Once your business reaches the toddler stage, you let it venture out cautiously to explore and expand in the world.

Paula and I felt that this analogy of "raising a business" would be very real to women. And though we equate raising a business to raising a family, we don't necessarily mean a family in the traditional sense. Paula's family, for instance, doesn't happen to be of the two-legged variety. Her family is her husband Aidan (okay, he has two legs), her dog Sheila, and two cats. The analogy works for her, as it does for the hundreds of thousands of other women in different family units, whether a unit of one or a unit of blended families.

Raising Your Business chronicles the life cycle of a business. With my story as the glue, each chapter deals with a different part of the process, from conception of the business idea, the planning that goes into the birth of a business, the screaming meemies of the first year, and finally the toddler years, up to and including age five, when you are likely to be confronted with growth issues. Each chapter revisits the requirements and issues around human resources, accounting, financial management, technology, and sales and marketing, but as they pertain to that particular phase of the business and to you as a woman entrepreneur. The bottom line? You've got to read the whole book to get the whole story.

My mother laughs and says my role in life is to fall down, bump my chin, scrape my knee, get up, and write about it. In the spirit of my first book, *Balancing Act: A Canadian Woman's Financial Success Guide,* which chronicled my life as a financial reprobate, this book is filled with painfully honest details of the many mistakes that I've made as a struggling entrepreneur. After *Balancing Act* came out in 1994, my business accelerated into overdrive overnight. In 1995, I got pregnant. Having no benefits, I was unprepared financially to manage an unpaid maternity leave. The rapid growth and the pregnancy resulted in me almost losing my business. But not only did I survive, I thrived. Today I run a going concern and Kate is a daring, dynamic three-year-old.

This book is not just a business reference manual. It's not a storybook of "successful" women business owners. And it most assuredly is not just my story. It takes the technical and the experiential, the logical and emotional, and marries them. Kind of like life. We've included real-life examples of how women across the country, across industries, and across stage and size have dealt with their own entrepreneurial dilemmas. This book gives women entrepreneurs an opportunity to share their worlds, experiences, dreams, insanity, dilemmas, resolutions, temper tantrums, fumbles and victories.

Paula and I agree that writing this book has been a cathartic experience. As we sifted through the experiences of the last five years, we were both left feeling dumbfounded and very proud of what we had accomplished. The fact that I, who six short years ago didn't know the difference between accounts receivable and accounts payable, have gained enough in perspective and experience to collaborate on a book like this is nothing short of miraculous.

Trust me. You're in for the ride of your life.

Finding
Her Here

I am becoming the woman I've wanted,
grey at the temples,
cracked up by life
with a laugh that's known bitter
but, past it, got better,
knows she's a survivor —
that whatever comes,
she can outlast it.
I am becoming a deep
            weathered basket.

I am becoming the woman I've longed for,
the motherly lover
with arms strong and tender,
the growing up daughter
who blushes surprises.
I am becoming full moons
            and sunrises.

I find her becoming,
this woman I've wanted,
who knows she'll encompass,
who knows she's sufficient,
knows where she's going
and travels with passion.
Who remembers she's precious,
but knows she's not scarce —
who knows she is plenty
            plenty to share.

Jayne Raleford Brown

1 Becoming the Woman I Am

The Creation of an Entrepreneur

*Barbara Caldwell, National Chair of
the Canadian Woman Entrepreneur of the Year
Awards, spoke at a conference in Saskatchewan.
During the question-and-answer period,
a woman from the audience asked:
"I'm trying to decide whether to start a
business or have a child. What would
you suggest?" Barb answered, "Start a business.
At least if it doesn't work out, you can sell it."*

"My life is a quintessential *Seinfeld* episode," I groaned, staring at the labyrinth of frost designs developing on my kitchen window. It was a numbingly cold March day, the kind that makes even the heartiest of skiers cower deeper into their duvets.

I was utterly miserable.

"Let me, just once, meet one of those delusional Pollyannas who go around expounding the mythical joys of owning your own business...," I ranted aloud to no one in particular. It was 7:30 a.m. and I was indulging my recently developed sugar craving by mainlining a second piece of leftover angel food cake — the proverbial breakfast of champions. "These experts are smart enough to tell you how to run your own business and too smart to start one of their own." The kitchen clock stared blankly back in silent agreement. Muttering, I slammed the refrigerator door shut with my foot while precariously balancing the jug of milk and a mountain-sized piece of cake. "What I wouldn't give to run into one of them now." An image of a car bumper flashed quickly through my mind. Only slightly horrified, I dismissed the image.

Though I was totally responsible for the mess I was in, I still found myself contemplating the media's much-hyped picture of the self-employed. Once upon a time I believed all that enthusiastic hype about being your own boss. I opined with the best of them about the benefits of controlling your destiny, balancing work and family life, being independent, and helping others to achieve a true sense of purpose in their work life. Lately, however, I felt more and more like I was attached to a bungee cord balanced at the edge of a very steep cliff with someone else's foot planted squarely on my butt. The sign on my office door read, "You might as well come in. Everything else has gone wrong today."

In the spirit of the avid X-Filer that I was, I was convinced that this self-employment craze was all illusory, some kind of evil plot instigated by a mysterious, elitist corporate and government consortium to suck dry the free will and contrarian spirit of millions of innocent victims and drive them back into the waiting arms of a grinning and solicitous "big brother."

As a business owner, I could control when I went to the washroom, but my destiny? Ask the bank. Independent? Ask the bank. Balancing work and family? Not so far. I did, however, tenaciously hold on to the last credo. I was making a difference. It was just sometimes hard to remember that when you see all your sweat, passion, and money sink into a big black hole.

I was having a really bad 120 days.

Fuelled by sugar and adrenalin, my fingers tapped incessantly on the phone as my stomach and mind churned over the heartbreaking call I had just received. Michelle MacIsaac, my general manager and chief cheerleader, had been with me a short six months, but in those six months she had seen a thriving, going concern do an abrupt about-face. An escapee from corporate Canada, Michelle was overwhelmed at the monumental stress that had become a permanent companion since she also fell into the clutches of the evil plot. Her voice was cracking with emotion as she ended our difficult conversation. "I need the weekend to figure things out. I'll let you know on Monday if I can stick it out with you."

Her call came as no surprise. If there was someone I could call to say "I quit," I'd be burning up the old Alexander Graham Bell myself. The reality was, however, as chief cheese, I'd be having the conversation with myself. Not that that was an issue, really. Talking to myself was not an uncommon occurrence these days.

Michelle's call was just one more disaster in the maelstrom called my life. Everything felt like it was in shambles. This day, like the last 120 or so, dawned with my self-esteem completely battered. Falling and staying asleep was a daunting challenge. As a result, I suffered from unbearable exhaustion. My healthy eating and exercise regime that had been consistent for years totally vanished. These days, my only exercise came from strenuous acts of phone slamming, head pounding, and hair pulling. I had become aware of a chronic soreness developing in my jaw, neck, and back from clenched teeth and tensed muscles. Every time I got up out of a chair, I heaved a sigh that carried the weight of angst and worry of a person far older than myself.

Most startling was my memory loss. I prided myself on having a near photographic memory. I had an uncanny ability to remember things like my paper carrier's aunt's daughter-in-law's birthday. Lately, however, it was a supreme effort to remember my address. I would call the office with an urgent issue and by the time Michelle picked up the phone, I had completely forgotten why I had called. Though we often laughed about it and chalked up these memory meltdowns to severe sensory overload, I was beginning to grow alarmed. Even my razor-sharp decision-making faculties were being affected. Michelle broke up one day when I snapped at her, "My decision is maybe and that's final!" Later I learned that sleep disturbances, memory loss, difficulty making decisions, and a sense of being constantly overwhelmed are all signs of serious medical conditions that run the gamut from chronic fatigue syndrome to clinical depression. But I was too tired, too overwhelmed; I just plain forgot to do anything about it.

I would attempt to boost myself with a daily "Cheer up, it can't get worse," only to be dumbfounded as things got worse. Much worse. I lurched from one catastrophe to another. Each day brought relentless worry, mind-numbing confusion from rushed hiring decisions, non-performing salespeople, escalating financial obligations, a vanishing market, the hair-raising costs of developing new markets, declining revenues, an obliterated bank balance, spiralling debt load, and desperate manoeuvring with suppliers, clients, bankers, and anxious employees. Things were so bad I couldn't wait for them to improve so I could afford to have a nervous breakdown.

Gulping down stale cake, I asked myself for the umpteenth time, "Exactly why the hell am I doing this? Do I really hate steady paycheques, stable work environments, and company benefits that much?"

I could hardly believe that I was a mere hairsbreadth away from throwing in the towel and taking huge personal, professional, and financial losses. And this after growing, in under 12 months, from a one-person basement operation to a company with three full-time and two part-time staff and a quarter-million dollars in revenue. And that quarter million was solely from the first part of the company's mission statement, *"educating women about money."* We had yet to delve into the other seriously needed and lucrative part of our mission — *"educating financial institutions about women."*

Swallowing hard, I struggled to stuff down a surge of panic. I was slowly coming to the realization that I had been woefully ill equipped to handle this new world of being responsible for my own business. I had not been prepared to reach this zenith (albeit small, but a zenith nonetheless) in such a relatively short time. I mused aloud, "If I had known then what I know now...would I have done it anyway? What would I have done differently? What could I have done differently?" Then I got hit with a wild case of "theshoulduvs": "I should have researched more....I should have done a better business plan....I should have done more sales and marketing....I should have spent less...."

Wearily I slumped back in my chair, resting my aching head, and closed my eyes. In order to escape the trauma and searing isolation I was feeling, my mind began to wander, leaving that place where bad things were happening.

Let me say straight out that I had never run a business, never aspired to run a business, and was never trained to run a business. Though I came from a long line of entrepreneurs, my father's bankruptcy when I was at the tender age of 18 cured me of that aspiration. But I was never comfortable as a corporate animal either. I did my own thing my own way, always pushing the envelope. Sometimes this worked. Often it didn't. I was characterized as being an "excellent performer, but often operating outside the lines."

As a senior account executive for a major computer company, I was responsible for managing major national accounts and routinely handled transactions in the hundreds of thousands of dollars. And even though I had made ridiculous amounts of money during the '80s computer boom, I lived my life as a financial reprobate. I had no personal savings of any kind and was buried under an avalanche of debt. My credit cards were showing symptoms of chronic fatigue syndrome. The only thing I knew about an RRSP was how to spell it. Here I was, year after year earning a six-digit income, and I still found myself peering out from behind the curtain when the doorbell rang in fear of those pit bulls disguised as bill collectors. I discovered that one of my clients, an insurance company, had developed a marketing concept targeting women. The idea was to provide financial planning for women in the hope that women would then buy the company's financial products. I decided to become one of *their* clients.

It was a slow process, but I pulled myself out of the financial quagmire I had created. The healthier my financial picture got, the more fascinated I became with the issues of women and their attitudes and belief systems around money. Perplexed and disturbed at how many women of every age bracket end up in dire financial straits (my grandmother, my mother, my sister, myself …), I turned my sights on becoming a specialist in understanding these issues. Even though I wasn't an accountant or a tax lawyer, an investment counsellor or an economist, my undeniable expertise in money management came from the fact I had none. Anyone could learn the technical stuff. I shocked my peers not only by resigning, but by taking six months off to get the required licensing to start a new life in a new career specializing in financial planning for women. I then went to work for my client.

I was hired by the insurance company as an independent contractor or "intrapreneur." This meant I was more or less on my own, responsible for running my "own company" as it were, but I still had an umbilical cord attached to some of the benefits of corporate Canada, such as a group RRSP, tax deducted at source, brochures, paper clips, administrative support, a phone, and, as long as my sales figures remained high, an office to sweeten the pie. This type of independent contractor set-up provided the perfect first step in the direction of running my own business.

Over the five years I spent as a financial adviser, I discovered a reality that would eventually become my *raison d'être*. I saw first hand how pronounced the differences were between women and men in their perceptions of and motivations to understand money. I also witnessed disturbing examples of women receiving imbalanced and stereotypical financial advice. For example, I overheard my co-worker Bob say, "Being a young woman, she's likely to be very risk-averse. So she can sleep at night, I recommended her $100,000 go into GICs." Yech.

I conducted monthly focus groups for research purposes. The focus groups were pivotal in my understanding of how women were different from men in so many areas of our lives. Women told me they didn't trust the financial services industry and hated cold calls and high-pressure sales. These women told me they were annoyed at constantly being referred to as "risk-averse" when, once equipped with information, they would invest in the stock market and mutual funds as quickly as any man. They were gratified to see their economic power finally recognized by purveyors of goods and services, but they were generally suspicious of superficial "marketing to women" campaigns.

They all agreed women's communication style was very different from men's and that the difference often led to misunderstandings and wrong impressions. These same women were gravely concerned about the financial price tag attached to child bearing. While off on maternity leave or home full-time raising families, women suffered a dramatic loss of contribution power to RRSPs and CPP.

These and other revelations had considerable impact on me. Being inside the financial services industry, I was in an interesting position to witness how few advisers actually got it. There were the beginnings of attempts to attract women investors and entrepreneurs. This was typically in the form of "women-only" seminars, complete with pink invitations and a free rose. I was offended, as were many like me. Pink is a colour, not a marketing strategy. I listened to my male peers as they expressed confusion about the motivations and methodology of many of their women clients. I heard the stereotypical view that the only women who had real money were those who married it or outlived their partners. If women were business owners, it was because Dr. Hubby had enough money to let her go out and dabble in her "little hobby."

I had established a thriving, well-known financial planning practice so it made sense to begin thinking about establishing an identity of my own. I was growing more frustrated seeing my blood, sweat, and tears being poured into something entirely for the benefit of someone else. As well, my income was into six digits. So, for identity and tax purposes, I decided to incorporate and become Women and Money Inc. I was still supported by the corporation but I now had my own personal shingle to hang. The vision of my company was to provide relevant quality financial advice to women. But in short order, it was clear that God in her infinite wisdom had other plans for me.

I had developed a relationship with the media as an expert on women and money. I guess this caught my publisher's eye, because they approached me to write a book on financial planning for women. After lengthy discussions with Mom and with my mentor, Dave Chilton of *Wealthy Barber* fame, as well as a few sleepless nights of soul-searching, I took the plunge and re-signed. In one dramatic moment, I went from the creature comforts of cor-porate life to being "Me Inc." I traded in the corporate navy blues and manicures for sweat pants and green fuzzy slippers. The only word that de-scribed the feeling was a gigantic "GULP."

I now had to figure out how I was going write a book. My closest expe-rience to writing was a diary I had kept for approximately three weeks when I was 13. Trusting the only thing I had to go on — instinct — I leaped into action. My first major task as president and CEO of the now independent Women and Money Inc. was to give myself a year off. I put all my belongings in storage and moved to a friend's farm near a small hamlet called Everett. I lived off my book advance and my savings for a year. Considering a night out was a trip into town to Pizza Hut, I believed my money would hold out.

A year later, *Balancing Act: A Canadian Woman's Financial Success Guide* was a reality. I was absolutely heartbroken at the prospect of returning to the city. But it doesn't take a rocket scientist to figure out that running a business that targets corporate Canada was going to be tough from a barn located al-most two hours away. Luckily, a friend who was a single mom with two ac-tive kids offered to share her home as a stop gap for a few months until I could see what kind of income would be generated by my ideas. I set up shop in her basement, which I nicknamed "The Pit." I relaunched Women and Money Inc. in April 1994, one month after moving into "The Pit," more than a year after I had incorporated, and the month *Balancing Act* hit the bookstores. Nothing could have prepared me for the wild ride.

Originally, Women and Money Inc. was to be a financial planning com-pany. However, after a year away communing with nature, I had an epiphany. I was haunted by the fact that 79 percent of the financial advisers in this country are men. I figured out that I needed to get to the place where most of the advice to women was being disseminated — the *educators* themselves. I was committed to the idea that if I could educate the educators — mostly male bankers, brokers, advisers, and planners — about the realities of women's lives, women would benefit on two fronts. That is how the vision became a company mission statement: *Women and Money Inc. — Educating women about money and educating financial institutions about women.*

I was in rather interesting shape to start a business. All I had was a book and a business concept. I had no office, no staff, and no clients. And, after a year without money or any source of income, going to the bank would have been a suicide mission. I had to use my personal line of credit not only to get started, but also to pay the rent.

Writing cheque after cheque for pens, paper, computer, software, printer, fax machine, desk, chair, waste paper basket, mouse pad, brochures, letterhead and business card design and printing, calculator, desk lamp, the occasional lunch with clients, postage, couriers, photocopies, occasional contract administrative help, accounting help, phone installation costs, long-distance phone bills, and so on, and so on was a heart-gripping experience. The cheque writing didn't stop there. My RRSP contribution, life and disability insurance payments were now absolutely mandatory since I had joined the ranks of the self-employed.

One of the toughest adjustments was having to make decisions in areas I knew absolutely nothing about. In fact, I knew nothing about 80 percent of what had now become my standard job description. At first glance, anyone with an IQ over 60 would wonder why I would embark on such folly as becoming president and chief everything officer of my own company. As my mother was quick to point out, my personality would make for some interesting dynamics in this new role. I had always detested math and any of its derivatives, especially anything to do with money (outside of making it). My eyes glazed over at talk of balance sheets and I stumbled over the difference between accounts receivable and accounts payable. Consequently, I was a natural for the accounting function. Being a big picture, arm-wavy sales and marketing type, I came well prepared for dealing with the gruelling, minute details of business planning. Having the attention span of a gnat helped me remain organized in the face of the 19 things that needed to be dealt with immediately. This made me a prime candidate for the painstaking, time-consuming job of hiring staff and choosing suppliers.

But, when *Balancing Act* hit the shelves, the heart and soul of the company emerged with a vengeance. The first half of the company's mission statement — *educating women about money* — was a huge success. The book held a message whose time had come. It took off like a rocket, selling a mind-boggling 50,000 copies. Overnight, the pace of my life went from a laid-back farm lifestyle to insanity. I was working around the clock trying to keep up with the media demand and speaking requests. I found myself crisscrossing the country at a furious rate on the circuit speaking to thousands of women. As if I wasn't kept busy enough on the speaking circuit, the media created what amounted to another full-time job. I must have been interviewed by every television and radio station, newspaper, and magazine in this country. I also began writing feature pieces for a variety of newspapers and magazines as well as a monthly personal finance column for *Chatelaine*.

I clearly needed help. So at way too early a stage, I took the plunge and hired a salesperson, and shortly thereafter, an admin person to help me manage the chaos. Barb and Michelle offered tremendous support and in the beginning eased the workload considerably. But that would change. Right in the middle of this meltdown, Barb would leave the company under the worst possible circumstances. Think lawyers and the Ministry of Labour.

This frenetic lifestyle concealed two phenomena: I was becoming more and more isolated without a constant network of peers and co-workers, and my personal life decreased proportionately with the increase in business responsibilities. Eventually, work took over completely. Every day I got out of bed, made coffee, and stumbled into my office across from the bedroom anywhere between 5:00 and 6:00 a.m. Though I loved not battling Toronto's revolting traffic, a home office made it easier to abuse the sought-after dream of balance. It was much too easy to slip into the office "for a quick minute" on Saturdays or Sundays, only to discover the entire afternoon had disappeared. Still, I reasoned, it was my life, my creation, and my essence. It was worth every anxiety-filled moment and all those Friday and Saturday nights home alone with the cache of chocolate and videos.

The strenuous pace was made possible by the fact that I was single and had no life. By no life I mean any significant, insignificant, or even imaginary other. I had no children, which I had very much wanted since the age of four. I hadn't been in touch with any of my friends other than three-minute hits on the phone every few months. I wanted more than anything to create a job description for myself that was more normal, but *I* was the company. Along with running the business, I and only I did the speaking, the writing, and the media relations. The next monumental task was to create something that was relevant and remained in the context of my mission statement but one that other life forms could do as well as or instead of me.

I saw the *educating financial institutions about women* part of the mission statement as the answer. I began to develop training courses to teach bankers, brokers, and financial planners how to properly reach the women's market. I often joked that my job was to teach financial service professionals how to stop pissing off women investors and entrepreneurs. All seemed relatively co-pacetic as money from the speaking business began to flow in. Yet strangely enough, we were always in a cash crunch.

Enter Paula Jubinville.

Paula's company, AQUEOUS Advisory Group, specialized in helping women entrepreneurs start and grow their businesses. For our first meeting, we agreed to meet at the King Edward Hotel in downtown Toronto for high tea. As we settled in for a very civilized hour of tea and scones, I found myself chuckling at Paula's introduction of herself — an accountant by trade, not by nature.

During the course of the conversation, I casually alluded to some of the headaches I was experiencing with the business. She listened patiently and offered a few well-chosen words of empathy, encouragement, and support. It suddenly hit me how alone I was. Her quiet compassion and innate understanding of what I was going through struck a chord. I had been convinced I was the only person in the universe experiencing what I was experiencing and that everything was my fault because I was incompetent and a lousy person all the way around. You can't imagine the relief when she told me both she and her clients often felt the same way. The connection with her was not an intellectual one but a gut-level emotional one born of shared experience. I hired her on the spot.

Meanwhile, back at the ranch, it was becoming increasingly difficult to fit my work into someone else's family life. The activity being generated in that basement was astounding and began to change the dynamic of the home I was a boarder in. Once again, it was time to go. Barb and Michelle also worked from their own homes. It doesn't take a genius to figure out that this arrangement, if not managed properly, could be hell. So, while keeping an office in my new home, I decided to move the rest of the staff into a central office in downtown Toronto. I also hired the services of a bookeeper and of Paula to help manage the dreaded accounting function. My heart rate increased proportionally with the size of the cheques that now had to be written.

You can guess what happened next. Approximately 12 minutes after I took on these huge additional financial obligations, the shoe dropped. It was February 1995 and the market crashed big time. The speaking business came to a grinding halt. Our intention had always been to offer a full range of services to our market, and to do it in a step-by-step, organized, and well-planned manner. But now we had to launch into hyperspeed. Throughout this period I kept thinking, "Thank God I had corporate training programs as part of the plan." However, it wasn't too long before we all began to feel overworked, underappreciated, misunderstood, deeply stressed, and financially strained. There was no way to cut costs because we were already running as lean and mean as possible.

In the midst of all these crises, what little that was left of my personal life evaporated. I began saying no to all social engagements because invariably some catastrophe would intervene and I would have to cancel at the last minute. Close friends began the annoying habit of tsk-tsking and gravely shaking their heads when the topic of my social life came up. Words like celibacy, old maid, and monk sprinkled our conversations. One day in mid-November, I got a call from a friend who allowed absolutely no wiggle room when I attempted to hedge out of her invitation to a Grey Cup party. Very grudgingly, I agreed to go. Besides the host and her mate, and one of the two men in attendance, I knew not a soul. Making the requisite small talk with people I didn't know was a monumental effort. I looked at my watch every 10 minutes. I remember thinking, "I didn't know hell was catered."

Because there were six women present, the inevitable war over the remote control ensued, the women hijacking the remote and flipping over to the "Barbra Streisand in Concert" special that was on the other channel. It made for an eclectic evening — snowstorm, chili, football, Streisand, and strangers. Oh yes, and love. I met my husband, Michael, that night.

On our first date (I asked him) we talked about how much we wanted to settle down and have a family someday. By the second date, the conversation was about how much we wanted to settle down and have a family with each other.

Opening my eyes, I stared out at the bright March morning. I sat, momentarily peaceful, listening to Michael brush his teeth upstairs. My hand instinctively went to my tummy. The beginnings of a bulge were noticeable under my sweatsuit. At first glance it might have seemed the result of my newly acquired angel-food-cake habit. But a craving for cake was only the symptom.

I flashed back to a couple of months earlier, to when I had committed a supreme act of stupidity that could only be attributed to a massive collision of my last two remaining brain cells. I had been in Vancouver giving a keynote speech. A mere two hours before the speech, I decided to take a home pregnancy test. When I checked the results my heart literally skipped a dozen beats as I stood there, staring at two brilliant red lines. Staring at this magic little wand, I realized that, at the tender age of 37, my life dream was about to be realized. I was, as they say, with child.

I needed to be face to face when I broke the news to Michael, but I also badly needed to tell someone, a cab driver, bell boy, anyone! So I called Mom. Her first reaction was, "Excuse me, you're alone in a hotel room, thousands of miles from home about to speak to an audience of a thousand people, and you did what?!?!" I don't remember a word I said on stage that night. My now-husband, then-boyfriend grinned for days with the news and we upped our marriage plans to the sooner rather than later category.

I now stood up in the middle of my kitchen, fighting the urge to giggle — not the giggling that stems from humour but the kind that comes from rising hysteria. My mind went back to earlier that week. I had had a rather stern discussion with God, essentially telling her to "back off a bit 'cause I've had my fill of surprises and challenges." Two days later the bank called. We had run out of money. I had no idea how I was going to make payroll.

So there it was. I was pregnant, exhausted, and completely broke. And very, very frightened. The dialogue in my head boomed, "I'm losing everything I've worked for. What am I to do next? There is absolutely no way out. Dear God, this feels like it's really over."

Then, without any conscious thought, I turned around and walked upstairs to my office. I sat at my desk, turned on my computer, and, as I had done every day before that one, took a deep breath and started to work. On the surface, this was an incredibly simple action, one I had taken gazillions of times before. I sat down at my desk and began to work. Big deal.

But it was — a very, very big deal. I had to write a speech, so I picked up a women's quotation book that was sitting on my desk. I flipped to a quote by Eleanor Roosevelt. It read: "You gain strength, courage, and confidence by every experience in which you really stop to look fear in the face....You must do the thing which you think you cannot do."[1] A lump grew in my throat and my eyes stung with tears as this resonated in my mind. To be able to put one foot in front of the other, to even consider turning on my computer and continue working under these gruelling circumstances, I could be only one thing. Certifiable or...

An entrepreneur.

Conception

2

*I have met brave women who are
exploring the outer edge of human possibility,
with no history to guide them, and a
courage to make themselves vulnerable that
I find moving beyond words.*

Gloria Steinem

What Moves Us?

Paula was enjoying a second helping of my world-famous homemade Italian chicken soup. Her laptop and stacks of papers competed for table space with the Tabasco sauce and Parmesan cheese. Contrary to what Paula's fashion model waistline suggested, this woman sure could put it away.

Six months had seemed to evaporate since my entrepreneurial epiphany. My girlish figure was blossoming as I advanced effortlessly through maternity. Even though I had never looked better, it was still a heart-stopping experience to peer over my stomach and see the scale register 170 pounds. I swore it groaned each time I stepped on it.

Eating lunch with our customary gusto, Paula and I sashayed down memory lane. Even though only six months had passed since the meltdown, it felt like a lifetime. After a weekend of communing in peace and quiet, Michelle showed up on time Monday morning, energized and fully committed to her job. When she told me she was back I said, "You, my friend, are a glowing example of entrepreneurial spirit. Either that or you need serious mental help. I hope you aren't making a mistake." Michelle laughed. "If you don't make mistakes, you may live and die without ever hearing your name mentioned."

Though the road was still rocky and arduous, we didn't look back. We had closed a large training contract and, for the moment anyway, we were out of the proverbial woods.

Polishing off her soup, Paula said, "You know, Joanne, your story is typical of so many women. You got caught by the hype and image of being a business owner. Don't believe everything you think, my friend." Paula was shaking her head as she reached for more bread.

"As much as it pains me to admit, O great guru," I said, "you're so right. By working faithfully eight hours a day, I eventually got to be my own boss and work 12 hours a day. But it's only now, after the dust has settled somewhat, that I really see how tough it was. Still is, frankly, but I feel that making it through that period has had a substantial maturing effect. I think it's our intense desire to be business owners that makes the pain disappear so soon after such an event has passed. Kind of like labour. I truly believe this mechanism is what allows us to endure.

"You know, Paula, I tried to take it one day at a time, but sometimes several days attacked me at once. I remember one day calling my mother and doing my customary kvetching. 'Mom,' I said, 'I'm up to my ears in trouble.' I'll never forget her answer. 'Yes, I know, dear,' she replied. 'Try using the part that's not submerged.' It felt like the first time I laughed in months."

"Joanne, if you had thought through the business idea more fully and considered its consequences to your personal life, would you have done anything differently?" Paula asked knowingly.

"Probably not. Long-range planning has never been my strong suit. I'm stymied figuring out tonight's dinner," I answered truthfully.

"So, stop beating yourself up. In a perfect world, the decision to start a business should be made as carefully as the decision to start a family…" Paula stopped in mid-sentence. She burst out laughing while looking at my soup bowl. It was balanced precariously on top of my immense stomach, which had become a highly useful built-in shelf.

"Well, then," I said, "my biological and business baby have a lot in common." Images of standing alone in a hotel bathroom, stunned and staring at a completely unexpected positive pregnancy test, flashed through my mind.

Paula conceded, "Your family planning does bear a certain resemblance to your business planning — the 'How the Hell Did That Happen?!' school. But seriously, isn't it weird how the two experiences parallel each other? It's not rocket science that conception and the pregnancy phase, birth, the first year, and the toddler years are very different from each other. Not only are the issues different, your ability to handle them changes as you mature and become more confident and experienced. The parallels with running a business are amazingly close. You conceive the business idea and grow it to a point that it can finally be born strong and healthy. You take the first year to nurture the business, tenderly guiding it, looking after all of its most basic needs. You fumble with the newness. It's a daunting task just trying to keep up with the rate of change. Once your business reaches the toddler stage, you flip back and forth, testing its independence by letting go, albeit just a little, to let it venture out cautiously to explore and expand in the world. This letting go collides with an overwhelming desire to keep it close to home. You begin to leave your business toddler with babysitters the odd time. You hire out certain functions to independent contractors. The time will come, when the toddler becomes older, that you will have to decide upon part-time or full-time care. You will need employees."

I was quite impressed with Paula's comprehension. Paula and her husband Aidan don't have kids in the traditional sense, yet she beautifully articulated the parallel. You'd only have to know Paula for 30 seconds before the pictures of her family — Sheila (the family dog) and the boys, Martin and George (the two family cats) — come flying out. Paula is both parts in *Green Acres* wrapped in one person. She comes from solid farming stock but loves her city life, fine clothes, and seven pairs of different-coloured Converse running shoes. Paula loves every living breathing organism on this earth.

After 12 years of continual whining that she was going through animal withdrawal Paula launched an all-out, weekend-long assault on Aidan while they were away on vacation. ("Nowhere to hide," she justified.) She opened the negotiation high, "I just can't live another day without a dog." Noting her loved one's fatigue, but stubborn disagreement, she modified her opening bid and said that perhaps a cat, which required less time to attend to, would do. Aidan caved on Sunday. Paula started her family by adopting five-week-old Martin from the animal shelter by 9:30 Monday morning.

For a year and a half Martin commuted with Paula from Aurora to her downtown Toronto office. When Paula resigned her position and started her company from home, she argued that Martin needed a pal to fill in the hours of the day. Enter cat #2, George, who is handsome but not very bright.

Paula figured she had the ultimate angle when Aidan expressed concern over the long hours she was putting in at her now out-of-the-home office and about her having to walk to the parking lot in the dark since the office was close to a questionable part of town. Paula argued that if she had a dog for protection, she could work the hours she needed to and be safe at the same time. So before poor Aidan knew it, they had Sheila on a leash and all of them were enrolled in obedience class. Boom! Paula's family was born. Sheila is now a regular fixture at her office.

Paula continued her musings. "Joanne, you don't have to have a traditional family to understand the correlation between raising a business and raising a family. I've given my mom three grand pets and I'm a surrogate aunt to my business partner's kids. We have nieces and nephews. Most of us have been close to enough friends and family who have been through this life-changing event to develop a fine appreciation for the general principles. But even if not, we were all a kid once ourselves. You know what, Joanne? My reasons and methods for starting my kind of family, and my business for that matter, may be different from other people's, but they're absolutely valid just the same."

"You've got that right," I emphatically agreed.

Paula continued. "I've also seen tons of research that shows there are endless permutations and combinations of reasons why women go into business. You know that research from the NFWBO (National Foundation for Women Business Owners) called *Paths to Entrepreneurship*? It proves that not only are women different from each other, we are different from men in our reasons for starting businesses, our business goals, our management styles, and our definitions of success.

"That other study — 'Myths and Realities' that was supported by the Bank of Montreal's Institute for Small Business — was a bit of an eye-opener too. There was lots of anecdotal evidence that women-owned businesses were a strong economic engine in Canada, but until this study was done, no one really knew the size and impact of these businesses."

"Some things in that study surprised even me," I said. "I loved the fact that women-led businesses employ more people than the 100 biggest corporations in Canada. The score? Corporations, 1.5 million: Women, 1.7 million. I felt very proud that we are creating jobs at four times the national rate. Even in provinces where business ownership was actually declining, like in Saskatchewan and Prince Edward Island, women-owned businesses still increased by 10 percent. We own one-third of all the companies in Canada and StatsCan anticipates we will be one-half by the year 2000. But what I liked about this study most of all was that it uncovered that the greatest growth areas for women entrepreneurs are not the service and retail sectors as everyone seems to think. They are, in fact, in agribusiness and the finance, insurance, and real estate sectors. It estimates that there are over 700,000 women entrepreneurs in Canada, but other estimates I've seen say upwards to 1.5 million."[2]

"That means there have been over a million reasons for starting a business," Paula observed. "But even though women start for a wide variety of reasons, there are some common ones. One of the most common I've seen is women's desire to make the world a better place. I know personally many women in the corporate and domestic world who experience a missing link in both their personal and professional lives. They feel a lack of ability to exercise control over their environment, which creates a sense of unfulfillment. These women commonly ask me and themselves, 'Is what I do important and worthwhile?' You've lived this yourself, Joanne. Most often in the corporate world, you don't get to define what you do. Ah, but not so in the entrepreneurial world. Your skills and experience are needed for your business merely to exist, let alone succeed."

"That's a big reason why I left, Paula. And I've discovered another reason women head into entrepreneurship," I added. "I call it 'The Suit Jacket Doesn't Fit.' Women want and need flexibility. I was intrigued to see that nearly half the women business owners in the NFWBO study said that this need for flexibility was one of the major reasons they started their own business. Interestingly enough, the study goes on to show that over one-third of the women from the private sector who are now entrepreneurs did not start their companies because of some long-held dream. They were leaving something behind, such as boredom with their job, or seeking something more, such as greater personal and professional growth. These women moved away from an environment that they didn't like in order to become business owners. I was sure part of that crowd."

"It's what Bobby Gaunt, president of Ford Canada, calls 'The Plastic Ceiling,'" Paula said.

"Oh, that one is hilarious," I said. "How did it go again? Something like 'the term glass ceiling should be replaced with plastic ceiling. Glass creates the impression it can be broken.' I thought it was compelling that 22 percent of women who have been in business for less than 10 years are entrepreneurs mainly because they hit a glass ceiling in their former careers. Compare this to just nine percent of women who owned their firms for 20 years or more. So much for the theory that things are improving. Something that zinged me right between the eyes was the fact that the glass ceiling constituency most frequently cited not having their contributions recognized and not being taken seriously as their biggest complaints in the corporate world." I paused, shaking my head. "This is a classic W-FACTOR."

"W-FACTOR?" Paula queried.

"Entrepreneurial dilemmas specific to women," I replied. "Women use entrepreneurship as a glass ceiling detour. If we can't work our way from the bottom up, we'll damn well start from the top down."

Paula laughed, snorting soup through her nose.

"Ouch," I said. "That's gotta hurt."

"That Tabasco sauce is a killer," she replied, wiping her nose with a napkin. "Anyway, I say Amen to that. Let's create our own corporate culture. And what about plain and simply putting food on the table?" Paula asked. "My Aunt Mary retired from her grocery store over 50 years ago. She maintains that she hasn't done anything special. She just did what she needed to do to make a living and provide for her retirement. 'Oh,' she will add, 'and support my brother and care for my father.'

"You know, today things like corporate downsizing and automating administrative jobs have expanded Aunt Mary's category of entrepreneurs, the ones evolving from financial need. There's also things like having difficulty re-entering the work force after family or health leave, not being able to afford daycare for the kids, non-custodial dads who don't pay child support, pink-collar ghettos, high unemployment rates for graduates, and being a new Canadian that all add up to that financial incentive. We all know that women and children make up the majority of people living below the poverty line in this country. Many women are starting their own business as a way to break out of this vicious cycle. Heavens, anything from home daycare to construction companies, from dog-walkers to multimedia companies, young and old women are starting businesses at an unprecedented rate. Another 1998 Statistics Canada survey showed a 46 percent increase in women-owned businesses between 1991 and 1996. This was dramatic compared to the increase in men-owned businesses. They hovered around the 20 percent mark."

Something struck me as hilarious as Paula was talking. "Paula," I said slowly. "Tell me, who talks like this in real life? If anyone was listening to us now, they'd think we were *both* accountants. My reputation would be sullied."

"Not hard to tell that both our worlds revolve around the women's market," Paula said, smiling.

"You know," I said, leaping back into the fray, "for the most part, corporate Canada still thinks women are either career women *or* mothers. The work place is still too rigid and protocols for promotion still too hierarchical. This makes life hard for working mothers, a term I personally hate. 'Working mother' — talk about a redundant term. Women often have to have the proverbial telephone booth handy so that we can duck in to make a quick change in roles. I have been in several presentations where women have had to leave because of a call from daycare saying little Ben or Beth is sick. And how many women get calls during family time, evenings, and weekends from the office? Because we still do the lion's share of child and home care this dual responsibility affects us more. What ends up happening is increased anxiety created by living a life of multiple and sometimes conflicting personalities, roles, and objectives. I really believe entrepreneurship offers the opportunity for women to integrate both roles of mother and business person. I love feminist philosopher Leslie McIntyre's take on this, though. She says, 'Nobody objects to a woman being a good writer or sculptor or geneticist if at the same time she manages to be a good wife, good mother, good looking, good tempered, well groomed, and unaggressive.'"

"It's sad that this is still somewhat true today," Paula said. "But you know Joanne, for many women who have traded in their computers for cradles, there is another interesting W-FACTOR that emerges. It comes when there is a fundamental realization that raising kids is only one part of life, not life itself. As business owners, these women have an opportunity to fill another need that is of equal importance to raising a family. Entrepreneurship can be a big step towards successfully mixing parenthood and businesshood, an otherwise water and oil tonic.

"Yes," I agreed. "But let me be quick to say to those proponents of the entrepreneurship-is-the-perfect-solution-to-your-life-balance-problem —

get a grip. If it's more time I was looking for, whether it be for kids, my partner, hobbies, or my dog for that matter, I need to give my head a reality shake. Starting and running a business is profoundly time- and mind-consuming. Even so, you could not drag me back to corporate Canada with a team of Clydesdales. In fact, it seems that you couldn't drag most women entrepreneurs back. Almost 60 percent of women business owners say that nothing would attract them back to a position within a corporation."

"Same deal with the women I talk to, even though entrepreneurship can often be the tougher path," Paula agreed.

"From my perspective," I continued, "even though I now deal with all the headaches, uncertainties, and turmoil, they're *my* headaches, uncertainties, and turmoil. Even though there is a financial cost to taking Friday afternoons off or three weeks in the summer, technically I can. Psychologically, it's about having control and that's worth a great deal. What it boils down to is that entrepreneurship may allow choice but you will probably find you have less time at your disposal than you did while in corporate Canada. Control, however, should not be confused with balance. Since I've become an entrepreneur, balance is a lot more difficult to get because of my increased responsibilities and increased stakes. But somehow, these don't seem as onerous or stressful as when I was employed in corporate Canada. I now have the power to make choices based on my own value system."

"Regardless of the specific catalyst, control — over one's time, environment, rewards, and manner of fulfillment — seems to be the common denominator for most women entrepreneurs," Paula said.

"Yeah," I agreed. "But like having kids, the personal sacrifices of being an entrepreneur are immense."

"Sacrifices indeed," Paula said patting my belly. "Instead of your new winter coat, it will be a car seat and crib. Instead of working out, you'll be leaping over furniture after a toddler. Instead of being responsible for only you as it's been for the last 37 years, you are actually going to be somebody's mother."

A stab of anxiety pierced my heart and made me catch my breath. "Intellectually, I get it that the changes that motherhood brings are so huge that I'm incapable of understanding them before it happens," I said quietly. "Even though I understand this thing is bigger than I am, on another level, I would really appreciate knowing in advance a little of what I'm getting into."

"Patience, my friend. Grass eventually turns into milk," Paula said.

"Well, it appears I'll learn about parenthood the same way I learned to be an entrepreneur. To conceive a workable business idea, I had to rely totally on instinct, guesswork, and wrong turns to be my teacher. I often felt like I was running a marathon with one foot nailed to the floor. I had the speed, but I was dizzy most of the time."

"You are supposed to be dazed and confused in that particular business phase," Paula commented.

"Business phase?" I countered. "That wasn't a business phase. I was just thinking, testing the waters, mostly. Nothing concrete, by any stretch of the imagination."

"I beg to differ," Paula said. "People are surprised to learn that 'just thinking' is a business phase, but one that is the most often poorly defined and articulated. It's the most important link in the chain because it's here that your *big idea* is born. Just like any other stage of business development, coming up with the right idea is best accomplished with some sense of process in mind. What I've found to have worked well with many new entrepreneurs kind of looks like this: First, you identify one or ten ideas that are appealing and possible. Then you have to figure out which ones best suit you personally. This step implies that you understand your personal and financial motivation for wanting to own your own business. And lastly and most importantly, you have to figure out whether one, two, ten, or none of your ideas is, in fact, viable. This is done by researching whether there are enough customers for you to reach, that will buy what you've decided to sell, at a price that makes you the money you want. To complicate matters all the more, there is no single approach to any of these steps that is 'the right way to do it.' You can choose the one that suits you best from a whole range of options."

And that's exactly what we are going to explore in the rest of this chapter.

So, What Do You Want to Be When You Grow Up?

Starting a business presents the historic problem of the blank slate. Inspiration generally just happens. It is far more difficult to summon deliberately. Add the entrepreneurial dilemma — how do I know what I don't know — and the difficulty becomes "What do I do in this new business, not having ever done this business before?"

Selecting the business you want to start, one that is viable and is aligned with your personal interests, values, and natural behaviours, is no small task. So, what are the ingredients you need to develop your own business concept? First, start with yourself. And this, folks, ain't easy. You need to take stock of your skills, experience, expertise, and the areas in which your interests and values lie. This process may mean actually saying something nice about yourself. When you go through the process of choosing an idea, think of what you love to do and what you show some talent for. You don't necessarily need to be well qualified now. Your plan can include how to become so. Use what talents you possess; the woods would be very silent if no birds sang there except those that sang best.

The following is an inspirational story to keep in mind when you search for your own idea. It comes from *Chicken Soup for the Woman's Soul*.

I had one of those serendipitous moments a few weeks ago. I was in the bedroom changing one of the babies when our five-year-old, Alyssa, came and plopped down beside me on the bed.

"Mommy, what do you want to be when you grow up?" she asked.

I assumed she was playing some little imaginary game, and so to play along I responded with, "H'mmmmm. I think I would like to be a mommy when I grow up."

"You can't be that 'cause you already are one. What do you want to be?"

"Okay, maybe I'll be a pastor when I grow up," I answered a second time.

"Mommy, no, you're already one of those!"

"I'm sorry, honey," I said, "but I don't understand what I'm supposed to say then."

"Mommy, just answer what you want to be when you grow up. You can be anything you want to be!"

At that point I was so moved by the experience that I could not immediately respond, and Alyssa gave up on me and left the room.

That experience—that tiny five-minute experience—touched a place deep within me. I was touched because in my daughter's young eyes, I could still be anything I wanted to be! My age, my present career, my five children, my husband, my bachelor's degree, my master's degree: none of that mattered. In her eyes I could still dream dreams and reach for the stars. In her young eyes my future was not over. In her young eyes I could still be an astronaut or a piano player or even an opera singer, perhaps. In her young eyes I still had some growing to do and a lot of "being" left in my life.

The real beauty in that encounter with my daughter was when I realized that in all her honesty and innocence, she would ask the very same question of her grandparents and of her great-grandparent.

It has been written, "The old woman I shall become will be quite different from the woman I am now. Another I is beginning...."

So...what do you want to be when you grow up?[2]

I wasn't an accountant or economist when I started Women and Money Inc. I didn't have a PhD in gender differences. But I did feel qualified to run with the concept of the business. And for the strangest of reasons. It was because, when it came to money, I knew about the dark side. Because of my personal experience in the financial services industry as a client and as an adviser, I was more than qualified to proceed down my path. I was also able to choose a business concept that blended with my personal values to form a firm foundation for the unbelievable level of commitment I was going to need later on. I don't even want to imagine where I would have been through those awful months if I hadn't had that integration of business and personal values.

Many people want to become business owners because they don't like what they are doing now. But be aware that there is a chance you may not like entrepreneurship either. If you find that your business doesn't fit with your personal goals, values, and skills, consider discontinuing the journey or taking another road. A goal is nothing more than a dream with a deadline and in life deadlines change all the time. Stopping or changing a business is a natural part of its evolution. The search for your initial business concept is also a part of the process. This searching may well be a contributing factor to the sobering statistic that nine out of ten new small businesses "fail." I take exception to the term "fail." The following is more to the point: Nine out of ten businesses *discontinue the first time around.* If you think about it, most successful entrepreneurs will leave a string of discontinued businesses behind them before they finally hit the formula that spells success for them.

The Big Idea — Market Needs Versus Market Wants

How did a million-plus women manage to find their ideas to start their businesses? It would be naïve to think that there can be so many unmet needs out there given the number of businesses that actually exist. Most experts will tell you that finding a way to provide something of value to the market is the essential ingredient in starting a successful business. So how do you explain the huge phenomenon of pet rocks? Or jewellery? Or becoming blonde?

While it is essential that a good business idea meet needs in the market, ironically, an unmet need does not, necessarily and solely, a business make. It's people's desires or wants that more often than not create a market. When brainstorming an idea for a business, never underestimate the power of want versus need.

It is relatively unlikely, but not impossible, that a market need has simply gone unnoticed. What you have more likely found is another, perhaps better, way to meet an existing market need. If you think you have found an unmet need, you may want to consider seriously the reasons why it remains "unmet." My grandmother once told me, "Don't ever take a fence down until you know the reason why it was put up." There could be some hard lessons just waiting to be learned. There are millions of new business concepts hatching each and every day. It is more likely that each market or consumer need is being serviced in some way, shape, or form. You need to ask yourself, "How is it exactly that I'm different from the pack?"

And don't be afraid to really reach. I can't tell you how often my ideas have been called "unreasonable." I once said to a senior guy at a brokerage firm who fought me all the way on the viability of targeting the women's market, "Those who say it cannot be done should not interrupt those who are doing it." He didn't have a clue what I was talking about. It's often a matter of "right place, right time, and right mind."

Some Different Ways to Conceive Business Ideas

Starting is the most exciting, most onerous, most terrifying, most difficult part of any project. But how do you come up with a viable, interesting, fulfilling business idea in the first place? There isn't a recipe book or Web site of terrific business ideas that magically guarantees success if you just add your time, money, and effort. It is very tempting to charge ahead, scouring the sources of "good business ideas," trying to spot the next brilliant, undiscovered product or service. But remember, kids and ideas are the same: Everyone thinks theirs is the best. In reality ideas are a dime a dozen. It's the people who put them into action who are priceless.

It doesn't matter what route you take to get the idea, you still have to do some advance thinking and investigation. Even if it doesn't feel like a formal process with business plans and chats with experts, all the stuff you do — lying awake at night mulling over a thought, coming to terms with the fact your boss is a goof, getting steamed over a poorly designed kid's toy — all these activities are, in a business sense, assessing market opportunities. The 1998 study, *Paths to Entrepreneurship*, shows that the pull of an entrepreneurial idea is the single greatest reason for entrepreneurship among women and men. Forty-four percent of women and 36 percent of men who own businesses have become business owners primarily because they had a winning idea or came to realize that they could do for themselves what they had been doing for an employer.

There are many ways to conceive a business idea. Here are a few of the more common approaches. The first way was actually Paula's path. It was kind of like the idea came at her from the left while she was looking right. She was really just looking around to see what was out there.

Spontaneous Brilliance — The Lightbulb Goes Off Paula explains: "I spent six months mentally and physically recuperating after extracting myself from a senior position in a terrible and demoralizing company. In those six months, my husband, Aidan, claimed that I had become the busiest unemployed person he knew. Those months were spent voraciously reading, learning, basically reconnecting with the real world. My wonderfully good-natured husband patiently tolerated my daily interrogations and acted as the dutiful guinea pig on whom I tested my new ideas, hypotheses, and insights.

"The unifying concept that tied my past with my present and my future came to light in a rough idea I had of a business advisory team of entrepreneurs helping other entrepreneurs. My personal experience acted as a focus group of one, identifying the need for business advisers who understood the entrepreneurial mind, environment, and *modus operandi*. Then I read a book by Dr. Deborah Tannen, a linguistics professor from Georgetown University who specializes in gender differences in communication styles. My lightbulb went off. It answered for me the question of which entrepreneurs to start with. In her book *You Just Don't Understand*, Dr. Tannen said that women were avid seekers and consumers of advice. And that's what I wanted to sell — advice. Women were going to be my first and primary target market. Because of my recent reconnection with many talented women, my instincts told me I had the makings of a very good idea."

Your Passion — A Possible Pursuit? Managing was a way of life for Indira. When she wasn't managing her three children aged four to nine, she was the den mother to a staff of 30 in a busy customer service call centre. Her life, she joked, was like an episode of *Grace Under Fire*. Her stained glass studio was her evening haven. There, surrounded by brilliant slabs of glass and beadings of lead and copper, Indira created instead of managed. Her vintage Victorian pieces were back-ordered by friends, family, and others who had been referred to her. She was regularly congratulated on her booming business. Indira's reply was that of a classic closet entrepreneur — "Business? You mean this thing I'm doing at night while working by day is a business?"

A business sometimes sneaks up on us before we know it, and it often comes from the thing we love the most. But turning up our amateur status that last notch so that the business will be viable requires a couple of adjustments. Instead of just covering the cost of materials, we now need to factor in overhead, labour, and profit. Instead of sitting down to our beloved activity whenever we need a break from the real world, it becomes the real world, with orders and deadlines and accounting. There is one thing to watch for when converting a passion to a possible pursuit: Sometimes when we change the spirit of why we do something, like sewing for pleasure or cooking for fun, it can change the feeling we have towards the activity.

The clear advantage to starting a business from a personal passion is that we already know we love what we are doing. It is so much easier, therefore, to integrate what we do with who we are. This is one of the most important ingredients of success.

A Little Bit of This, a Pinch of That In a span of 20 years and between sailing junkets, Maya's career included holding senior executive positions at a consumer products company, a technology company, and an international consulting firm. Maya was very good at a large number of things. Even after she exited corporate Canada, the stream of requests to help with this or that didn't stop. As a result, Maya had a steady flow of business. But they were disparate opportunities. Maya felt like she was the sum total of different and unrelated parts. She was really struggling with defining who and what she was in a way that wasn't so fragmented. Her paramount challenge was to develop a unifying business theme that encompassed all that she could do and was doing. Her solution? A business card with the only constant on it — her name.

Many women with a wide variety of skills, experience, and ideas, like Maya, still struggle when trying to figure out how to tie it all together into one business identity. As you search for a unifying theme that ties in the appealing aspects of each business idea, you may end up with a camel that started out as a race horse. All business ideas go through an evolutionary process and often end up looking nothing like the original concept. Don't fret. The world needs camels just as much as it needs race horses. Just be sure to take care when piecing together a little bit from each idea (like financial planning and gender awareness, for example) that, in the end, you want a camel.

Women, especially technicians or professionals who want to move beyond their training and experience, often find that their business concept looks a little like Frankenstein's monster. They tend to pursue their new future while still holding on to the comfort of their past. It's normal to worry whether people will hire an accountant to create a corporate image, a lawyer to decorate their house, or a computer specialist to help with strategic business planning. The *Paths to Entrepreneurship* study shows an interesting gender difference when it comes to the kinds of businesses women and men start. While the businesses started by men are more likely to be closely related to their earlier career, women will start a business totally unrelated to their previous job. Fifty-nine percent of male business owners are in a business that is very similar to what they used to do. Fifty-six percent of women, on the other hand, own businesses that are totally unrelated to their previous careers.

Here's a good gauge of how successful you have been in integrating all your ideas. When someone inquires as to what you do for a living, do you hesitate, then laugh as you answer, "Well, that's a good question"; answer, "Everything"; or have a snappy one-line motto that sums up everything you do? The last one means you've finally hit it. In our case, we had to figure out how to blend financial planning for women and corporate gender awareness training into one motto. We hit pay dirt with *"Educating women about money and educating financial institutions about women."*

Rent an Idea Simone describes herself as a free spirit who was getting crushed in the nine-to-five scene. The three-hour commute each day was also a strong negative factor. Her employer agreed that her services could be provided to the company while she worked from home, which she did for a year and a half. Telecommuting made the severing of her connection with corporate Canada far less painful when the opportunity came to take a voluntary severance package. However, Simone needed to expand her horizons.

She knew she wanted to dip her feet into entrepreneurial waters, but only a toe or two at a time. In business, sometimes we avoid investing in ourselves by not naming our company, not developing our own corporate identity, not printing our own business card, or not installing a separate business phone number. We protect our real and independent identity by carrying the card of our client/old employer. But the problem is you can't wait for your ship to come in if you haven't sent one out.

The Rent an Idea approach goes kind of like this: "Shhhhh — don't let anyone think I'm seriously doing something on my own. I'm not going to run a real business quite yet. I'm just going to be an independent contractor — a pseudo-independent *employee* for hire."

Simone soon realized that this approach would only work for so long. So two and a half years after her self-induced liberation from corporate Canada, she launched her own business under her own identity. The time was right to get her hair wet by jumping into the deep end of the pool.

Regardless of whether you arrived at your idea by having an epiphany, borrowing someone else's for a while, or assembling it piece by piece, just be aware that all methods have inherent risks and benefits. And remember that great ideas need landing gear as well as wings. Whether you are contemplating creating your own business concept, buying a business from someone else, or taking over where someone else left off, whether you are planning to do this solo or with a partner — guess what? — you *are* in business. This conception stage of business is not often legitimized as a real business stage, but it is. This thinking/idea/assessment stage is the necessary first leg of the entrepreneurial journey.

It's here we have to learn to think really big and get comfortable stepping outside of the box. The state of the world today demands that women become less modest and dream/plan/act on a larger scale. Peter Drucker says people who don't take risks generally make about two mistakes a year. People who do take risks generally make about two mistakes a year.

Taking Stock of Your Business Idea — From the Inside Out

Regardless of whether you plan to convert your passion into a business or run with the lightbulb, you need to look forward and register your feelings about the future. You need to be able to take stock of your business idea from the inside out.

Women often catalogue their experiences in life, both personal and business, according to how an event made them feel. This emotional Dewey Decimal System is the place we constantly make reference to when we relate to others. Men don't usually bring such an emotional component to the world of business. Countless times I've had men look at me as if I had two heads and green hair when I explained a business issue in language that included phrases like "I was frightened" or "My neighbour went through the same feelings…."

And though the emotions do vary from person to person, every one of us has experienced and will continue to experience the full range. Often within five minutes. Your emotions range from ecstacy to terror, liberation to paralysis, confidence to doubt, from being absolutely sure to completely pretending. You'll swing from loneliness to being overwhelmed, and from feeling integrated to falling apart. One minute you're sure you're going to be a millionaire, the next you're convinced you're going the route of bag lady. Regardless of where you are on the emotional continuum, know this — you are not alone.

Business conception is like a romantic courtship. The one thing that you can count on is that you will have lots and lots of endless questions … WHY am I doing this? WHAT am I doing? WHY am I doing this? HOW am I going to do this? WHY am I doing this? WHO will I be doing this for? WHY am I doing this? WHEN should I be doing this? WHY am I doing this? WHERE should I be doing this? WHY am I doing this?…

Why is such a good word for the entrepreneur, providing it doesn't become negatively coupled with hair-pulling and self-flagellation. *Why* acts as a clarifier of thought and commitment. Ambition without determination has no destination. "Why am I doing this" is a complex question that will help you define your destination and establish what you want out of the journey. But be prepared. As your life and the marketplace changes, so will the answers to these and other questions.

Defining Your Own Personal Meaning of Success

"More soup?" I asked, wide-eyed with wonder. Paula groaned as she undid the top button of her pants. I took that as a no.

"Paula, how do I know if my business is successful?" I asked.

"Pretty big question, Joanne," Paula replied. "But it's one I get asked a lot. The fledgling entrepreneur may be overwhelmed by the challenge of choosing what she wants to be when she grows up. Conventional wisdom says you should choose the most viable business concept that has the greatest opportunity for success. Yeah, but how do you define success? The research is clear on one thing. Women define success very differently from men."

"You know, we billed a quarter of a million dollars in our first year and I personally thought that was good, especially with that internal meltdown," I said. "But if I use a traditional model of defining success, I doubt very much that the business would be classified as successful."

"Remember, it's not how much you make, but how much you keep," Paula said. "That aside, how does it feel?" she queried.

"Well, you'll notice I said a quarter million instead of two hundred and fifty thousand. A quarter mil sounds like so much more. And frankly, I was thrilled. I think it was a noble start."

Paula smiled sadly. "I'm amazed at how many women business owners get the old guilt trip, 'You need to be big in order to be taken seriously.' You hear it all the time. Businesses aren't considered successful if they are under $250K. Joanne, whatever you do, don't fall into this trap. Set your own benchmark.

"The media often concentrate on only one facet of the 'return on investment' or ROI in a business — the financial return. This aspect involves the fascinating world of dividend streams, options, bonuses, capitalization rates, earnings multiples, and price/earning ratios. Of course, we as women entrepreneurs know the absolute importance of making money in business, but we also recognize that there's much more to it than that. The traditional definition that *only* factors in the money is incomplete because it doesn't factor in the equally important and intangible personal payoffs that result from entrepreneurship. These are often the most compelling reasons that women start businesses."

"Paula, that is so right on," I agreed. "As is often the case, traditional (read: male) perspectives collide with the way women do things. I've seen research that shows men take more money out of their business than women do and that women start businesses for more personal reasons than men.[3] I have yet to hear from a woman entrepreneur that it was solely the opportunity to generate really great financial ROI that inspired her to work so hard creating her own income stream. More often we hear women refer to the emotional ROI they expect from going into business for themselves."

"I have devised a 'Top Five List' as to 'Why Women Leave the Creature Comforts of Corporate Canada to Dive Into the Completely Insane World of Entrepreneurship,'" Paula said. "It goes like this:

1. I want to control my destiny.
2. I want my personal and business life to match/balance/integrate.
3. I want to write my own paycheque, a big one, based on my own efforts and ideas.
4. I want my work to jive with my personal values and beliefs.
5. I want to be limited only by the limits of my own imagination.

Bottom line, Joanne? Clearly figuring out your emotional and financial ROI in your own business — your personal definition of success — is a task to be tackled right from your business's earliest conception."

"This is a big one, Paula. Arriving at a personal definition of success involves some serious soul searching and a few runs around the block."

"That's true, Joanne. But frankly, time spent here is as important as the market research you do while conceiving your business idea. It is critical that you figure out how to self assess and define your personal meaning of success because, while you will change it occasionally, it will act as a stabilizing force in your business life.

"Considering all the societal influences we endure as well as the business culture with its firmly entrenched male definition of success, it's no wonder women struggle with this."

"Paula," I said, "I have to realign my definition of success if I'm going to maintain any self-respect or sanity. I've always measured my professional success by praise from colleagues, being of use and value to others, and earning a decent paycheque. I think some of this is going to have to change now that I'm a full-fledged business owner. I've noticed that now that I'm the owner, I regularly have to make people mad. That makes the praise part of the equation a lot tougher to achieve. When Kate comes, my priorities are also going to change radically. It's really tough trying to find a definition of success that I can live with, one that suits my life, my goals, and my personality, when my life, goals, and personality have changed so much."

Paula understood. "Think about it. Defining your own benchmark against which to measure success for your business leads to another interesting entrepreneurial dilemma: What do you want versus what do you need versus what can you live with. You need to consider all three."

I pondered this for a minute. When I thought back over the early stages of my entrepreneurial life, I had accepted *what I could live with* more often than not over *what I wanted* or *what I needed* because that was simply what life had dealt me. If I had understood and articulated these boundaries beforehand, chances are it wouldn't have felt so much like failure when life happened. By setting this stuff out in advance, it would have helped me at the very least acknowledge that the *what I could live with* part of the equation actually happens and, as I found out, usually far more frequently in entrepreneurial life than the *what I wanted or needed* part.

"Something else too, Paula. As women, we sometimes get frustrated, demoralized, and feel guilty when our intentions are good, our efforts immense, but we still don't get what we are after. Just open a fashion magazine." I shook my head, thinking of those perfectly coiffed, elaborately dressed, impossibly thin, and eerily tall models, air brushed to perfection, who couldn't remember the last time they did a face plant in a plate of ribs. Yeah, like they really reflect my reality.

"Rightly or wrongly," I continued, "we seem to gain a sense of accomplishment from what we actually achieve. It's much harder to gain any sense of accomplishment from an attempt or an effort to achieve. This is the same for both women and men, but I can't help but wonder if women deal with an additional layer. Think about it. It's impossible to gain any sense of accomplishment if your goal is unrealistic, imposed, or someone else's. Like those stupid fashion magazines. Men don't deal with the role conflict to the same extent that women do. This is a classic W-FACTOR. Women are supposed to be lovers, mothers, partners, housecleaners, chauffeurs, business owners, chefs, daughters, nurses, friends, teachers, mentors, workers...."

"I get it, I get it," Paula interrupted. "And we really have to be careful of this attitude in our businesses. Effort does mean something and there's got to be a way to measure it. A good focal point for entrepreneurs to keep in mind is that success isn't just whether or not you reached the goal, but also the distance that you travelled. Therefore, there has to be a link established between the 'how' and the 'what' — *how* your actions will get you *what* you wanted in the first place. This is the heart of the plan for your business."

"But what about when what I want changes, Paula? As I think back, I realize that what I want from my business today is quite different from what I wanted a few years ago. Then, I considered myself a roaring success if I could pay my bills. Today, however, I define success with a lot more complexity. My business is successful if I can have a semblance of balance in my life. It is successful if my staff feel they are an integral part of the organization, both financially and emotionally. The business gets a thumbs up if I am in a position to spend a little, save a little, and give a little. It is successful if I can continue to feel pride and accomplishment in what I do every day."

"Would it have been helpful to you in the beginning to have understood that 'success' is a growing, evolving thing?" Paula asked.

"Big time," I replied. "I would have avoided putting things in narrow and confining boxes like Success = $250,000. I would have cut myself a lot more slack. I was unaware that the meaning of success would evolve and change dramatically with the maturation of my business and personal life."

Paula agreed. "Because your business success is defined by your personal and financial objectives, there tends to be as many different definitions of success as there are entrepreneurs. My personal favourite is Ralph Waldo Emerson's definition of success:

To laugh often and much;

To win the respect of intelligent people and the affection of children;

To earn the appreciation of honest critics and endure the betrayal of false friends;

To appreciate beauty;

To find the best in others;

To leave the world a bit better, whether by a healthy child, a garden patch or a redeemed social condition;

To know even one life has breathed easier because you have lived.

This is to have succeeded.

"Wise words," I commented, "but I think there are only three people on earth who manage to live them out. You know, I need to be clear what my own beliefs are regarding money, lifestyle, family, and accomplishment. These are what go into making up my personal definition of success."

Paula leaned back in her chair with her hands behind her head in an attitude of thoughtfulness. "Joanne, do you want to run a national organization?"

"Sure."

"Do you want to put $100,000 a year in your pocket?"

"Yeah, I think I could find pockets big enough for that."

"How much time off do you want with your babies?"

"The rest of my life."

Paula shot me a "be serious" glance.

"Ideally nine months."

"Do you want to spend every Tuesday and Thursday with Kate after she is born?"

"I'd love that."

"Can you afford to spend every Tuesday and Thursday with Kate?"

I sadly shook my head no.

"Do you want to work close to home?"

"Absolutely. I'll continue to work from home and keep an office downtown for the staff."

"If you could do most of these things, would you consider yourself successful?" Paula asked.

"You bet. But earning $100,000 a year, having a nine-month maternity leave, and having two days off a week with Kate are inconsistent goals right now. But, the most important priority is a no-brainer, Paula. I want to be with Kate during her first nine months. I want to breastfeed her for as long as she'll have me. But I am going to have to go into debt to do it." I smiled, "I suspect it's going to be a small price to pay."

If people think through what success really means to them, they can then decide whether business success is the end or the means. Is a successful business what you want or is it the medium through which you plan to achieve personal, that is, emotional, spiritual, and financial dreams? Answering this little gem of a question in advance will determine your entire view of your business. It will set the tone for your attitude towards it. It will affect how you make decisions as well as the actual decisions themselves. It will determine how you choose to run your business and how you live your personal life.

Am I an Entrepreneur Yet?

By now, we had moved to my front porch to take in the kaleidoscope of colour that only a Canadian fall can provide. "Paula, when do you know that you're an entrepreneur? I mean, there's no checklist to follow."

Paula replied, "Relax, Joanne, it's not a test. And you are right, there is no checklist for either parenthood or entrepreneurship. In both cases, we do whatever we have to do, regardless of what the checklists say.

"Women entrepreneurs are not only extroverted, ambitious, structure-busting, risk-thirsty, high-flying, self-assured, brilliantly creative rebels, they are also conservative, content, self-aware, quietly competent mere mortals. My experience with close to 1000 entrepreneurs tells me they come in all shapes, sizes, backgrounds, and behavioural profiles, with varying kinds of dreams, ambitions, and goals. Checklists can be unnecessary barriers to entering the world of entrepreneurship if you take them too seriously. Depending on how and what you decide to do and for whom, who you are may be exactly what is needed. I always advocate self-awareness and an exploration of what you love, your interests, and your behavioural style in advance of looking to the marketplace. If you do this, the probabilities are very high that you will conceive a business and a place in it that is perfect for you."

"That's encouraging," I said. "You know, Paula, most pundits state unequivocally that entrepreneurs are born not made. This is a myth. The truth is, entrepreneurs are born and made. It's actually all in the timing, not the person — there is no entrepreneurial gene. It's more a matter of grit and determination to make it through the inevitable tough times. The explosion of people starting businesses in the last five years has far more to do with economics than it does with genetics. The media hype has brought entrepreneurship out of the closet, so to speak, and given it the status of 'the sexy thing to do.' This outlook didn't exist a few years ago when running your own business was something you did because you couldn't get a real job."

Paula and I sat in comfortable silence. I looked down at my protruding belly. For the moment, I was feeling remarkably at peace. With the difficulties of the conception phase of both the business and baby behind me, I had the anticipation of Kate's imminent arrival. Having been through a birth of sorts already, that of my business, I felt secure in the knowledge that I didn't have a clue what was about to happen. And that was okay. The only thing I was certain of was that Kate was going to come a-callin' soon.

Giving Birth 3

Women's liberation is just a lot of foolishness.
It's the men who are discriminated against.
They can't bear children. And no one's
likely to do anything about that.

Golda Meir (1898–1978)

I glanced over at the digital clock. The neon glow seared into my brain. "Again with the 3:00 a.m.!" I moaned, heaving my girth to a more comfortable position. "My brain is going to shrivel up from exhaustion."

At eight and a half months pregnant, I battled nightly for sleep. What with my mind whirling, my crushed bladder, and Kate's internal triathlon, sleep had become life's scarcest commodity. Deep in the darkness of morning's earliest hours, the same questions played out in my head: "Is Kate going to be healthy? Am I going to be a good mother? What will she be when she grows up? What opportunities will be there for her? Will she always need me? When will she outgrow me and begin to need others? How will I keep her safe while allowing her enough room to grow? What will be her strengths and weaknesses? How can I be sure I'll always give Kate my best?" I could stand what I knew. It was what I didn't know that was making me anxious.

And my dear, loving, supportive husband Michael lay beside me, snoring away in blissful, deep, restorative REM sleep.

Struggling, I got out of bed to pee for the four hundredth time that night. My feet hit the floor with such a reverberating thud I was sure I had awoken the dead. But I didn't care about the dead — just that snoring lump beside me. When the bed finally stopped vibrating, Michael stirred and said sleepily, "I'm awake now."

"Good," I muttered as I waddled off to the bathroom, vacillating between shame and delight. Naturally, by the time I had returned a scant minute and a half later, he was out cold again.

"How the hell does he do that?!" I wondered as I attempted to find a comfortable position. Not an easy feat considering the Queen Mary had recently docked in my stomach. I knew Michael thought about the same things I did. We talked about them often enough. The difference was, however, he thought about them but I thought *and worried* about them. That's why he was asleep and I was developing a passionate hatred for clocks.

By morning, I would normally have returned to my joyful self. But not this particular morning. I was still groping with lack of sleep when a way-too-cheerful "Hello, I'm here!!!" hailed from the front door as Paula appeared with some forms to sign.

"I'll be down in a decade," I retorted, referring to my rapidly declining mobility. I could hear Paula laugh as she made her way to her favourite room in our house, the kitchen. When I rounded the corner I was greeted by the sight of her posterior sticking out as her head was reappearing from deep inside our refrigerator.

Paula immediately caught my expression and smiled sympathetically. "Howya feeling today, girlfriend?"

I settled gingerly into the breakfast nook. "Ask my sleep-deprived hormones," I answered. "Paula, I know that I'm a smart, capable woman with many talents. But could you explain to me what happens to that person every night at 3:00 a.m.? She goes into deep hiding and this Neurotic Nellie emerges. I second-guess myself to death and deluge myself with thousands of questions I can't ever hope to answer."

"3:00 a.m.? Yikes." Paula looked sympathetic as she snacked on leftover chicken. "I suspect all these worries are natural and to be expected. I haven't had kids yet so I may be presuming here, but frankly, I remember lying awake nights and feeling totally neurotic when I started my company. I spent a ton of time, energy, and money trying to prepare in advance for the so-called birth of my business baby. And I sure remember the anxiety around it, especially at the 3:00 a.m. witching hour. I was plagued with uncertainty that, strangely enough, diminished when the sun came up. I'd pummel myself with questions like, 'Is my business going to survive? Do I have what it takes to be an entrepreneur? What is the company going to be when it grows up? What opportunities exist for it? Will the business always be so intrinsically tied to me or will I ever be able to depend on others to help with it? How can I keep it safe while I take the necessary calculated risks venturing into new territory? What will be the company's strengths and weaknesses? What will I do about them? How can I be sure I'll *always* have what it takes to give my business my best?' I gotta tell you, Joanne, that night-time insanity seemed like it went on forever."

I sat back amazed at what I had just heard. "Paula, change the names and you would have just described the anxiety attack I had last night and every night for the last month about life with baby. Now that you mention it, how could I forget that same searing night-time paranoia I endured when I launched Women and Money Inc. Criminey, I almost what-ifed myself to death. And not the constructive 'what-if' like 'If I got pregnant, how would I manage?' or 'If the market turned, what would be my plan B?' It was the much more counter-productive 'What will I do if I fail?' or 'What will I do if people find out I'm not who they think I am?' Honestly, Paula, giving birth to Kate better be less painful than giving birth to the business."

Paula snorted, "Oh yeah, that's pretty likely."

Choosing to ignore her jibe, I continued, "I can't keep track of all the things I'm worried sick about now. Am I going to have the money and more importantly, the emotional fortitude to keep this business going after Kate comes? And I'd be lying if I said it didn't concern me if I was going to phys-ically recover quickly enough to be able to handle the immense demands." I glanced down at my stomach trying to imagine how something so big was going to gracefully exit my body.

Paula thought for a moment. "Every woman worries about what hap-pens after the pain of birth. Whether you are a mother or business owner you wonder how you will be able to foresee and plan for what's coming around the corner. You have no idea how you are going to integrate all the pieces of your life into your new role of mom or entrepreneur. Because things are so crazy, you wonder how you'll find the time to brush your hair, work out, spend time with the business and your friends and family. How are you supposed to find time to figure out your short-, medium-, and long-term plans? You wonder where to go to get help and advice on all the gazil-lion areas you know nothing about. You worry about what to do when things go wrong. You panic that you are going to run out of money. As for your busi-ness, you don't even know who your customers are and how much to charge them. You wonder if you should play by yourself or take on a 'business part-ner.' You ask yourself, 'Is it true that there is no place like home for my busi-ness or that my business has no place at home?' You haven't even figured out what business face or image you want to present to the world. But trust me, Joanne. All these questions get answered eventually."

Different Types of Business Births

The Natural Birth — The Classic Business Start-up

A natural birth is one where you conceived and incubated the business idea and gave birth to it yourself. This is the typical start-up situation that will be dealt with at length throughout this book. The classic business start-up car-ries your DNA, your unique skills, experience, and passion. This type of birth results in an extraordinary bond between you and your business. You expe-rience everything, from start to finish.

However, unlike biological births, the pain of the actual launch or labour can be mitigated by how well you take care and plan during the pre-birth period. You have 100 percent control of your concept during this time. All of the choices are yours.

Adopting a Business — The Classic Business Purchase

A teacher once told me of an exchange that took place in her first-grade class. The kids were discussing a picture of a family. One little boy in the picture had different hair colour than the other family members. One child suggested that he was adopted. A little girl named Jocelyn said, "I know all about adoptions because I'm adopted." "What does it mean to be adopted?" asked another child. "It means," Jocelyn said, "that you grew in your mommy's heart instead of in her tummy." Adopting a business does entail many of the same emotions and processes as a business start-up, with a few notable exceptions.

The gestation period of a business adoption, as with a natural birth, also involves choice. You have to choose which business you buy. As the purchaser, you have to determine the value of the business. You have the difficult task of negotiating or choosing a price that works for both you and the owner. There is always the worry and risk that existing clients will leave when you take over, especially if you are in a personal service business, so you have to choose how to handle the transition from the previous owner. For example, are you going to "clean house" in order to implement rapid change, or choose the slower lane by having the previous owner stay on for a period of time? You also have to choose how to move the business forward and choose how you will form your own relationship with the clients, employees, and suppliers.

Another difference between a classic start-up and adopting an already existing business is an emotional one. Negotiating with the previous owner can often be more painful than delivering the business to market yourself. To the seller, it can feel like losing a child. Parents often — no, always — have an over-inflated opinion of how great their own kids are. The incumbent owner of a business is no different. Many business purchases falter because the previous owner feels that the business is worth far more than it is to a prospective new owner. Even though the existing owner wants to sell, sometimes it's tougher to create a win/win situation.

The upside of purchasing a business is that it already exists. You actually get to see it up and running before you have to make the choice. And you can check out its sterling (one hopes) track record. Technically "valuing" a business is the job of accountants who have been specially trained as Chartered Business Valuators, or CBVs. These folks apply certain reasonable general rules to the operations, assets, and potential of the business. In order to arrive at a range of value that can be substantiated by the financial history and outlook of the business, they will look at the quality of:

- the stuff owned and owed that's listed on the financial statements. For example: receivables, inventory, fixed assets, payables, and loans.
- assets not on the financial statements — things like the company's customer base, relationship with suppliers and creditors, including what terms

are available. There are assets like employees, location, patents or trademarks, brand names, and exclusivity of territory.

- income and profit potential of the business and the ability of the business to generate cold hard cash.

This is the art of accounting at its best. But before you get the accountants involved, do your homework. If you are seriously considering buying into or buying an existing business outright, you may want to consider completing the comprehensive checklist in Doug and Diana Gray's book, *The Complete Canadian Small Business Guide*. It's a gazillion pages long but it's a good step in determining whether the business is worthy of investing the fees for a CBV.

Because you have not been part of the business's life from the outset, there is a possibility that problems exist beneath the surface that you cannot see. At a minimum you should involve a lawyer and an accountant with business purchase/sale experience before you make an offer to purchase. Get them involved again when you actually ink the agreement, which is a legally binding contract. They should both be familiar with buying businesses and will help ensure that your letter of intent includes the deadline for sign-backs of both the letter of intent and the purchase-and-sale agreement, the conditions or the results of your investigation that will allow you to walk away, your proposed terms of payment, and whether you are buying the assets or shares (if incorporated) of the business. If the business is incorporated, most sellers want to sell the shares, which means both the assets *and* the liabilities of the company. Your lawyer will help you determine if what the seller has claimed and represented to you is true by checking to see if there are any liens against the assets, any lawsuits pending, or claims registered against the business.

Not only will you have to deal with the ego of the previous owner during the negotiations, you will also have to deal with the established behaviour patterns of the people already involved in the business who, like most, probably hate change. If you are lucky, there will be a talented pool of experience. If you are not so lucky, you will have slackers whom the previous owner didn't have the heart to fire. Establishing your authority and operating style may be difficult because people have become used to the ways of the previous owner. Just be aware that usually a business sale/purchase will result in loss of employees as well as possible client and supplier attrition. The good news is that bringing in new blood may help the business reach new heights.

While adopting an existing business is not entirely a fresh start, it can be a quicker start. It could even act as the catalyst in taking the business to the next level. It can release untapped talent among the staff and ignite new networks and market opportunities. Sometimes all it takes is a new owner to realize potential in a business that hadn't been realized before.

In summary, here are the steps to keep in mind when buying a business:

- Define the kind of business you want to buy *first* and then go out and find the right company to purchase.

- Do research before setting the initial price. Don't overestimate the value of the status quo.

- Make sure your letter of intent is very specific. Don't worry about offending the integrity of the seller. Put everything in writing.

- Do the best "due diligence" that you can afford to do. Go into it with the mindset that you are *not* going to buy the company and look for the reasons that you should. Err on the side of being too skeptical and be prepared to walk away.

Surrogate Business Ownership — The Classic Franchise

Franchising is a hybrid model and technically embodies the best of both worlds. It can offer the "wonder of creation" of the start-up. At the same time franchising offers the security of working with the support system of an established operation.

Or so I thought.

Paula and I spent an afternoon wandering around a small business trade show. There were the usual suspects from the world of computers, financial services, and phone companies. We passed by a row of exhibitors hawking franchising opportunities. Seemed innocent enough to me until I heard Paula mutter, "These people remind me of being at a timeshare salespersons' convention. Prospects better keep their eyes wide, wide open."

"Huh?" I asked, mystified at Paula's comment. "I thought franchising was a good thing. I know lots of people, including my Uncle Gerry, who got into franchising. What's this about 'eyes wide open'?"

"Joanne, the truth of the matter is that theory and reality tend to diverge in the practical light of day. Think of franchising as joint custody. Technically, joint custody is supposed to be better than sole custody and oftentimes it is. But sometimes it's just a bad experience spread out over more real estate." I sensed Paula getting ready to step up to the accountant pulpit.

"Okay, girl," I prompted. "I'll put my quarter in. Go."

"In Canada, with the exception of Alberta, there is no strong legislation overlooking the activities and claims of franchisors. Many unsuspecting wannabe entrepreneurs are lured by the possibility of 'starting their own business' but not having to be entirely on their own. Many fall prey to the high-pressure sales tactics and overinflated claims of those franchisors who treat franchising as a financing strategy instead of what it really is, a business format."

"What does that mean?" I asked. "I'm confused, what's wrong with franchisors using franchising as a financing strategy?"

"I've been on both sides of the deal," Paula continued. "I've worked as an executive of a national franchisor and I've been at street level as a co-franchisee. I have seen far too many franchisors selling franchises for all the wrong reasons. They need that next franchise sale to pay for *their* mortgage and lifestyle instead of investing in the health and well-being of the franchisee support structure."

"Oops. I see your point. It's like some commissioned salespeople?" I offered.

"Exactly. The problem is that sometimes people approach buying a franchise with more trust and less diligence than if they were purchasing a stand-alone business from another person or starting their own from scratch. The reality is, there should be *more* diligence. That's because you are purchasing a business from someone else and you are tying your fate and reputation to the franchisor and every other franchisee in the network. The old 'we are only as strong as our weakest link' takes on a whole new meaning."

"But I thought one of the main attractions to buying a franchise is not having to go it alone. Isn't the franchisor there to support you and make sure you succeed?" I queried.

"A good one does and the industry is making great efforts to promote those who do. That's why the Canadian Franchise Association screens its potential members and refuses membership to those not living up to the standard that they have set. This association supports a self-governance model for the industry. Unfortunately, some franchisors are primarily sales organizations with aggressive sales targets and very little time, money, or diversity of business skills left over to support the franchisees," Paula said.

"Well, surely you can mitigate that risk by checking them out thoroughly," I said.

"What's interesting, Joanne, is that many people remember to check out the other franchisees but few apply the same rigour to their investigation of the franchisor. And that's if they do an investigation at all. They take the franchisor at their word. Even when investigating the franchisees, people often talk only to the franchisees that the franchisor directs them to. People need to make sure the list of franchisees that the franchisor provides is complete and that they are allowed to choose randomly from it."

"Yikes. A strong example of *caveat emptor* or "buyer beware," I commented.

"Absolutely. There are excellent opportunities out there but there are bad ones too. I swear in today's world, just about anything can be franchised. I have seen some pretty wanky, fly-by-night operations. Once I received a letter from a lawyer trying to sell a cat-skinning franchise in Mexico. I actually deliberated whether or not this was serious, that's how weird things have become."

Appalled, I said, "Cat-skinning? That is seriously disgusting and hopefully a really bad joke."

"Yeah, it probably was," Paula agreed. "It's far easier to identify and steer clear of the strange concept operations, like that one. What's tough is identifying the ones that appear normal, everyday, and for every person, but really aren't. And it's even harder to figure out which ones haven't laid a strong operational or financial foundation. Believe me, there are a lot more casualties in this category."

"Does the public know how to avoid falling for the wrong ones?" I asked.

Shaking her head, Paula replied, "Not as well as they should. What people really have to figure out is how to get the information they'll need to make good business decisions. They need to protect themselves by asking tough questions. People should also be aware of the typical responses they'll get."

"Such as?" I asked. It was getting tougher to act uninterested. "Let's say I took leave of every one of my God-given senses and decided to buy that cat-skinning franchise. What should I ask about in advance?"

"Would that be before or after the throttling I'd give you?" Paula laughed. "The first thing you'd do is make sure that the concept works in Canada. A great example is Mail Boxes Etc. (MBE). It started out in 1980 in the U.S. and now has 3700 franchisees in over 58 countries. Gregg Kuperstein, the director of marketing over there told me that the MBE concept is set to take advantage of one of the most significant sociological transformations since we moved from the farmhouse to the factory. The original concept was to be a post office alternative but it quickly evolved into a full-service centre for business. Since 1991, the concept has ridden the wave of the growing number of entrepreneurs in Canada. Now with 219 franchises established, they are poised to grow to 600 by the year 2005."

"Wow," I said. "By that time almost 40 percent of all Canadians will wear 'entrepreneur' as a job title. It's a good example of how opportunities drop in your lap if you have your lap where opportunities drop. Okay, so, let's assume the concept works, what next?"

"Get a handle on the financial stability of the franchisor. Ask to see a copy of their most recent and preferably audited financial statements. What they may tell you is, 'We are a private company and do not release our financial information to anyone.' If you are refused financial information or not given other ways to get it, throw up a red flag. You need to ask for credit references from trade suppliers, employees, and franchisees. Ask them if the bills are paid on time and how they would describe their relationship with the franchisor. Positive answers are usually a good indicator of the company's financial health and well-being."

"That's going to be a lot harder than it sounds. My mother always taught me it's rude to ask people about their financial affairs," I said.

"Get over it, friend," Paula said. "Because you've got to dig even deeper. Knowing that the franchisor pays the bills on time won't tell you anything about their growth trends. And if you can't get the information about growth trends from an outside third party, you have to ask the franchisor."

"Ask for what?" I asked, fearing that I was sounding exceptionally clueless.

"Ask for a report showing the number of locations opened each year by both the franchisor and franchisees. Ask how many are still owned by the original franchisee. You also need to know how many were closed and how many the franchisor took over and why. You need access to plans for the future to get a fix on whether the franchisor's projected franchise growth rates are realistic or suicidal. If head office is unwilling to share these numbers with you, send red flag number two up the pole. It may be the case that the franchisor just plain doesn't have a plan for growth. Joanne, I can't say this strongly enough — *if the franchisor does not have a business plan they shouldn't be franchising.* After all, that is really what you are buying — a tested and proven business plan. The franchisor's own actions in the planning area will speak volumes either in support of or in contradiction to their claim that their franchise package is worth buying. At an absolute minimum, be sure that you look at the annual rate of growth in the number of franchises that have actually been opened."

"It's like putting your money where your mouth is," I said.

"Precisely. Now, in a perfect world, you should look at the performance of the franchisees that started no fewer than three years ago. Ask to see a comparison of the projections given to them and what really happened — the actual financial results. This will give you the comfort of knowing that in the projections you are given, the sales are not overstated and expenses understated. You may be told, 'We don't do those types of comparisons. Besides, the financial information of franchisees is confidential. However, our franchisees always overachieve because our projections are very conservative.' Get bold. Tell them they are missing a great selling point. Emphasize that this is an important decision point for you so you are happy to wait until the analysis is complete. If you are still meeting with resistance, dig into your supply of red flags. The good news is many franchisors, like MBE, will give you summary sales figures to show you the performance of their franchise network. That way they can keep the individual information confidential."

"I'm running out of red flags, Paula," I said.

"Oh? Well, hold one in reserve," Paula said. "One of the most common franchise benefits touted by franchisors is the 'strength in numbers' philosophy. You'll hear, 'Our pricing to our franchisees is the most competitive because we buy on volume.' Notice the word is *buy* on volume, not *sell*. Sometimes the only benefactor of the volume discount is the franchisor themselves. Ensure that the tools and supplies needed for your business and stuff like the signs, marketing brochures, and training programs that the head office provides are priced competitively. You are often required to buy all this directly from the franchisor. Don't take their word on it that it's the best price you'll get. Comparison shop and deal with the restriction on whom you can buy from up front and before you sign any agreement. After all, you may have a sister-in-law who is a printer and family prices are usually the best in town."

"I learned that one with one of our large bank clients," I said. "It seems some of their suppliers actually put a premium on their price because they are perceived to have deep pockets. So, what else do I need to watch for before deciding whether or not to buy that cat-skinning franchise?"

Paula rolled her eyes as she answered, "You would seek out information on the business experience, expertise, and reputation of the franchisor."

"Check out the reputation of the cat-skinning lawyer, eh? Somehow I can see a lawyer being good at skinning. It seems to me that many of them have related experience," I joked.

Paula laughed as she continued. "Ask for CVs of all of the key managers and the owners themselves. Get business references. Check with the Better Business Bureau, the Ministry of Labour, the media, and former franchisees if you can find them."

"That may be tough. Can't say I've run into many cat skinners in my circle," I deadpanned.

"The last thing I'd recommend is to get the franchisor to amortize the up-front franchise fee over the course of the first couple of years. Try to tie the instalment payment to the performance of the business. Of course, there is a good chance they'll say, 'The up-front franchise fee just barely covers the up-front support and inventory of materials and goods you need to get started. What if *you* don't work hard enough to make your targets?' Recognize that if you don't skin enough cats, that is, make your targets, it might be because of a lack of support or a problem with the franchise system. It's a possible clue that the franchisor might have a possible cash flow issue if they need your money to get you started."

"Well, as usual, you have a strong opinion on this matter. I'm not sure I'm comfortable being seen with you here on Franchisors' Row," I said to Paula, nervously looking about. "There's gotta be some upside here. Franchising is a huge business."

"Relax," Paula said. "I don't want to leave you with the impression that all franchise opportunities are suspect. There are clear and distinct advantages to owning and operating a franchise of a healthy, reputable, and responsible franchisor, one with a proven system. I'll share with you some of the pros, just so long as you pay attention to my 'been there — done that' pointers. Frankly, I think one of the greatest upsides to franchising is that the business plan has already been developed and tested."

I quickly agreed. "I, for one, would love that, being the planning genius that I have been in the past. So tying into a proven business plan is a good thing. What else?"

"Whoa," Paula said. "Make sure that the operational plan, or as it's sometimes called, the operations manual, is in writing."

"I'm getting a headache," I said.

"Joanne," Paula continued, "this document is especially important in the franchise scenario. In most cases, the standard franchise agreement, which is your legal contract, uses this operations manual to set out what is acceptable operational procedure according to the franchisor."

"I know what you are going to say, *'Read it carefully!!!'* " I mimicked in my almost perfect Paula-the-Accountant voice.

Again ignoring me completely, Paula said, "Just make sure you understand each guideline and why things are required to be done the way that's being suggested. Take the time to note which guidelines may not apply to your franchise location. You may find out later that you do not have any choice whether or not to follow them. The bad news is that not following the guidelines could result in your breaching your franchise agreement."

"Give me an example of what you mean. What things should I be on the lookout for?" I inquired.

"Well," Paula thought for a moment. "Maybe your business is the first of its kind in a particular region, province, or country. You have to be sure that the way the franchisor expects you to operate does not violate or offend any laws, cultural norms, or generally accepted standards. We have incredible diversity just within Canada: language laws are different in Quebec, franchise laws are different in Alberta. Another example is that with new and better technology, you may wish to operate your business virtually or from a home office. Some franchisors require that you set up a retail location even when your operation mostly takes orders by phone. Reducing your overhead would increase your profits; however, most franchisors focus on revenue because that's the baseline on which royalties are calculated. Another thing to look out for would be if the minimum sales targets established by the franchisor exceed your personal financial objectives. At this point in your life, whether because you have a young family or you have already worked hard for a lot of years, you may not want to become a one-person multinational. Talk to a lawyer experienced in dealing with franchise law. They can walk you through your obligations and rights in the franchise agreement."

"Okay, so I've got the plan in writing, I've actually read it, and it's good. I buy it all. I've considered how my operation may be unique. Why else would I consider franchising?" I asked.

"If you were to rate all your challenges and headaches on a scale, you'd probably come up with some variation of the following list — attracting new customers, getting financing (living in a cave is the only way to have avoided hearing the repeated outrage of small business owners when it comes to this one), and the loneliness of being on your own. The popularity of franchising has a lot to do with some of the benefits it offers on all three of these fronts," Paula said, but without coming to a full stop.

"First of all, the marketing costs and responsibility in a franchise system are shared. But this is only a plus if the franchisor's marketing and advertising plans benefit your franchise operation. Make sure the franchisor involves you in the marketing planning process. For example, MBE has an established franchise advisory council, with a representative from each major region. It meets three times a year and keeps in regular contact so that it can act as a sounding board for new products and processes. They maintain an informal ad hoc volunteer committee that meets four times a year before each promotional season in order to get feedback and input on marketing programs. You may also want the franchisor to provide an accounting of how your marketing dollars are being used.

"Here's something else to consider. One of the best ways to assess the financial stability of a company is to ask someone else who has and is privy to information that you can't get at. Enter the banks. In fact, the mere existence of a formal franchise financing package from one of the banks can go a long way to making sure you sleep at night. The bank has had to determine the financial health of the franchisee system in advance to ensure that it is even bankable. And most franchisors have made the rounds to most of the banks with the intent of establishing a third-party financing program for new franchise owners. They are willing to share more detailed plans and financial information in the hopes that the bank will agree to establish this pre-authorized financing arrangement. This type of program is attractive to franchisors because it adds value to the franchisee sales package. Not only does it give the organization credibility, but it gives them the added bonus of not having to use their own funds to provide financial support. But this information is only to augment, not replace, your exercising due diligence.

"People who get into franchising tell me that one of the greatest benefits is not having to go it entirely alone, that they love the fact they can leverage off the business experience of not only the franchisor, but the other franchisees as well. You just need to be sure the franchisor has dedicated paid staff to answer your questions and provide you with support. It would be terrific if the staff's performance were tied to that of the franchises they supported. You can be guaranteed that this would ensure their attention and priorities stayed focused on you. It also really helps if there is some kind of formal communication channel or forum, like a network for example, for the franchisees only. MBE franchisees, for example, are guaranteed 48-hour response time to queries of head office. In addition, there is a bi-monthly support newsletter, continuing education programs, as well as monthly networking and support meetings at the regional office level. It's also important to figure out if they have accessible, collaborative leadership at head office. This goes a long way to mitigating the 'me versus them' attitude that is very prevalent and so often a destructive force within franchise systems.

"As a franchisee you will definitely not be alone. You will have many relationships to consider and manage. Like an independent business owner, you will have the relationships with your customers, staff, suppliers, banker, accountant, referral sources, and the media. Like an employee, you have your relationship with the franchisor and their staff. Like a business partner, you have your relationship with your fellow franchisees. Because the web of relationships in this business model is very extensive and interdependent, it is so important that you clearly spell out, in writing, any and all of the terms of the relationship that can be identified in advance. The franchisor will likely have a stock franchise agreement already prepared. As with most agreements, it will likely be biased towards the preparer. Make sure you read it very carefully to ensure that your needs, the claims that you feel are important, are included. If you want to make sure that you have any rights that extend beyond the posturing of the courting period, make sure it becomes part of your franchise agreement. This is your only protection if things start to go wrong. Above all, get and listen to professional advice from a lawyer who is familiar with franchise agreements."

By the time Paula had come up for breath, I had learned more about franchising than I may have cared to know and we had come full circle at the trade show. As we were preparing to take our leave, I turned to Paula and said, "Let's put the sarcasm aside for a brief moment, shall we? I really believe a single conversation with a wise person is worth a month of study in books. It's obvious that your experience in the world of franchising can be of extreme value to someone considering a cat-skinning venture. I think I have a bit more work to do before going down this road."

"Yeah, like getting a lobotomy reversed," Paula said, as we stepped out into the cold. The doors closed behind us.

If you're seriously considering buying a franchise, Doug Gray has a book on franchising called *The Complete Canadian Franchise Guide*. And no. He's not paying us a commission, but he has written a mere 16 Canadian business books, all excellent and ranging from starting a home-based business to financing your entrepreneurial venture.

Planning for a Healthy Business Birth

In Chapter 2, we talked about how essential it is to consider the emotional and financial return on your investment when conceiving your business. We discussed what had to go into using entrepreneurship as a means to achieve your emotional and financial goals. In this chapter, we are dealing with the "how's" — the "how to" start or give birth to your business, regardless of what form it takes — the "how to" plan and prepare your business for survival and growth in the real world. This chapter deals with what you should think about practically before giving birth to your business.

Regardless of whether your time conceiving your business was easy or hard, your business birth will be sometimes difficult, mostly wonderful, and always profound. Some births are long and protracted, some quick and easy, and many are plagued with false starts. But know this: You have to plan. And although it is always best to do as much planning as possible in advance, the reality is often quite different. Entrepreneurs understand that they can't examine every option, limit every threat, and eliminate every risk. Entrepreneurs don't wait until everything is perfect. When Champlain's boat hit the shore, someone had to jump off first. But studies show that women entrepreneurs do plan more than their male counterparts. That's why we will spend so much time in this chapter talking about the art of business planning.

What, Me Worry?

Research bears out the following: Women worry more than men. Witness Michael's ability to sleep at night while I mamboed with the night demons. This worry thing may be a major factor contributing to why women use *"what if"* or *scenario planning* as a key decision-making methodology. Dr. Deborah Tannen's research shows that women do consider many ways to accomplish the desired end and consider *all* the angles before making a decision. Being holistic creatures, we make business decisions in concert with other parts of our lives. In our world, everything is connected. We are connected to our friends and families, who are connected to our businesses, which are connected to our financial lives, which are connected to our spiritual, emotional, and physical health. Our businesses are made up of the vital connections we make when we network, sell, market, advertise, and look for suppliers, clients, and employees. When creating and starting a business, this tendency to consider all the angles, whether natural or learned, is a huge asset because it means we are usually better prepared. The downside is that we get less sleep because our brains can't stop churning as we spin our plans.

My mom tells a great story of the time she and Dad pulled their car over to ask a teenager how far it was to their destination. They were told, "If you keep going the way you are headed it will be about 50,000 kilometres. But if you turn around, it will be about 3 kilometres." A plan keeps you going in the right direction.

Marrying our personal experience and practical expertise, Paula and I came up with five key planning areas to think about before you nail up the Open *For Business* sign on your door. The intent is to help you take a more direct route to your goals, not the dizzying route I took. We'll look at these briefly here and go into more detail later.

1. The Art of Planning Your Business

Suppose you were on a non-stop flight to the Orient and heard this announcement: "Ladies and gentlemen, this is your captain speaking. We're travelling west across the Pacific Ocean. In a few hours, you'll be able to look down and see land. When that happens, we're going to start looking for a big city with an airport. If we find one, before our fuel runs out, we'll land. Then we'll figure out where we are and decide where we want to go next. In the meantime, folks, just sit back, relax, and enjoy your trip."

A case for planning? I think so.

I know so many companies that have all the ingredients of success but have never come up with a suitable recipe. A plan is a suitable recipe. Peter Drucker says long-range planning does not deal with future decisions, but with the future of present decisions.

So, it is always wise to have a Plan B, C, or even Z in your back pocket. Can you think of some ways other than what you are doing now to accomplish what you want? Walk the perimeter of your business concept, looking at it from different vantage points. Solicit insight and feedback from as wildly divergent sources as you can find. Remember, your goal is to identify and investigate other ways of doing business. It is not to convince the other person that your idea or methods are right or the best. This process ensures that you don't jump to conclusions and that you actually plan.

2. Stay in Touch With Your Goals

What would you need to have in place today to consider yourself and your business successful? Think in both financial and personal terms — both matter deeply. What about next year? Five years from now? Don't worry about being out in la-la land. I would have told anyone who said I was going to be married and pregnant — oh, excuse me, pregnant and married — one year after I started the business that they were not of this planet.

Mary Kay Ash, founder of Mary Kay Cosmetics, never lost sight of her goals. When she wanted to borrow $12 from a friend to attend a sales conference, the friend told her she'd be better off using the money to buy her children shoes instead of wasting it on some dream. Yet it is these dreams and goals that make women successful. Golda Meir, a "common" woman in her culture, became the prime minister of Israel. Margaret Thatcher lived over her father's grocery store until she was 21. Grandma Moses started painting in her seventies and became a revered and world-renowned artist.

3. Test the Waters

Said another way, before bringing a product to market, make sure the product has a market. You can do this to a certain degree by research and running your ideas by "those in the know" — your prospects and peers. It is important to understand who is buying your product. You need to study the market so you can better understand how to sell to it. I know a real estate broker in Vancouver who joined a local real estate office. The first thing she did, which no one else had done before, was to make a map of all the houses in the area, attaching a price and recent sales history to each one. This showed her where the least and the most expensive areas were. It also revealed that people were constantly trading up from a home of about $300,000 to something more expensive. She decided to go after the market segment that was trading up. Four years later, at the age of 22, she owned the real estate agency.

4. Anticipate Life's Little Bumps

I wake up each morning torn between a desire to make the world a better place and a desire to enjoy it. This makes it hard to plan the day. Before we can have a plan, we have to know what we are planning for. This is what we call the "what-if" stage. This is where you can let your imagination run wild. Think about what events, both from within your company and outside it, would trigger which alternative plan.

I know a hilarious story of a woman who was asked to "what-if" during a job interview. She had applied for a job as a flag person at a railroad crossing and was told she would be given the job if she could pass a test consisting of a single question. Agreeing, she was told to imagine she was a flagger at a crossing having but a single track where she suddenly observed a freight train approaching from the east at 170 kilometres per hour and, looking in the other direction, saw another freight train bearing down from the west at 190 kilometres per hour. Having further been told that the two trains were at the time 90 metres apart, the job-seeker was then asked what she would do under such circumstances. Without hesitation, the would-be flagger responded that she would go and get her brother-in-law. Puzzled, the railroad's examiner inquired what good that would do, to which the job-seeker replied, "He ain't ever seen a train wreck."

5. Show Me the Money

This is not calculus. There has to be money around when you need it. Which, unfortunately, is pretty much all of the time. However, what can sometimes feel like calculus is trying to figure out a way to consistently and accurately project how much cash is coming in and when. In ugly accounting terms, this process is called projecting cash flow. This is one of the most important business concepts to master in the pre-birth and birth stage. To illustrate: If a sales manager hired a new salesperson in January and agreed to pay her $100,000 a year, the sales manager should hold back her paycheque during the first 11 months and pay her entire salary in December. This would be a great way to demonstrate how difficult it is to run a company with no cash. If you don't, you'll do as I did: scramble too often to "beg, borrow, and contemplate stealing" to pay the rent or make payroll.

The Art of Planning Your Business

Prebirth business planning ensures that you will have the resources ready — sanity, energy, time, and money — to care properly for the business once it is born. Of course you don't have to plan. You could just start and see what happens. If you are tempted to go this route, stop reading immediately. Go back and reread chapter 1.

Not planning puts your business at serious risk — risk of possible failure. I endured terrible growing pains because I didn't take the time to really think everything through. I just showed up for work each day, teeth gritted and ready for battle.

In Paula's experience, planning and being proactive are always difficult for everyone. I, for one, justified not doing long-range planning because of the busyness of managing day to day. I made the mistake of thinking time spent there was of more value than time spent in some airy-fairy arm-wavy head game. I couldn't have been more wrong. The time spent in putting out fires that resulted from lack of *"what-iffing"* was a hundredfold what I would have spent in a simple constructive exercise of asking "what if." And I don't mean the nasty what-iffing I tortured myself with at 3:00 a.m.: "What if I go bankrupt?" or "What if everyone thinks I'm some kind of wing nut?" With the exception of the last point, none of the nasty what-ifs came to light.

Planning Your Business Versus Writing Your Plan

Kate was having an active day. As I sat in my chair watching her elbow or knee glide across my stomach, I said, "Get a load of this, Paula." Paula turned in time to see Kate kick with such a wallop that I jumped a good foot off my chair. Her eyes wide in amazement, she said, "Why does the movie *Alien* leap to mind?" I suggested we take one of our strolls through a local park to get my mind off the football game going on inside.

The reality of Kate's imminent arrival was growing stronger with every passing day. "I think I need to write a new business plan, Paula. One based on zero revenue for the next six months. Zip, naught, nada, goose egg."

Paula zeroed right in on the word "write." "My dear misguided friend," she began, "on one level you are right. Regardless of where you are in the life cycle of your business — conception, birth, or the raising stage — you do need to plan. But please take particular note that I did not say 'write' a plan. Please don't confuse the act of planning with the act of documentation.

"Technically, planning is 100 percent thinking, investigating, analyzing, choosing, and decision making. How and if you choose to communicate the results of these activities is entirely up to you. You can keep it in your head, share it with your colleagues, or tell your butcher, for that matter. You can draw a picture, record it on cassette, or, if you wish, write it down. Business pundits are quick to point out that you are 'doomed to failure' and could never be entirely 'successful,' whatever that means, without a written business plan. Guess the majority of the companies that made it to *Profit's 100 Fastest Growing Companies* list missed that newsflash. Get this. 1998's *Profit 100* were surveyed and asked whether or not they started and ran their business with a formal written business plan. Less than half said yes. However, when asked how many use such a plan today, the number shot up to 84 percent. This illustrates that a written business plan does become necessary later when it becomes more likely that you will have to share your plan with others, like a banker."

"Oy, don't hold back, Paula," I exclaimed. "If I hear you correctly, and I'm praying beyond all hope that I have, I don't have to write a business plan? That's contrary to everything I've ever read or been told by bankers, academics, and business experts. I mean, if I wanted to build a house, the first thing the contractor would ask for would be the plans. The lumber and concrete are no good unless I have a plan to put them together into some kind of finished product."

"Joanne, all successful entrepreneurs have a plan for their business, but as the survey showed, not necessarily in writing. They have identified the assumptions that their business is based on as well as its key success formula. They have tested their assumptions to ensure that they work. And most importantly, these entrepreneurs have figured out how to stay connected with that success formula. Look, both you and I are married to engineers. We know that thousands of engineers can design bridges, calculate strains and stresses, and draw up specifications for machines, but the great engineer is the person who can tell whether the bridge or machine should be built at all, where it should be built, and when.

"While I absolutely advocate and support the need to plan your business, I have seen it time and time again — many new entrepreneurs hyperfocus on *writing the plan* instead of *planning the business*."

"Well, Paula," I said. "I'd like to lock you and 10 other business pundits in a small room and let you all slug out the way business planning should be done. There seem to be as many different opinions on this issue as there are experts."

Never Forget the Business Is You

It seemed to me our pace quickened considerably as Paula continued with her business planning rant. I felt two heart rates climbing, both mine and Kate's, as we moved from stroll to brisk walk. "Most business books and academics focus on the importance of the document itself: its content, presentation, and format," Paula continued. But that's only part of the equation. A proper plan is impossible without reference to its key asset — you. You are the key contributor, the main ingredient, the maker. What most people forget is that ensuring that both you and your business are healthy involves preparing both a personal and a business plan that are compatible and are integrated. Joanne, the perfect business plan is where Richard Bolles, author of *What Color is Your Parachute*, meets the more technical Doug and Diana Gray. A healthy business ownership plan is a plan that considers the *how* part — how are you going to start and raise a healthy business? And, unless you are an engineer, it's this 'how' part that is the toughest to figure out."

Stay in Touch With Your Goals

Goals make work more fun. They are nothing more than dreams with a time limit. When you are starting out on a journey, it helps to know the destination. Your emotional and financial goals are supposed to act as a rudder for your business. Your endpoint is simply where you want to end up eventually. If you don't have a very clear idea of what your goals are, the endpoint becomes a moving target. The good news is that just having a general idea of where you want to end up can limit the number of options you have to process or decisions you have to make. Consequently, your actions are tied to some reference point and aren't just random. This endpoint or goal gives you a vision that will keep you pressing on. Here's an example.

The California coast was shrouded in fog that Fourth of July morning in 1952. Twenty-one miles to the west on Catalina Island, a 34-year-old woman waded into the water and began swimming towards California, determined to be the first woman to make it across. Her name was Florence Chadwick and she was already the first woman to swim the English Channel in both directions.

The water was numbingly cold that July morning and the fog was so thick she could hardly see the boats in her own party. Millions were watching on national television. Several times sharks, which had gotten too close, had to be driven away with rifles to protect the lone figure in the water. As the hours ticked by, she swam on. Fatigue had never been her big problem in these swims. The danger was the bone-chilling cold of the water.

More than 15 hours later, numbed with cold, she asked to be taken out. She couldn't go on. Her mother and trainer in the boat alongside told her they were near land. They urged her not to quit. But when she looked towards the California coast, all she could see was dense fog.

She was pulled out only half a mile from her destination.

Later, she told news reporters, "I'm not offering excuses, but I think I could have made it if I had been able to *see* my goal." She figured out that she had been licked not by fatigue or even the cold. It was the fog that defeated her — it obscured her goal. It was the only time Florence Chadwick quit.

She decided to try again. This time, she concentrated on developing a mental image of the coast of California. She memorized every feature of the distant coast and fixed it clearly in her mind. Two months later, she swam the same channel and encountered all of the choppy waters and fog she had met before. This time she made it. Not only was she the first woman to swim the Catalina Channel, she beat the men's record by two hours.

Remember, your endpoint is a focus point not just a target. Don't fret too much about being perfectly clear as to what lies ahead. Just go as far as you can go. From there you can see farther. There is no falling short, only moving closer to or away from your goal.

Progress is by no means a fluid experience. There are fits and starts; you go one way, then another, but it's progress just the same. No one knows this better than these two intrepid hunters:

> Luke and Anton hired a seaplane to take them hunting in our great Canadian north. They were to fly in at sunrise and fly out at sunset. All went well on the way in, but when the pilot returned to pick them up, he found Luke, Anton, and two large moose.
>
> "You'll have to leave one of those moose behind," the pilot said. "I can't handle the weight."
>
> "No way!" cried Luke. "Last year we chartered a plane just like yours and the pilot took us *and* the two moose."
>
> "Hmmm," mused the pilot. "I'm the best there is and if he did it last year, I can do it today. Let's load up."
>
> The plane was soon loaded with both moose, Luke and Anton, their gear, and the pilot. The little plane roared down the lake struggling to gain altitude, barely clearing the treetops. The pilot managed to keep the plane airborne for a while but the weight proved too much. The little plane plopped down on an adjoining lake.
>
> Anton looked around and saw that no one was hurt. Turning to Luke he asked, "How did we do?"
>
> "Pretty good," said Luke. "I think we got a few miles farther than last year."

I guess it's all in how you define progress.

Paula and I were in my downtown office, grimly going over the company's financial statements in preparation for Kate's impending arrival. Kate, still in utero, was demanding to be fed for the ninth time that day. And it was only 11:00 a.m. Thankfully, Paula was always up for a food break. We headed down to Tom's, the building's quite serviceable restaurant.

"Here we go again, back in survival mode. Lord knows, Paula, I can't wait until I know whether this business is really a viable one. How long does it take to move beyond mere survival and become a real business?" I asked.

"Well, first of all, you are a real business. Viability simply means that something can exist in the real world under normal circumstances." She glanced down at my stomach. "Joanne, it's just like birth, there is a point in the baby's development when the baby can be born and survive outside the womb."

I remained thoughtful for a moment. "Yeah, but there is always the risk that if the baby is born too soon, it may not survive." I was thinking much more in terms of the business baby. Kate felt so huge at the moment that I wouldn't have been the least bit surprised if she came out looking for a football to punt.

"Yes, that's also possible," Paula concurred. "When you feel like you are in survival mode, and until you pass through it, there is always the chance that the complications from a premature birth could limit your chances for survival and future success. In a business sense, it can mean, for the short term anyway, that your personal and financial goals are still out of reach. But with some additional effort and struggles, even preemie businesses can develop into healthy and successful enterprises. A truly successful business birth just means your business has been born equipped to propel you towards and within reach of your goals, whether that be so many dollars in the bank or spending every morning until 10:00 a.m. with your children. It means you have a proper foundation to support getting both the emotional and financial ROI that you set as your benchmark of success."

"Hmmm, so viability is an absolute prerequisite to business success. Your business has to first survive in the real world before it can evolve to the next stage of serving you. What a profound concept."

"It's way too early for you to be panicking." Smiling, Paula patted my tummy. " You, girlfriend, are about to find out just how viable your business really is."

A Need Is a Need and a Want Is a Want and Often the Two Collide

What's the true difference between a viable business and a successful business? Viability relates to fulfilling basic daily needs. Success, on the other hand, notches objective-setting up one more level, to getting our wants fulfilled. Cue the W-FACTOR. While satisfying needs is acceptable, women have been conditioned to believe that satisfying their wants is selfish.

I never thought consciously about the difference between my wants and my needs and, frankly, didn't understand the fundamental difference between the two. It was a conversation with the wisest woman I know that put it sharply into perspective for me.

I was talking to my mother on the phone one evening, commenting on how gloriously the pregnancy was progressing. I didn't have morning sickness and was a fine example of the proverbial maternal glow. I had never looked or felt better. I was two weeks away from my due date and had gained 40 pounds, 10 in the last two weeks. I was admitting to her that as much as I'd like to say it was baby weight, I knew in my heart it was baklava weight. We were living near Toronto's Danforth area, a Greek community with an abundance of the city's finest eateries. My friends and I single-handedly hit every one of them in a scant two weeks.

I went on to say that I had my exercise equipment dusted off and was eagerly waiting to have it strut its stuff again right after Kate was born. I figured I would lose the weight within the first three months. I also casually mentioned a documentary on teenagers Michael and I had recently watched and told Mom I had a firm "no tongue-piercing" policy for Kate in place.

In her classic, understated style Mom said, "Well, my love, when Kate comes, reality is going to knock you square between the eyes. Don't be surprised if your exercise stuff sits idle for a long, long time. And you will be so exhausted, a strict no-anything policy will be a waste of time. Conserve energy for the big stuff, Joanne. You need to appreciate the subtle difference between real-life needs and what you want. Your desire to lose weight is important but you will desperately need sleep first. Wanting Kate to be a sane and rational teenager is honourable but she needs to learn to walk and talk first."

Bingo.

This conversation with my mother about the difference between wants and needs helped my personal and business life and my sanity more than just about anything else. In my business life, needs tended to be those annoying short-term problems that generally required some kind of immediate action. Like exercise and sleep, they often weren't consistent with what I wanted. Sometimes, I had to spend more money than I had to get the right person or I had to borrow from my personal line of credit to make payroll. Needs are like a newborn — they have short-term and immediate requirements. My business wants, on the other hand, are the goals for the future that I intend to achieve with the help of adequate intellectual and financial capital.

But, until I learned the difference between the two, my business needs and what I wanted seemed to be in constant collision, especially in the early years. If I had understood the difference between the two, I could have been better prepared psychologically. I wouldn't have felt I screwed up so often when short-term needs temporarily interfered with long-term goals. Having a long-term view from the very inception would have made it easier to prevent the company from becoming derailed and to stay on track. I could have saved a ton of emotional energy.

Test the Waters

By now, you probably have a fix on what you want to be when you grow up. You have a preliminary handle on what your business and personal goals are. Now you need to test to see if your goals within the context of your business are actually workable. The best way to test your business concept is to create a prototype.

To properly set the stage, you need to unpack the basics to construct the set. There are several things you need to ask yourself in advance of giving birth to your business. For example, do you have a one-line answer to the "And what do you do?" question? Who exactly are your clients going to be? How big is your market? Who's the competition? What's your mission statement? How do you figure out how much to charge for what you do? How are you going to tell people about what you do? How do you even begin to research the market?

To best help you with this most essential of planning stages, Paula and I will share our own experiences as well as those of two other women entrepreneurs. The first is Christine Magee, president and co-founder of the outrageously successful mattress retailer, Sleep Country Canada. The other is Sabine Schleese, of Schleese Saddlery, whom we'll introduce later.

Christine Magee: Good Homework, Great Results

I had the opportunity to chair a two-day conference in Toronto on Successful Management Strategies for Women. Christine, a banker-cum-entrepreneur, was part of a panel that presented at the conference. As she describes it, the rigour she has gone through in this stage of her business — testing the waters — absolutely guaranteed her company's success.

When I met Christine after the panel, I asked her, "Christine, why mattresses?"

"Oh, come on, Joanne," she replied. "Who hasn't aspired to be known as the 'mattress lady' since they were seven years old? Banking and mattress sales are both challenging and rewarding...but I sleep better at night now."

No wonder. The Vancouver-based operation has grown to over 50 stores throughout B.C., Alberta, and Ontario and employs 285 people.

"Is there anything about the business you don't like?" I asked.

"Yeah, people who ask 'Is she really the president?'"

Christine is married to Allen, a television producer. She was also 37 when they had a beautiful baby daughter. On several occasions during her tenure in the

Ontario Commercial Lending Unit at National Bank, Christine had extended financing to two men who were mattress manufacturers. As manufacturers, they were in a perfect position to see that there was a serious lack of retail presence in the mattress market. They came to Christine with an idea, and instead of dismissing mattress retailing as a supremely boring idea, the three decided to seize an incredible opportunity. Christine saw gold in them thar' mattresses. She says, "All you have to do is consider for a moment the reaction most people have to buying a mattress. It ranges from lack of interest to absolute abhorrence. But why?"

This is what Christine and her new business partners figured out. Selling mattresses to the public wasn't being done well. The first thing Christine uncovered in her research was that people buy mattresses very infrequently, maybe one every ten years. This fact, combined with the difficulty people have in assessing the product, means people have to rely on the retailer and its sales staff to assist them in selecting the right mattress. They estimated 50 percent of the market share was dominated by the department stores, which were not dedicated to this segment in either selection or sales training. The other 50 percent was highly fragmented among local furniture and specialty shops, with no significant national brand awareness in this field. The specialty shops were typically adorned in warehouse decor and generally adopted a pushy or hard sales approach. They also used a commodity discount pricing approach that markets only on price, not on individual needs.

Not only was the market not being well served but the stable demand for mattresses made the market very appealing. The fact that, as a retailer, Christine would have an automatically qualified customer walk through the door eliminated the question of browsers (people don't browse mattress stores like they do book stores). This really appealed to her. Her market research proved the economics would work and the need in the marketplace was there. But first, like Paula and me, Christine needed to figure out how to make it really happen.

So What Is It That You Do Again?

Like most new entrepreneurs, Paula and I sometimes run out of breath when trying to answer this question. I am not fond of the real answer which, in short form, looks something like: "I'm a mother/writer/wife/consultant/friend/speaker/rabblerouser/mediaspokesperson/daughter/television host/mentor/blahblahblah." Keeping it short and simple when you are trying to do justice to something as important as who you are or what your business is is unbelievably tough. It's not unusual at this stage to find that you may have decided what you want to do when you grow up but you don't have a clue how to articulate it. Enter your value proposition, sometimes referred to as your positioning statement.

Your value proposition articulates your business's positioning within your chosen market. It describes what you do, who your best customer is, and why they will pay you rather than someone else. Paula's, for example, is "Through a multi-disciplinary team of professionals who share our clients' entrepreneurial reality, AQUEOUS provides real-life, real-time business advice and support *(what they do that is unique)* to individuals starting, running, and growing their own business *(their best customer)*, enabling them to achieve their business and personal goals faster and easier *(why they pay AQUEOUS rather than anyone else)*."

A mission statement, on the other hand, says why you are motivated to do what you are doing. In my company's case, our mission statement is to make the world a better place by improving the overall financial and business education levels of girls and women. This includes educating the financial services sector on the economic power and realities of women's lives.

A slogan tries to capture why your target client is motivated to buy from you. It is an advertising byline that is crafted to catch the attention of your target customer by communicating a sentiment or attitude that your customer can identify with. A good example is Nike's "Just Do It." Sleep Country's is "Why buy a mattress anywhere else?" I hear this tag line so often it will be second in memory only to Pizza Pizza's phone number. A slogan can capture the main feature or benefit offered. It can even say what you do and occasionally for whom. This is where ours falls — "Educating women about money and educating financial services about women." But my personal favourite is "Aeroflot Airlines: You Have Made the Right Choice." This slogan was for an ad campaign for the only airline in the then Soviet Union.

But the mother of all business statements is really the value proposition because it says it all. It is the basis of your competitive advantage and the foundation of your marketing and sales efforts. Bottom line? It's why you get paid. As you will soon discover, creating this one statement is harder than it looks. So let's break the process down to make it easier to tackle crafting your value proposition.

Who Am I Really?

Think up one simple, concise sentence that describes what you offer and what is unique about it. Remember the key to unique is to focus on what makes your product or service different, not necessarily better. Ours was easy. We educate women about money and financial institutions about women.

Christine says, "I'm a sleep expert. I'm in the business of selling the service of sleep." Paula emphasizes the shared entrepreneurial reality she and her associates have with their clients.

Who Do I Want to Play With and Why?

Ask yourself: In a perfect world, who would be my best customer? A typical answer is "Everyone." There seems to be a widely held view, especially among new entrepreneurs, that limiting the definition of who your customers are will limit your success.

Generally speaking, business owners who believe that everyone is their customer are usually bound for failure. Why? They become nothing to nobody. Harry Beckwith, in his book *Selling the Invisible: A Field Guide to Modern Marketing*, captured the true benefit of being specific about who your best customer is in one statement: "Narrow your focus to broaden your position."[4] In Christine's case, it wasn't much of a stretch to realize that everyone needs a mattress. So, in essence, everyone was her target market. But her research indicated that women were the decision-makers in the choice of which mattress gets bought. That helped define who her customer was in a much more purposeful way.

The March 1998 *Marketing Magazine* said that the way to keep shoppers loyal is to segment the market. "Segmentation provides a way to understand and enhance customer loyalty by enabling marketers to tailor their products and efforts to the needs of particular groups of customers. If they meet their needs well, these customers become or stay loyal. Segmentation is simply a grouping process. Common ways to segment consumers are shopper loyalty, product purchasing, attitudes, and geo-demography. Directing marketing programs to satisfy the needs of groups in households is more complex than mass marketing, but far easier than trying to market to individuals."

For my company, it was much easier to position selling and marketing to women to the financial services industry than it was to absolutely everyone. I knew where the industry players were, where they were going, and how they thought. I knew exactly what the industry needed.

Here is an example of what I would define as the epitome of a product niche: "We want to go after those situations where we know there is a high propensity for people to want to communicate outside of where they are staying." This is a quote from MCI's John Jacquay on the prison pay phone product niche.

Sabine Schleese: Specific Need, Untapped Market

On the more serious side, we have a classic story of someone finding a very specific need in a very specific market. Enter Sabine Schleese. Sabine is a wickedly busy mother of three. With her husband, Jochen, she also manages a custom saddlery company and a retail equine accessories shop.

Most of the Schleeses' clients are women, since dressage, according to Sabine, is a very popular pastime with the 'moneyed fairer sex.' Ironically, traditionally riding saddles have been made by men for men, with the exception of those silly side saddles. Here's the kicker. No one got it that, anatomically, women are built quite differently.

One of the Schleeses' clients, who was an important horse show judge, was having recurring bladder infections and was experiencing bleeding in the urogenital tract. She was rubbing herself raw every time she rode. She went to the Schleeses with her problem. She wanted to continue riding but obviously not at this physical cost. The light bulb went on.

It became apparent to the Schleeses that these physiological differences, evident in the sport of dressage, hindered women in riding properly. Because of the angle of women's hip articulation, the width of our pubic bones, and the depth of our seat bones, women are fighting the saddle, the very tool that is supposed to help them achieve the proper position. What the Schleeses came up with was a design that would allow women to achieve the proper position and be able to concentrate on riding properly, rather than trying to sit properly at the same time as trying to avoid pain.

What makes the Schleeses' work unique is their mission to build saddles that accommodate the specific anatomy of every individual rider. They did this by using their plaster cast method to customize each mould. Sabine said she always wondered why most of Jochen's saddles felt so uncomfortable, until looking at her own cast. She saw quite vividly how wide her pubic bones were, probably from childbirth, yet how narrow she was in the seat.

The saddle tree they designed, with its integrated air pocket, has been awarded a U.S. patent and is referred to in the vernacular as the "crotch comfort saddle." The initial premise of their technology was to service an unmet need of women riders. It turns out that, eventually, the customization feature became an innovation that was also highly regarded by their male clientele for, uh, obvious reasons.

Sabine is a networker extraordinaire, which has helped her business greatly. But a definite advantage is the fact that her market segment is 95 percent women. Interestingly enough, she doesn't need to develop sales and marketing materials specifically for women because the Schleeses have a product that speaks for them. This is the ultimate in market segmentation. They also didn't need to do much conventional advertising because of another indisputable fact: Women are a fabulous referral base. Word-of-mouth has been the main source of the Schlesses' advertising. And has it worked?

Sales for the Schleeses have increased over the last five years by almost 150 percent. They have tripled their work space. Schleese Saddlery is the supplier to the U.S. and Canadian Olympic equestrian teams. In 1990 they set up a three-year apprenticeship program with the Ministry of Skills Development to make saddlery a registered and certifiable trade in Ontario and, as such, became the only authorized training facility in Canada. The company won an Award of Merit from the Ontario Chamber of Commerce in 1997. Even the *Wall Street Journal* and the Discovery Channel have found their story compelling enough to profile them.

Sabine's words of wisdom for baby entrepreneurs? "Find something that needs to be done and then go out and do it. It's what you do and how you do it that may be just that little bit different from what's already available that will gain you a position in the marketplace. Oh, yeah, and be sure to blow your own horn because nobody else will."

Does Your Business Concept Make Sense?

Now it's time to walk through the act of offering your product or service to your best client. For this exercise to really work, there are a few important rules to follow.

- Don't ask just anyone for feedback on your product or service. Ask your potential best customers and ask more than one. I asked everyone I knew in the industry. But here is a caveat. When you ask your friends, family, and colleagues whether they believe your product or service is absolutely needed, remember to consider the source. They may not fit the profile of your best customer. If you are lucky enough to have 1000 prospects, you can quite safely test out your value proposition and adjust it based on market feedback. However, if you only have a few, be careful not to blow any possible leads. And I learned something else the hard way. I spoke at length with a colleague about my idea of training financial service professionals on how to sell to women. Lo and behold, guess who had set up a similar shop not a year later? When you ask for feedback, take pains that whoever you are talking to won't run off and "do your idea" themselves. If you are concerned about this at all, consider getting a confidentiality/non-compete agreement signed.
- Ask why after every statement, both positive and negative. The answers that you need lie not in the actual statements but in why they are made. For example, if your sample customer makes the statement "I would feel really

comfortable recommending this product to someone else," and you stop the conversation there, you may walk away feeling confident that you have a terrific product that this customer would buy. If you ask why, you may be surprised when the answer comes back, "Well, I don't really need it but my patients would." Turning a good idea into a good business is an interactive process. It's like adding a little more seasoning to a dish throughout preparation to make it just right. In Christine's case, she and her business partners weren't afraid to ask for advice, assistance, or both. She was able to do a large part of her concept testing anecdotally, through acquaintances, family, and friends. She conducted focus groups. She also took the extra step of going south of the border to see if anyone was successfully employing her approach in the marketplace so she could adopt a "best practices" approach.

- Don't bother asking for feedback if you are not prepared to listen to it.

Make sure you leave this part of the planning exercise with the following knowledge:

- Would the person you ask use you, your product or service, and why? You do not just want to know what they think of the idea.
- Would they actually pay for your product or service, and how much? Is this a good idea but not a good business?
- Would they use your product or service but not buy from you? Would they buy from you and why? There may be reasons why they would or would not prefer to buy from you, reasons like accessibility, affordability, other value-added benefits, convenience, selection, and quality.

I use this method extensively. I discovered the best way to learn about my market fully was to jump into the fire with both feet. Now I'm not talking about a blind leap here. I did have research and some experience under my belt, but the real learning came after being in the fray for a while. I had clients who believed wholeheartedly in what I was trying to do. They let me evolve my courses by using their staff as human guinea pigs. After each session, we would debrief and make the necessary changes. After the first year of training, I had the unprecedented experience of talking openly and honestly, in a totally unthreatening forum, to over 1000 brokers and bankers. There was no way I could have "market researched" all of the invaluable insights I derived from this experience. I was now able to take my "in the field" experience and improve the courses to an immeasurable degree. Not everyone will be lucky enough to have clients who are willing to pay you as you learn. But you may be surprised to discover how far your clients are willing to go if you sell them on what's in it for them instead of on the product or service itself.

How Many of Them Are Out There? And How Many Can You Get?

Now you've got to fully understand the demographics of your market. The financial services sector was my ideal customer so I needed to learn everything I could about them.

Market Size

I asked myself, "How many of my prospects are actually in the geographic area where I intend to operate?" Since we wanted to be a national organization, Canada was our geographic market. But the good news was that the head offices for most of our target customers were located right here at home, in Toronto. When Paula started her company, she had to extrapolate her estimate of the number of women entrepreneurs from patchwork statistics on the number of self-employed persons and the growing rate of women becoming business owners. Christine relied on industry data. But be prepared if you are considering a similar source; her market size is an estimate since most companies in her industry are private. Actual numbers are often difficult to get.

Market Trends

Next, you need to figure out if the numbers of your ideal customers are growing or declining. In my case that was easy. Financial services were exploding. I came to that conclusion rather easily by being inside the industry myself and witnessing the growth of advisers to the ranks. Paula looked to Statistics Canada reports, studies done by the Canadian Federation of Independent Business, research from the Business Development Bank, and the more comprehensive and primary research done in the U.S. by NFWBO and the SBA (Small Business Administration). Christine determined her industry market trends through focus groups, information from Statistics Canada, and over 300 personal store visits. It's also wise to uncover what things are actually causing the trend so that you can register early any change that may turn it from positive to negative.

Reaching Your Target Market

I then asked myself, "How easy is it going to be to reach my ideal customer? Are they diverse or homogeneous? Can they be easily grouped by characteristics? It was easy for me — banks, financial planning firms, and brokerages. Financial institutions were small in number but big in dollars and people. With most having their head office in Toronto, I could just call each one of them and market one on one.

Sleep Country determined that women aged 24 to 54 were the decision makers when it came to buying mattresses. This allowed Christine to target her media purchase to reach that market. She wanted to ensure that customers who were in the market for a mattress were compelled to visit Sleep Country and take advantage of the current promotion.

For Paula, it was easier to reach women who had already started their businesses and more difficult to reach those women just about to start their businesses — often the ones most in need of professional advice and support. So, Paula packaged some of her services into a corporate program for firms that were downsizing, specifically targeting people entertaining the idea of self-employment rather than re-employment.

Market Share

Next, I had to ask myself, "How many customers could I reasonably manage to get from my competitors and still service them well?" After all, no business opportunity is ever lost. If you fumble it, your competitor will find it. Considering I was a market pioneer, this was a no-brainer. Consider the following factors when attempting to answer this question and determine your market share:

- the total value of sales recorded for the industry
- the total number of customers available
- the total number of other competitive businesses angling for their share of customers and sales.

Remember to restrict your calculations to the geographical area and specific market segment that you intend to serve.

To Wrap...

There are a lot of resources available to get "market" information. My primary resource was having been in the industry for several years. Practical experience is a huge asset. Other secondary sources of information include:

- directories like *Scott's Directory* that list companies by type and geography. I used *The Guide to the Canadian Financial Services Industry* published by *The Globe and Mail*, which is updated every year. It listed every piece of information I would ever need. There are directories like this for almost every industry. If associations are your bag, there is a fabulous directory from CSAE (Canadian Society of Association Executives) called *Associations Canada*.
- national census information from Statistics Canada
- reports and studies published by industry and trade associations
- articles from business or trade journals

- books written by demographic and market experts like *The Pig and the Python, Boom, Bust & Echo,* or *Sex in the Snow.*

Who and What Else Is Vying for Your Customers' Attention?

Now it's time to go shopping — comparison shopping. Not a bad way to spice up boring, mundane research. The way I chose to scope out the competition is to put on my customers' shoes and begin looking for a solution to my (their) problem. That's how I found out I was the only player at that time. Christine took this comparison shopping to a new level — she and her business partners made over 300 visits to other stores.

This is what you gotta do: Metamorphose and become your customer. As your customer, where would you start looking for you or your product or service — the Internet, the Yellow Pages, friends, family, co-workers, the streets where you drive around the community, local and national newspapers, or trade, technical, and consumer magazines? Next, think about what matters most to you. Remember, you are play-acting here. You have to stretch your imagination because being your target customer may mean you are a different age with different values, preferences, and needs.

Christine was easily able to think like a customer. Being consumers of mattresses themselves, she and her business partners considered any and all the concerns they would have when shopping for, buying, and receiving a mattress. They donned the customer's hat and asked, "Where am I going to buy? What am I going to buy? How much should I pay? How am I going to get it home? How am I going to set it up? What will I do with my old one? What if I find the mattress uncomfortable? What happens if there is a warranty issue? Who would I contact?"

After your phantom shopping experience, it is time for reflection on what you did find and what you didn't. Which supplier would you choose? Why? What expectation gaps aren't being filled? Where is the real opportunity?

What really struck Christine was, knowing what she did about mattresses, she still walked out of many stores totally confused, just as real customers would. Through this exercise Christine was able to narrow the criteria for what would be of value to her customers. It started with knowledgeable, helpful, courteous sales assistance, and continued with selection, delivery service, and comfort. She figured out that things like store appearance and warranty issues were important to her customers. That isn't to say that some of these areas weren't being addressed by her competition. It was that no one was offering these comprehensively as a total package. Take, for example, home delivery. Everyone's had a bad experience with home delivery. Christine considers home delivery an essential part of Sleep Country's service. The delivery person is the last face her customer sees, so Sleep Country attempts to hire delivery people who are caring and courteous. They do the little extras to enhance their service: wearing uniforms, donning booties to prevent mud being tracked through the house, giving the client a three-hour window for delivery time. They advise their customers to clear the pathway, especially stairs and hallways, to prevent accidents.

Christine and her gang stuck with the general results of their market research, but they added another layer by asking themselves what *they* wanted. They also realized that if you educate the customer on good body alignment, comfort, support, and size, price would not be a barrier to introducing a high-end product. Christine says, "Market research is only as good as the questions you ask, your sampling, and asking 'Compared to what?' If the customer has only ever experienced A they won't suggest a need for B. But we still need to service the entire spectrum. Research is key not only to assist in designing the concept but also to lend a helping hand in executing the approach. What are other companies doing successfully and why? Adapt ideas to your marketplace...now that is innovative."

New entrepreneurs are usually pretty gung-ho at the first go-around of competitive research. But after getting this market intelligence, "gung-ho" turns to "oh, no" when the time comes to make changes to their own product or service. There is a huge pit out there filled with new business owners who overestimated the demand for their product or service. The pit next to the pit of the overestimating entrepreneur is even more crowded with the entrepreneurs who underestimated the competition. The overzealous crowd got that way because they didn't define their service area or population of potential customers clearly enough. The underzealous group tended to consider only competitors who offer identical products. They didn't ask themselves a pivotal question, "What exactly am I selling?" A microwave oven manufacturer doesn't just compete with other manufacturers of microwaves. It competes with anybody trying to find an easier way for people to cook meals. They share the pit with entrepreneurs who underestimated how tough it is to get a sale or enough sales. You have to have both your head and feet planted firmly on the ground (interesting mental picture) when estimating your sales potential. It's the very heartbeat of making the right business decisions.

How Will You Get Your Customers to Buy From You?

Not only buy, but *continue* to buy your product or service. I recognized I needed to provide exemplary customer service. As my dad says, "Anyone who thinks the customer isn't of supreme importance should try going without them for 90 days." But you've got to break the buying process down step by step. Your first step is to let your target market know you exist — make them aware of your offering. The next step is to convince them that their life will be meaningless without your product or service. The last step is to persuade them that they not only need your product or service but also need to buy it from *you*. Most new entrepreneurs think that step two is the same as step three. It's not. Here is how each step works.

Generating Awareness With the Right Folks

Getting your product or service recognized by the right people is often one of the biggest entrepreneurial dilemmas. Take the following case in point. The chief buyer of one particular company was extremely inaccessible to sales people. He called you, you didn't call him. On several occasions when people did make it in, they were summarily tossed out. One saleswoman finally broke through his defenses. She sent him a homing pigeon with her card attached to one leg. On the card she had written, "If you want to know more about our product, just throw our representative out the window." As evidenced by this story, there is no shortage of ways to communicate with your target market. The tough part is getting access to the right person. The wrong person is usually a piece of cake.

Find the most effective way to inform your potential customer about your product or service. I had a magic door opener — my first book, *Balancing Act*. It became my business card. In Christine's case, her advertising campaign created a high expectation as to Sleep Country's level of service, selection, and expertise.

The one, two, or any combination of communication vehicles that you choose will depend on your budget and the number of people you want to reach. A "big P" point that we entrepreneurs sometimes overlook is that it only counts when our communications reach includes those people from our target market, not every Jane, Dick, or Suhana who might hear about us. For example, don't get too discouraged if your interview on CTV at 6:00 p.m. did not make the phones ring off the hook if your target client is a small business owner. After all, how many small business owners do you know who are home watching TV at that time of the day? I have done no fewer than 42 million media appearances — TV, print, and radio. But only a tiny percentage gets me attention from people within my target audience — financial institutions. I've had full-page profiles in *The Montreal Gazette* and *The Toronto Star*. Dead silence. But, minor one-line references in articles in *The Globe and Mail* or *The Financial Post*, or my profile on the *Globe and Mail's* Managing page, get tons of responses. Similarly, Paula's office received 350 calls, 50 percent of which were prospective clients, in the 48 hours following CBC's *Venture* profile of AQUEOUS.

It was a different story for Christine. Sleep Country launched a highly targeted and massive media campaign. Christine's company conducted focus groups to test what messages their advertising and market approach would actually be sending. Christine wanted to know whether these messages were valuable to her customer. She got her answers. That media campaign put her company on the map.

Sleep Country made significant radio and television buys in the markets they wanted to do business in. They hoped a catchy jingle would attract people. (Believe me, it worked.) They wanted a spokesperson who would be perceived as credible and sincere. Why not *el presidente* herself? Christine became the centrepiece of the entire ad campaign. They also found their five-ton delivery trucks provided a nice form of brand awareness. They got the most from their stores by carefully selecting high-traffic, high-visibility areas and by using as big a sign as the law would allow. The strength of their advertising campaign generated incredible recognition very early on in the company's life.

Convincing the Folks That Your Product or Service Meets Their Needs

You need to be sure that your product or service will meet the buyer's needs. Something clicked with me once on a flight to Vancouver years ago that has shaped the way I do business to this very day. I was trying to get some work done but I, and everyone else on the plane, was having difficulty concentrating. A four-year-old boy was insisting on being a four-year-old boy. He ran up and down the aisles, spilling people's drinks, knocking into people's computers and calculators, and generally creating havoc. One passenger, obviously without kid experience, finally insisted the boy be strapped in his seat. He screamed blue murder. I decided to talk to the flight attendant. I whispered in her ear and she disappeared into the cockpit. The man next to me asked, "What did you say to her?"

"I suggested that instead of trying to solve our problem with the little guy, we should try to solve his problem." A minute later, the second officer came out and asked if the boy would like to fly the airplane. The boy was soon sitting in the jump seat in the cockpit, "flying" the rest of the way. Not a peep was heard from him again.

Convincing your target customer that they need *your* product can be simple. All you need to do is determine, out of the 50 unique things your product or service does well, which one or combination of features matters to that customer the most. People buy for their own reasons, not yours. Then you never stop reminding the client you are around. Case in point:

> *Store owner:* "I've been in business for 50 years and never once needed to tell folks I was still around."
> *Business consultant:* "Excuse me. But what is that building on the hill?"
> *Store owner:* "It's the village church."
> *Business consultant:* "Been there long?"
> *Store owner:* "Over a hundred years."
> *Business consultant:* "Well, they still ring the bells."

People want to hear about themselves, not you. So when you shine the spotlight on your star feature, make sure you're talking about the benefits to your target customer first. I *always* put myself in my customer's headspace. What makes them tick? I found a verse that helps put it into perspective.

> Don't sell me books, sell me knowledge.
> Don't sell me insurance, sell peace of mind and a secure future for my family.
> Don't sell me a house, sell me comfort and pride of ownership.
> Don't sell me clothes, sell style, attractiveness, and a sharper image.
> Don't sell me a computer, sell me the time saved.
> Don't sell me things. Sell me ideas, feelings, happiness and whatever else I
>   may be interested in.

You see, if you sell things, you run the risk of hearing "So what?" People don't buy newspapers, they buy news. Last year, Canadians bought millions of quarter-inch drills. Not one of them wanted a drill. What they really wanted was a quarter-inch hole. But you gotta buy a drill to get the holes. Good salespeople do not sell product. They sell the benefits.

Persuading the Folks to Buy From You

A mediocre salesperson tells. A good salesperson explains. A superior salesperson demonstrates. A truly great salesperson inspires the buyer to see the benefits on her own. I saw an ad in my local paper that was guaranteed to get a huge response. It said, "I can fix anything your husband can. *And I'll do it now.*" I immediately jotted the number down.

Once you get the prospective client convinced that your product or service does get their job done, getting them to buy often involves reducing or eliminating their pain. This means that the investment of time and money necessary to acquire your product or service is less painful than the pain they may be experiencing as a result of their unsatisfied desire, unfulfilled need, or unresolved guilt. However, you need to be able to identify the source and magnitude of your prospect's pain before you can get to work on reducing or eliminating it.

The Price Is Right

Most people are very anxious about establishing their first pricing strategy. It's a common dilemma for new entrepreneurs: "What if I charge too much and nobody buys?" or "What if I don't charge enough and I can't make enough money to pay the bills?" The key here is to determine how much is too much and how little is not enough. To do so you need to put a stake in the ground. In other words, rough up a test product or service price. Don't worry about getting it right the first time. The objective is to get as close to the price that your best customer will pay. And in our imaginary test world, you can safely make adjustments. Ultimately, it will be your "real" best customer who will determine how close you got to the true number. You have to know your costs and how they relate to your activities as well as your profit margin, inside and out, which is discussed in detail in chapter 5. Christine warns that a common mistake in a competitive environment is for a company to lower their price. "The reality is, it doesn't necessarily work. A reduction in price might not be the factor swaying a customer's decision. It may be things like selection, trust in the person offering the service, and the timing of the need." I have always said that competition may be the life of trade but it's often the death of profit. Lord knows you don't want to be in the position of the business owner who had the following sign in her window, "Staying-in-business sale now in progress."

You first need to identify a range of values that has some basis in fact. Your range will have two endpoints. At the low end, you will have one that represents the absolute lowest price you dare to go and not go completely broke. In other words, you need to be able to cover your costs. *All of your costs.* At the high end, you have an endpoint that represents the price that may already be charged in the marketplace for a similar product or service. Note it doesn't say the same product or service. You need to compete with other products or services that offer similar benefits to the customer. For instance, you could substitute reading this book for going to a small business consultant or finding free information on the Internet. Just be sure that your product or service is properly positioned within its competitive environment and that it is properly priced, keeping in mind the benefits it provides. Use the following as guideposts to help you establish your range.

A Price You Can Live With

Start the process of figuring out the proper price by calculating an amount that will cover costs and produce enough profit to meet your personal and financial objectives. And not just for today but for later as you become more established. I know people who establish their price of service based on their reality today, meaning a home office, a 10-year-old clunker of a car, and no employees. That may not be the case for you forever. Try to avoid a "cost plus" approach and determine a price more on market value. Don't forget to include a fair salary for yourself and your co-workers. Many baby entrepreneurs look at their new business's revenue potential and assume that the more sales they make, the more successful their business will be. However, when you consider all of the expenses, salaries, and free services usually required in the start-up phase, the reality is your concept may not now, or will never, make money.

A Price That Your Customers Can Live With

Another trap many new entrepreneurs fall into is believing that to be competitive, your product or service must be cheaper or better than similar offerings in the marketplace. While it may be that your target or best customer is looking for "less expensive" or "better quality," don't automatically assume that they are. Many businesses find niches based on differentiating themselves on the basis of convenience, speed, availability, selection, suitability-to-task, or novelty. Women and Money Inc. is a classic example of a niche player. So is Paula's company. So is Speedy Muffler. Make sure you ask your client outright, "What will make you buy? Is it price, quality, service...?" You need to go back to your target customer's purchasing and usage patterns and then rank them in order of importance.

A Price Equal to Value

The reason why it's smart to focus on what it is that you do differently from anyone else is that it is often those intangible or sometimes tangible differences that create unique benefits for your customer, benefits that they may be prepared to pay more for. There is a subtle yet mission-critical point here: Your customer will not pay you for what you do differently — they will pay you for the benefits they get from what you do that is different.

Torang offers a unique feature at her day spa. You can purchase already prepared low-fat meals that can be taken home. The unique benefit to her very busy, higher income customers is that they get to maintain their health not only by getting a massage but also by eating well. They love the fact that they can do all of this with not an extra ounce of energy being expended. This one-stop shopping experience provides extra value and Torang's clients are only too prepared to pay a premium because of the convenience and quality she offers.

If you are hit with the "It costs too much" objection, remember the immortal words of selling superstar Zig Ziglar: "Yes, the price is high. I don't think there's any question about the price being high, but when you add the benefits of quality, subtract the disappointments of cheapness, multiply the pleasure of buying something good, and divide the cost over a period of time, the math comes out in your favour....If it costs you a hundred dollars but does you a thousand dollars worth of good, then by any yardstick you've bought a bargain, haven't you?"

So, now you have acted out the common and not-so-common situations. You have set the stage, unpacked the basics, and constructed your set. Now ask yourself:

- Did walk-throughs and practice help you anticipate possible situations you might find yourself in?
- How could you have either avoided or resolved any of these situations?
- Where would you have needed help, either in skills, additional people, or money?

Christine Magee is a master at practice and play-acting. She says that walking through business scenarios made life infinitely easier all around when the company was finally launched. But she warns, "I think it is very hard to try to imagine every possible reaction or concern of a customer. Experience indicates that it is impossible. What is better is to empower your team to have the authority to make decisions that are aligned with your company's objectives...to service the customer."

Amen.

Anticipate Life's Little Bumps

You have created a prototype of your business. Now it's time for you to go into major *what-if* mode. Don't worry about being outrageous. Think of Alice and the Queen in Lewis Carroll's *Through the Looking Glass:*

Alice laughed. "There's no use trying," she said. "One can't believe impossible things."

"I daresay you haven't had much practice," said the Queen. "When I was your age, I always did it for a half hour each day. Why, sometimes, I've believed as many as six impossible things before breakfast."

Start with this exercise. Think of your personal and business life in as grandiose terms as possible. Imagine you have just closed a huge contract with the country's largest bank. Imagine you have to hire salespeople to keep up with the demand. Imagine you are able to pay all your bills and buy new furniture for your home. Imagine you have met the man of your dreams and you run off and elope. You get married in a romantic chapel nestled on a beautiful lake. Imagine you have just realized a lifelong dream — you're pregnant. Life could not be more perfect.

As the song says, this ain't necessarily so.

This idyllic scenario (yes, it was mine) could have remained so if I had spent a minute or two thinking through the long-term ramifications of each of these events on my life. There are zillions of different things to ask *what-if* about. It really depends on the circumstances of your life. I had three major areas where if I had asked *what-if*, life would have improved immeasurably. For example, if I had taken the time to ask, "What happens when I close my first big contract?" life might have gone much more smoothly. I had no clue how much it was going to cost me, financially, physically, and emotionally, to close and maintain a big deal. I just concentrated on bringing the business in with little regard for the impact on cash flow, staff resources, and my sanity.

Another place I should have *what-iffed*, "What if I hire a salesperson to sell my vision? How would that work?" If I'd asked those questions I would have found out that it was only I who could successfully sell my vision, certainly in the early stages. I would have saved a small fortune and tons of heartache. The business concept was a natural extension of who I was fundamentally as a person. How could I expect someone else to get it across the way I could?

Another huge area I should have *what-iffed*, "What would happen if I actually got a date? Married him? Had a baby?" By asking those questions I wouldn't have had to endure so much financial uncertainty. Mind you, when I started the business, dating was as foreign an activity as caber tossing so babies weren't an imminent reality. The problem with this short-sightedness, however, was that having babies was one of my life's most important goals. But I had simply adopted a laissez-faire attitude, "I'll deal with it when it happens." When I did get pregnant a year after the business started, I had to go into serious scramble mode.

I had no idea how I was going to keep my business going, look after an infant, a new marriage, and myself at the same time. My refusal to project into the future was understandable. Not smart, but understandable. I thanked God Michael had an excellent job with a big computer company and that he would provide some financial stability until I figured out a way to balance work and family. I knew I was going to take a serious financial hit while I was off looking after Kate. Since the pregnancy was a surprise, there had been little time to prepare financially. The big picture was fine. We both had RRSPs, scads of life insurance, and wills.

But even with the Royal Bank's deposit on a future training program in our pockets, I had to resign myself to the fact that I would have to go into debt, using the company's line of credit to fund the time I was going to be away from the business. Not that I could really be away. That was a luxury I could ill afford, especially with staff payroll to meet. I was sensing that the financial domino effect of being away would take years to recover from. Michael would be required to pay the majority of the household bills for a while as I would need to repay the debt that would be incurred through my nine-month pseudo maternity leave. Just as my financial life was affected by the birth of my business, it was to be hugely affected by Kate's birth.

Spending some time thinking about the financial ramifications of your life as an entrepreneur on your personal life is essential. As a baby entrepreneur, I discovered that separating business and personal money is difficult because they seem so totally integrated. Technically you can separate the money into a personal and a business account, but the reality is a decision in one realm will have a lasting effect in the other. Because everything is so connected, a thoughtless manoeuvre over here could have a huge impact on things way over there and way down the road. Without a well-thought-out financial plan during the conception and pre-birth phase of the business, things like pregnancy, market downturns, and bad hiring choices can have catastrophic impact. They do under the best of circumstances. Increase the effect exponentially if there is no financial contingency plan in place.

I no longer had an employer to depend on for luxuries like life, health, and disability insurance. Pension plans were a thing of the past. Questions like, "What if I get sick? What if I divorce? What if I die? What if I don't want to do this any longer?" took on a whole new dimension.

There is so much I would have done differently. I would have taken the time to sit down and do a proper financial analysis of the real costs of my business endeavour. I would have spent the money to sit down with a qualified accountant to plan ahead instead of the more costly option of hiring one after the fact to bail us out. I would have done a financial forecast a lot more regularly so I could have prepared for the valleys when they inevitably occurred. I would have taken a percentage of money when times were good and put an emergency fund aside. I would have hired fewer people — one instead of three. I would have thought through the financial implications of a baby on the business and involved my major clients and my business adviser to help me strategize how to make it work. I concentrated on what I believed to be really critical and I let the financial side of the business fall down the priority ladder. And as I discovered, the ladder of life is full of splinters, but you never realize it until you slide down.

This experience, coupled with some serious arm-twisting from Paula, has now put financial management close to the top of my business priority list. As you have probably determined by now, there is much to ingest and digest when experimenting with the different ingredients needed to make your dreams happen. So far, the creation of the concept of your business has included planning, goal-setting, testing your market on an imaginary stage, and anticipating what could go wrong. It's now time to identify the resources needed to transform your concept into reality.

What Do You Need to Make Your Dream Happen?

To best illustrate the key elements in taking your business dream from vision to form, we have unapologetically revised a well-known fairy tale, *Rumpelstiltskin*. This is the fairy tale as it appears in Kate's book on nursery rhymes, word for word, with our entrepreneurial spin. In our story, we have three quintessential entrepreneurs, the miller, his daughter, and, of course, Rumpelstiltskin. The miller and his daughter started with a goal, to land the royal account. Rumpelstiltskin was in the right place at the right time with the right offering (his magic) to get paid a handsome sum to help the miller's family achieve their goal. Given the only resources he had on hand — time, bails of straw, a spinning wheel, and his energy — he seized the opportunity created by the family's lack of technology and process, only to be one-upped in the end by the entrepreneur with the plan. So without further adieu....

Rumpelstiltskin

Cast of Characters

Established Entrepreneur played by the Poor Miller

Emerging Entrepreneur played by the Princess

Target Client played by the King

Key Supplier and ex-Banker played by Rumpelstiltskin

There was once a poor miller who, together with his daughter, ran the family business. One day he had to go inside the King's palace on a sales call, being that the sales and marketing end of the family business was his responsibility. He was very pleased that he had managed finally to get an appointment with the King. He became so determined to close the sale that he exaggerated the claims he was making and made the classic mistake that many sales people do — he overpromised in order to win the business.

He told the King that he had patented a unique process by which his beautiful daughter could spin gold out of straw.

"You may bring her to see me," the King told the miller, who was already beginning to regret some of his overzealous sales tactics. "I would like her to do a pilot project and benchmark some of that wonderful spinning for me."

The next day the frightened miller took his poor daughter on a follow-up call to the King. The King was very impressed by the professional appearance of the girl. He directed her to the test site that he had prepared as the first stage of the pilot — a small room that was full from floor to ceiling with straw.

The King pointed to the spinning wheel. "Set to work. For this part of the pilot, you have until dawn to spin," he told the poor girl.

The miller's daughter had no idea how to spin straw into gold and all she could do was sit and weep, a kind of verbal request for proposal. She decided that her only hope would be to start networking in an effort to find someone who could help her out of her dilemma.

Suddenly the door opened wide and in peeped a tiny man. "Why are you crying?" he asked.

"I must spin straw into gold by dawn," she wept, "and I don't know how to do it." (Women are so much better at admitting what they don't know.)

"Do not worry about that!" cried the little man. (Men do tend to like to rescue women and try to fix their problems.) "I will help you, but first, what will you give me if I do?" (Which goes to show that business ain't altruistic, even with a damsel in distress in the picture.)

The girl, strong in the art of negotiating as a result of good mentoring from her father, said, "I will give you my ring." Since it was a pay before you play type of situation, she gave it to him, then he sat down at the spinning wheel. It began to turn and twist. The little man fed straw on to the whirring bobbin and the more he put there, the more golden coins fell to the floor.

When the dawn came there was no straw left and the room was full of gold!

When the King came to see the girl, he could hardly believe his eyes. He was so pleased with the results of the first stage of the pilot that he had another room prepared. Since most clients are like juries in terms of needing to be convinced beyond all reasonable doubt — this time it was an even bigger room and there was still more straw in it.

"As the second stage of the pilot, spin more gold for me, my dear!" cried the King. (Unfortunately, even today the recurring plight of the female entrepreneur is to be called dear.) He shut the door, leaving the poor girl alone with the straw and the spinning wheel.

She did not know what she was going to do without the little man's help. She decided she needed to put out another request for proposal to find the technology to complete her task. The door opened a crack and he peeped round at her once more.

"What will you give me this time if I spin the straw into gold for you?" he asked.

"I will give you my necklace," cried the girl, confident that he would accept her proposed fee for service.

The little man took the necklace, then he sat down at the spinning wheel. Whirr, twist, and twirl went the wheel. The bobbin caught in the straw and cast it out again in the shape of hundreds of golden coins, just as it had done before.

When dawn broke all the straw had gone and the room was full of glittering gold. The second stage of the pilot was deemed to be a raving success.

This time the King was so overjoyed that he had a still larger room filled with straw, which was tightly stacked from floor to ceiling.

"Now, for the final stage of the pilot…if you spin all this straw into gold I will make you my exclusive partner — my Queen," he cried to the miller's daughter.

The girl knew that she could not do it without the little man's help and, confident of the relationship she had developed with him, she waited hopefully for him to appear. Sure enough he came.

"What will you give me this time if I spin the straw into gold?" he asked.

"Alas, right now my cash flow is tight because we have been doing bigger and bigger jobs and we are just about to land the contract of our life. At this moment, I have nothing to give," wailed the girl.

Having previously been a banker, the little man recalled the principle of collateral. (Unfortunately, the girl did not have a husband whom he could get to co-sign a promissory note.) He took what seemed like an eternity to make what seemed like such a simple decision. After all, the miller's daughter had made good on all her other payments and he could see that they had this big job in the hopper. Finally, he came back with an answer.

"Then promise me that when you are Queen you will give me your first son," demanded the little man.

The girl could do nothing but promise as there were no other sources of financing available within the time frame to which she was bound. She went for the far-from-perfect deal because she desperately needed a solution to her problem, albeit only short term. (Oh-oh: short-term gain, long-term pain.) At once the little man seated himself at the spinning wheel and began to spin.

The wheel whirred until the room was full of gold, then the sun shone in through the window and the little man went away.

The rich King kept his promise and he made the miller's daughter his Queen.

A year later a son was born to the Queen and she was so happy that she forgot all about the little man and her promise to him until, one day, he appeared in her room and pointed to her baby. And, as was foreshadowed, there is no free lunch, no yin without yang, no buy now without a pay later.

"Give me the child as you promised!" he cried.

The Queen begged him to take anything except her baby and, as he felt rather sorry for her, he bent a bit by giving her what seemed to be an impossible task in an unreasonable time frame. (This was his banker side coming out.) He told her if she could guess his name within three days, she could keep her son.

The Queen tried all the names she knew that day, but she could not guess the little man's name and he went away. He came the next day and she tried with hundreds more, but the little man's name was not one of them.

Before the third day dawned the poor Queen sent a messenger all over the land to bring back the strangest names he could find. (It was her entrepreneurial experience that made her move from reacting by just guessing to a real plan, that of deploying the messenger to uncover the name.) Alas, there were none left.

"But I did see one strange thing," he told the Queen. "I was passing a little house where a tiny man danced and jumped round a fire burning in front of it. He was singing a song (ignoring the supreme importance of confidentiality at this stage of the game) and this is what he sang:

Tomorrow I brew, today I bake,

And then the child away I'll take;

For little deems my royal dame

That Rumpelstiltskin is my name!

The Queen was delighted to hear this strange name and was very happy when the little man came next time. As it is with self-made success stories, the harder you work the more luck it seems you have.

She waited for him to speak before she asked him about it, and teased him a little before she said the name her messenger had told her.

"Now, dear lady, what is my name?" asked her visitor.

"Is it Harry?" she asked.

"No!" laughed the little man.

"Is your name Conrad?" she asked.

"No, no!" cried the little man.

"Is your name Timothy?"

"No, no, *no!*" shouted the little man.

"Then your name is Rumpelstiltskin!" said the Queen.

"Some witch told you that! Some witch told you that!" cried the little man, and he was so angry that he stamped his foot so hard he sank right down into the ground out of sight (as do most who underestimate their competition or take their relationship with their clients for granted) and never troubled the Queen again.

Our recast tale works well to illustrate the resources that are required by most entrepreneurs to convert their vision into reality. In the case of our cash-poor friend who bootstrapped her way to achieving her personal and financial goals, her resources could be categorized as follows:

- people/materials — a good little techie, straw, room, board, and administrative support provided free of charge by the palace
- process/know-how — old 486 spinning wheel, the traditional spinning process adapted with "the secret straw conversion process" acquired by hiring the right people
- money — funds on hand (ring and necklace) as well as the funds generated by the creation of gold were used to cover the costs of the "free" support provided by the King while the balance was retained earnings placed into the royal coffers.

How are you going to convert your vision into reality? Who are the people? What are the materials/processes/know-how? How much money do you need to spin your straw into gold?

Who Does What?

It is very important to determine what it is you do for your company. While it is accurate to refer to the CEO of a small business as *Chief Everything Officer*, "everything" may not be strictly correct. Very few people are such complete self-starters that they can make it without any help. As a baby entrepreneur in your first year, it takes no time at all to discover that your personal support network of friends and family has just been incorporated into your business.

So, here are more choices to make in your first year — what will you do and what will others do. In the others category, we have employees, suppliers, clients who get their own coffee and use the voice mail system's auto attendant to get your telephone extension, temporary help to stuff envelopes, the staff at the Business Depot, your brother who is a technical whiz and keeps your computers healthy, your spouse or life partner who needs a job description just to get some of your time, the courier who fetches the cheques from your clients' payables department, your mom who doesn't have to teach in the summer and pitches in, your pal who you trust to keep your grandiose schemes grounded and your other pal whose job it is to pick you up when you fall down and you don't think you can get up. It's a big support network.

It is important to break down "everything" into the key functions within any company regardless of who does it. Consider:

- who is going to find and get the customers (sales/marketing)
- who is going to find, train, motivate, manage, and keep the workers (human resources)
- who is going to do the actual work (production)
- who is going to keep track of the work you have done, make sure there is enough cash, billing, and collections, and that your payables are being paid (accounting/finance)
- who is going to plan for the future (research and development)
- who is going to plan and support today's business (administration/information systems).

You just have to map out all the jobs, big and small, that need doing. Then figure out who is going to do them (even though it will likely be you in the beginning), how long they need to do them, and how much you are going to have to pay to have them done.

The Straw, the Wheel, and the Process

What are the equivalents of the straw, the wheel, and the process in your business venture? Your straw could include tangibles like raw materials, parts, paper, toner, and coffee, or intangibles like information. Your wheel could be computers, photocopiers, machines, factory or office equipment, phones, and phone lines. And how you produce your gold, be it how you make your product or how you deliver your service, constitutes your production process.

Often these elements are the basis for your competitive edge in the marketplace. Think about why you buy from others.

- They call you back.
- You like them and want to do business with them.
- They told you what they had to offer.
- They have the answers to your questions at their fingertips.
- They deliver on their promises.
- They deliver when they promise.
- They deliver faster than everyone else.
- They are the only supplier of that product/service.

Now the usual suspects in our version of *Rumplestiltskin* have fit the bill on all accounts except the last one, that of being the only supplier of a product or service. Obviously there were other sources of gold in the kingdom. We can assume the King already had his fair share so he wasn't suffering from some unmet need. It was a manufactured case to demonstrate the value of being in the right place, with the right product, at the right time. And delivering.

The Costs of Doing It

Naturally, a huge part of the planning process is around the cost of your endeavour. There are three types of costs to consider:

Variable Costs

This is the cost of *doing* business. These costs are the kind that increase or decrease depending on your sales or production volumes. You incur these costs only if you make a sale. The best examples of variable costs are:

- labour directly associated with doing the work, creating the product, or providing the service
- supplies and materials
- credit card discounts (Note: These are the percentages of the sales charged on credit cards that the credit card companies keep, usually from 1.5 percent to 6 percent. Small businesses usually pay the higher percentages

because of smaller volumes, unless they belong to a trade or industry association that has negotiated a group rate. The membership fee to the Retail Council of Canada is worth paying just for the terrific break on this fee.)

- preferred customer or other promotional discount costs
- delivery costs
- packaging
- long-distance charges related to making the sale or servicing the customer.

Fixed or Overhead Costs

This is the cost of *having* a business. These costs are incurred on an annual basis or are based on the timing (not volume) of transactions. The best way to go into business is with high hopes and low overhead. Some examples of overhead costs include:

- telephone
- Internet connections
- depreciation on furniture, computers, and equipment — estimate of the cost of using this stuff during the year
- payroll expenses for office staff
- benefits (RRSP contributions, health, life, and disability insurance premiums)
- insurances (auto, business, key person)
- rent and utilities
- parking
- advertising and promotion design, materials, and programs
- office supplies and services
- professional fees
- technical support
- income taxes
- bank charges and interest.

Hidden or Opportunity Costs

These costs are the costs of *not* doing something else with your time, money, and talents. Unfortunately, these costs are rarely factored into any pricing model, but they are really important to identify upfront. How else can you be sure that what you're doing is competitive with what you could be doing? At the very least, ask yourself the following question as a reference point: "What could I be making as an employee working for someone else?" keeping in mind the value of your talents and your ability to contribute value to the organization.

Now it's time to translate your word plan for spinning your straw into gold into your numbers plan.

Show Me the Money

Ugly Accounting Terms — Cash Flow and Projections

Paula and I were discussing business over a pseudo-picnic lunch one day. As we strolled through the park with our sandwiches I was bemoaning the fact that I was being forced to learn about an area that had historically lulled me to sleep — accounting. "Paula, to me accounting — stuff like cash flow and projections — sounds about as friendly as quantitative statistics," I sulked.

"Whatever gave you the idea that projecting and managing your cash flow is accounting?" Paula asked. "That would be like saying that writing cheques and making deposits is banking. Banking is what happens after you do the deed. The same holds true for accounting. Accounting is what happens after you do the deeds related to running your business, like making sales, paying bills, and managing your cash flow. Managing your cash flow does involve numbers and a spreadsheet, but that certainly does not make it accounting. This is a big misconception of many business owners.

"Let's put cash flow in its proper perspective. I'll try to explain the concept in terms that mean something to you." She gently rested her hand on my stomach as we strolled through piles of leaves on the sidewalk. "Oxygen breathed in from the air will become the essential and life-sustaining element the very second Kate joins us in the real world. Oxygen, as you know, will continue to fuel her health and well-being as she grows. Cash flow, Joanne, is the equivalent of oxygen for your business once your business is born. Some people define survival as a business's ability to sustain a positive cash flow — more coming in than going out. Businesses that don't generate sufficient cash flow will inevitably suffocate. The thing to watch as a new entrepreneur is that you don't confuse cash flow with revenue or sales, or even cash in the bank. What cash flow is, in reality, is a hybrid concept that focuses on the *timing* and not just the actual amount of cash flowing in and out of your business. Remember the crunch you experienced when you closed your first big contract? You had lots of revenue, just not enough cash when you needed it."

"Good Lord, that's so simple it's almost embarrassing," I replied.

Paula reached up and pulled a leaf from a low-hanging branch. "Think back to before your business was born. It was your ideas that kept it going, the *what is it going to do, for whom and how* stuff. But, once your business was born, it needed both ideas and cash flow to stand on its own two feet. And sometimes your business needs some extra help, like outside money, until it grows up, goes out on its own, and generates enough of a cash flow from its own sales to sustain itself."

"I guess the real challenge comes in the form of guessing when the cash peaks and valleys will happen," I mused aloud. "That's what I find the toughest. It's like a fantasy exercise. I mean, how do you really know for sure how much you'll need and when?"

"That's where projections come in," Paula answered. "Think of it this way: Cash flow is the oxygen that is necessary for the business to survive. Projections are the planning tools that tell you how the business will breathe and sustain its own supply of oxygen. This whole exercise of sketching out these guesses causes entrepreneurs to deconstruct their estimates or projections into component parts such as units, orders, hours, and minutes. This helps us understand the relationship between all of the factors at play in our business."

"How does it do that?" I asked.

"For one thing, it makes it easier to properly evaluate our estimates. For example, I know two entrepreneurs, sisters Mara and Emer, who owned their own organic bakery. They wanted to generate $15,600 in sales each month. The average purchase was $4.50. They planned to be open six days a week from 8:00 a.m. to 6:00 p.m. So, in order to reach their monthly sales target, they figured out they would have to make a sale every four minutes." Paula smiled. "It makes it a lot easier to decide what is do-able when you look at having to make a sale every four minutes rather than by looking at a total monthly sales number. The trick is to break down your monthly target into the number of sales you have to make using the value of your average sale and then figuring out how many orders or contracts you have to take each week, each working day, and finally each hour to make that number. This process will, in no short order, show you whether or not you are of this planet. It will also help you evaluate whether you have the capacity to handle that kind of sales volume."

"What did Mara and Emer do?" I asked.

"Well, in their case the average sale included a loaf of bread and six bagels or buns. Mara and her sister figured out they had to make and sell 134 loaves and 804 bagels or buns each day. I asked them if that was physically possible given how long they take to make, the size of the bakery, and the number of staff. Mara expelled the breath she had been holding while we worked through the calculation, along with a relieved 'Yes.'

"Proper forecasting also helps in a big way in another area. New entrepreneurs need a lot of time and money. In my boring accountant world, this stock of money is called a capital reserve. Think of a capital reserve as the air in a diver's tank: It will eventually diminish to the point where it can no longer sustain life. Think of it as the barometer that shows how long our business can be sustained before it must breathe on its own by consistently generating sufficient cash flow from its operations."

"Oh, dear friend, you don't actually think that your accountant's world is boring?" I asked, with mock disbelief. Not willing to let this prime opportunity disappear, I asked, "Paula, what does an accountant do for birth control?" Paula braced herself for the inevitable insult. "She talks about her business." I launched into gales of laughter. Alone, I might add. Once I regained my composure, I continued. "This is not rocket science," I said, wiping the tears from my eyes. "Is it not just a question of having more money coming in than going out?"

"Yes," Paula replied, apparently impervious to my bad accountant jokes. "That and having enough of it to do what you want to do in life. At the risk of sounding like a broken record, what qualifies as capital reserve and how much is sufficient is something emerging entrepreneurs must know before diving in. Most businesses start out undercapitalized." Paula continued, "This means that during the period your company is trying to breathe on its own, there isn't enough money around from other sources to supplement your company's own internally generated supply. There is no shortage of stories about people who couldn't get a loan or didn't have enough personal money to put into the business when they needed it. Too many of us in our initial planning only consider our short-term needs."

"Why do we do that, Paula?" I asked, bewildered.

"Because," Paula answered, "we underestimate the length of time that our business will really need outside support in money, time, and talent."

"Yeech," I concurred. "Heaven knows I learned that lesson the hard way. I must say that having an outside adviser review my assumptions, goals, and projections before I leapt out of the gates, as I am wont to do, has been really helpful."

"That's my job. I get you to push the limits of your imagination and to consider things you might not have thought about before. The best part, though, is that I get to tell you when I think you've lost your mind. I love my work."

Paula shrieked as an armload of leaves descended on her head.

We will talk about cash flow throughout the book because it needs to be considered in the different growth stages. How you manage your cash flow will either make or break your company. The trigger to something being amiss with your cash flow is if you are working very hard — harder than you ever have — and you are not moving ahead financially. Here are three of the possible causes of your cash flow problems and some possible solutions. Before you jump on any one of these solutions, make sure you have accurately diagnosed the cause of your cash flow crisis. Otherwise you run the risk of driving yourself deeper into the pit.

1. Running Out of Air

When there is not enough oxygen in the tank to sustain the diver for the length of time she needs to be underwater, the diver will suffocate. As we mentioned, this is what your capital reserve is all about — it kicks in when your company's cash flow is running at low levels and you need to bridge the tight spots. A sure route to trouble is if your revenues are increasing and you take out too much cash too soon. Doing this deprives the company of the cash it needs to get through the growth period or start-up phase. This is often a problem if you have been paying yourself only a small draw from the company coffers during the first few years and you need to replenish your diminished personal financial reserves.

Bolstering your company's capital reserve isn't rocket science, but it ain't easy either. Your choices in this situation are:

- You can increase your revenues even more by kicking up your sales activity, then cut your expenses so that you have more profits to leave in the company. Sometimes this solution takes too long and may not be good enough when you are in crisis, unless of course you are willing to make very deep cuts in your expenses.
- You can put more of your personal money into the company.
- You can take less money out of the company.
- And, of course, you can put someone else's money into the company. This is where bankers will likely cry, "Not me!!!" They are in the business of renting money to help you out with the cash flow crunches resulting from timing problems. An outside investor may be a more appropriate choice if you find yourself plagued by running out of air.

2. It's All in the Timing

Another problem may be matching the timing of your incoming cash with your outgoing payments. There are four common situations that will cause this timing problem.

- You have to pay for stuff before you can charge for it, for example, inventory.
- You are very slow in collecting money from your customers because either your customers have a very long payment period or you are very shy when it comes to hounding people for your money.
- You have not established billing terms that coincide with your payment terms.
- You are too busy to invoice your customers on a timely basis, but you can't collect what you haven't billed. This is the least talked about and most

embarrassing offender. And to compound matters, the further from the delivery date you bill your client, the harder it is to collect.

Solutions to cash flow timing problems should be considered in this order:

1. Sit down and figure out where you can change your billing or payment terms in order to make them work for you. I pay our trainers only after we have been paid. Paula's agreement with her associates is the same. We both accept credit cards in an effort to reduce our receivables. My company bills for our large contracts on a quarterly basis, which really helps even out cash flow.

2. Make invoicing your first priority, not your last. Create your invoices at the point of sale or agreement to buy and hold them until it is time to deliver. Then put the bill on the table with the product or the service deliverable.

3. Explain your billing and collection policy in advance of starting to produce the product or deliver the service. Send out friendly account reminders as soon as an account passes the number of days established in your credit policy. This way you don't have to be shy in following up those outstanding accounts. If it is too painful for you to do it, don't *not* do it — get someone else to do it. Paula has a client whose mother collects her accounts for her.

4. Try to negotiate (you can, you know) shorter payment terms with your customers.

5. Ask for payment up-front. This may be a tough one. For clients who are notorious for long payment terms, I ask to be paid 50 percent in advance of my service. When they ask why, I tell them, "You guys suck at paying your bills." No one has ever argued the point with me and I always get the 50 percent. Companies know when they are bad. I then give them an invoice for the remainder owed with the actual letter of intent to do business. If this doesn't work, don't accept business from customers whose payment terms are too long. You will simply be unable to afford to do the work. The Schleeses' motto? "In God we trust. All others pay cash."

6. Get an operating line of credit to buffer the remaining differences in cash flow timing. This worked really well for me.

3. No Profit Zones

Then there is the plain and simple possibility that your negative cash flow is a result of an unprofitable product or service line or company. You know, the old *more going out than coming in* syndrome. This can be caused by one of, a combination of, or all of the following reasons:

- You are not charging enough for your product/service.

- You cannot charge enough for your product/service.
- You are paying too much to produce your product/service.
- You are spending too much on running the business.

Most new entrepreneurs have a problem with each and every one of these points. It is important to know that not having enough cash is a symptom of the illnesses noted above. Most new entrepreneurs tend to react to this symptom rather than figure out which one or combination of issues is causing the problem. To further aggravate the condition, the new business owner reacts by trying to sell more products or services or by putting more of her own money in or trying to get additional money from banks/credit cards/investors. We are going to throw a yellow flag on these reactions.

- Selling more unprofitable products and services simply increases the speed at which you are creating losses. It will eat up whatever cash reserve you have.
- Trying to finance a business that is producing unprofitable products or is operating at a loss can result in your wasting more money and time pursuing a futile quest instead of solving the real problem. Or, possibly even worse, loading your company up with a debt that it may not be able to repay.

These remedies should only be considered once you have rolled up your sleeves and dug around to see if there are less than stellar operating practices in your company, things like painfully slow invoicing, not following up in a timely manner on receivables, or not charging enough for your product or service. Left unchecked, these practices will eventually erode your cash reserve, if you had one, and put you out of business. But don't lose heart. If your business is experiencing some of these difficulties, it is never too late to put a plan of action in place.

To recap:

- Don't confuse cash with cash flow.
- Cash flow is the oxygen of your business.
- Cash is generated by sales and consumed by expenses. The extra sits as cash in your bank account. However, cash flow is the *timing* of the actual amount of cash that flows in and out of your business.
- Before opening your doors, know how much cash from sources other than operations will be needed to keep your business afloat while you get started and until your business can generate enough cash, at the right times, on its own.

To Wrap Up the Art of Planning...

So there you have it. You can see where planning will help anticipate and mitigate your business risks. Let's review.

- Know where you want to go and how you see your new business helping you get there. No sense climbing the wrong mountain.

- Always solicit the opinions of others who matter. The best source is your prospects and ideal customers. Get them to tell you if your thinking is on the mark.

- Be clear on what your role will be and what role you are best at. Figure out a way to remind yourself of that each day so that you don't end up losing yourself in your business.

- Get your head around the notion that, no matter how well you prepare and plan, you will need to arrange for some extra help, both in hands and dollars, at the outset. Why? Because the demands will be immense and unexpected things happen. You may even have to change your lifestyle to afford the additional mouth to feed.

- Think about what happens to the business if something happens to you. You have to set up your support structure in advance so that you can call on it at a moment's notice. This means both a personal and business support group. Whether it be your staff that fills the void by restructuring existing responsibilities or an organization that sells support services like payroll and marketing by the hour, know who your choices are in advance. It's so much easier than having to search for the right support once you are already in need.

- Trying to predict the future falls far short of a science. So it is important to be honest with yourself about where your projections are strong and where they are weak. Figure out where you have made logical estimates, where you have made educated guesses, and where you just plain don't have a clue. Be specific and write down the assumptions you have made in each case. There are a lot of interdependencies at play within your financial projections. Therefore, you must be cognizant of the domino effect at work here. It's the numbers in your projections that are the product of your assumptions and not the other way around. That's why you need to focus your time and energy on getting the assumptions as right as they can be.

Now it's time to focus on a few remaining logistical issues, like where you are going to operate from and in what legal form, before you fling open your doors.

Should You Move Away From Home? Pros and Cons of a Home Office

An important choice in the life of all new business owners is whether they are going to operate from home or from a rented office. Things that need to be thought about include:

- **Costs** Could your overhead costs be better minimized by sharing a location with another like-minded entrepreneur or by the attractive tax benefits of having a home office? You need to consult an accountant to get the low-down on the tax rules governing home-office expenses.
- **Accessibility** What's worse? Parking in downtown Moncton or in the suburb of Riverview? Then there is traffic. Traffic in places like Vancouver, Toronto, and Montreal is nothing short of horrendous. People plan their entire lives around avoiding it. You need to think about this for your staff and customers. Do you need to be close to your customers? Your competition? A good example is the pack mentality of music stores. They all tend to hang together. What about complementary businesses?
- **Expansion Capability** Does your neighbourhood allow your type of business to operate? Think about zoning and licence or permit restrictions. I can't tell you how many home-based entrepreneurs I know who have been booted out into the streets because neighbours have complained about the cars and people coming and going at all times of the day and night. A friend of mine operated his computer business from his home. Good thing it was a monster home because by the time his neighbours called the city to complain, he had 13 people working for him out of his basement.

A home office can give you certain competitive advantages. The fact that the commute to the office consists of a traffic jam in the bathroom makes this option one of the rapidly growing choices. A home office is flexible since you are the one who determines whether working until 2:00 a.m. is reasonable or not. The operating costs are more manageable since your kitchen table can double for the boardroom table and the sewing room or son Jamie's old bedroom can be made into an office. But, as Dolly Parton says, "If you want the rainbow, you gotta put up with the rain." Sometimes home offices can stunt your ability to grow. And setting up a home office is not as easy as it might look. Thousands of Canadians have discovered that working effectively from home involves more than plunking a desk in the basement. A home office can take over your house if you aren't careful.

Avoid the Basement Pit

When I had my office in the basement ("The Pit"), going to work had the feeling of going down to the dungeon. It was windowless, quite dark, and not at all conducive to creative thinking. Working with staff became a nightmare. Besides the cramped space and lack of phones, copiers, and other resources, I had to deal with people seeing how messy I really was. I finally moved to another house, purposely chosen for its extra bedroom. It offered lots of space and natural light. The one thing that really shocked me as my business grew was the amount of storage space I needed. When I started the company, I had a fistful of files. I now have two full filing cabinets and 20 shelves, the biggest and most useful being the floor. This doesn't include the 15-odd boxes that I have stored in the basement and all of the stuff in our downtown office.

The Workspace

In order to work productively at home, you absolutely must have a comfortable working environment. I got creative when developing my first work space. I went to a used furniture store and bought not only functional but nice cabinets. I made sure they were the same colour as the walls so they would blend in with the surroundings. I also discovered that a centrally located home office is more likely to have phone access (like an outlet) than, for example, "The Pit."

The Family

Another writer friend of mine managed to squeeze her desk into the upstairs TV room. She says the situation is a lot less than ideal. There's no door, so when her son is home sick and the caregiver is looking after him, she's in plain view and an easy target. When she wants to work evenings but hubby wants to watch the game, there is friction. Her mother went out and bought them a set of headphones. Problem solved.

The Isolation

Being a social animal, I really wondered whether I could hack working alone. But being social and being able to work independently aren't mutually exclusive. I soon found out that I actually got energy from working alone, especially when writing. But I'd be lying if I said that the isolation never gets to me. Even though I'm in constant contact with people by fax and phone, I still occasionally miss the human contact of an office. So, I compensate a little bit. I make an effort to get out once in a blue moon. My neighbourhood happens to be filled to the brim with entrepreneurs who work from home. There is also a large population of mothers who are home raising their families. If I find I'm getting cabin fever, the knowledge that I can phone someone up and ask them if they want to go for a walk can be very liberating.

The Routine

I also worried about whether I would have the self-discipline to meet my work commitments. Though I didn't need to keep the conventional 9 to 5, I did need to keep regular hours. My work required at least 40 hours a week. I had to figure out where I was going to fit eight hours of work into each day. That turned out to be the least of my worries. I found working at home made it far too easy to work too much. It was a simple matter of opening a door and sitting down.

The Mess

I've heard many home-based entrepreneurs say that housework, often in full view, poses another distraction. I did not have that problem in the least. I was brilliant in my ability to ignore housework. I just closed the door so I didn't see it. I put housework right up there with barium enemas. I believe I can put my time to better use so I hired a weekly house-cleaning service.

The Unexpected Perils

Be sure to keep a spare set of clothes in your office! I kid you not, this could be one of the most important pieces of advice for the home-based entrepreneur.

I had just gotten out of the shower one day when my business line rang. I was expecting a vitally important call from a prospect who we hoped was soon to be a client. Taking just a milli-second to debate the wisdom of answering the phone in my naked state, I decided to go for it. For some reason, I dropped the towel as I dashed for the phone. Sure enough, it was the call I had been waiting for. I can't tell you how strange it feels to be chatting with the executive vice-president of a huge financial institution, totally and completely in the buff, albeit via a phone. The news was good. As we began to get into the logistics of how the training was to roll out, I realized this was going to be a long call. I began to feel little twinges of discomfort.

Well, that twinge turned into an all-out stab of fear when I heard a key in the front door. Michael was in Boston, so I knew it wasn't him. Then it hit me. It was Tuesday. Lorna and her mom were here to clean. To add to the confusion, I heard a man's deep voice. I tried to remain calm and not burst out laughing as I contemplated myself standing in my office, naked as a jaybird, talking to a new client in a calm, professional voice while frantically trying to shut my office door. The cord wouldn't reach. I winced as I asked my client if I could put her on hold for a very quick second. Lorna called up to me from the front hall to tell me that a courier was there and needed my signature. I groaned in disbelief.

I looked around my office for anything, anything at all that I could cover myself with. There was absolutely nothing. Meanwhile, the incessant flashing red light of the hold button was driving my anxiety level through the roof. I didn't know what to do. I could call downstairs and tell everyone to disappear so I could streak to my bedroom, a scant 10 footsteps away. But I couldn't bring myself to that level of humiliation. I was trapped.

Then I saw it. It was my only ticket out of this mess. I picked up the phone and asked my client if she would mind if I called her back in two minutes. I apologized profusely and said an unavoidable emergency had just cropped up. I then walked over to the other side of my office and took down a large framed picture of Nellie McClung, Canada's first and one of her most famous suffragettes. I positioned her strategically in front of me, took a deep breath, and walked out. The picture was so large that the only thing that showed was from the top of my calves down. I adopted an air of complete normalcy. I casually mentioned as I strode by that I would be right down. When I got to my bedroom, I began to giggle. Before long, I was hanging on to the edge of my dresser, bent over gasping for breath, laughing hysterically with relief. I composed myself, got dressed, and walked downstairs as nonchalantly as possible. No one suspected a thing.

After I had signed for the delivery and gotten Lorna set up, I called my client back. In keeping with my twisted sense of humour, I decided to tell her what had just happened. She couldn't talk for 10 minutes, she laughed so hard.

Family Dynamics and the Home Office

There is another possible downside to working from home that few ever weigh in their decision-making process. Exactly what happens when the family dynamics break down? And I'm not talking just about divorce — what about issues like juvenile delinquent behaviour or chronic illness?

I have an old high school friend named Sue Fraser. Sue is an accomplished hairstylist with a shop in her home in Dartmouth, Nova Scotia. I spoke in Halifax one time and had joined Sue for dinner. That's when she told me of the nightmare she had endured when her marriage began to disintegrate. Sue said, "I can look back and laugh at some of the stuff now. But I often wonder how I ever got through it. I deserved an Academy Award because none of my clients had a clue of the disaster I was living in. Imagine, Joanne, having a huge argument with your husband who is going out the front door while a client is coming in the back door. Imagine sitting on the kitchen floor sobbing in despair, then hearing the click of the door as your client walks in. The only time you have to pull yourself together is the time it takes that person to cross the threshold. Then the performance begins. You don't have the luxury of walking around the block. Business people who work outside the home get to separate work and home. Work couldn't be my refuge."

Sue's survival instinct concerning her business kicked into high gear when the possibility of single parenthood loomed. The worst of the marriage break-down lasted a year. She finally had to take action. Contrary to his promises, her husband would not leave the house. One day, while he slept on the couch, Sue took his house keys off his key ring, packed all of his clothes and other belongings, and put them in his car, all during the five to fifteen min-utes she had between her clients that day. Sue laughs sadly at the memory of this wild woman, bitterly cramming clothes into a suitcase, angry as hell, throwing her husband's suitcase down the stairs, then having to go back to her in-home shop to greet her clients, cheerfully and professionally, over and over again. She said she felt like she was in an episode of *The Twilight Zone*.

Divorce is a horrible thing at the best of times, but Sue claims that her nine-year-old son found it stabilizing having his mom at home while the family went through this terrible time. Sue said it was a bittersweet upside to having a home-based business. There isn't much you can do if your marriage breaks down, but it doesn't hurt to have some contingency plans in the back of your mind in case something disastrous happens on the home front.

Incorporate? Sole Proprietor? Partnership?

Me "Incorporated"?

I was showing Paula a solicitation letter I had received. It was addressed to *Women and Money Ink*. We absolutely howled. It started a conversation that again made me think about the importance of having some idea of what you are doing before you give birth to a business.

"What made you decide to incorporate yourself, girlfriend?" Paula asked.

"Danged if I know. I'm sure it had something to do with taxes. It also made the company sound bigger than it really was," I said.

"That kills me," Paula responded. "Most new business owners think that the key consideration in choosing what form their business will take is taxes. That's because they talk to their accountant too soon."

I laughed uproariously at this. It was rare that Paula got to up me on a good accountant joke.

"No, really, Joanne, I don't know who the public relations agents are for accountants, but it amazes me that new entrepreneurs, when faced with the 'incorporate or not' decision, believe that their choice should first and foremost be based on tax issues. In my opinion, it's your legal position when it comes to protecting yourself from liability that should dictate which way you go, not your tax position. It's really a case of form following substance. After you have decided on the substance of your business and have a general idea of how you are going to do your business day by day, that's the time to think about the legal form of your business. There are choices, you know. There is the route you took, incorporation, and there is the unincorporated route. In either form, you can share the ownership and/or management of the business with another person. This is technically referred to as a partner in an unincorporated business or a shareholder in an incorporated business. I tend to be extremely conservative on the matter of the legal form of one's business. I want to first make sure I don't lose what I've got. Then I can breathe easily and concern myself with how to keep more of what I make."

"Actually, I remember thinking about that when I incorporated," I interrupted. "I figured I needed to look at some of the potential origins of the nasty word — legal liability."

"Exactly. You need to worry about legal liability if your business involves touching someone or something someone cares about, or if you share responsibility with another person or company that you do not control. If you make a product or provide a service that, if used or applied improperly could cause either personal or financial harm, do not pass go, do not collect $200 — *incorporate*. If something were to go wrong, incorporating will limit your personal financial responsibility. If you haven't provided any personal guarantees, you would not be personally liable and your personal assets would be safe and secure."

"It sounds like a corporation is an ingenious device for obtaining individual profit without individual responsibility," I said.

Paula deftly let this one go as she continued, "If you're a doctor or lawyer who can't incorporate — *insure*."

I was surprised. "I didn't know professionals couldn't incorporate. What about my brother-in-law, John, who is a country doctor up in Espanola?"

"Espanola?" Paula asked.

"It's exactly 45 minutes north of nowhere. So what would he do?"

"Most professional governing bodies or associations offer comprehensive insurance packages that their members can, or sometimes, must purchase. This group approach really helps those professionals who are on their own or running a smaller practice. John, and anyone else who is running an unincorporated business for that matter, may wish to transfer the ownership of his large personal assets, like his house, to his spouse or partner. The downside to this is what happens if the relationship were to break down. Again, he should talk to his lawyer to put measures in place to mitigate the personal and financial impact of these circumstances."

Intrigued, I kicked my shoes off and curled up in my office chair. I asked, "So what else should I have thought about before deciding to incorporate? Tell me so I know whether I made the right decision. Not that there's much I could do about it now, anyway."

Before my very eyes I witnessed the most amazing transformation, one that I never tire of watching. Paula turned into an accountant. Now, I'm of the mind that accountants are so boring that if they were drowning and their life flashed before their eyes, they'd probably fall asleep. But Paula had a way about her. Remember her motto? Accountant by trade, not by nature.

"On top of the liability issue," she began, "you need to consider things like 'How much money have I got?' That may determine what you can afford to do. 'Do I want more protection for the name of my company, a significant part of my company image?' Incorporating automatically ensures that no one else can use the same or similar name in the same type of business and in the provincial or federal jurisdiction that you're in. This may be important to you if you are investing a lot of time and money in creating a brand and producing marketing materials and you don't have the money to trademark your name right away. This point alone may justify incorporating, Joanne.

"One of the main reasons that many people go the unincorporated route is because it's easy to register the business and saves the legal and other fees involved in incorporating, such as name registration. However, if you were planning to go with an unincorporated business (sole proprietor or partnership), you could still get the same level of name protection as an incorporated business if you registered your trade name with the provincial or federal registry.

Paula paused only for a moment, then forged on. "Did you think about whether you would ever need access to really big money that would need to be raised from outside parties? Granted, you can always incorporate later for this purpose if you want to. Is it a possibility you might some day transfer ownership to someone else, like your kids or maybe even another company? Are you going to keep significant amounts of what the company earns in the business to fuel future growth and expansion? Do you need to ensure that the legal identity of the company continues even if something happens to you? Did you consider that if you needed to incur debt, would you use company assets or your own as security? Do you want to be able to deal with the issues of ownership and control separately? Think about this — it's important if some day you plan to increase the number of owners without affecting your control of the company. Or even if you would like to share profits some other way than percentage ownership of the company. And finally, did you think about whether you would some day sell your company?"

Paula could talk longer than anyone I knew without taking a breath. I sat back, feigning awe. She looked down at me with a big grin. "You really hate it when I do this, don't you?"

I grimaced. "More than you know. I probably should have consulted a tax accountant and corporate lawyer to get better direction."

"Joanne, something else people should consider. If you think about these questions before you start the professional meter running, you will end up with a smaller bill."

"Well, be all that as it may, for better or for worse, I'm incorporated. Is that a good thing or a bad thing?" I asked.

"Well, luck is an accident that happens to the competent. You happened to do the right thing."

Technically...

A corporation is a legal entity that exists separate and apart from you, the shareholder.

- It has its own official and unique name that enjoys a certain level of protection under the law.
- It is responsible for its own liabilities that do not become the responsibility of the owners if the company fails to handle them (keeping in mind that banks and other creditors more often than not ask for personal guarantees on amounts borrowed). The government also holds owners personally liable for things like unpaid wages or unremitted income tax withholdings as well.
- It has its own diary, called the minute book, that keeps a record of all the decisions made by the corporation through the directors and officers.

- It must pay its own taxes each year within two to three months of its year end.
- It has its own tax rate, usually around 25 percent for the first $200,000 of profit. This is half of the top personal tax rate, so more money can be kept from the government if it is kept inside the corporation.
- It can choose if, when, and how to distribute its own earnings or profits.

This legal form of business offers the most flexibility and protection to its owners. However, you get what you pay for, or rather, you pay for what you get. The cost to incorporate can range from $400 (the do-it-yourself version) to $1500 and up, depending on the amount of work your lawyer has to do. Whether you become an Inc., a Ltd., a Corp., a Ltée, an Incorporated, a Limitée, a Corporation, or a Limited, the process is the same. Here are some of the things that you may need the help of a lawyer to figure out.

The Name

Is the name you wish to use legally available? Choose one that is distinctive and includes one of the identifiers above. My company became Women and Money *Inc.* and Paula's company became AQUEOUS Advisory Group *Inc.* The Schleeses named their company Schleese Saddlery Service Limited. There is a brochure from the government that outlines its approval guidelines for corporate names. The name has to be sufficiently different from other business names, trademarks or well-known names. So a NUANS (New Updated Automated Name Search) that shows other registered business names would have to be conducted by a lawyer, a search house, or a paralegal.

The other type of registered name for a business is often referred to as a trade name. While not the incorporated name, a trade name is the name that the marketplace knows the company as. This approach is often used if you need to set up separate identifiable divisions of the same company for marketing purposes. A trade name can also be used if you decide to go with a numbered company, for example, 123456 Alberta Inc. Sabine set up the retail division of her company as Schleese Saddlery Service Ltd. (35 Ltd.) Retail o/a "Caparison." You'd go the numbered company route because it is faster to set up, you don't have to go through the NUANS name search. You would also go this way if you don't intend to advertise or use the name of your company publicly, for example, a company for an investment property. We'll assume that you do want a public face so it will be the trade name that will appear on your official company materials, like invoices and letterhead. You just have to ensure that you include "operating as" or "a division of" the legal name of your company on all official company correspondence (for example, Just-in-Time Drycleaners — a division of 123456 Ontario Inc.). Again, you would be well advised to order a NUANS on your trade name so that it has the same protection it would as the registered name of your business.

Speaking of your public face, coming up with a name for your business is one of the most exciting and intimate parts of the business birth process. There are competing schools of thought on how to name a business. Some believe emphatically that you need to choose a name that says what you do. Lawyers usually fall into this category because it lessens the chance that your business name will be confusing or too similar to another company's name. There are some great examples of this approach, like Toys "R" Us and Women and Money Inc. Then there are others who opine that names should be easily identified with and create an image about the company, its product, or its founders, like Eaton's. Still others go for names that mean nothing other than what they make them mean — like Loblaws for example.

Your company name represents your company identity and will appear on your business card, signage, Web site, invoices, cheques, envelopes, vehicle, brochures, ads, forehead (just kidding). It is important that all applications of your name be well thought out. It's important to be thinking about these things now, preferably before you give birth to your business and "legally" name it. We will deal with the marketing side of your identity in more detail when we talk about life (or lack thereof) in your first year of business.

The Shares

As the owner, you select which types of shares will be issued and to whom. Your company is like your house: It's a separate, legal entity from you, the person. As a result, you have to show who the people are who own it. Now the shares in your company are like the deed to your house. Shares are what are used to define who owns how much of your company. But, unlike the deed of your house, shares come in different flavours and colours. Different types of shares let you have different types of owners. What differentiates them are their rights and privileges, things like the right to vote on corporate matters and whether you stand first, second, or third in line to share in company profits.

When your company is registered, you determine with your lawyer and accountant how many different types or "classes" of shares you need and how many of each class the company may need, now and in the future. The most common type of shares used are called *common shares*. The number of shares can range from 1 to 1,000,000 plus. You may consider authorizing additional classes of shares if you think you might need to raise money from outside investors or if you plan to share the ownership with other people (like your children or life partner). Doing this when you incorporate may help you avoid additional expenses to change the share structure of your company later on. However, this can of worms is better left to be opened in the presence of a corporate lawyer and accountant because everyone is different with different needs.

If I want to find out how many shares and what type I have, I need to contact my lawyer to get my company's minute book. (A minute book is sort of like a corporate diary that is used to record important corporate matters such as your share structure, different decisions such as declaration of dividends, and who your accountant is, as well as legal correspondence such as the minutes of shareholder meetings and forms such as your Articles of Incorporation.) I personally own all 100 shares in my company. Why 100? It is hard to divide one share if I ever want to sell a percentage to someone else. There is also too much legal administrivia to change the total number. In Paula's case, she has two classes of shares, common and special. Her common shares are used to establish how much control each owner has by way of their voting rights while she uses the special shares to determine who shares in the profits of her company and by how much. She needed to go with two classes of shares because the votes and the profits were not distributed according to the same percentage.

The Decision Makers

You've really only got two sides to your company's team — the side that manages the big picture of the corporation (the shareholders and directors) and the side that handles the day-to-day operation of the business (the executive team or officers of the company, the CEO and/or president and VPs). On each side, there are different players, with different roles, making different contributions, with different ways of getting compensated. You will likely need a plain-speaking lawyer to help you demystify the legal morass of the incorporated world.

Plainly put, owners who hold common shares are said to "control" the company because they have the right to elect the company's directors who decide on matters like the company's structure, what type of shares will be offered, and how many are available to be purchased. They also vote on how much of the company profits get distributed to the shareholders. Because directors in a small company are usually synonymous with the common shareholders, they are the people who are responsible for making sure the corporation operates within the law and the regulations that govern its activity, like the Tax Act and the Human Rights Code.

If it sounds confusing, it's because it is. Especially when it is the same person who is wearing more than one of the hats. Don't fear, the good news is that in our smaller businesses, we are it — the shareholder, the director, the president, and the cleaning staff. I often joke that I can hold a board of directors meeting on the toilet. As our companies get larger, we may consider electing outside individuals to our board of directors to bring in outside expertise or because their spheres of influence are important to the organization.

The Year End

You get to pick your own tax year end. Let's look at Women and Money Inc. as an example. Because the corporation is a separate legal entity, Women and Money Inc. has its own birthday. Actually it has two. WMI's first birthday is the date of our incorporation, which is the day that our Articles of Incorporation (the actual legal registration form) were filed and approved by the government. For us, this birthday is February 11, 1993. The second is the day that we will refer to forever amen as our year end. We got to choose our own year end, but it had to fall within the 53 weeks of the day we incorporated. The date we chose determined the period for which we had to pay taxes. We consulted a bookkeeper for advice on which year end date would be best for us to minimize tax in our first year. He advised the end of February. In retrospect, that turned out to be a bit of an "oh-oh." Long afterwards, when Paula came on the scene, the advice was different. (There is a lesson here, folks. Bookkeepers do fabulous work as bookkeepers. Resist getting them to do an accountant's job. Bookkeepers are terrific at recording the financial transactions in the business while accountants are better at providing planning advice that requires professional judgement in areas like taxation and how to handle transactions.)

Paula suggested we should have had a year end of January 31. For us, February, being RRSP month, has always been a very big sales month because of the inhuman number of personal finance keynote speeches that I do. Paula explained that by choosing January 31 as our year end in our first year, we could have deferred the tax payable on those February sales for a whole year. And deferring as much of your payable tax as possible is what it's all about. Please note that deferring is not avoiding, which is illegal.

The Complete Canadian Small Business Guide includes a comprehensive treatment of this topic as well as all the steps to incorporation. If you want to learn a truckload more about the advantages and disadvantages of incorporation or unincorporated businesses such as sole proprietors or partnerships before going to a professional, buy this book. We'll provide you with some of the highlights of the unincorporated alternatives in the following sections.

Just Me: The Sole Proprietor

My street is as typical a suburban street as you can get. The two things it has in abundance are kids and minivans. My neighbour, Jeanette Greenwood, is the 40-year-old mother of three of those seemingly thousands of kids who populate our street. And yes, she drives a forest-green minivan.

When she's not running.

Next to raising three children, this is what Jeanette does best. She's a marathon runner. Living next to her can be pretty tough as I squeeze my spreading hips and thighs into jeans a tad larger than in my younger days. I watch her run almost every day on the path that winds its way through the ravine behind our houses. It's enough to make you want to sit down and devour a bag of cookies. Now, being that my experience with running is limited to the distance between the fridge and the family room, I was unaware of how important a runner's log is to a serious runner. Both Jeanette and my husband Michael, a triathlete in a former life, look at me as if I'm some pitiful waif, shaking their heads sadly at my lack of sophistication about running. They humour me as I feign interest in their efforts to run as fast or as long as they can to go nowhere in particular. I share Erma Bombeck's sentiment that the only reason I would take up running is so that I could hear heavy breathing again. But one thing I do get. A lot of people take running extremely seriously. And a runner's log is a vital part of this world.

Having used these logs for years, one day Jeanette suddenly had an exclamation point hover over her head. Having seen most of the logs out there, she realized that they were all written by men, appealing mostly to men. Filled with tables and charts listing pacing rates, wind-chill readings, and metric distance conversions, they included nothing that would inspire women runners. Jeanette figured that if "extraordinary ordinary women" could share their experiences of how running had changed their lives, it would be a far more powerful motivator than elite male runners sharing training tips on how to run faster. She decided to write her own running log. Not only that, she decided to start women-only running clinics. She called her company "Forever Running." When Jeanette set up shop, she decided to go the sole proprietor route. This meant that essentially she and her business were one and the same. As she was the sole proprietor, Jeanette's company name was going to be either shared with her own or a name registered by her. The upside for Jeanette in going the sole proprietor route was that she didn't have to go through any lengthy or costly process of incorporation. She got to leap out of the starting gate right away.

But Jeanette realized at the outset that there were issues she needed to be aware of as a sole proprietor. She discovered that even though the process was faster and cheaper, her registered name was not as protected as it would have been had she incorporated. (Unless she ordered a NUANS on her business name and registered it with the provincial ministry of consumer and commercial affairs.) She also recognized that her company's liabilities were her personal liabilities. (However, even if she were to incorporate, she could be asked to personally guarantee some of her company's debts.) The profit from her company was her income. Because there was no separate corporate entity, this meant she had to pay taxes at her personal tax rate on all the profits her business made, not just the amount that she needed to pay herself. Jeanette was happy to discover, however, that as a sole proprietor, she was able to deduct all of the same expenses from her income as someone like myself who had an incorporated business.

One thing that Jeanette liked about the sole proprietor arrangement was that her company's tax rate was her tax rate. The advantages to her depended on the level of her annual profit. If her profits were low the first year or two, they would be taxed at her lower personal tax rate. This rate was below the small business tax rate for incorporated businesses. The whole tax thing was so much easier, in fact. Forever Running's tax year was her tax year, the calendar year. The company's tax return was her tax return that had a deadline of April 30 every year. And since this business was a personal extension of who Jeanette Greenwood, woman extraordinaire, was, it didn't bother her at all that the life of Forever Running would end when hers did.

Jeanette had to go through the same office as I did when registering her business, even though hers was a sole proprietorship. Her choice was that she or a hired law clerk or paralegal could stand in an interminably long line or she could log in via her computer to get to the provincial Ministry of Consumer and Commercial Affairs. Or she could have gone directly to a lawyer. She did have the option of using the computers in the local library or in any self-help business office. Most provinces are in the process of decentralizing access to business registrations. Check with your provincial Ministry of Consumer and Commercial Affairs to see if they are online.

Jeanette paid the government $70 to get Forever Running registered. She received a photocopy of her application with a red stamp and seal on it. This was her "official" copy of her business registration which she needed to open a separate business bank account.

Now, these kind government folks asked if she wanted to search the name she had chosen for a mere $10 charge. Jeanette was like many unsuspecting new business owners in thinking that to say yes meant the same thing as initiating a corporate name search. She discovered in short order that it wasn't the same at all. This name search that was being offered to Jeanette was simply to let her know if Forever Running was being used by any other businesses, but it offered none of the protection of actually registering her business name. So Jeanette opted for the free alternative to this name search and made a good start by looking through the white and yellow pages of the phone book in the areas she intended to do business.

Jeanette couldn't afford to incorporate her business right away but thought that she might like to some day. If she has contracts and agreements signed under her sole proprietor name, they may actually be transferrable to a company that she or her family owns. She also considered what could be described as an interim solution, a kind of hybrid arrangement. In this scenario, she would choose her name Forever Running, as well as a couple of variations, so she wouldn't be disappointed if what she had her heart set on doesn't fly. Then all she would need to do is get her lawyer or a paralegal to order the corporate name search, or NUANS. This would cost her less than $150. Assuming that the name comes back cleared, just doing the name search would hold and protect it for 90 days. That's three months that she would have to get the business going and to earn some money to pay for her incorporation. She could move ahead with creating her logo, stationery, business cards, and marketing materials without any risk that she may have to change her business name when it comes time to incorporate. Then she would register her business using the soon-to-be corporate name (minus the Inc., Ltd., etc.) so that she could open her bank account.

In the end Jeanette decided to run her business initially as a sole proprietorship. This approach was best suited to the nature of her business in the short term. In the longer term, when the business becomes an expanding entity, she will definitely reconsider. Incorporating will put her in a better position to build equity in the business by reinvesting her profits into the business at a lower corporate tax rate. Incorporation will also help to further separate her personal finances from those of the business and to limit her personal liability as it relates to the business.

The Unincorporated We: Partnerships

Partnerships look a lot like sole proprietorships except there is more than one person who owns the business. Just like a sole proprietorship, the income of the business is the income of the partners, except that it is split according to each person's percentage of ownership. People in partnerships include their business income or losses on their personal tax returns and they are personally responsible for all the business's liabilities, even those created by the other partner.

In partnerships, the risks tend to outweigh the rewards. Unfortunately, as we mentioned, some professionals are not permitted to incorporate, so partnership is the only way they can expand their business beyond themselves. Some professionals segment their business into the type of work that can be incorporated (i.e., consulting) and the type that can't, for example, their core practice.

Should I Get Married? Bringing in a "Business Partner"

Bringing in a business partner, whether it be a partner in an unincorporated business or a shareholder in an incorporated business, is exactly like getting married. You start out thinking the union will last forever; then, just like almost half of all marriages, the union needs to end sometime before forever. People change and forget to tell each other. While the reasons for divorce in both the personal and the business sense are varied and often mutually beneficial, most business break-ups could have been predicted from the start. We've all heard the following:

"We wanted to take the business in two different directions."
"She just wasn't putting as much into the business as I was — she had other priorities."
"We weren't compatible — we had different work and business ethics."
"We weren't making enough money to support both of us."
"She was a good friend but a lousy business partner."
"We needed someone with different skills and experience as we grew."

A great example of business partners is that of our very own Paula and her counterpart, Debbie Shinehoft. Paula tells me often how fortunate she is to have a business partner like Debbie. In a business sense, these two had actually lived together for over two years since they had both worked for the same company, a national service franchisor, before tying the corporate knot. In fact, Paula had the privilege of hiring Debbie as the firm's director of marketing and advertising. So it was to be that common ground as well as individual differences helped them to build a strong, rich, and successful business relationship.

Making Difference a Good Thing

Paula and Debbie both say that anyone who knows them understands why their relationship works. Debbie is the only person Paula knows who finishes as many things as she likes to start. Debbie gets more done in an hour than Paula can manage to accomplish in a day. Paula loves to initiate, Debbie likes to conclude. Paula likes to be out front, Debbie prefers the role of the strong supporter. Paula sees things in terms of grey, which results in either break-through solutions or outright paralysis. Debbie, on the other hand, distills things down to black and white. This either focuses them on the essence of the situation or creates a strong preconception that may be difficult to debunk. They allow each other to do what they love and do best. They respect the impor-tance of each other's contribution and value each other's perspective.

How do they manage to reconcile their sometimes divergent perspectives? They practice the art of respectful yet passionate discussion. Sometimes Paula caves in and parks some of her scathingly brilliant ideas. And sometimes Debbie indulges Paula by letting her add yet another item to the corporate slate, but only if she brings it up more than once. Despite their differences, they have the important things in common. They are strongly aligned on how cus-tomers, staff, and suppliers should be treated. They share a value system and a cultural background (Paula is half Lebanese, though I'm not sure which half, and Debbie is Jewish). They both have a healthy sense of who they are, and most importantly, trust each other implicitly.

Who Gets What

Once Paula and Debbie decided to incorporate, they sat down to figure out what would be an appropriate split in ownership. They wanted to structure the company fairly and they both agreed that fairness should be based on the proportion of value that each could create for the company. They let substance determine form, rather than choosing the easier but more arbi-trary route of equality. In determining their individual contribution, they looked beyond the obvious inputs of time and money and tried to capture the value they could generate based on their individual talents, roles, and re-sponsibilities. They agreed that Paula would be primarily responsible for cor-porate leadership, strategy, and sales, and that Deb would be primarily responsible for the management and administration of the company. They would both do client work relative to their experience. So Deb handled the creative design, communications production, and administration work, while Paula took on the strategic planning, finance, technology, and marketing end. They also tried to look beyond their start-up contributions to what they thought their sustainable long-term commitment could be. Based on all of this and some serious *"what-iffing,"* they agreed to a split in which Paula owned two-thirds and Deb one-third of the company.

At the same time they also decided how they would be compensated. Again, they decided that their salaries would be based on the market equivalent of what they could earn doing the same job elsewhere. In the beginning, of course, they could not afford to pay themselves market rates. So they settled on paying themselves the same percentage of their respective market rates. There was one exception that they had to make. (Having the ability to make exceptions to the rules is one of the entrepreneurial luxuries.) One of the principal values in Paula's and Deb's organization is the importance of family. Deb had one child and therefore an onerous financial responsibility that Paula did not have — daycare. It was necessary that they rework the compensation to pay Deb more at the beginning so that she could deal with that economic reality. They kept track so that they could compensate Paula once the company could afford it.

Agreeing on who gets what at the start of the relationship eliminates one of the common causes of business breakdown.

Breaking Up Is Hard to Do

The number of times that I had seriously considered taking on a partner in an effort to "lessen the load" was considerable. I had, on a couple of occasions, even entered into preliminary negotiations with other larger firms to test the waters. I wanted so badly to continue with the work I was doing, but still have a sane life and a regular paycheque, especially with a baby coming. But, for whatever reasons, nothing ever materialized. Providence, I suspect.

I ran into Paula at a function that was sponsoring former prime minister Kim Campbell as the keynote speaker. We didn't get to hear a single word. Paula and I sat next to each other, and before I knew it, I had poured out my heart and soul, confessing that I didn't feel up to the pronounced rigorous challenges of being a solo act anymore. I told Paula I so desperately wanted to lessen the burden by taking on a partner. She said something that really made me think twice: "If you think that taking on a partner will lessen your load, absolutely do not do it. More often, partnerships can double the trouble. Before you even begin to consider selling or giving shares to someone in return for their money or sweat equity, stop. Even if it's because you don't want to start the business on your own. Partnerships are meant to be permanent. Getting out of one is very tough and often very expensive, both financially and emotionally."

"I know that in my heart," I answered, "but I still find myself daydreaming about finding a business partner to make all my problems vanish. I know such a business relationship is no stronger than the people in it. I remember a story my mother told me of an 80-year-old woman who was about to give up her beloved golf because of her failing eyesight. She could still hit the ball well, but she couldn't see where it went. So her doctor teamed her up with a 90-year-old with perfect eyesight. The first day they played, the 80-year-old hit her first drive and asked her golfing partner if she had seen where it landed. The partner answered, 'Yep.' She asked, 'Where did it go?' Her partner answered, 'I don't remember.'"

Paula and I were killing ourselves laughing when the waitress came by to top up our coffee. Paula fell quiet for a moment and stared introspectively into her coffee cup. Taking a sip, she began to share her philosophy on business partners. "Formally partnering with someone else in your business has to be one of the most human aspects of owning a business. Personalities, ambitions, quirks, and eccentricities are all magnified when you add earning a living to the equation. The really wise ones get a second opinion before they go public with the announcement of marriage in order to avoid the potential pitfalls of a 'not right' relationship. Just like living together or marriage, it may have been 'not right' from the beginning or is no longer right because of changes in circumstances. Even if you have known your potential business partner for a long time and you know that their values, ethics, and skills are right for your company, things change. That's why I tend to use 'not right' instead of 'wrong' when talking about these types of issues.

"Most often it's not that the people have really changed," she continued thoughtfully. "Sometimes, a person holds themselves out to be more than they are or overpromises on what they can deliver. But then they can't hold the pose forever. What they promised up front as their contribution turns out to be only that — a promise. I've been there. I chose to confront the issue right away when the discrepancy between promise and reality became evident. I had that business partner resign his stake in the company by transferring back his shares. Because this person was someone of integrity, he understood and complied."

"I can't imagine how hard that must have been. I detest confrontation. How did you handle it? Did it get nasty? Didn't it feel like a kick in the gut?" I asked.

"Not at all," Paula answered. "While I had considerable anxiety leading up to the meeting, once we were sitting across from each other, it turned into a simple discussion about the contribution of value in the company. I told him that we believed that his other responsibilities precluded him from making the contribution that was needed to maintain his share in the company. He agreed. I then told him that the return of his shares would remove his obligation to us. If he should ever be in a position to contribute in the future, we'd pay him more appropriately, like a referral fee, for example. This worked out well because it more accurately reflected the nature of our relationship.

"Let me tell you, Joanne, the more common cause of difficulty in a partnership or shareholdership is when the needs of one person, the company, or both change. Unfortunately, because imbalance in the business relationship causes a lot of anxiety and stress, most people attribute this type of change to the people themselves. But it is important to differentiate between changes in the business partners and changes in the company. Remember, the company is a separate entity, it has a life of its own and needs that go with it. These needs are constantly changing as well as expanding. Sometimes, despite best intentions and efforts all the way around, the gap between need and ability to contribute widens."

"Isn't it ironic," I said, "that a divorce is what people agree on when they can't agree on anything else. I heard George Burns interviewed. He said lots of people asked him what he and Gracie did to make their marriage work. I'll never forget his response: 'It's simple — we didn't do anything. I think the trouble with a lot of people is that they work too hard at staying married. They make a business out of it. When you work too hard at a business, you get grouchy; and when you get grouchy, you start fighting; and when you start fighting, you're out of business.' You can't force a healthy relationship, personal or business. And you can't reduce what makes a relationship work to a black-and-white document."

Paula agreed. "That's true; nevertheless, I always recommend that people who are considering becoming business partners sit down and go through the exercise of divorce. This act forces both parties to put themselves in the position of the break-up and walk through the difficult act of claiming what they believe to be rightfully theirs. It is usually enough to bring out people's true colours. Believe me, you will get a glimpse at whether a business divorce is likely to generate a big legal bill. It will help you make a better decision on whether to say 'I do' or 'I don't.' That's what Deb and I did. We walked through the process of what we would do and what would happen to the shares in the company if either or both of us got sick or went insane, for longer than a week, which was allowed, or if either of us had to be away from the business for an extended period of time. What would happen if we kicked the bucket? What about if we divorced, then remarried? What if we wanted to move on? Wanted the other one to move on? What if one of us wanted to sell to another party? We had to think about these things carefully. These are some of the key issues covered in a formal shareholders agreement."

"So should I ever decide to bring in a business partner and make it legal, then I assume that I, and everyone else in the deal, get independent counsel from a corporate lawyer?" I asked.

"Yep," came the short reply. "There are other options besides co-ownership, Joanne. People enter into partnerships or share the ownership of their businesses for the wrong reasons. Most first-time business unions result from people getting together on the rebound. You are working your guts out, you just can't do it all, you need to do so much more, and you can't afford to pay anyone to help you out."

I shook my head at the futility of it all. "I guess the real issue is trying to determine whether you are in rebound mode or if the co-ownership idea is legit and makes business sense. I'm sure Hewlett and Packard, Procter and Gamble, and Rolls and Royce figured out that sharing the risks and rewards was a good thing. I guess I'd better think about this co-ownership idea more carefully, especially since I'm feeling vulnerable and financially and emotionally stretched. I feel like such a baby entrepreneur, Paula."

"Soon to be toddler," Paula said.

We dove into dessert.

Business, Government, and Tax Accounts

So many choices, so little time. "Where will my business live? Do I incorporate or not? What about taking on a business partner?" Hang in there. There are still a few matters — having to do with bank accounts, taxes, and your corporate identity — that need to be looked after.

Bank and Credit Card Accounts

Regardless of what form of business you choose, we recommend that you set up a separate bank account to handle your business transactions. There is not a lot of choice here for small business. Each bank offers business bank accounts, payroll services, electronic bank access through ATM or Internet, and many service fees, which vary greatly. Specific information will become out of date 12 minutes after this book is published, so talk with your bank manager for details.

Government and Tax Accounts

I find it fascinating that we small business owners — you know, the busiest people on the planet — are responsible for charging, collecting, and remitting taxes on behalf of our municipal, provincial, and federal governments. In some instances, they allow you to reduce what you have to remit by a set calculated amount in recognition of your efforts. But don't plan your vacation yet. The amount doesn't even cover the time you need to add it to each invoice. Consult your business adviser, accountant, lawyer, or the appropriate government office to figure out whether you should register for any of the following.

Goods and Services Tax

GST (or TVQ, the Quebec equivalent) — is a 7 percent tax charged on most goods and services sold in Canada; GST is administered by Revenue Canada using your Business Number (BN). Mandatory registration gives you the privilege of collecting GST on your sales and gives you the job of doing the math, netting what you collected against what you paid, and sending it off to Revenue Canada. This can be done either monthly, quarterly, or annually. Registration is only required for those businesses that make over $30,000 per year in revenue. However, even if you will not be making over this amount in your first year, you may still wish to register if you expect that the total value of goods and services you purchased to set up and operate your business will exceed your revenue. In this case you will be eligible for a refund for some of the GST that you paid. It may also be a good idea to do this from a marketing perspective. Do you want your potential clients to know that your company is making less than $30,000? By registering, you will appear larger, meaning, higher than the GST threshold.

Provincial Sales Tax

These tax rates (0 percent in Alberta, 8 percent in Ontario, etc.) are required to be charged on most goods and some services sold within the province; PST is administered by the provincial Ministry of Finance. Check with this office to see if you will be responsible for charging, collecting, and remitting this tax on your product or service.

Harmonized Sales Tax in New Brunswick, Nova Scotia, and Newfoundland

As of April 1, 1997, the new 15 percent HST replaces the GST and the previous total federal and provincial sales taxes in three of the four Atlantic provinces. The HST is administered by Revenue Canada and applies to goods and services sold in or delivered to these provinces in the same way that the GST used to be. The result of this new taxation approach? A tax savings of almost four percentage points in Nova Scotia and New Brunswick, and almost five percentage points in Newfoundland. If you are registered for GST, the government will automatically register you for HST and you can continue using your current GST return to calculate how much you have to remit. Remember, you don't have to have a business located in New Brunswick, Nova Scotia, or Newfoundland to be required to collect and remit the HST. You must do so if you sell or deliver goods or services to clients located in these provinces. For more information on this relatively new tax approach, check out Revenue Canada's Web site at http://www.rc.gc.ca.

Employee Remittances

Your business number is also used to keep track of your employer accounts for the remittance of income tax withheld as well as the employer and employee portions of Employment Insurance (EI) premiums and Canada Pension Plan (CPP) contributions. Consult your accountant to determine the rates that apply to you and your business.

Employer Health Tax

EHT is a provincial payroll tax that helps the government fund the public health care system. In Ontario, it is assessed as a percentage of your total payroll expense and needs to be paid at least annually. Small business has been given some additional breaks when it comes to this tax. You do not have to remit in your first year of business or if your payroll is under a certain amount ($350,000 in Ontario and going up to $400,000 as of 1999). Check with your local Ministry of Finance for your provincial guidelines.

Workers' Compensation

Businesses in which there is a risk of personal injury while on the job are required to pay monthly premiums to the Workers' Compensation Board. These fees are mandatory and are treated like your payroll taxes. If you are required to pay WCB for your employees and subcontractors and you don't, you'll get slammed with penalties and the directors of the company will be held liable. Be sure to check with your local WCB office to see if your company is required to maintain this benefit for its workers. You may be exempt if your business has a low risk for personal injury while on the job.

Business Taxes

These are municipal taxes charged to you usually based on the size of your office, sort of like your home property taxes. It's an estimate as to how much of the town's or city's services you use. Many municipalities are starting to charge the landlords with the responsibility of administering this tax and you may now have it included in your rent instead of getting a separate bill from the city. This change came from the fact that municipal offices could not keep up with identifying let alone visiting all of the new businesses that started each year.

The Business Birth Experience

You are about as ready as you are going to be. You have done your homework in the personal and business *what-if* department. You have a short-, medium-, and long-term plan, either in your head or carved in your rec room wall. You have planned (in a big-picture sense) for whatever life may throw at you. You have sought out advice from all those you care about and have internalized it or chucked it. You have given your ideas the acid test and they have passed. You are crystal clear on your endpoint or goals. You have prepared in advance by knowing on whom you can call when you need an extra pair of hands. You have contingency plans in place for when things don't work out quite the way you figured they would. You know the difference between a want and a need. You know who your "best" customer is. You know what your cash reserves are and how long they will last before you need to push the panic button. You know if you need to incorporate or not. You've decided that there is no place like home for your business or that your business has no place at home. You have picked a name for your business baby. And you have resigned yourself to the fact that you will always worry about how much you worry.

You are ready. In other words, you are a full nine months pregnant. Take a deep breath. It's time.

The Biological Birth Experience — Welcoming Kate

It was Saturday and I was now only days away from my due date. My girth had expanded so much in the last month that my only chance of finding something comfortable to wear would have been from *Joe's Tent and Awning*. The day began as it usually did, breakfast, shopping at St. Lawrence Market, and home by lunch. The biggest difference was that I had technically gone into labour earlier that morning, but didn't know it. What prompted us to go to the hospital that afternoon was the fact my water had broken, hours earlier, but I felt not an ounce of pain. Feeling remarkably calm, we headed off just to be sure everything was where it should be. We arrived at the hospital, and the nurse hooked me up to a machine to see if I was really in labour. According to the monitor, I was, indeed, in labour. The nurse announced, "Looks like your contractions are five minutes apart." Every ounce of calmness fled.

"How is that possible?" I asked incredulously. "I don't feel anything! Is it possible that I won't feel anything?"

The nurse smiled. She said simply, "No," and left it at that.

"Why don't you guys go home or go out for dinner?" she suggested casually. "This could take hours."

So, as mind-boggling as it seemed, we went home with the knowledge that our little girl was on her way. I couldn't wait to meet her. Michael and I couldn't stop grinning. All the while, I got this incessant little thought niggling at the back of my mind that I was going to breeze through this with little pain. I couldn't shake the fact that my contractions were five minutes apart and I wasn't feeling anything worse than the dull ache similar to a period.

Around 7:00 that evening, Michael decided to take a nap in preparation for the very long night ahead. My intellectual side agreed that was a good idea. My emotional side wanted to drive a steamroller over him. He went to sleep and I was left alone feeling bereft, abandoned, and completely neglected. I paced for two hours solid, planning ways that I could make him pay.

At 9:00 p.m., the nurse's patient smile when I had asked if I might not feel pain flashed briefly through my mind as an intense contraction ripped through my body, taking my breath away and doubling me over in a split second. A wave of fear and incredible excitement passed through me simultaneously.

So imagine this. The woman who dared entertain the thought that her labour was going to be painless is now on the way to the hospital, screaming like she was being murdered. At one point, my beloved husband was forced to make a U-turn in the middle of a major street, driving over the sidewalk in the process, because the police had blocked off the main road to the hospital. Apparently there was a shoot-out of some sort going on. Welcome to Toronto.

When we finally did get to the hospital, Michael and I took the time to have a fight about whether he should park in public parking (since he had no idea when he would get back to the car) or, my preference, drive the car right into the damned lobby. Thankfully, calmer heads prevailed and he parked in the lot that was only a few feet away from the entrance.

Which turned out to be locked.

A sign said to use the south entrance after midnight. It was now close to 1:00 a.m. Michael remarked innocently that we needed to use another door. I launched straight into the stratosphere. In between contractions, which were coming at a fast and furious rate, I yelled to no one in particular that I had no idea where north let alone south was and as far as I knew all women had their babies in the wee hours of the morning and this had to be some kind of plot from some bonehead, probably a man, who didn't realize this small, minor detail and if someone didn't let us in immediately, I was going to have this baby on the front lawn of this esteemed establishment and I would sue the pants off whoever was the closest.

Someone from the cleaning staff happened to walk by. I started to pound on the door. This whole thing began to seem very unreal. I'm having a baby, for God's sake, and Michael and I were pounding on the front door of the hospital to let us in. The woman shook her head and pointed to the sign that had sent me into a fit the first time around. I pounded even harder, threatening to burn the entire building down with her in it if she didn't open the door. She opened the door a tiny crack with the intention of telling us to go to another entrance. It was all we needed. Her eyes flew wide open in astonishment as I pushed the door open and marched right past her. She began gesticulating wildly as Michael and I hurried over to the elevators. By the time we got to the labour room, my contractions were less than two minutes apart. Kate was making her way — fast.

A scant four hours later, at 5:00 a.m., my darling husband, with a little help from the nurse, delivered a stunningly beautiful 7-pound 8-ounce ball of perfection. Thirty-seven years I had waited for such a moment. The circle was completed.

By now I had completely forgiven Michael for his earlier transgression of falling asleep. It seemed so minor compared to the miracle we had created.

The First Year

Because of their age-long training in human
relations — for that is what feminine
intuition really is — women have a special
contribution to make to any group enterprise.

Margaret Mead

Giving Birth — Separating Yourself From Your Business

Oh, how I envied Michael. Those last few hours of uninterrupted sleep he managed to steal the night I went into labour were his last for several months. But at least he got some. What a ride it became when Kate exploded on the scene. Why is it that change is always greater than we anticipate? It harkened back to those early, insane days when my business first started. I had it all planned. I was going to breastfeed and, when Kate napped, I'd do a couple of hours of work in order to keep my finger on the pulse of the company so I could ward off bankruptcy.

Yeah, right.

Needless to say, the majority of women have wonderful, smooth experiences with breastfeeding. Unfortunately, I was not one of them. It seems Kate had her own way to feed, which unfortunately hurt. A lot. Forty-eight hours after she was born, we found ourselves heading home, even though we still hadn't resolved how to breastfeed. But it's amazing what we can do when we need to do it. In my business life, I had learned I didn't need to have all the answers before figuring out a solution. It was this attitude that made me breathe a little easier about taking Kate home so soon.

Kate fed 10 to 12 times a day. The pain was so bad each time, I had to put a pencil between my teeth to help bear it. I spent the next six weeks talking to every conceivable expert, trying to figure out why it hurt so much. Everyone kept concentrating on me and my technique. I felt like it was my fault, that I was doing something wrong.

Michael was fantastic. This dear man got up with Kate and me every single night for every one of those arduous feedings. Being the technical one, he helped with all the tubes, tape, and syringes if Kate and I couldn't get it right the natural way. We could only rely on our own instincts and what the so-called experts and books told us.

But I refused to give up, though people were starting to suggest that I do. Six weeks were enough to figure out if it would or would not work. But I really believe my entrepreneurial personality emerged here. Entrepreneurs are like fire fighters running into a situation everyone else is trying to leave. It was strictly passion that carried me until I could figure out the solution. Or, as my mother is fond of saying, "You will succeed because you don't have the sense to quit."

Getting more and more desperate as the weeks marched by, we made a call to a lactation consultant. (Can you believe it? There actually is such a thing.)

It turned out that this woman, Anne, was the same consultant I had seen at the breastfeeding clinic the day after Kate was born. At that time she had very casually mentioned the possibility of a yeast infection but let it drop. When Anne came to the house, she mentioned infection again, along with 99 other things Kate and I could be doing wrong. Again, the infection comment got buried in the avalanche of advice. But nothing helped. Frankly, I couldn't imagine things getting worse. That's when I got hit with the most severe breast infection — mastitis — on the planet.

I had never been that sick in my entire adult life. The only hope for clearing mastitis is antibiotics, hot compresses, and, ironically, to nurse your way through it. Every two hours, Michael had to carry me from the bed to the rocking chair so I could feed Kate. It had now been five-and-a-half weeks of breastfeeding hell. I now had to face the very real prospect of giving it up. I made a last-ditch effort and called Anne to come back one more time.

As a last resort she suggested, not too hopefully, that I try an over-the-counter cream for yeast infections. She thought my breasts looked too red. (I couldn't imagine how else they could look given what they had been through.) Lo and behold, things started to improve immediately. In no time at all, the breastfeeding kicked in and Kate and I became a dynamic team. I fluctuated between joy and anger when I realized that six weeks of unadulterated hell could have been eliminated by a stupid five-dollar tube of cream.

That experience of the first six weeks of Kate's life has come to symbolize so much for me. It was the first real adversity Kate and I had encountered and we came through like pros. Kate's tenacity was unbelievable. She gained weight steadily from the minute she was born, even though she almost killed her mother doing it.

The saddest day for me was the day I entered the following into my journal: "*September 1, 1996*. Officially weaned. You are ten months old. I miss you terribly."

There is a lesson here — a big one. There will always be curveballs when a baby or a business is born. No amount of planning can change that immutable fact. As first-time business or biological parents, we are so new to everything. And like most new parents, we often never get a chance to recover because we hit the ground running.

But I learned something critical. Shortly after my business was born, a new regulation changed my target market. After Kate was born, there was the breastfeeding experience. That's just what happens. The reality is the first year can be traumatic, no matter how you cut it. What compounds the problem is the utter exhaustion, whether you are a biological or business parent.

And if you are anything like me when I'm tired, the whole world takes on a far more ominous face. In this and the following chapters, we are going to talk about the entrepreneurial dilemmas common to your business's first and toddler years of operation. You need to keep a sense of humour throughout the traumatic experience of the birth of your business. There's an old joke about a woman business owner who ordered a fancy floral arrangement for her grand opening. She was furious when it arrived adorned with a ribbon that read, "May You Rest in Peace." Apologizing profusely, the florist finally got her to calm down with a reminder that in some funeral home in Regina stood an arrangement bearing the words, "Good Luck in Your New Location."

Oh yes, and no matter how traumatic or life-altering the experience of giving birth to your business is, don't panic. As I discovered, it's often only a five-dollar solution that's needed.

Surviving the First Year — 365 Days and Not One the Same

In your first year both you and your business baby will be growing and changing daily. Don't blink. It's exciting, terrifying, and the start of a whole new stage of your business life. The year will continue on as a year of firsts — your first phone call, your first customer, your first employee, your first bad debt, your first computer crash, your first nervous breakdown, your first set of financial statements, your first business card, your first lost sale, your second nervous breakdown. It is impossible not to feel overwhelmed and inspired. Take heart. You have to live it all in order to figure it out.

Human Resources — The Team

Oh, the incredible thrill of seeing "President" on my business card for the first time. In reality it should have read *president, janitor, VP sales, VP marketing, receptionist, office manager, filing clerk, office equipment repair technician, bill collector, Chief Everything Officer.*

I thought I knew "busy" before I started my own business. But in short order I came to realize that I had outgrown my own personal time and talent pool. I desperately needed help managing customers, writing cheques, making decisions, and even sweeping the proverbial shop. I had to face it — I needed to hire more staff. Letting go of some of my responsibilities and entrusting them to others was a huge leap.

Because the business had accelerated from zero into overdrive almost overnight, I was doing everything at half capacity and nothing exceptionally well. Now, in a perfect world, which an entrepreneurial world never is, I would have taken at least a wee bit of time to sit back and reflect. I needed to decide, preferably in advance, if I really needed to hire someone, who to hire first, where to find them, how to choose, how to pay, and, as it turned out, how to quickly replace. But I didn't. I let my frantic, overwhelming short-term needs dictate my actions. Consequently, I added more to my growing list of bad decisions.

Running a business is 95 percent about people and 5 percent about economics. Before bringing in another person, I should have made sure that I had ways to know if that employee was happy and if they were properly doing what I needed them to do. I should have thought of ways to determine if they were thinking of leaving or were ready to advance within the company. Did I know how to tell if they were fulfilled and doing quality work? I should have had all these key indicators set out even before placing the ad. As it was, though, I took 12 minutes to complete the whole process. In fact, I managed to commit every one of the most common hiring mistakes in my first attempt. Let's keep in mind, however, when we say "mistakes" we don't mean in the traditional negative sense. It's more like my mother's definition of mistake: "It doesn't matter how much milk you spill, just so long as you don't lose your cow."

The Most Common Mistakes People Make in Hiring

1. Not first considering alternatives to hiring.
2. Thinking that anybody is better than nobody.
3. Hiring for today and hoping that tomorrow will take care of itself.
4. Doing it yourself. (Don't.)
5. Hiring the résumé, not the person.
6. Paying too little.
7. Hiring for humanitarian reasons.
8. Hiring based on referral alone.
9. Not considering how to fire someone.
10. Paying too much.
11. Not setting the terms and conditions of employment in advance.

Though it seemed pretty clear to me that I needed another full-time set of hands, the company hadn't been operating long enough to know what cash flow was going to look like. I was having a hard time imagining how I was going to support myself let alone be responsible for someone else's bread and butter. So I began to entertain the idea of trying to find someone who would see working for Women and Money Inc. as an opportunity to "write their own paycheque" instead of being paid a set salary. I could outsource sales because the results are tangible and quantifiable and can be compensated out of the cash generated by the sales. Hiring a salesperson made sense because I figured they would only be paid when they brought in business — no cash flow hit before a sale was made. Also, having someone else keeping the funnel full would allow me to take three or four minutes off without a dip in business activity. So here it is — *Hiring Mistake #1* — I did not consider alternatives to hiring first. This was no environment to bring in someone new. There was no structure, policy, procedures, or money. I should have looked at a better use of technology. I could have contracted out a lot of the work I was doing to free myself to concentrate on sales, which was what I was good at. I could have established a more efficient system to streamline my work. Hell, a system, period, would have been good. Then of course I could have cut back on the work that wasn't creating value for the company. But who has the courage to say no when you are a baby entrepreneur.

Peter, my business adviser at the time, confirmed my fledgling thought. Find someone who shared the passion for this work and who was willing to work on a performance basis until revenue started to come in more regularly. At that point, though, I was so desperate for help I would have happily hired Leona Helmsley. That's where I made *Hiring Mistake #2* — anybody is better than nobody. The reality? Hire the right person or stay home. Feeling creative one day, I wrote what I considered a "must" list for the ideal candidate.

WANTED

Someone with previous sales experience willing to work on commission who is energetic, entrepreneurial, independent, and schizophrenic. Must be willing to work absurd hours for no or low pay and be willing to perform no less than 427 tasks simultaneously that may not be within their skill set. The successful candidate must thrive on previously unimagined stress levels and completely unreasonable project completion deadlines. Also must show affection for dark, windowless basements with low ceiling beams that regularly knock down anyone over 5' 5". They should feel at ease in a war-zone environment and thrive on cycles of manic highs and deep lows at least four times a day. The successful candidate will show great creativity and no remorse in spending money not currently available. When in a cash crunch, the ideal candidate will show no outward manifestations of fear towards bankers, suppliers, or other such unsavoury characters.

Mothers and those with front-line military experience preferred.

"Oh yeah, this is going to be real easy," I said to myself, looking over my list. I showed it to Peter, who laughed out loud. His advice was good. He said, "Look at the person more than your list. Pro football coaches always say they want quarterbacks who are six foot four and weigh 230 pounds, but they bend a little when a Doug Flutie shows up." Men and their sports speak.

Enter *Hiring Mistake #3*. I was attempting to hire for today with the hope that tomorrow would take care of itself. I was only concerned with "getting out of this mess." It turned out tomorrow didn't take care of itself. What I really needed to do was to try and picture the role I would need this person to be playing in a couple of years. If I couldn't, then I shouldn't be hiring. My first employees were to be the bedrock of my company. Ideally, I needed to leverage their growing knowledge base as the company grew.

My research assistant on *Balancing Act*, Kim Speers, recommended that I talk to a young woman that she had gone to university with. Kim's referral, Barb, called me on a Friday morning quite anxious to meet. I looked at my calendar and saw I was free at the end of the day. "Come over today!" I exclaimed brightly, giving absolutely no thought to what I was going to say at the interview. I didn't even consider having someone else there to provide a more objective point of view. Yep. You guessed it. *Hiring Mistake #4*. If you feel the need to do the recruiting and hiring yourself, don't, especially if you are in desperate need or have never done it for yourself before.

Barb and I met at 5:00 that Friday evening. I was gravely concerned the minute I laid eyes on her. She was 5' 7." Peter's dumb Doug Flutie example came to mind. I brought her downstairs into "The Pit" and was heartened to watch her deftly manoeuvre under the low ceiling, avoiding the inevitable collision that had rendered many flat on their backs. Lying unconscious on the floor is not a great way to conduct an interview.

It wasn't a standard interview. In retrospect, I now understand why you need to go through all the paces. There is the right way to do it and the way I did it. The right way? The interviews (note the plural) should take longer than 12 minutes. I hired Barb after one hour-long meeting. The right way? You actually need to plan for the interview. My way? No planning. Zero, zip, nada. I don't think I even had coffee in the house. The right way? Use a variety of means, like personality tests and second opinions, to assess the candidate. My way? I eyeballed her suit (good quality). I trusted that desperate little voice screaming inside my head, "You need sleep/balance/and at least six extra pairs of hands, *now*. Here's someone who can start right away. What more do you need?" The right way? Conducting an interview entails a battery of well-thought-out, thought-provoking questions to give you a good overall sense of the candidate. My way? "So, tell me a bit about yourself." Of course, the right way includes actually checking references. My way? I didn't even ask for any.

But we hit it off right away. Her unbridled enthusiasm and dissatisfaction with her status quo and my desperate state made an immediate and ideal combination. It was intoxicating having someone totally in love with your vision. She was smart, savvy, optimistic, and incredibly dynamic. I always believed you hired an optimist as a sales person and a pessimist to run the accounting area. Her résumé said she had extensive telemarketing experience as well as some media training. It looked like Barb met the criteria. Hallelujah, folks, there you have it — *Hiring Mistake #5*. I hired the résumé, not the person. There was no way I could have hired the person considering the speed with which we consummated the deal. The problem with just looking at a résumé is that you are only looking at a claim of skills and past experience. A résumé gave me little insight into how she would perform this new job at this point in her life.

Something Barb said had a huge impact on me. She was so anxious to get out of her current work environment that she was prepared to work for free for the first six months. This was said to someone with erratic cash flow and who was high up on the desperation scale. Her words couldn't have been sweeter. I justified hiring Barb for next to nothing financially because I was giving her a significant opportunity at a new career. Alas, *Hiring Mistake #6*. Paying too little meant the chances were good that in the long run Barb wouldn't be happy. She would eventually feel undervalued and, eventually, the market would call to her. People need a living wage, no matter what they tell you. Offering her a new chance in life was part of the reason for me making *Hiring Mistake #7*. Boy, did I discover first hand that altruism is not a solid ground for hiring. Hiring is not a humanitarian act.

After one meeting, a handshake, and absolutely no reference checks, I hired Barb. The very next morning she quit her job. She leaped into the dizzying fray of the self-employed and started with me down the road on what proved to be an unbelievable adventure. Can you believe it? Here was *Hiring Mistake #8*. I hired Barb based on Kim's referral, though Kim was quick to point out that she had only known Barb from school. Would it have made a difference if I had asked for and checked her references? Probably not. But at the very least I should have set up a probationary period where we could have tried each other out before finalizing the terms of the job. Hiring strictly on referral is often a lazy substitute for a thorough hiring procedure.

In no time at all, Barb became my lifeline, my right and left hand, and sometimes my brain, when I was reduced to three or four brain cells from overwork. I learned first hand the truth behind the saying, "It's better to have one person working with you than three people working for you." It's amazing how dependent you become on others when you work in a small business. We were virtually inseparable in all aspects of our lives. Because there were so many long hours, our personal and professional lives blended. In fact, our professional lives overtook our personal lives, which, for the most part, ceased to exist. Peter used to laugh at us, referring to us often as an old married couple.

With only two pairs of hands doing the work of a dozen, it was a relatively organized version of "every woman for herself." Job descriptions changed daily in order to keep abreast of the explosive growth. What was policy one day had to be discarded the next in order to accommodate new business. While we grew, we had to hire another set of hands to handle the administrative workload. That's when Michelle, and eventually Rosa, came into the picture.

Though technically Barb was in charge of sales, we worked as a team for the first few months so I could show her the ropes. The idea was that after she got up to speed, she would go off on her own and continue to develop the market. Believe me, I did think about the trade-off in this arrangement. It was a big one. It came down to who owned and controlled the relationship with the customer, the lifeline of any business. I was constantly on the road doing keynote speeches, which made being around for sales calls somewhat challenging. It was incredibly easy to justify transferring the sales responsibility to someone else. However, this was a mistake from day one. There was a whole variety of reasons for this but the biggest one was the fact that the client or prospect really wanted to talk to me. I was the product. Sales needed to be handled by the most responsible and accountable person, namely me. When I was out there, I would be able to hear first hand what would have enabled the business to move from being viable to being successful. Most importantly, my presence would have ensured that the lifeblood of my business would not be restricted if Barb ever moved on.

And move on she did. *Hiring Mistake #9* — I hadn't considered in advance how I would ever fire someone. Working through what constituted grounds for firing before I hired Barb wouldn't have necessarily predestined our relationship to failure; it likely would have strengthened it. We would have discussed what wasn't acceptable and how a termination would be handled when we were not actually in the heated situation. A proactive approach is more likely to prevent these types of circumstances from boiling over.

Because start-up usually requires everybody doing everything, it was really hard to dedicate oneself to a specific task. Realizing this, we decided to put Barb on a monthly non-recoverable draw (meaning she didn't have to pay it back) once our cash flow got better to tide her over until sales started coming in. In my opinion, I was paying Barb a considerably large draw for the size of the company. *Hiring Mistake #10* — I now paid too much. Barb's work in the beginning had been excellent so the draw was easier to justify in my own mind. But I was a bit concerned that, based on good performance and compensation reviews, I would likely have to add to this salary. There was a possibility that her salary would then shoot above the market rate.

Barb had been with me for nine months, and her verve was gone. This was extremely painful to witness since we had grown up in our entrepreneurial lives together. I knew I had to do something drastic but wanted to maintain the friendship, so I had resisted doing anything for several months. Instead of letting go when it was prudent to do so, we both hung on and on, making excuses and unrealistic promises to each other in an effort to salvage the relationship. But Barb's decreasing ability to perform and the company's need for more money created a very unhappy dynamic.

I needed big help in a big way. Everyone wanted to remain committed to the concept but there had to be serious changes. Enter Paula. Again.

One of Paula's first orders of business was to find a way to control the negative swell that was cascading over everything. She did behavioural profiles of each one of us to determine our strengths and weaknesses so that we could understand why the clashes were occurring. Most of the staff fell right in the middle of the behavioural continuum and got along fine with each other. But when you had people who deviated from the centre to the extreme nether regions of the behavioural map as Barb and I did, trouble naturally brewed. Paula submitted to me a lengthy report outlining her findings and recommendations.

I implemented the first of Paula's 764 recommendations immediately. I had her facilitate a couple of group sessions where all the staff came together to put our concerns on the table. It was pretty powerful stuff with lots of tears, laughter, and generally serious down-home emoting. Each one of us walked away from the exercise believing the sessions had helped to focus us. It seemed to begin reversing the negative spin and to move us in a more positive direction. A couple of weeks later, I took everyone away to a country retreat for a weekend to further establish equilibrium. Everyone felt much better.

Except Barb and me.

The problems between us were so deep, it became evident they were beyond repair. Very sadly and not at all easily, we finally agreed to part company. Our discussion was emotional but amiable as we tried to support each other through the difficult severance process.

Barb had some issues around her final compensation package that she wanted time to work through. I agreed and gave her what I felt was a reasonable timeline to come back to me with her request. However, weeks went by and there was no resolution in sight. From my perspective as an employer, she was taking far too much time to work through whatever her issues were. I was nearing the end of my rope. In an effort to see a swift but fair end to what was already a gruelling and protracted death scene, I decided to put a timeline on how long I was prepared to negotiate with her. I sent a letter off to her by fax giving her a deadline to respond or all negotiations were off. What a mistake. Negotiation depends on communication.

She promptly slammed the door shut to any direct discussions. Communication now took the form of lawyers' letters. A couple of days later I received a terse letter via fax. Barb had chosen to involve the Ministry of Labour to go after a whopping claim of $24,000 for "back wages." She felt our verbal agreement that she was an independent contractor on commission was not accurate, that in fact she was an employee. That meant her compensation became based on hours, not sales. She justified this charge because she had to perform numerous jobs during her stint with me. She agreed she had originally been hired as a commissioned sales person but the reality was she performed duties other than sales. And she was right. That's why we paid her a monthly draw, to cover those additional tasks. But Barb didn't see it that way. So here was my last *Hiring Mistake, #11*. It turned out to be the biggest one. It was, simply put, not setting the terms and conditions of employment in advance.

People have a right to know what constitutes success and failure and what they can expect to happen in either case. Obviously, I should have put our agreement in writing. Barb felt she had good reason to reverse our agreement and every right to pursue her case. However, if we had had everything in writing, none of this would have happened. Needless to say, I was stunned. I called her back and left a terse message of my own: "Be prepared for the fight of your life."

The company's financial picture was so tight there wasn't even a single extra nickel to hire a lawyer. Thankfully, I was able to find an employment lawyer who took our case on for free. Every single morning, until we settled a year and a half later, I awoke with a feeling of great personal loss. The irony? I would have readily settled on the final amount, which was one-quarter the original claim, without any outside influences. All she had to do was come to me directly and present her case.

Meanwhile, while all this was happening, my publisher came to me and suggested I revise and update *Balancing Act*. I agreed and, as a result, took myself out of the revenue-generating loop completely for two more months. As unbelievable as this may seem, because we needed money in a major hurry, a sales replacement was quickly hired. I still laboured under the illusion that someone else could sell the services we offered. And I made many of the same hiring mistakes that I had made with Barb. Her replacement lasted a month.

Call me slow, but I think I was beginning to see a pattern here. Nobody but me could sell my vision. I had to revamp everything so I could work selling into my already bulging job description. That was the bad news. The good news was that selling was as natural to me as breathing. It topped the list of my skills.

Sales and the Customer

Columbus was definitely the world's most amazing sales person. He started out not knowing where he was going. When he got there, he didn't know where it was so when he got back, he couldn't say where he'd been. He did it all on a big cash advance and he got a repeat order.

Entrepreneurship attracts the full spectrum of people — tall, short, introverted, extraverted, analytical, and creative. But there is one thing they all have in common. They have to sell. It's not that they *can* sell, they *have* to sell. This necessity is the bane of many a business owner's existence. Why? Selling is not a skill everyone is born with. Most aren't. For instance: A plumber went into a shop owner's store basement and noticed that the walls were lined with sacks of salt. The plumber commented, "You must sell lots of salt." The shop owner said, "Mister, I couldn't sell a pinch of salt, but the woman who sells me salt — she can sell salt."

Selling Myths

Most first-time salespeople suffer incredible anxiety and pain. As soon as the word "sales" is uttered they start to sweat and busy themselves with the thousand other things that "absolutely need to get done." Some misconceptions about selling are particularly paralysing for women. So let's reduce some of this anxiety by telling you what selling is *not*.

1. *Selling does not require a certain personality.* The best salespeople are good listeners, knowledgeable about solutions to their prospects' needs, understanding of their limitations of budget and time, and genuinely helpful and considerate. Aggressive salespeople are just plain unprofessional and untrained. The most effective salespersons are those who are just themselves and are comfortable sharing who they are with others. Sales is just a focused conversation with a specific person who has a specific need for which you have a solution.

2. *Great salespeople are not born that way.* They are trained and have practised (a lot). People often tell me that I'm a natural born salesperson. Well, if you count 21 years of experience with several professional sales training courses under my belt, then indeed I'm a natural. But always keep in mind that old expression, "Never teach a pig to sing. It just wastes your time and annoys the pig." The right training should be given to the right people.

   One of my oldest friends, Shaune Martin, is very fond of telling the story of my first sales call. She was the seasoned veteran who was given the responsibility of taking me, the rookie, cold calling one afternoon. She passed on some very sage advice about the phenomenon called "Doorknob

Phobia." She told me that every time I'm out cold calling and I feel the urge to bolt instead of knocking on the door, I should hold a debate with myself before turning the doorknob. The debate goes like this: "Where am I?" "In the hall." "Where do I want to be?" "In the decision maker's office." "What will happen if I go inside?" "The worst that could happen is that I'd be thrown back into the hall." "Well, that's where I am now, so what do I have to lose?" It worked every time.

3. *Selling is not coercion.* You can't sell something to someone that they do not want or need. Selling is the art of helping customers identify their needs and wants and showing how your product or service can satisfy them. We lived in the Maritimes for 15 years where my dad worked in sales. There was a prospect he had been trying to get for years, to no avail. Dad said he'll never forget what the old guy said to him. "In this part of the country," he said, "every want ain't a need." Customer service and sales are no longer two separate functions. People today want to be assisted by salespeople who they can trust to put their needs first. If you care about what you do, the passion comes through and that is what gets people excited, not some canned sales pitch and persuasive closing technique. Take care of your customers and take care of your people and the market will take care of you.

4. *Selling is not primarily about closing the sale.* The objective of being a sales person is not to make sales. It's to make customers. Today's top salespeople seldom spend much time on closing. Instead they focus on finding customer needs, demonstrating benefits, and asking for customer feedback. Your job is to be like a good cook. You need to create an appetite when the buyer doesn't seem to be hungry. After making sure that the client has all the information needed to make a decision, the professional salesperson simply asks if he or she would like to take the next step. I can't tell you the last time I had to ask for an order. If you take care of everything at the front end, the chances increase significantly that the sale just evolves. Check out *The Spin Selling Fieldbook: Practical Tools, Methods, Exercises, and Resources,* by Neil Rackham. It's a great guide to selling.

5. *Selling is not marketing.* Selling is a necessary part of the marketing process but it's downstream from marketing. While marketing makes your "ideal" customers aware of your product or service, selling is one way of getting them to try it by buying it. However, to confuse matters, you can also use direct selling as a means to reach and build awareness in your target market and some marketing tactics like direct mail to close sales. Take all of those "not right now, not interested" cold calls. You didn't get to sell but you did make the prospect aware of what you were in the market to sell.

Assessing Your Comfort and Skill at Selling

Most entrepreneurs fall into the category of "sales novice." Check out the following questions and see if any apply to you. If so, pay careful attention to the suggestions to ease the pain of selling.

Do You Feel Like You Have to Do All the Talking?

Sales is more about sparking revelations than about begging, badgering, or arm-twisting. In order to help others come to new realizations, you need to listen. Most neophyte salespersons immediately launch into a verbal dump about everything they know. The client sits there with a thought bubble over her head that reads, *"Way too much information!!!!!"* Don't let your tongue cut your throat. Nobody ever listens herself out of a sale.

Don't presume that your prospective customer actually knows and can articulate what her real problem is. Sometimes your product or service is a solution to a problem that she doesn't even realize she has. So don't worry too much about getting to the punchline or hurrying to close. Turn the tables. Getting your customers to close themselves isn't as impossible as you may think. The way to do this is by asking questions. Start off easy by asking questions about their situation. This prompts them to lay out the facts. Next, ask questions designed to get them to articulate the nature and extent of their problem. Now it's time (through careful questioning, not telling) to help them focus their attention on how much pain they are actually in as a result of their problem. Once they realize that they have a problem and that fixing it is important, you then ask questions designed to get *them* to explain how your solution could benefit them.

A case in point: I knew financial institutions were having serious credibility problems with women prospects and existing clients. I also knew that the opinions within these institutions on this issue ranged from "we have no problem" to "we have a serious one but don't really know what to do about it." So I made an appointment with Charlie Coffey, executive VP of Business Banking at Royal Bank Financial Group. Thankfully, his mind was so open, you could drive a truck through it. When I first met with Charlie, he good-naturedly positioned our meeting by saying "Prove to me there is a women's market." By asking a series of well-positioned questions like, "In your personal experience, would you say women are as happy with their bankers as men are?" and "Would you generally describe women-owned businesses as being the same as men's?" I eventually got him to acknowledge that not only was there a difference in women- and men-owned businesses, but that his industry had a problem. The second Charlie admitted that banks had a serious perception problem around women entrepreneurs, the sales cycle began. I watched as Charlie's questions went from "Why do women have such a bad view of us?" to "What can you do to change that?"

Four years and a half-a-million-dollar training contract later, he and his bank found out.

Do You Make a Lot of Assumptions?

> After an accident, a women stepped forward and prepared to help the victim. She was asked to step aside by a man who announced, "Step back, please! I've taken a course in first aid." The woman watched his procedures for a few moments, then tapped him on the shoulder. "When you get to the part about calling the doctor," she said, "I'm already here."

Whatever you do, don't make assumptions. This is a check to ensure you are not talking too much. If you don't ask enough of the right questions, or you don't listen for the answers, you will be forced to fill in the gaps yourself. That means it's your assumptions that become the basis of the sale, not the customer's needs. Treat generating business like developing relationships. Don't rush it by making assumptions. You run the risk of being wrong.

Do You Feel Compelled to Discount Your Price or Fee?

Most novice salespersons, inexperienced and anxious about selling, try to close the sale too soon. Because the customer hasn't realized why they should buy, they hesitate. Convinced that price is the main issue (the entrepreneur's most common assumption), you start to feel pressure to lower the price in order to remove your perceived barrier to closing the sale.

This is such a mistake. Charge what you think you are worth. This is a classic W-FACTOR. Women are socialized to "give it away." We do 99 percent of the volunteer work that gets done in society. I can't tell you how many times I have had to tell women whom I am doing business with to charge me what they think their service is worth. They are so uncomfortable even talking about money. Before I even get a chance to ask, I'm being offered a discount. I shake my head in disbelief. "Stop it!" I yell. "This is your business. What is it worth?" (This is not to say I wouldn't attempt to negotiate where appropriate, however.) I've had to do this with everyone from my walking partner to the trainers I have hired. You need to project confidence in the quality and worth of your product. After all, you don't expect to pay hamburger prices for filet mignon. When Eastman Kodak entered the copier market, it made Xerox improve its quality. With Kodak being a quality-oriented and well-financed competitor, Xerox was forced to compete on quality, not price.[1]

Do You Know if the Prospect Is Able to Buy Your Product or Service?

One of the most important things a first-time seller needs to figure out is whether the person to whom they are speaking is actually a customer or just an interested party but with no buying authority. The next most important thing is whether this person has the means (read: the cash) to do the deal. Don't be shy. When it's appropriate, just ask. "Do you have the budget and authority to make this purchase decision?" Or try, "Who, besides yourself, will be making the final purchasing decision?" Both questions will serve to flush out to whom you should really be talking. And whatever you do, don't hesitate to ask that the decision maker be included in all of your conversations. Bottom line? Talk to not only the right person, but the right group or organization. 3M Post-it Notes, so familiar in offices all over North America today, weren't well received initially. When the idea was presented to office supply distributors, they thought the idea was a bad one. They took market surveys that were negative. Eventually the little notepads became successful after samples were mailed to the administrative assistants of the CEOs of the Fortune 500 companies.

Do You Prefer Indecision to Rejection?

Are you afraid of "No"? Most entrepreneurs are and that is why they prefer to hear "I'll think it over." The problem with this response is that you don't know where you stand. Even with "no" there are many meanings that you have to work at to make sure you properly understand what the customer is saying. Consider the "no" that means "No, not right now; no forever; or no, I don't like you." Or then there is the "partial no" — "no" to only part of what you are offering. "No" is often the beginning of the sales cycle.

Do You Have a Systematic Approach to Selling?

A young life insurance agent walked into a factory and asked to see the sales manager. When the manager finally greeted her in his office, the agent nervously said, "You don't want to buy any life insurance, do you?"

"No," replied the sales manager, curtly.

"I didn't think you would," said the agent, as she got up and headed for the door.

"Wait a minute!" said the sales manager. "Come back here."

"Yes, sir," she said, obviously nervous and frightened.

"You are without a doubt the worst sales person I've ever seen."

The agent looked down. "Yes, I know."

"Listen, you've got to have enthusiasm when you sell, you have to be positive, not negative. You have to believe in yourself."

"Yes, sir."

"Now look, I'm a very busy man, but I'll show you how." And for the next 30 minutes the sales manager gave the young agent all the benefits of his experience and wisdom.

"I don't know how to thank you," said the agent.

"That's all right," said the sales manager. "Now because you're obviously new at this, I'll buy a small policy from you."

The agent quickly dug out a policy. The sales manager signed it and said, "Remember, don't go in cold, not knowing what you are going to say. Work out a planned and organized sales presentation."

The agent smiled, "Oh, I have. What you've just seen is my organized approach to sales managers."[2]

Have a system. Following a specific set of steps can help the novice master the selling process. It is most important, however, not to let the selling process dwarf your customer's buying process. The only way to prevent this is to prepare diligently every time before stepping on to the selling stage so that you have confidence, forget yourself, and play to the crowd. The real art of selling is keeping the customer in the foreground and your process in the background so that you are always in control and moving the process forward.

Mom Said Talking About Money Is Impolite

Just as many new entrepreneurs feel uneasy about their role as salespeople, so it is normal for them to shy away from the inevitable discussion with the client that involves price and payment. Here are some pointers to help you get paid what you are worth:

- As long as your customer is convinced that your product/service will provide more value than it costs, they will pay your price. So don't be afraid to disclose it and defend it.

- Remember, it's your uniqueness that has the customer willing to pay you. Therefore, you better know what your competition is charging and how what you are offering is different. Point out to your customers the positive side of doing business with you. A woman was eating in an Italian restaurant in Toronto. She told the owner, "Your veal parmigiana is better than the one I had in Italy last week." The owner replied, "Of course it is. You see, they use domestic cheese and ours is imported."[3]

- For service providers, get customers to focus on results, not dollars. When potential clients ask about your rates, tell them, "My fees are based on the results I produce for you. Therefore, I need to know more about your needs before I can give you a price." Ask Picasso. He had this concept firmly in mind many years ago while working in the streets of Paris. A woman recognized him and requested that he do her portrait. She sat down and five hours later she had an original Picasso. She was very pleased and asked how much she owed. He responded, "Five thousand dollars." She said, "But it only took you five hours." He corrected her, "No, madam, it didn't. It took me all my life."

- Offer "value added" incentives to attract business, preferably the kind that doesn't cost a lot. Try things like free delivery over a certain volume or dollar value, subscription to your company newsletter, free parking or someone who will watch the parking meter. When you offer the customer a service, make sure it's what the customer wants. Jonathon Tisch, president of Loews Hotels, says, "We believe many hotels get distracted by advertising, promotions, and giveaways and lose sight of the basics. The only real way to differentiate yourself from the competition is through service. For instance, we believe in guest recognition rather than guest rewards. What's more, we've found that guests prefer it that way. They prefer to be upgraded to a suite, to be remembered by name, and to receive their favourite amenity rather than pay a higher room rate so that we can afford to send them on a free trip to Europe."

- Get a price as close as possible to what the market will bear by raising your prices 15 percent until your prospects or customers say "ouch!" I did this with the keynote speaking. There was no way to determine the market value of what I did since I was the only one doing it. So, every year, I increased my price $500 until we started to hear, "Oh, wow. That's too much for us." That's how we finally knew what to charge. The amount of increase really depends on how much you charge and what the competitive environment is like. And remember to revisit this process as you grow and add products or services. It's okay to lose the lower-margin customers to make room for the higher-margin ones. But always keep in mind that profit is like health. You need it, and the more the better. But it's not why you exist.

- Fire the customers who consume too much of your time, energy, or resources. Adrian Slywotzky, co-author of *The Profit Zone: How Strategic Business Design Will Lead You to Tomorrow's Profits,* says, "Business people are a little shocked when we tell them that probably about 15 percent of your customers right now are creating a drain on profitability, and you have to be willing to get rid of them. Too often first-time entrepreneurs treat the customer as though they are the boss and relinquish their control in the relationship. But remember, you are in control and it is your choice who you serve and who you don't. Cocky? Yep. But it is also the attitude of successful business people who run their own business instead of the other way around."

Actually, the best time to fire this kind of client is before they become one. I had a meeting once with the VP of marketing at one of the country's largest brokerage firms. He was interested in having me as a keynote speaker but not until I could guarantee him the income level of the audience. Implicit in his demand was his belief that women had little or no money. You can be guaranteed that other financial speakers who spoke to general audiences never had to do that. There was going to be too much involved in bringing this guy into the 20th, let alone the 21st century. I packed up my stuff, graciously extended my hand, and promptly bid him farewell. It was then I realized that I had the right to choose my clients. I could fire a client or turn down a prospect.

Sandra Goertzen is a classic example of a woman entrepreneur who has mastered the art of "the customer comes first" selling. As you read her story, take note not only of her innovative sales approach, but also how she has applied many of the themes we've talked about. Sandra's story beautifully illustrates how most women want to make a difference and a good living.

Sandra Goertzen: The Customer Comes First

Sandra Goertzen is bracing herself for an impending midlife crisis since her 45th birthday is just around the corner. She is the mother of three grown kids, one of whom works in her business. She is the owner of two Manitoba franchises of MEDIchair in Dauphin and Brandon. MEDIchair is the retailer of an extensive selection of home health products such as bathing and walking aids, motorized scooters, and wheelchairs.

In her previous life, Sandra was an occupational therapy assistant at the Dauphin Regional Health Centre, where she set up programs for the rehab and the chronic-care wards that included general exercise, social activities, and wellness discussions.

Sandra explains, "We purchased some equipment from the local MEDIchair store for my father-in-law when he had a stroke, and I felt these people treated their clients quite fairly. I approached the owner of MEDIchair in my capacity with the Health Centre, asking if I might be able to do some in-service for seniors in the community. His response was 'Why don't you buy the business? I am getting tired of it and would like to do something different.' I was totally unprepared for this answer. I don't think I slept for three weeks until my husband and I made a decision."

"The first chance I got I made a trip to the Brandon store. I just showed up on a Saturday and began to ask the sales rep questions that a professional might ask on discharge of a patient from the hospital. He couldn't answer all my questions. I thought to myself, 'I know more than this young fellow. I can do this.' So I did.

"I felt it was very beneficial to be involved with a franchise. MEDIchair provided a product catalogue, an advertising department offering camera-ready art and professional TV commercials, product consultants, a database of new products, and a sharing of ideas of what worked and what didn't work. The negotiation for the Dauphin store went very smoothly because of the owner's desire to sell. But Brandon was different. The previous owner had engaged in some questionable business practices, so after a long and ugly court battle, MEDIchair took control of the franchise. With both stores there were some bridges to be mended with the public. The Dauphin store, while it treated people fairly monetarily, lacked proper and prompt service. The Brandon store, before being taken over by MEDIchair, did not always treat their customers fairly."

So this is what Sandra inherited. It was her remarkable ability to understand the sales and marketing process that enabled her to turn the business around and be named MEDIchair's Franchisee of the Year for 1998. In the pages that follow, we will share with you some of Sandra's secrets of success.

Keeping the Sales Funnel Full

So let's assume you have landed the first client. If it is a big one, you have to work fast to eliminate the "one customer dependency" problem. If it's a small customer, you have to work fast to get more business so you can turn a profit. Sandra nets out her recipe for keeping her sales funnel full this way: Find out what is out there and what the competition is doing. She was up against some pretty big players. But she realized that what counts is not necessarily the size of the dog in the fight; it's the size of the fight in the dog. Sandra also spent time figuring out what "sold her on things." She took business courses and used the Internet for ideas. And lastly, she wasn't afraid to be visible.

But before we start randomly screaming our message from the highest mountain top, let's just make sure that we focus our time and money on picking the right message and the right mountain top. Let's look at the basic and all-important 5 Ps that make up the holy grail of marketing: product, positioning, packaging, price, and promotion.[4]

Product

> "Marketing has to encompass the definition of what a product is. Marketing is not just promotion, advertising, and sales. Marketing includes product planning. Any engineer who does not see herself as a marketer is not doing her job."[5]

The marketplace changes with the speed of light. So, in your first year, you need to reconsider how similar your product is to what is already being offered by others. Ask yourself again, "How is my product or service different? Are the differences still relevant and valuable to my chosen target market?" If the differences are not important to your prospects, you need to rethink either your product design or your target market. When I started out in this business I was the only competitor I had, but the market around "marketing to women" has exploded. I need to ask myself these questions at least every six months now.

Now that you have some actual experience under your belt, you will be better able to define what your customers are really buying. Note: We did not say what you are selling. Peter Drucker says the aim of marketing is to know and understand the customer so well, the product or service fits him or her and sells itself. Sandra really gets this. Let's look at what Sandra's customers are buying.

- Imagine a 75-year-old man who has being going to his local coffee shop twice a day for the last who knows how many years. He has a stroke and can no longer drive his car because his licence has been taken away. He now has to depend on his wife to drive him. He has lost his independence. This gentleman decides to try a scooter. All of a sudden he feels he has some control back. He can go to the coffee shop and not have to wait until his wife takes the bread out of the oven. That's independence and freedom.
- Imagine a 39-year-old mother and her 10-year-old daughter. Mom has MS and says how badly she feels because she can no longer go for a walk with her daughter. At the trade show, her husband will not even look at Sandra's booth, but his wife perseveres and purchases a scooter. The next year at the trade show, hubby stops by the booth and says how great the scooter is; Mom stops by and says how much freedom the scooter has given her. She shares how she rides her scooter alongside her daughter who rides her bike. She talks about how she rode her scooter around Jasper. That's independence and freedom.
- Imagine a 9-year-old boy in a wheelchair with cerebral palsy. Every time he wants to go outside he has to call his mom, dad, or brothers to

open the door so he can go through with his power chair. MEDIchair installed a power door opener for this young man. It's now his job to let the cat in and out. That's independence and freedom.

What do you think Sandra sells when she talks to her customers? You can bet your bottom dollar that price and features rate lower on the scale than the real selling points — independence and freedom.

Another consideration when defining your product involves identifying what "extras" you can offer that your clients will value and that will clearly set you apart from your competitors. Small additional services for little or no charge can also be the things that create loyalty among current clients and often require significantly less investment than going out and getting new business.

Positioning

A critical aspect of marketing is positioning your product or service properly in your market. Case in point: Lazzari Fuel initially marketed its mesquite charcoal as a fuel. Sales weren't great. Then they decided to position the mesquites as an ingredient instead of a fuel. Sales soared.

Make sure the target market you established in your research phase is still the one of greatest opportunity. Does your target client still have the same set of potential vendors to look to in order to get their need met or has the market supply shifted or expanded in some way? Constantly and diligently be looking for a gap in the current market that you can fill, instead of copying something that is already out there. Your unique market position can be based on price, level of service, understanding of your target's needs, or the extras that you offer. Remember, to beat your competition, don't depart from your area of superiority. How can you beat Bobby Fischer, the greatest chess player of all time? Get him to play you any game but chess.

Packaging

Walk down the aisle of any grocery store. Every package on the shelf has behind it a tremendous amount of research on what it should look like. We don't give Kate candy or junk food of any kind. Yet when we walk into a store, she makes a bee-line for the candy section. I'm amazed (and not particularly pleased, in this case) at how well packaging works. She has never eaten a Smartie in her life, yet she will have a total meltdown when I tell her, "This lives at the store and it needs to stay here with its brothers and sisters." She doesn't buy it for a second. The colour, the cartoon characters, the bright, bold lettering all say, "I'm over here, little girl. Come over here, little boy." Think of how often you feel compelled to buy a product because of its unusual or appealing packaging.

With that in mind, think not only of how your product's packaging looks but how your business cards, stationery, Web site, and office environment make a statement about you and your business. We invited two Toronto-based entrepreneurs to share their perspective on company image. Liz and Rod Nash have been life partners for 35 years and business partners for 25 years. Besides building their own successful advertising and design business, they've helped build and maintain identities for dozens of businesses, large and small, over the years.

The Nashes believe that from the split second you decide you are going to start your own business, you are beginning the process of establishing your corporate identity. You are thinking about what you want the business to be and what you feel it may grow into. You may not realize it at first, but your company identity is about:

- the kinds of products or services you'll make or sell
- what kind of facility you'll operate from
- how you will treat your customers and associates
- how you will describe what it is you do
- how all of this is presented visually through business cards, advertising, and promotion.

Liz and Rod also say it is important for every start-up entrepreneur to understand that whether you consciously develop your identity or not, you have one. So always try to stay aware of the identity you and your business project, from your products and services right on through to your company's overall visual identity. And be sure that the identity works *for* you, not *against* you. A company selling expensive second-hand Porches, Ferraris, and Mercedes had developed carefully crafted, well-printed stationery and business cards. But the sales staff were uncomfortable using the materials. The design was clever but unintentionally reflected an image of "used car sales." To the sales staff and customers, there was all the baggage that goes with being seen as "a used car salesman." The Nashes used some of the original elements but redesigned the materials to create a more refined corporate image, an image that increased the potential for the company to reach its goals.

The cornerstone of a good identity is a good logo or symbol used consistently in all the materials you produce. The actual designing of your new company signature, logo, or symbol is generally best left to a professional designer. If you give the designer all the tools they'll need to produce a sound visual identity for your company, it can be affordable for you and still profitable for the designer.

The Nashes believe that designing comes out of knowledge, and the design part actually comes last. Liz and Rod suggest your designer know the context of your industry, your competitors, your company history, and any new developments in your industry. As for a visual context, you start by collecting business cards, letterhead, mailings, ads, and packaging of your competitors and your clients. This will show what the industry seems comfortable with and what prospective clients are used to seeing. It's also important to have a clear idea of your target audience, the "publics" you are talking to. These include existing and potential customers, of course, but also media, the financial community, government, prospective employees, and your current staff and suppliers.

They also suggest that you save what you *don't* like in the way of brochures, business cards, etc. This will make it easier for your designer to understand more about you and where you are coming from. Since we are in the electronic age, it's useful to list what office equipment, computers, and software you'll be using, including the file formats for importing graphics or text into your computer documents. Next, get out your written mission statement for reference and write down briefly what you want your company to be in five years. And while you're looking ahead, identify all the areas where your logo will need to be placed in the future. Dream in technicolour: A 40-foot tractor trailer? A large sign on a new location? A billboard? Will it need to work on video? Do you need a version for the Internet? Is it likely to be animated?

From all this material you should be able to write a short, clear, and concise description of what's needed for your corporate identity. What is key is that the description must clearly spell out guidelines that will keep the designer on the right track, descriptions like a strong image, or a feminine image, or a trendy image. After meeting with you and looking over your research, the designer may help you clarify this description. This is often called "The Brief." It's important that you both agree on the wording up front. Tell them your budget up front and also tell them which other designers you are talking to. This sets the stage and lets the designer know you mean business. Designers earn their income by selling their time. If you are respectful of their time, they'll give you more of it.

The Nashes emphasize that, more than likely, what you are starting here is a long-term relationship that can be very valuable to you. Often what you are looking for is a designer or design firm that can offer more than design alone, that can help you with your overall communications strategy. You are looking for someone who has a sense of how your identity can "play out." So think of the money as an investment. Liz and Rod say, "Even if you do all your preparations, research, and homework, don't expect a good designer to be able to work with you for less than $1500 on your first project." But it will be money well spent.

And they offer another tidbit about copyright — have the designer sign over ownership of the new logo and symbol to you. You may even want to have it registered as a trademark.

I spent about $1500 to have my first identity established. But that was when the plan was to do financial planning for women, when *Balancing Act* was a mere gleam in my eye. That included logo design, business cards, and letterhead. Though the logo was (and still is) serviceable, it didn't fax or reproduce particularly well. It also didn't say much about what we do now. We needed to review our identity to see that it actually said what we were. So, add another zero to the above cost. That's what it cost us to do it right the second time around, including a new design for letterhead, business cards, labels, and the design of several brochures including our corporate brochure. I love our corporate brochure and there's quite a story behind it.

As part of the creative process, the design agency came up with all kinds of ideas to incorporate our theme of women, money, and entrepreneurship. We saw everything from the extremely overused Mona Lisa to pink dollar bills (!?). We weren't happy.

This to-ing and fro-ing went on for months. A few months earlier, I had been to Alberta for a keynote speaking event. While out there, I stayed for a weekend to visit friends. Meandering through a museum in Banff, I came across a quilt exhibit that caught my eye. One in particular really appealed to me because of its deeply rich earth tones and texture. As I leaned forward to take a closer look, I was completely blown away. Each panel represented traditional work women do in the home. There was a pair of hands gardening, another pouring milk from a jug, another pair was crocheting, more serving a piece of pie, hanging clothes on a clothesline, ironing, drying dishes, holding a baby, and cutting vegetables. There was another panel showing a mother breastfeeding. But what really got me was the title of this gorgeous piece of work — "No Wife of Mine Is Gonna Work." I absolutely howled. I had to have it. I tracked down the curator of the museum who, after artful badgering, gave me the artist's name, Wendy Lewington Coulter, and her phone number. When I called her, I was crushed to learn that there was only one of these quilts on the planet, the one I had seen in the museum. It belonged to her husband who would rather be struck by lightning than sell it. She also only did "one of a kinds." I think it's when I started to cry on the phone that she finally relented.

Four months later, Michelle, Barb, and I were looking over the latest batch of less-than-stellar ideas for our corporate brochure when the doorbell rang. It was a delivery service bringing my long-awaited new quilt. As we opened the package and laid the quilt out over the dining room table, we stood back in silence, staring at the most magnificent piece of work we had ever seen. It brought tears to my eyes all over again. Michelle was the first to speak. She said quietly, "There's our brochure cover."

It took a minute to sink in, but then light bulbs started going off. We jumped around and screamed like a bunch of adolescent school girls.

I cannot tell you how many comments we get on that brochure and they are all fabulous. Men bring it home from the office to show their wives and girlfriends.

Price

Particularly in the service professions, price can make a strong statement about your position in the marketplace. As you did in the research phase, check out your competitors again and make sure that you're priced appropriately. Figure out what elements of your product or service some people will pay a premium for, things like same-day delivery or after-hours consultation. You may be able to separate these out from your standard product offering and charge additional amounts for these extras. This allows you to attract both kinds of customers, those who want the extras as well as those who don't care so much. Remember, the price is what they pay; the value is what they receive. For example, I could put a higher premium on our training because of my media profile. I don't. But I certainly could. The value my customer receives tends to be greater "buy-in" by the participants. Paula is able to charge a premium for people who call needing immediate assistance with an entrepreneurial dilemma or who require after- or before-hours appointments. Find out if there are certain features (or lack thereof) that could suggest you need to reduce your price relative to that of your competitors. For instance, if your major competitor offers a premium-priced same-day service your advantage may lie in providing the less costly alternative solution of providing next-day delivery.

And by the way, don't assume that your competitors have gotten it right. Your competition may be doing their own trial and error thing and may or may not have done their research to make sure that they have set the right price. Feeling compelled to follow suit without doing your own evaluation beyond "what the competition is doing" may result in making twice as many mistakes.

Promotion

Susan RoAne, author of *How to Work a Room*, tells of a financial planner who put his designation "financial planner" on his name tag at a meeting. No one looked twice. But when he wrote "MONEY" beneath his name, he was approached by scads of people who wanted to know more. I find the same thing happens when I attend an event. The company name "Women and Money" invites all kinds of interested responses. I had that marketing advantage in mind when I chose the name.

Sandra Goertzen believes that it wasn't just one thing but several right things that helped build her business, especially in the first year. Look at the wide array of marketing tactics that Sandra uses, including promotional programs that provide direct purchase incentives and advertising (both paid and word of mouth) that informs, reminds, and attempts to convince her customers to buy from her instead of her competition. She also uses her public relations efforts to get free publicity for her company in order to leverage and tie these marketing elements together. Sandra's approach to marketing and sales helped her send out the right message to the right people to get the right response — a satisfied customer.

- Sandra attended local *trade shows* in her franchise area. At the first two trade shows, she featured the major items, scooters, lift chairs, and bathlifts. She found that people would just walk past the booth, because "I'm not old enough." Or "I'm not an invalid so why would I need that stuff?" Sandra changed her tack along with the appearance of the booth. She still had all the major items, but she set up a table with door prizes that anyone could use like a "Good Grips Vegetable Peeler" or a back massager. As people filled out the draw slip, their eyes would look over the table at the items she had out, and eventually scan the rest of the booth. Many times the kids would want to know how the scooter worked and would ask if they could take it for a ride. Sandra's approach to promoting her product started with decreasing the traditional stigma attached to owning this equipment.
- Sandra set up *interactive workshops* in each of the major centres within the Dauphin franchise area. She invited health professionals, therapists, third-party funders (such as the Department of Veterans' Affairs, Medical Service, and insurance companies) and family service workers to attend "lunch and learns." Here, new products were showcased and ideas of what works and what doesn't were shared.
- Believe it or not, Sandra made *house calls*. This is a traditional method of promotion for a market that prefers traditional things.
- She implemented a *customer loyalty program* with cards and coupons to use for future purchases.
- She created a *customer newsletter*.

- Sandra started a *Local Hero promotion* where professionals, therapists, and people in the community can nominate a person who they feel has gone above and beyond the call of duty to help out the less fortunate or to provide special community service.
- Her franchises started *selling people's used equipment* on consignment when they no longer needed it. Families find this service reassuring when they are trying to tie up the loose ends of an estate.
- Sandra offered *wellness presentations* in seniors' housing. She provided education on what products and services were available as well as lunch, which gave that all-important social aspect.
- Sandra and her team developed therapist binders (a *catalogue* of sorts) that offer a comprehensive view of the types of products Sandra carries from various manufacturers.
- Sandra entered into an active and extensive *network* — Chamber of Commerce, Women Business Owners of Manitoba — as well as maintaining her existing contacts with the activity therapists. These all add to her credibility in the marketplace.
- She has been, from the beginning, a *good corporate citizen*. MEDIchair donates several pieces of demo wheelchairs and cushions to therapy departments.
- Naturally, Sandra *advertised*. The first month at the Dauphin store, she went to the local TV station, radio station, and newspaper to see what she could do to get local exposure. She negotiated her advertising on a weekly basis, 52 weeks of the year, which gave the best rates.
- She *extended the store hours*. Neither store had been open on Saturdays under the previous ownership. Sandra's research discovered that it was on Saturdays that kids take their aging parents shopping. That's when family members come home to visit and seniors can get their kids' opinions on these major purchases. Sandra knows that they have scored additional sales because their competitors were closed.
- Finally, the profile of her stores has increased since she *changed locations*. When Sandra first bought the Dauphin store, it was located on a little side street off Main Street. People would come in only when they needed something but no one ever stopped to browse. Sandra was able to secure a five-year lease in the only mall in town at a fair rate. People would actually stop in and look around, and subsequently, traffic increased dramatically.

Sandra was pretty busy that first year.

Now, you may not need to do any or all of these things, but Sandra's examples do provide a comprehensive look at what one successful entrepreneur has done and what has worked. But there are other practical and affordable ways to get yourself and your business known by your target customers.

Ask for Referrals

Referrals are the best business continuation method that I know of. Once your client is pleased with your service, always ask, "Who else do you know who would benefit from my expertise?" Referrals serve a variety of purposes, not the least of which is warming up a cold call. As we can all attest, getting and making cold calls ranks right up there with getting your wisdom teeth removed.

Interestingly enough, referrals are why many organizations are specifically targeting the women's market. Women give far more referrals than men. Referrals from women can be gotten differently than from men. With men, it's wise to wait until the business is concluded and a good relationship has been developed, usually during the follow-up process, before you ask for referrals. Not necessarily so with women. During my days as a financial adviser, I targeted women lawyers. I never made a single cold call. Even if it was determined there wasn't any need for my services, not a single person left without hearing me ask, "Do you have friends and family who can benefit from my services?" I always got names. My financial planning business was generated solely by referrals and seminars.

But if you think referrals are great in the women's market, you gotta see them work in the mommy market. It's common knowledge that most women have two full-time jobs, one paid and one unpaid, and suffer severe time poverty. As a result, the support system around moms is very intricate, complex, and sophisticated. If one person has done the research on a particular school or some consumer product, that information is shared with everyone in order to save people time. I've sent Kate to a certain gym program, even though there are tons to choose from, based on advice from my neighbour. I've gotten my hairdresser, mechanic, doctor, lawyer, homeopath, accountant, dentist, and Kate's nursery school all through this "jungle telegraph." Though it's very informal, it is extremely powerful. Why? You do a good job and the chances are you will be included in this referral system.

Even as I shifted to corporate clients, referrals still played a major part in my marketing. Once my client was satisfied with our training, I would invariably ask if other areas of the organization would benefit from our service. For example, after training 1400 business banking account managers at Royal Bank and establishing a successful track record, I asked this question. They now intend to roll out our program to train account managers in different areas of the bank, all 10,000 or so of them. Asking for referrals should become as second nature to you in your business as breathing and complaining.

But be careful how you ask for referrals. It's easy to bark up the wrong tree. The following story is a case in point.

> With university expenses in mind, a working mother made some investments for her young daughter. One of the things she did was buy stock in a bank in her daughter's name. Two months later, the bank sent the following form letter to her daughter: "It has come to our attention that you recently became an owner in our stock. May we suggest you recommend our bank and its services to your friends and business associates?"
>
> The woman replied, "My daughter, who is 19 months old, has asked me to thank you for your letter and to explain that she has no business associates, only half a dozen acquaintances and two of what she regards as real friends, a cat named Misty and a dog named Woof. Unfortunately, she pulled Misty's tail and bit Woof's ear yesterday, leaving her, at the moment, without friends *or* business associates. However, she graciously extends her cordial greetings and says she is looking forward to receiving your next quarterly report."

Keeping the sales funnel full is a layered process. Before seeking out total strangers, first look to the people you already know and have a relationship with. These are called centres of influence and take the shape of suppliers, customers, friends, family members, your dentist, accountant, insurance broker, lawyer, therapist, shareholder, fellow volunteers, and clergy. They make willing agents. Just make sure they are armed with a clear understanding of what benefits your product or service offers and who your ideal customer is before unleashing them on their own personal and business network. Now let's find some strangers. What do we do with them?

The N-Word — Networking

I was talking to Paula on the phone one morning. It turned out that we had both received an invitation to an event billed as an "excellent networking opportunity." I was feeling exasperated as I always did when I got invitations to things like this. I knew I should probably go but I never had the time. I always felt like I was missing something.

"I have to confess, Paula," I began, "when I hear the term 'networking' it conjures up less than stellar images. I imagine coffee klatches or cocktail parties with business cards being wielded about like swords. My mind fills with images of inane conversation, bad food, boring speeches, and heaps and heaps of false sincerity. Phrases like 'a total waste of time' and 'I'd rather stick needles in my eyes' leap to mind."

"Oh, I know," Paula said. "We all feel the same way about those events designed solely for the purpose of standing around in a room full of strangers, dreading the moment when you will be called upon to share a little bit about yourself. You are then rated at the end of the ordeal by how many business cards you managed to part with. However, I do think that real networking is far broader and requires much more thought, preparation, and effort than just milling around a room with your business card on permanent attention, ready and waiting to be drawn."

Paula continued, "Call it a clan, call it a network, call it a tribe, call it a family: Whatever you call it, whoever you are, you need one. All networking is, really, is a means of building an infrastructure of mutually beneficial relationships with other people. That can run the gamut from customer referrals, a good photographer, an available administrative assistant, a shoulder to cry on, or a skill that you are presently missing and need. You need to be choosy and nurture only the relationships that are beneficial to you. Part of the reason people hate the notion of networking is the amount of worry and energy it takes to figure out both sides of the 'What's-In-It-For-Me?' equation."

"That's true," I said. "I'm always uncomfortable asking for something from someone unless I can give something back. Often I make a promise that just makes more work for myself with little or no return on my investment. But what about people who are starting from ground zero, Paula? It's all well and good for those with an established network, say from a previous career. But what about when you don't have a starting place? What if you have ventured into something entirely new or you have been out of the business environment for a while? How do people like that get their network started?"

"You have to get out of the office and into the real world. Set aside one evening, one morning, or one lunch a week to be with new people either socially, professionally, or as a volunteer. Learn to golf," Paula replied.

"Golf?" I exclaimed. "If I wanted to find a way to embarrass myself more, I couldn't. And that's too bad because I've heard golf is a game that gives you something to do while you're nailing down a business deal. All this stuff means taking time away from my family and new business. This is exactly what I mean when I say this networking thing is not realistic."

"Joanne, you are forgetting that establishing a network is marketing," Paula countered. "Marketing is a significant part of doing business so you aren't really taking time away. As for family conflicts, just go to events that happen during the day. Trade an afternoon to take Kate to the zoo for an evening with colleagues and prospects."

"Okay. I'll give you that one. I do that now. What else can I do then?" I asked.

"Don't shy away from positions of leadership or responsibility. It's here that you will be able to meet the most new people. Chair a conference, be on an organizing committee, be a board member, organize a charitable fund raiser," Paula suggested.

"I didn't really think of all this as networking, it was my way of giving back," I said.

"Think of the people you have met while doing this stuff. From a professional and personal point of view, has it been worthwhile?" Paula asked.

"Most assuredly," I answered. "I was a member of the board of directors for Lester B. Pearson Airport in Toronto for four years. I remember when they asked me, I laughed and said, 'I'm a good choice. I, uh, have been to the airport.' It seemed so unrelated to what I did for a living, but I was intrigued by the opportunity to sit on a major board. I couldn't even begin to tell you how much I learned about running a company from that experience. And the board meetings were only once a month at 7:30 in the morning. It didn't prove to be a family or business conflict at all."

"And what about our trip to the theatre last Saturday?" Paula asked.

"I'm still in shock over that one," I said, shaking my head. "Here I am in the market for another trainer. Two days before, Cynthia, our senior trainer, had told me about a woman she used to work with who had just joined the ranks of the unemployed. Cynthia thought this woman would be an excellent addition to our training staff but had no idea how to get hold of her. And then we ended up sitting beside a woman whose brother dated her for a year! I got a call from her the very next day."

"You never know where the gold is, do you? One of the things I do," Paula continued, "is to chair a roundtable of customers, prospects, vendors, and other entrepreneurs to brainstorm solutions for business, industry problems, or issues that concern everyone. I've done these in person and virtually on a conference call. You get the benefit of doing market research and marketing at the same time."

"I conducted focus groups as well when I first started the company to get a handle on the issues around women, money, and entrepreneurship," I added. "These focus groups started out small, but they had grown so much in popularity that I continued them long after the original purpose for them ceased. They became a forum for women to speak their minds freely. The focus groups became a great marketing opportunity for me."

"Substitute marketing for networking, Joanne. It's the same thing," Paula said. "You could take a course or attend a conference where you get to learn, develop skills, and meet people at the same time. And this option is available both in physical and virtual space. The phone and the Internet have brought us closer to each other in many ways. The anonymity of cyberspace puts everyone, introverts and extroverts alike, on the same level. It gives those who cringe at the idea of mingling in real life the opportunity to mingle virtually. There are tons of people who meet and talk at these electronic cocktail parties."

Karen Fraser runs a Toronto-based company called Women Like Me that publishes a women's networking directory. She says, "Networking is an art form. The tossing about of business cards is not. You could say networking is a Renoir and card-tossing is an Elvis on black velvet. They both hang on the wall, but they are not the same. Men grasp this. After all, networking is how they run the world. Formal networks are just one form. There are countless others and it's your skill that makes any of them work. It is vital to have this skill in this era of change. You can't possibly know everything, but you can know who does."

Affordable Marketing Tactics

Networking is a great way to build awareness about your business. But you need to use other means to let people know you exist and to get those who are interested to contact you. Whether you decide to buy ad space, deliver flyers, hand out coupons, run contests, give away gifts with purchases, write articles, send out press releases, put your logo on your car, sponsor community events, or host a golf tournament, if it doesn't produce the sales results that you expect, don't do it.

In your first year of business, you usually have more time than money. So, here is a look at some of the more affordable marketing tactics.

- Refer business to those who are in close and frequent contact with your prospects, but only keep referring if the sentiment is returned.
- Write an article for a publication that your target customer is known to read. Find out by asking them which ones they buy. For example, I wanted to break into the association market as a speaker for their annual conferences. I wrote an article for *Associations,* the trade magazine for the Canadian Society of Association Executives. It got my name and area of expertise better known. In fact, I got to speak at the Canadian Construction Association's annual conference in of all places, Maui.

- Offer a seminar, class, or workshop as a way to get in front of more than one person at a time. Holding it at your office will keep expenses in check. Consider charging a nominal fee. It helps minimize cancellations and increases the perceived value of the seminar.
- Close the loop by sending a thank-you e-mail, fax, or letter to those who refer you business.
- Publish your marketing materials to the Web, e-mail, or diskette. That way you can change your copy as you refine what it is about your business that works without losing your investment in printed materials that can't be changed.

Overcoming "Small Company Syndrome"

There are great benefits to being small. I was a mega–conglomerate of three people when I landed the country's largest bank as a client. I was quick to point out that my size was an advantage. I could respond to the bank's requirements much more quickly than many big companies. I was more flexible. I had lower overhead and offered more opportunity to customize in order to meet the bank's need.

But being small is not necessarily beautiful when you are just starting out and trying to convince new customers that you can do the job as well as the big guns. Here are some tactics to promote your credibility and inspire confidence in your prospects:

- Always ask for testimonials from your existing customers. If your client list is a bit sparse, supplement your business testimonials with personal testimonials from past careers and jobs. Don't forget to get their permission to use their testimonial in your marketing materials.
- Give away samples. Let your customer try out your product or service, whether it's a free demo for software or real-time advice over the telephone or agreeing to do a complimentary speech at a charitable function. Let people actually experience what you want them to buy. Then they can take their own word for it. I had to provide no fewer than three free training or pilot sessions until we got it the way one brokerage firm wanted it.
- Guarantee your work. Guarantees take on all shapes and sizes and include every creative iteration from money back to doing the job again or replacing the product until the customer is 100 percent satisfied.
- It's all in the packaging. Appearance is 90 percent of perception. Embellish your own presence by teaming up with other established businesses. This will spawn a halo effect. Some accomplish this by being an approved supplier of a particular product or brand. Others manage to project the "bigger"

image by sharing a physical location without specifically identifying the individual companies on doors, signage, or directories so that each can create the impression of occupying the whole place.

- Work downstream from a big fish. Acting as a subcontractor or supplier to a larger or higher profile company allows you to do what you do best without necessarily having to do it all. Many of the business counsellors at the Business Development Bank (BDC) are, in fact, independent consultants who are contracted to deliver their workshops and programs.

- And you can do as I did. Market your smaller size as a distinct customer advantage. Make the most of how being small but mighty allows you to provide more customized and personal service to your customers.

Transcending Customer Service

You should already be starting to think of how you are going to get the next sale before you close the first one. That usually means providing serious customer service. In today's world meeting or even exceeding customer expectations may not be enough to keep a customer loyal to you. Transcending, and being able to actually anticipate customer needs, is what will keep your customers coming back.

You need to start thinking now, in your first year, how you are going to keep those first customers who are worth keeping. Most people only plan as far as getting to yes the first time, but making additional sales to the same customer usually translates into more profit.

Here are a few inexpensive ideas to help you anticipate your customers' needs and thereby increase your chances for repeat business:

- Put on your customer's shoes every so often and go through every motion of doing business with yourself. Customer walk-throughs are a great way to identify inconsistencies in your image or in the delivery of your product.

- Establish a survey for your customers to tell you how they think you're doing. This tactic lets customers know their opinion is important to you. It also acts as a subtle reminder that you are there and ready to serve them as the need arises.

- Create good reasons to be in touch with your customers often. A new look, product, employee, or policy are all great reasons to talk to your customers.

- Communicate everything that is new and great in your organization using e-mail, fax, or mail. Remind customers of your special niche or unique services. For example, when I was a financial adviser, every time I was noted in the press, I sent clients and prospects a copy. I felt a little self-conscious

about self-promotion in the beginning, but I had to get over it or get someone else to do it for me. I got over it.

- Make plain, old-fashioned follow-up calls. Get on the phone and ask how
  your customer is enjoying or benefiting from the use of your product or service. This reinforces the benefits once again and allows you to see if there
  is anything else that you can help them with. It also gives you an opportunity to uncover any flaws in your product or service. Fixing a problem ASAP
  goes a long way to encourage customer loyalty.

- Make the effort to acknowledge things that matter to your customer on a
  personal level — a child's first birthday, a long-deserved vacation.
  Acknowledge in writing significant events, number of years in business, a
  business expansion, landing a big contract, or any kind of publicity received. This may go even further to inspire loyalty and trust than most
  standard and traditional communications about your product or service.

- Pass along information like a potential resource or contact that you think
  may be helpful to your client or prospect.

- Add a dose of humour to your customer's day by faxing or e-mailing interesting and tasteful cartoons and quotes.

- Use the unused space on your fax cover pages, at the end of each e-mail, or
  in your daily voicemail or answering machine message to remind customers of
  your value proposition or to announce new product updates, company
  achievements, special events, contests, and any other information relating to
  the company. Include your marketing materials in your product packaging,
  your bill payments to suppliers, and your invoices to customers.

These tactics, when adapted to your business, marketplace, client and budget,
will keep those sales flowing. You may start small, but before you know it
you'll be catching lots more — or even that big fish.

The Human and Financial Cost of Closing the Big Ones

This is what every entrepreneur dreams of — the one big contract that will
ensure your company will not only survive, but flourish. However, next to
breastfeeding, the most closely guarded secret is the financial and human
cost of closing big contracts. Like many others, I spent so much time and effort closing the big deal, I forgot to consider what happens after the big
deal closes. When I closed my first big contract, I was shocked to see how
much hell and havoc was wreaked on my cash flow, people flow, and my
energy and sanity.

Both Paula and I deal with a lot of big players in corporate Canada. These are some of the potential downsides to closing "the big one":

- Your business can become too dependent on one contract. You may be at risk if client expectations are not perfectly managed.

- The resources required are often underestimated. I didn't consider the administration requirements to manage large projects. This left projects undercapitalized in both time and money. Rosa, Michelle, and I almost collapsed under the pressure.

- My sales skills landed the contracts but I discovered large contracts require project management skills to execute them. These latter skills, I quickly learned, are quite different.

- You have to have contingency amounts, a financial buffer, a rainy-day line item, a "what if/what if not" allowance. Contingency amounts are necessary so that there can be some flexibility in the management of the project. Things *will* change and it's unlikely that you will have anticipated 100 percent of the requirements.

- I didn't think about projecting cash flow. The timing of our client's payments did not coincide with the financial needs of the project. In fact, I became appalled at how little the big corporations understood or perhaps even cared about the small entrepreneur. Many corporate business practices shocked me. Many took three to four months to pay their bills. When they finally made a decision as to whether or not they were going to deal with us, after dangling a carrot for an interminable length of time, usually years, they wanted everything done yesterday.

- People on both the client and the supplier side can change. A multi-level, multi-person relationship should be thought out and secured in advance.

- Large accounts can often demand a price break and use the promise of "lots more opportunity here" to justify it. Don't necessarily buy it. It's penny pinching and it can crush your margins.

- A "big one" may require the flawless execution of volume orders. A large corporation can throw a lot of weight around if the orders aren't done right.

You might want to consider starting with smaller contracts until you have the cash flow, resources, and process in place to be able to withstand the pressure and deliver "the big one." It may be a better way to deal with the resource poverty that we as entrepreneurs seem to be always struggling with.

Full Circle and Back to Hiring

We've seen closing sales creates more work. When we have more business than we can personally manage, we need more hours in the day and more money in the bank. More hours often means more physical bodies. It's time to revisit that hiring thing again.

Today, the knowledge and skill that you need in the form of additional bodies is available from a number of sources and in a variety of arrangements, from full-time, long-term commitment to more of a just-in-time, as-needed basis. Figuring out what type of relationship to engage in is half the battle for the entrepreneur. So where do you find the right talent, under the right arrangement, and for the right price?

Job Description

Well, first you have to know what the job is. It's not wise to go shopping without a shopping list. What jobs get passed on to others will depend on what you prefer not to do, what you don't have the skill or experience to do, or what you just plain don't have time to do. The most common areas where new entrepreneurs generally need to hire or outsource in their first year are:

- general administration — order taking, phone answering, word processing, office organization, invoicing, paying bills, bookkeeping
- customer service and order fulfillment. In our case this involved booking speeches, getting slides and workbooks ready, ordering copies of *Balancing Act*, and shipping to the customer
- marketing plan development and execution
- and of course sales, but we've already beaten you over the head with that one.

Hiring someone either permanently or on a part-time basis, either as an employee or contractor, requires a significant investment of time, money, and, most of all, trust. Just make sure that you really do need to hire someone and that you don't just need to get better organized or more focused. Pick your toughest business critic and try to justify your need. If it floats, go for it. If it doesn't, reorganize.

So whether you are hiring your first employee or replacing one who started with you, before you start scouring the "available for hire" classifieds, make sure you can describe what the job entails. First, try to identify all the tasks and responsibilities associated with the position as well as how often those duties need to be done. For instance, do you expect your bookkeeper just to provide you with the listings of those people who owe you money and to whom you owe money? Or do you expect that she also place calls to your customers whose accounts have been outstanding for more than 30 days? How often do you expect your bookkeeper to process payments on the accounts that you owe? Then, consider the types of decisions that the person will have to make. Will they be expected to work independently, supervise other people, or interact with customers? The more accurate and comprehensive your job description, the more likely you are to find the right person to fill the bill.

A good description of the position is also a recipe for defining what qualifications are required to do the job well. You need to be clear about the know-how, experience, skill, education, behaviours, disposition, and attitude that a person will need in order to fill the position properly. (Malcolm Forbes once said, "Never hire someone who knows less than you do about what he's hired to do.") When settling on the right mix of talent, remember that people often get hired for having the "right" skills and fired for having the "wrong" behaviours. Also, when defining these qualifications, be very careful that you don't inadvertently do so in a way that is discriminatory or that violates basic human rights. This means differentiation on the basis of race, ancestry, place of origin, colour, ethnic origin, citizenship, creed, sex, sexual orientation, record of offenses, age, marital status, family status, or disability. Each province has its own Human Rights Commission where you can obtain a complete copy of not only the code, but examples of permissible and prohibited questions complete with a sample application form.

Employment Standards

This one came as a big surprise to me. I thought that, as the employer, I could determine the nature of any work arrangement that I entered into. Frankly, many small business owners fall into this trap. Once again using my favourite "two-by-four-to-the-back-of-the head" method of learning, I discovered most of the day-to-day administration of the employer/employee relationship comes under the jurisdiction of your provincial government's Employment Standards Act. Your provincial Ministry of Labour is responsible for the enforcement and administration of this legislation, which covers issues like:

- hours of work — what constitutes full-time, part-time, and overtime
- whether or not someone is an independent contractor or employee
- equal pay for equal work
- minimum wage

- overtime pay
- public holidays
- vacation pay
- parental leave
- pregnancy leave
- sick leave and bereavement leave
- termination of employment
- severance pay
- wrongful dismissal.

Even when I had only one employee, I should have familiarized myself with this legislation. But frankly, I didn't even know enough to ask the question. You can either obtain a copy from your local government office or review it online through the Internet by searching using the key words "employment standards" and the name of your province.

Keeping accurate records is a royal pain but of paramount importance when you are an employer. This hit home when we found ourselves in a defensive position with the Ministry of Labour. At a minimum, the personnel file on each employee should include their résumé or job application, starting date, starting salary and terms of employment (number of weeks of vacation, sick days, hours per week expected to work), days of vacation taken, sick days claimed, any extended time off work, all issues of performance, both good and bad, and any relevant supporting documentation. This file should be kept in a locked cabinet to which only those with sufficient authority in the company should have access.

Finding the Right Person

Good employees have to be searched for. Eagles don't flock, you have to find them one at a time. Employers' preferred method of finding new employees is still the referral. Almost three-quarters of small businesses rely mainly on referrals when looking for new employees. Referrals are trusted the most because they involve little cost and can be an effective part of the screening process. Advertising in a local paper is the second most common search technique.[6] Other sources for locating a new employee include personnel agencies, educational institutions, specialized training courses, Human Resource Development Canada, your provincial employment office postings, your employees, seniors in your community, the Internet (Job Shark, Career Track), your own Web site, or your competition. Don't neglect the human resource departments of large firms that may be downsizing or who may have the talent you are looking for in the form of people who are retiring soon.

The Interview

During the actual job interview, you can expand the scope of your questioning to include questions that will enable you to get to the heart of the applicant's qualifications or ability to do the job. If you are unsure about what you can or cannot ask, again look at your Human Rights Commission's guidelines on their Web site or at their office. To be on the safe side, refrain from asking for any supporting documentation such as a driver's licence, work permit, social insurance number, or educational transcript until you have made them a job offer. You can make it conditional, but you have to wait for the offer to be formally accepted before asking the new employee to take whatever medical examination may be required for insurance or benefits purposes.

That handles what you can and can't ask legally. But what about what you should ask in order to get a good read on whether this person is the right choice for the job and for the company? Both aspects are absolutely imperative in a small company. Your questions should be designed to get a sense of not only what the person has done but what they can do; not only what roles they have played but what role they could play; and lastly, not only what contributions they have made but what contributions they could make to your enterprise. Too often, novice employers concentrate on interviewees' past and whether they're likeable in the interview. Don't forget that you're trying to get a sense of how well you, other staff, and your customers could work with this person and how much value they could add to the company in doing so. This is all future-tense stuff that's hard to extrapolate from just looking at the past. So you may want to consider using typical scenarios to test out the extent of their initiative, decision-making ability, and how they would go about implementing solutions (for example, Are they flexible? Are they always referring to "I" as opposed to "we"? Do they appear to own responsibility or try to keep it resting on other's shoulders? How good are they at communicating and motivating?).

Remember that you'll need to consciously set aside the anxiety created by your immediate need so that you can focus on figuring out if this person can provide long-term value to the business. Because the future of your organization is only as good as that of your people, nobody is better than anybody. Also remember that the people you're interviewing are coming prepared (hopefully) to show you what they think you'll want to see, which makes it all the more important for you to be well prepared if you're going to be successful in uncovering the real scoop.

The Right Arrangement

Should you employ, hire on contract, or get a consultant? For one-time or infrequent requirements that need a specialized skill or talent, you have two choices — a consultant or a contractor. You might ask, "What's the difference?" The line can be drawn this way — if you need someone to help you figure out what and how you should do it, put a call into a consultant. They are set up best to advise, not to do. For instance, if you need to figure out how to pay as little tax as possible or you need to vet your strategic plan for your company — then it is a consultant you need. Using consultants can be expensive but worth it. Here's the story of the owner of a hair salon:

> As she was in a small town, she enjoyed the security of knowing she was the only game in town. She was responsible for cutting and styling the hair of every man, woman, and child in that town. Her income allowed her to live comfortably and even send her six children to university. Unfortunately for her, big business came to town. Right across the street from her busy salon sprang up one of those new full-service franchises.
>
> Immediately the media campaign began; ads in the newspapers and magazines and on billboards announced "EVERYTHING FOR $6.00! $6.00 haircuts, $6.00 perms, $6.00 manicures, everything for $6.00."
>
> Soon all of her customers began visiting the salon across the street, and her business sat empty. Desperate, she hired an expensive business consultant. "I'm finished!" she cried. "It's impossible for me, little me, to compete with them."
>
> The consultant squinted her eyes at the salon across the street. "Not just yet. Not just yet."
>
> With that the consultant picked up the phone and dialed the town's only billboard company.
>
> "Yes, on top of our salon...big letters...the message? WE FIX SIX DOLLAR HAIRCUTS."

However, if you need someone to *do, rather than advise* on a job for you as and when needed, like setting up and maintaining a computer system, you should probably be considering a contractor. Most new businesses don't generate enough need in the areas of public relations, technical support, or bookkeeping to justify having someone on payroll full- or part-time.

Don't fall prey to using friends for free or on the cheap. We did this when we needed someone to maintain and service our computer systems. I used a dear friend who was in that business. Our friendship almost ended as a result. We were always way down on their priority list because we weren't high-paying customers. When conflict arose, as it inevitably did, the friendship got in the way of proper resolution. I ended up letting him go and went with another firm to whom we pay full fee. The service is a darned sight better because they are accountable.

If you feel that your need is long-term, frequent, or not too specialized, then and only then consider hiring a part- or full-time employee. If you stick to this process of elimination when looking for extra help, you will be able to keep the overheads low while getting the right job done by the right person.

Regardless of who you hire, or which type of hiring arrangement you go with, make sure you can define what the terms and conditions of the position are and what the actual contract of service is. You may choose to put on paper the scope of the position, contract, or engagement, the responsibilities that the job entails, the terms of a probationary period, and standards and performance targets that are the basis for continued employment with you or payment of commission or fees. Or, like most new entrepreneurs you may not. (Guilty, Your Honour.) Just take a pointer from those of us who have gone before and landed flat on our face. Save yourself some money, time, and a whole bunch of frustration: *Put it in writing.* (Have I said that before? Believe me, it bears repeating.) This written document pays for itself a thousand times over by helping you pick the right people and by better orienting them to their role and the company. It will more easily and less subjectively help you evaluate their performance. And when all else fails, it will provide evidence of your employment practices or contractual arrangement should you ever be called upon to defend them.

Selecting a Consultant

There is no shortage of consultant jokes these days. One of my favourites: A consultant is a man who knows 146 ways to make love, but doesn't know any women. For new entrepreneurs, consultants may be a way to eliminate the need to hire an employee. And, just like with new employees, entrepreneurs tend to source consultants by referral. This is a good thing but don't forget to do your homework before signing on the dotted line. Before you settle on hiring any consultant, make sure you have been diligent in your selection process.

Widen the Search Don't just look in your own back yard. With technology, many consultants can work with you virtually, therefore keeping the cost of doing business lower. A long-distance call still costs less than a plane ticket.

Check References Try to check references beyond the ones that they offer by contacting their professional association, possible suppliers, or even their competitors. Gauge their objectivity and independence — find out if their advice is really customized to the individual client or whether it is just the same stuff sold to different people. This can be done by comparing the references' responses. Ask clients what they would have preferred that the consultant had done differently. Check with their local trade or professional association to see how they are perceived by their peers and whether they have adhered to their professional code of conduct, if governed by one.

Get It in Writing Insist on a written proposal or contract that will outline the scope, consultant's approach, and the resources that will be committed as well as what is *not* included in the job to ensure complete and mutual understanding. Make sure that you set the milestones that coincide with when you will pay the consultant. This is how you know if the job is getting done and done properly. Don't presume that the consultant will know all of this and offer it unsolicited — *ask!* I didn't do this. I hired a consultant to help with the customizing of our training course. Though this person had tremendous technical expertise, she had never dealt in the gender awareness arena before. But because of her technical background, I chose to go ahead. At the end of the assignment, I had an $8000 invoice and not one piece of useable material. Again, I had nothing in writing. Granted, I still continue to use this person on other projects with good results, but she was the wrong person for that particular job. Had I been more diligent, I would have come to that conclusion long before the $8000 invoice arrived in the mail. It's still under dispute.

Independent Contractor or Employee?

This is an age-old question, and one that deserves careful consideration. Whether those you pay to provide a service are employed or on contract will depend on the circumstances, in particular, on how much control you exercise over the person. For example, if you control the person's work hours or if they provide their own tools, if you tell them how to do the job, if they don't have the risk of profit and loss, if they're seen as an integral part of your organization to the outside world, and if they're economically dependent on your company, that person would likely be considered an employee in the eyes of Revenue Canada. However, if they provide services to a number of different people or businesses, if they determine the nature and extent of the service and they can prioritize their own demands, these people are likely considered to be running their own businesses and are contracting their services to you. That makes them independent contractors. So, why all the fuss? Well, if you have a contractor whom you should have treated like an employee you may find yourself liable down the road for the taxes and employee benefits that should have been remitted to the government. You may even need to pay them vacation pay and the government penalties. Consider this issue carefully.

Part-time Help

Students and retirees make good employment or contract candidates for entrepreneurs with a part-time or short-term need. Students are usually affordable and up to date in terms of their understanding of technology, but they do tend to lack experience. Retirees, on the other hand, have the experience, are maybe not quite as affordable since you pay for their wisdom, and may lack some of the more current techno-know-how and market knowledge, particularly if they have been out of the workplace for a while. Consider which one or combination might work in your situation.

The Right Price

Remember, you don't pay for what someone knows. You pay for what the person does with what they know. Second only to finding the right person, figuring out what the job is worth is an entrepreneur's next biggest challenge. Of course, the minimum wage is always one benchmark for paying staff but is certainly not applicable in every circumstance. In fact, small businesses are slightly less likely than larger firms to employ people at minimum wage. Only 17 percent of very small businesses employ workers at the minimum wage, compared to 23 percent for larger firms.[7] I believe that if you pay your people the least amount possible, you'll get the same from them. If you are hiring a co-op student, ask their placement officer for the wage ranges for students in that particular faculty in that year. Most keep these kinds of statistics as a service to employers and a planning tool for the kids. Most industry associations survey their members and publish those salary surveys as a means by which to promote their trade, profession, or membership. Sometimes just looking in the classified ads in your local newspaper will help you establish a reasonable range for the position and level of responsibility you need filled.

In addition to setting the right pay level for the position, keep in mind that you might be eligible for some assistance in hiring that new staffer. Both the federal and provincial governments have a number of programs aimed at helping new employers and those in need of securing a position (like young people and the unemployed). We hired Rosa through one of these programs called Jobs Ontario. (Thank you, Mr. Rae.) Unfortunately, it's now defunct. (Thank you, Mr. Harris.)

For more information on the government programs available to help you hire, contact the Human Resources Development office in your province or visit them on-line at www.on.hrdc-drhc.gc.ca/english/hrdsites/.

Money Isn't Everything

Employees can be motivated by more than money. One afternoon Paula and I were having a debriefing session in her office. We were trying to establish the best possible working environment where all could flourish.

"So," I began, "what can I do to make sure I am giving Michelle and Rosa the best that I can give? I don't have a lot of money. I've even considered giving them a piece of the action. How do I get creative and give them what they deserve?"

"There are several things you can consider, Joanne," Paula replied. "Cash is only one of them. Basically, it nets out to this: Consider giving your people more money throughout the year. But since you can't do that yet, you could try bonuses based on individual performance. Go as far as profit-sharing, or company-performance-based payments. This doesn't mean you have to give up shares in your company. Maybe you could look at providing benefits such as health care, disability and life insurance, and making RRSP contributions."

"Sounds good but expensive. What else?" I asked.

"There is the tangible stuff that will cost you money but will also help them get the job done better. Think about environmental upgrades like new furniture, a good chair, a laptop computer, or even a parking spot so they don't have to circle the block for hours looking for one. You're not there yet, but eventually there's the prestige perks like cars, product or service discounts, expense accounts, and a larger office. You gave Barb a car phone. That's the kind of thing I'm referring to."

"Yeah, I read somewhere that companies are getting really smart about taking care of their employees. The Scherer Lumber Company, for example, has a motto, 'We have no sick pay, we have well pay.' For each month workers are not late or ill, they are given two extra hours of pay. At the end of the year, if they have missed no more than three days, they collect a $300 bonus. Lockheed Missiles and Space Company estimates that in five years it saved $1 million in life insurance costs through its wellness program. Absenteeism is 60 percent lower and turnover is 13 percent lower among regular exercisers. Atco pays $100 per pound lost during a five-month period, $500 to stop smoking, and $500 for regularly climbing the stairs. It's all quite remarkable, and there isn't a single reason why a small company couldn't do these things."

"Exactly!" Paula exclaimed. "It all adds up, Joanne."

"There's the ongoing professional and personal training I provide for everyone. That has to make for happier campers," I said. "When I really think about it, maybe what I need to be doing is spending more time figuring out the intangible stuff that makes people feel good — things like recognizing and acknowledging when they've done a job particularly well. I have already started increasing their authority and I include the staff in all high-level decisions. What I really need to work on is a way to give them more time off. This business can completely consume you and before you know it, you're working around the clock. What about my idea to share in the ownership of the company? Wouldn't that be a good incentive?"

"I don't recommend sharing ownership in the company during the early years," Paula said emphatically. "It is best to keep ownership and employment issues separate. Too often we use a share in the company as if it were non-cash compensation for doing a job and it's not intended for that. It's intended to represent the value of the time and money that have been invested long-term in the company over and above your employment responsibilities. Don't go down that road — yet."

Paying the Boss

Okay. You've figured out how to pay your staff. What about you? What do you think you are worth? To preserve cash in the first year, many (okay most) entrepreneurs don't put themselves on salary. In my case, I wasn't at all sure of the timing of my cash flow. I had no idea what the terms of payment by the financial institutions would be. I was so grateful they bought something, I didn't ask. More to the point, I was embarrassed to ask, thinking asking might make me sound needy and too much like a small player. As it turns out, I couldn't have been more wrong. The very savvy business owners are particularly adept at settling terms as part of the initial negotiation.

Yet clearly, like everyone, I needed money. So Paula set me up with a shareholder loan account. This meant I could borrow the cash I needed from the company on an ongoing basis. Not only did I take out money to live on, but I bought things that I believed to be business expenses, like furniture for my new home office. Now, I was expecting a whack of cash in the near future from the bank's training contract. The idea was that I would then pay myself a true salary and use that salary to pay back my shareholder loan. The loan had to be paid back within one year after my first corporate year-end. But try not to wait that long. And pay it back on time. Revenue Canada charges interest on overdue amounts at a prescribed rate plus 4 percent. Even worse, in some cases,

Revenue Canada might assume that the loan was really salary and you will have to pay the income tax that wasn't originally withheld, and probably a penalty.

The shock — when it came — came in two forms, the first being the amount I had to pay back. Lordy, did it add up fast. The second shock was the fact that the loan had to be paid back with personal after-tax dollars. I had a heck of a time with this one. "But it's my money! Why should I have to pay *my* company back *my* money?" Because you do. Period. The only way ultimately to get money out of your company is by salary or dividends. Paula told me to consider it like this: As an entrepreneur, you have two pockets, one business and one personal. Every time you move money from the business pocket to the personal pocket, the government wants its share unless you put it back. Unfortunately, it doesn't work the other way around. You don't get *extra* money when the cash flows from the personal to the business. It was tough to get it through my head that this loan had to be paid back. It's necessary, therefore, to track the shareholder's loan carefully and use it for as short a time as possible. Once your business is up and running, separate everything personal from the business. That's when it's time to go on salary.

Under certain circumstances, a shareholder loan can be a one-shot deal that doesn't have to be paid back within the year. These are the three circumstances: a home purchase loan through the company, a car loan provided the car is used for business, and a loan to purchase unissued shares, for example when an employee buys shares but the company is lending them the money to do it.

The option of going on salary is for incorporated businesses only. Sole proprietors often ask, "How much can I take out of my business?" The answer? Whatever the business profit is, is what the government considers you to have taken.

You might also consider looking into using pre-tax company dollars to provide yourself with some of the more common company benefits such as a company car or a laptop, and tacking on a couple of personal travel days to business travel. In some instances you will have to take what is considered to be the "personal benefit" converted to dollars into your personal income and pay taxes on that portion. The rules around the calculation of personal benefits are quite complicated, so get the help of a good tax accountant. But usually you will have contributed less to the national coffers if you have perks as a component of your compensation. Always check with your accountant because the rules around how much is deductible, what's deductible, and what's not change all the time.

While you can pay yourself bonuses and add some perks in your first year, it is not recommended until your business has proven itself to be viable and can handle more expenditures. As your company becomes stable, you may notch up the amount of money you take by giving yourself a year-end bonus. And as the company begins to thrive and become competitive, so will your total compensation package.

If you have an incorporated business, one of your more important decisions will be how to pay yourself — specifically, how will your compensation be split between salary and dividends. It is best to hire a tax accountant to review your tax position as the business owner and as the key employee. Remember to review your compensation mix annually to ensure that it is still the best for your circumstances.

Splitting Your Income

Salaries may be paid to family members as long as services are actually performed and the amount of salaries and wages is reasonable. My dad did income splitting with me and my mother. The objective of income splitting is to spread the total income among as many family members as is reasonable. That way the total tax paid is lower than if it were paid by one person at a higher tax rate. As a teenager, I cleaned Dad's offices on the weekends and went in occasionally to help when he was overloaded. Mom regularly provided him with administrative support. We were paid a reasonable salary — salaries that he would have had to pay others providing similar services. There were a number of great reasons for my dad to pay a family member.

- His company got a deduction for the expense, which reduced the company's taxable income.
- The money was taxed in mine and Mom's hands at a significantly lower tax rate.
- Mom and I would have been able to contribute to our own RRSPs if we had known what they were.
- Since I was going to university, I paid little or no tax on my salary because my tuition fee and education tax credits were sufficient to offset the tax.

The Separation Continues — Your Personal Finance Life

For a comprehensive treatment of personal finance, you need to read my first book, *Balancing Act: A Canadian Woman's Financial Success Guide*. But here are some of the more important aspects that you as a business owner need to deal with.

The first step to building your personal financial plan is learning to manage your personal debt. That includes knowing something about credit rating. For entrepreneurs, credit rating is of paramount importance, especially if you want to borrow money from the bank. Nowadays, a decision about a small business loan is based more often on your personal record than your business record. This is to make it easier for newer business owners to borrow cash.

How Credit Ratings and the Credit Bureau Work

Credit lenders decide on your credit worthiness based on three principles known as the three Cs of credit:

1. *Your Character*
   Are you dependable? Do you pay your bills on time, or at the very least, pay the minimum when it's due? (This is more important than paying more than the minimum late.) Does your past show you to be a financially responsible person?

2. *Your Capacity*
   Do you have a steady means to pay back what you are borrowing? Do you own a home or rent? Have you lived at your current address for long? Credit lenders like to see your name on one mailbox for at least a year.

3. *Your Collateral*
   When everything is added up, *is what you own worth more than what you owe?* Do you own something that is worth at least as much as your credit limit or the amount you want to borrow? This might include the equity in your house, household goods, a car, savings, investments, and life insurance.

If "yes" figures prominently in your answers, then you are a good candidate for credit.

What's a Credit Rating?

Your credit rating is a scorecard of your credit behaviour. Everything you do with credit is tracked and rated according to how responsible you have been in paying it back. Most of your credit transactions are kept on file at an independent credit bureau. These transactions include things like loans and credit cards but not rent or utility bills. It is your personal credit rating that will be used initially when your business is really new and has not established a track record. How you pay your personal expenses is held as a good indicator of how your business will pay its expenses.

Financial institutions, retailers and other lenders who have an interest in your financial status check your rating before deciding whether you get credit. To be sure your record is accurate, write the bureau for a free copy of your history every year.

Look After Your Own Affairs

The merits of having your own driver's licence and social insurance number are obvious. It is equally important to have your own credit rating. If you have lived under the umbrella of your partner's credit, for example by using a supplementary card instead of one in your own name, you may be surprised to learn the credit bureau doesn't even know you exist. This could be dangerous should you wake up one morning to find yourself on your own and handling money for the first time. Something you always took for granted — credit — is gone. To be sure you are establishing a credit history of your own, apply for credit in your own name, using your partner's name as a co-signer or guarantor only if absolutely necessary.

How Can You Establish Credit?

People looking to establish credit could include women who have recently survived the death or divorce of a partner. It could be graduating students or empty-nester moms earning their first full-time paycheques. Others might be coming off the seven-year credit ban after a bankruptcy.

No matter which group you belong to, the best way to create a credit rating that will allow you to borrow money is to borrow money. Confusing? Yes, but it's easier than you think. Credit lenders often like to see a good repayment history before lending money or offering credit. You can begin to develop this history by trying any of the following:

- Make regular deposits to a savings account.
- Pay all your bills, such as rent and utilities, on time.
- Get a credit or charge card at a department store with a $500 limit and repay it quickly. Pay the minimum on time.
- Get a joint card (not a supplemental card) with your partner so the credit reporting is done in your name.
- Obtain a small loan and have a friend or relative co-sign for you.
- Take out a car loan and pay it back promptly.

This is how you *establish* a good credit rating.

Keeping a Good Credit Rating

Your credit record begins the minute your first credit application has been approved. The way to *keep* a good rating is to make all payments, even if it's the minimum, on time and not take on more debt than you can handle.

Every 30 days, most of your major creditors, like The Bay or the phone company, pass along information to the credit bureau about your outstanding balance, missed payments, and current credit rating with that company. The bureau, in turn, passes along this information to anyone to whom you apply for credit.

So it's not the credit bureau that establishes your rating. Rather, each company you've dealt with gives you an R rating, beginning with *R0* (as soon as you've been approved for credit) and ranging from *R1* to *R9*, depending on your performance as a debtor.

An *R1* rating is like an A+ in school — it should be treasured. It's amazing how easy it is to get down-graded: Even if you go one day over the 30-day time frame, you're considered a payment behind and lose your coveted *R1* score, and so on down the scale. You are not informed when this happens. It's around *R3* that your potential credit grantor starts wondering if you're a little light in the financial discipline department.

Making the Credit Grade

Rating	R#
Too new to rate: approved but not yet used	R0
Pays within 30 days, and all payments are up to date	R1
Pays in 30 days to 60 days, and is not more than 1 payment behind	R2
Pays in 60 days to 90 days, or is 2 payments behind	R3
Pays in 90 days to 120 days or 3 or more payments behind	R4
Account at least 120 days overdue, but not in collection	R5*
Making regular payments under consolidation order or similar arrangements	R7
In repossession	R8
Account is in collection or debtor can't be found	R9

*There is no R6 rating

And don't think that paying off delinquent amounts gets you in the clear again. Your low rating remains unchanged, and the record of missed or late payments becomes part of your credit file for seven years, after which it is removed by law. Delinquent student loans, unpaid tax bills, and unpaid rent will not show up on your credit history. Credit bureaus are used mainly by private companies — such as banks or department stores — rather than by governments or landlords.

Although credit bureaus are under provincial jurisdiction and are required to maintain accurate records, their information is only as good as what's given to them. You have the right to dispute what's on your record. Equifax Canada, the country's largest credit bureau, handles over 800,000 customer requests for file inspections annually. You can get this information by mail (call your credit bureau for details) or by visiting your local office. Be prepared to show two pieces of photo ID.

Putting Yourself in Charge With Credit

It seems debts are about the only thing we can acquire without money. Credit card debt was responsible for my downward spiral into credit hell. I saw my cards as a natural extension of my income. Yet, credit cards are one of the greatest inventions on the planet. They are designed to give you 21 days free money. They are not, however, efficient means of financing purchases over the long term. It's a little known fact that there actually is a difference between credit cards and charge cards. Knowing this difference is the first step to making an informed choice.

Charge Cards Some oil companies and certain financial and travel service companies, like American Express, tend to be the issuers of these types of cards. Because they offer no pre-set spending limits, they must be paid in full every month. They don't charge interest per se but they do levy delinquency fees. Charge cards are really designed for short-term credit needs, usually 30 days or less.

Credit Cards Credit cards allow you to carry a balance from month to month as long as a minimum portion of the bill is paid each month. You are charged interest for this benefit. Unless, of course, you pay off your balances in full each month. You can choose from two categories of credit cards. The first is offered by banks, trust companies, credit unions, and other financial institutions. The second is offered by retailers and the oil companies who don't fall into the charge card category. The major difference is store and gas cards have higher interest rates and fewer features.

Supplementary Cards These cards are generally issued to the partner of the principal cardholder. Even though there may be two different names on the card, the responsibility for paying the bill remains with the principal cardholder. This kind of card does not establish a credit record for the partner since all credit reporting is done in the main cardholder's name.

What Are Your Choices? It used to be that a credit card was a credit card was a credit card. Choosing the right credit card has become almost as mind-boggling as choosing running shoes these days. In response to demand for options and added value, companies are introducing a large variety of products to address different consumer needs.

With all the choices, it still comes down to these main categories:

- **Low-rate Cards** These cards are generally stripped-down versions of standard cards without the added benefit of a points program and can offer interest rates up to six points below conventional cards. Many come with an annual fee so be sure to ask.
- **Standard Cards** These cards are offered by financial institutions, and carry interest rates in the 16–18 percent range; some offer various incentives like points towards travel, entertainment, and merchandise. Cards offered by retailers generally don't have incentive packages and charge interest rates as high as 28.8 percent.
- **Premium Cards** Otherwise known as gold cards, these are enhanced products with generally a higher annual fee and a range of benefits. Features may include higher credit limits, cash back, travel insurance, purchase protection plans, guaranteed hotel reservations, collision insurance on rental cars, health insurance, credit card registry services, and itemized annual spending records. The same incentive programs attached to standard cards apply to premium cards as well. Premium cards usually charge $50–$130 in annual fees.

Credit Card Line of Credit This is called a credit card line because the credit application is the same as the form that you use for a personal card. It bills you the same way with monthly statements and minimum payments based on the outstanding balance. If your business needs an operating line of credit, the credit card lines are a quick, easy, and efficient way to apply and they are better than a personal credit line because the credit history is built up in your company's name rather than in your name as an individual. For every "get" there is always a "give" — the interest rates are a little higher than you might be able to negotiate with a traditional line of credit.

Business Credit Cards At some point you should have a separate credit card to use for business purchases. You are not usually in a position to do this until after your first year end, however. A separate card will lessen your monthly administrative angst. If you are not eligible for a business credit card or would rather accumulate points on your personal card, you can request a second card and have it in your name as follows: Joanne Thomas Yaccato — exp. (for expenses). Then use it only for business purchases. Since the credit card companies provide you with a separate statement for each card, you will be one step farther down the housekeeping trail at the end of each month. In some cases, you can get a statement at the end of the year that summarizes your purchases by category (i.e., meals, car, entertainment, accommodation, travel, etc.). American Express offers this valuable service as part of the annual fee.

The Real Costs of Credit and Charge Cards

How Is Interest Calculated? It's pretty simple. Cards from financial institutions charge interest on daily outstanding balances. No interest is charged on new purchases if you pay the entire balance by the due date. In most cases, if the balance isn't paid by the due date, interest is charged from the date you made your purchase until the balance is paid in full. In this case, you lose any grace period. Retailers, on the other hand, tend to charge interest on monthly as opposed to daily balances. In most cases you'll pay less interest if you pay at least half the balance each month. If you only make the required minimum payment each month you will only cover the interest cost and never pay off the balance. This is the most expensive form of borrowing.

Grace Period The number of days you have on a card before a company starts charging you interest is called a grace period. Usually that period is the number of days between the statement date and the payment due date. Grace periods on credit cards are usually 21 days for financial services cards and 25 to 30 days for retail cards. Charge cards typically offer a period of 30 days. Be aware, though, that there are some low-interest cards that have no grace period at all. When you carry balances from month to month, there is no grace for balances carried forward from previous months.

Fees Watch for annual and administrative fees. Depending on your balance, the fee may end up costing you more than a card with a higher interest rate but no fee. For instance, on an average yearly outstanding balance of $1500, a card with an interest rate of 13.5 percent with a $60 annual fee ends up costing you the same as a no-fee card at 17.5 percent.

Matching Spending Habits With Card Features

Where do you belong?

- **Flunk.** If you constantly carry a balance or pay only the minimum requirement, rethink using credit cards. It is important and possible to find a less expensive form of borrowing. Using credit is borrowing money and it's a privilege you earn, not a consumer right.
- **Yellow Flag.** If you consistently take a couple of months to pay off balances and carry a balance of $400 a month, low-rate cards are your best bet. If you carry a monthly balance you should avoid the temptation to use your card more in order to accumulate points.
- **Pass.** If you generally pay off balances in full each month but have been known to occasionally take a couple of months, you can feel comfortable choosing just about any of the card options available. You are in the responsible range.
- **Sleep Well.** This is the credit card puritan. You pay off your cards each month. Your best option: any card, but in particular, the value-added ones. Your financial discipline means you're getting the financial institution to finance your purchases for 21 days. And with a value-added card, you'll also be earning points for trips and gifts. This is a great bonus, especially if you were planning to purchase the goods and services anyway.

Disability Insurance

Now that your credit house is in order, it is time to turn your attention to another crucial aspect of financial planning. Your business may be flying, you're taking out a healthy income, and you have the most sophisticated investment portfolio on the planet, but without disability insurance, it can all be reduced to hamburger overnight. With a disability policy, you get a monthly cheque from the insurance company if you're too sick or injured to work. It's that simple. (Note, however, that disability insurance does not pay you as much as you earn while working and it may not pay enough to replace you with an employee able to fill your shoes.)

But buying the right policy is about as simple as choosing a new car: You have to understand the options. Start with the question of where you buy; it can make a big difference. There are three main sources: your company job (group insurance), an association or university alma mater you belong to (association insurance), or, the only real option if you are an entrepreneur, a plan you own outright (private insurance). Each has merit, and each has drawbacks.

- **Group** insurance is dependent entirely on your employer's generosity, and it's only good while you work there. Obviously, if you are reading this book, you are thinking about or have ceased to work there. You can top up your group insurance with private insurance to a maximum of 65 to 70 percent of total income.
- **Association** insurance (e.g., offered by the Canadian Bar and Canadian Dental Associations) is an inexpensive option essentially the same as group policies, but the premiums can be subject to big increases if there are too many claims.
- **Private** policies give you the most control and security, but they cost a lot more. In fact, they can cost an average 30 percent more for women than for men. That's because women have higher claim rates; the insurance industry cites "superwoman syndrome" as part of the reason for this.

When investigating disability insurance, ask the following questions about any plan offered. And seek the help of a professional, preferably someone specializing in this area.

- What does disability mean? Do I have to be in a coma to receive benefits or can a broken finger qualify? Group plans can define disability as down-and-out with little chance of recovery: Anything short of that and they pay nothing. Private plans tend to have a more liberal definition of disability, which is why you pay more. Be sure to ask whether partial disability is covered.
- Can the benefits be reduced or cut off? This can't happen with private plans but can with group and association plans.
- How long will benefits continue? Some plans will pay until you are 65, others pay only for five years — even if you're disabled for life!
- Do the monthly benefits increase with inflation? If you become permanently disabled with a monthly benefit of $2000 with no provision for inflation, you could be in trouble down the road. Remember, a 1974 dollar is worth 29 cents today.
- What if I'm up to some other line of work? Some plans cease paying if you're well enough to do any job at all. Maybe you're a surgeon and lose a hand. The insurer might say, "Go sell widgets." Check for an "own occupation" clause.
- And the price? Get ready for the bad news about private plans: they cost. A 35-year-old healthy non-smoking woman would pay in the neighbourhood of

$100 a month for a $2100 monthly tax-free benefit beginning on the 31st day of her disability. The cost rises for those older or less healthy. A good way to reduce the cost is to lengthen the waiting period for benefits — if the above 35-year-old were willing to wait two or three months, her premium would drop to $70 or even $60.

Be forewarned: Getting private disability insurance may not be easy at any price. You need job stability, a certain level of guaranteed ongoing income, and, most importantly, good health. Already you can see the challenges small business owners face. Most insurance companies won't give you disability unless you have been in business at least a year. Exceptions will be made if the business you are going into is similar to the one you left behind in corporate Canada. If you are lucky enough to get disability insurance, make sure you pay for the premiums out of your personal pocket and not your business pocket. That way the benefit amount is tax free. If the company pays the premium, expect Revenue Canada to come and get its share if a benefit is ever paid out. Remember, health buys insurance, money only pays for it. That's why the time to buy is when you are well. Owning disability insurance is a bit like owning a parachute. Nice to have, but pray you'll never need it.

Life Insurance

According to the insurance association, LIMRA, 50 percent of women are poorly covered. More than 50 percent of couples with kids who look at life insurance never consider adequate coverage for the wife. And with so many women becoming entrepreneurs, the need for insurance has never been greater. So, what kind of life insurance do you need? Consider this Life Insurance 101, and talk to insurance professionals or an investment adviser before you decide on your strategy.

Do You Have to Own Life Insurance?

Maybe not, if you are single with no dependants. But as a business owner, don't forget that dependants are both human and corporate. It's prudent to be sure there will be enough money on hand to bury you and pay off any debts as well as sell, close, or continue the business.

For family breadwinners, the choice is obvious. But what if you work full- or part-time raising your family? Before you leave life insurance out of your plans, consider the cost of replacing the unpaid work you do at home. As a business owner, you not only need to consider the requirements of your life partner (if any) but your business partner as well.

Who Should You Call?

You can buy insurance from an agent (who is generally sponsored by one company) or an insurance broker (who can sell for more than one company). Fee-for-service financial planners don't usually sell financial products but do offer advice. Find someone who comes recommended and who asks detailed questions to help you determine exactly what you need. And shop around — prices vary greatly.

How Much Should You Buy?

Forget commonplace formulas like "10 times your salary." Get professional advice — and before deciding on a bottom-line number, make sure you have answered these questions:

- How much will it cost to provide for your children's education, child care, and housekeeping services as well as food and clothes?
- Do you want to establish a rent-payment fund or pay off your mortgage?
- What will your funeral cost? For that matter, how much will it cost to die? Medicare doesn't cover everything, and there will be lawyers, executors, and taxes to pay, too.
- How much capital will it take to provide a secure income for your family? How much will inflation eat into this capital?
- What is the average amount of money that you owe to suppliers, lenders, and shareholders? How much would it cost to replace you in the business?

For Now or Forever?

All insurance products on the market are variations on the following:

- **Permanent** insurance is commonly called whole life or universal life and provides guaranteed protection right up until the day you meet your maker. With whole life you will generally pay a set monthly premium for life; with universal you can vary your premiums and death benefit. These policies accumulate a cash value that is available to you if you decide to cancel your policy.
- **Term** insurance, on the other hand, is good for specific chunks of time like 5, 10, or 20 years. You can renew when the term is up, but at the rate for the age you will be then. A term policy is pure insurance with no cash value. It's ideal for financial obligations that will disappear, like mortgages and children.

- **Term-to-100** policies are gaining in popularity. They are actually permanent insurance with little or no cash value attached. Beware of advisers
  who trash one type of policy over the other. You can only decide based on
  your specific requirements.

Is It a Priority Now?

Owning life insurance can be even more important than starting a retirement plan. Maybe you can do both at the same time; a life policy can be
fairly cheap, and most investments can be started for as little as $50 a month.
But if you must choose, ask yourself: What happens to my family if I die six
months after I start my retirement fund?

Wills

Brace yourself for a vital snippet of financial information: You're mortal.
Unfortunately, most people live as though life never ends. A survey by the Trust
Companies Association of Canada found that only half of Canadian adults have
wills, and only one in three even talked to their executor about the contents
of their will. If you're in either group, here are five good reasons to make an
immortal statement of your financial wishes:

1. If you die without a will, the government writes one for you. This isn't a
   service they provide. It's just a set formula as to who gets what. This could
   mean that people you want to get stuff, won't, and people you don't want
   to get stuff, will.
2. Without a will, your assets are frozen. That means no one has access to
   any money or property (including your business) until the estate is settled.
   Since it's the government's job to do the settling, the process takes time.
3. A proper will can mean your heirs pay less tax, sometimes much less. When
   you die, your investments (such as your cottage) are considered sold. Unless
   you make provisions in a will, the "sale" can have expensive tax implications.
   Someone also has to file what's called a terminal tax return and pay your income tax for the current year up to the moment you left this earthly place.
4. A will lets you decide who will arrange your funeral and distribute your assets.
   In making your choice, don't rely on sentiment. Your executor is financially liable for any mistakes made in settling your estate, so choose someone competent. If you're considering a family member, weigh in personality: At an
   emotional time, some people are better at performing an executor's duties
   with an arm's-length attitude. It's sometimes wise to choose a co-executor —
   a lawyer, perhaps — if you have a complicated estate.

5. When you go out for an evening, you give the baby-sitter painstaking instructions and contact numbers. But who will care for the children if you don't come home?

Take a week or so to make yourself a will. Make sure your significant other (if any) has one, too. Your options range from a 35-cent stationer's special to the $150-plus will done by a lawyer. Consulting a lawyer is always the safest option, as the do-it-yourself versions may not stand up if contested in court and rarely include provisions to deal with your business asset.

Power of Attorney

When Michael and I were first married, we knew that the wills we had as single folk became null and void when we signed the marriage register. So, two weeks after our wedding, we took ourselves to a lawyer to tackle the gloom-and-doom portion of our financial plan. We had already drawn up new wills to name guardians for Kate and an executor to divvy up our immense estate (?!) should we die. Now it was time to consider powers of attorney for property and personal care. Both documents may come into play if you are mentally incapacitated. The person (or persons) you appoint acts as your hands, your head, and your voice in dealing with your assets, property, financial affairs, and, in some provinces, medical care, until you can act for yourself again.

Power of Attorney for Property

While at the lawyer's office, Michael asked what would happen if he had a car accident and lapsed into a coma. Wouldn't I, as his wife, naturally step in and take over his affairs?

"Unfortunately not," I said. "First, your financial affairs, personal and business, would be frozen pending the court's decision on who should act on your behalf. This means I couldn't get access to *anything* in your name until I proved I could manage your affairs.

"Second, the Public Guardian/Trustee/Curator could take control of everything. This should not make you feel warm and cozy. A 1992 provincial auditor's report showed that of 125 trust and estate files examined in Ontario, 55 percent had been handled deficiently."

Though the issue itself is difficult, getting a power of attorney may not be as hard as you think. A meeting with your lawyer is the only way to ensure the power of attorney is tailor-made to your needs; it'll take around an hour and cost you about $150. There are other less expensive options. Commercial do-it-yourself kits are available through provincial governments and some lawyers. You can also buy really cheap stationery-store versions. But the rules are complicated and vary among provinces, so it's smart to seek legal advice before signing anything.

Anyone over 18 can be appointed a power of attorney. Most people choose family members, but I've been named by some single friends. The key consideration is trust. This person will be responsible for doing your banking, making investment choices, and the like. Will they understand the mechanics of such decisions? Can they cope with the responsibility? Many people worry about giving one person too much power over their affairs. A simple way around this is to appoint two people to act jointly. Or, leave your power of attorney with your lawyer along with written instructions on when to release it. Your stand-in can't act without the physical document. But don't go overboard with your restrictions. You can always revise or revoke your power of attorney as circumstances change. Revoking it can be as simple as tearing up the piece of paper and all copies, if you are competent, that is. If you are deemed to be incompetent you are out of luck.

Power of Attorney for Personal Care

Next, Michael and I had the cheerful task of drafting our powers of attorney for personal care, also known as living wills, advance directives, or, in Quebec, mandates. Their primary function is to put your wishes in writing and to name someone to make medical decisions for you if accident or illness leaves you incapacitated. Until recently, living wills were not legally binding. However, Nova Scotia, Ontario, Quebec, British Columbia, and Manitoba have made living wills legally binding or are in the process of doing so.

Whether you have a lawyer draft your living will or decide to do it yourself, be specific. "Please avoid heroic measures" isn't very helpful. What's heroic to one physician may be standard procedure for another. Talk to your partner and doctor so you can draft a living will that exactly sets out your wishes.

Registered Retirement Savings Plans

Raise your hand. How many of you can afford to be unemployed for 20 or 30 years? Right. Because of women's extended life spans, our retirements can actually last longer than our careers. When you consider the explosive leap of women into entrepreneurship, we've really got to pay attention. Once you leave the comfy confines of corporate Canada, you've got to create your own company benefits like insurance and pension plans. That's where RRSPs come in. They are the great equalizer.

What Exactly Is an RRSP?

You don't really "buy" an RRSP, you purchase some kind of investment — such as a guaranteed investment certificate (GIC) or mutual fund — and that becomes part of your registered retirement savings plan.

Remember the First "R"

With an RRSP, the key word is "registered." This is how it works: Say you earned enough income to contribute $5000 to your RRSP this year, and you decide to buy a GIC. The standard purchase form includes a vital question that says something like, "Do you wish this plan to be registered?" For maximum retirement income, the right answer is yes. Your GIC (or whatever investment you choose) becomes registered with Revenue Canada, which means two things: You can deduct your contribution from your taxable income this year, and the tax on the interest that is payable every year will be deferred until you cash out your RRSP, which is hopefully when you retire. The result (assuming an average 8 percent rate of return): your annual $5000 becomes $394,772 in 25 years. But if you don't check that "yes" box, you end up with only $165,088, all because you lost the benefit of tax-sheltered compound interest and tax deductions.

Tax-Free? Not Likely

When you cash in any part of your RRSP, you have to pay tax. The idea is, however, if you wait until retirement to do so, you'll likely be in a lower tax bracket. As a result, you'll pay less tax than you would have in your prime earning years. You have until age 69 to protect your hard-earned money from Revenue Canada, but before the end of that calendar year, you must either cash the RRSP out or convert it to a registered retirement income fund or an annuity.

Growth Is Good

So, what kind of investment should you buy for your RRSP? Look for something that will yield maximum long-term growth, not a quick fix. An extremely popular RRSP choice is some form of mutual fund based in stocks and/or bonds. True, mutual funds are not free of risk — but then, nothing is. Guaranteed investments like GICs and Canada Savings Bonds can't lose you actual cash, but because of inflation, you may find yourself with a lot less purchasing power from your dollar at retirement. One of the fundamental laws of investing is that the riskier the investment, the higher the potential rate of return. So you've got to hang on to your mutual funds for the long term

— generally no fewer than 10 years. As you get closer to retirement, start shifting your RRSP portfolio into the more guaranteed-type investments — but still not exclusively. Remember, you hope to be living off this money for a long time, so you will continue to need some growth even in retirement.

The Good Spouse

A spousal RRSP — a plan in the name of the purchaser's partner — is an excellent option for women who work full-time unpaid in the home and for women like me who took a financial hit for the time off with Kate. If Michael buys a spousal RRSP, he will benefit from the tax deduction, but I will own the tax-sheltered investment.

No, Tomorrow Is Not Another Day

When my sister was 30, she told me she was going to forego contributing to her RRSP that year. She was going through a rough spell financially but said she'd make it up the following year. I did a quick calculation based on her $5000 allowable contribution and informed her that by postponing it one year, she would take roughly $105,000 out of her pocket at retirement. My sister borrowed that year to make her contribution. Borrowing for your RRSP makes sense because of the long-term benefits — as long as you can pay back the loan *within a year*. But note that the interest on your RRSP loan is not tax deductible. Some financial institutions will give you an RRSP loan at prime and/or on a deferred-payment basis provided you buy directly from them. Not a bad idea if you're comfortable with the company and its investment choices.

When you are considering what to pay yourself from your business, make sure you take sufficient salary to enable you to make maximum Canada or Quebec Pension Plan contributions, as well as to contribute the maximum to your RRSP. The contribution limit for your RRSP is based on 18 percent of your earned income in the previous year. The maximum you can contribute to your RRSP in 1998 is $13,500. That means you would have had to earn $75,000 in 1997 to make the maximum contribution to your RRSP in 1998. You will need the same amount of earned income in 1998 to make the $13,500 maximum RRSP contribution in 1999 as well.

Remember, an RRSP is more than just your ticket to a retirement villa in Venice. With the prospect of slim pickings at the social security trough in the near future, it's nothing less than a question of survival. It takes as little as $50 a month to start an RRSP. People who contribute to RRSPs now, today, tend to have the attitude that the first 65 years is just a warm-up. Always consult a well-recommended financial planner, banker, broker, insurance agent, or mutual fund dealer, and feed your plan every single year.

The key to personal financial planning is patience and perseverance. The road to financial success often runs uphill, so don't expect to break any speed records. If you don't think you can do it, remember that Ginger Rogers did everything Fred Astaire did, only backwards and in high heels.

There are three main steps you need to take to start the process of financial literacy:

- **Step One** Get organized. Assemble all of your insurance policies, tax returns, and investment and RRSP receipts.

- **Step Two** Start looking at what you own and what you owe. This is where you set your long- and short-term goals. It's always easier to begin with an end in mind. Think about what you want to be when you grow up. Write down exactly where you want to live when you retire. Write down the square footage of the villa in Italy. How many nights out to the theatre do you plan? Make the dream tangible.

- **Step Three** Ask yourself first, "Do I need investment advice?" The answer is likely to be, "Probably." The Canadian Association of Financial Planners suggests you ask yourself these questions: Are you confused about conflicting advice from different sources? Are you paying too much tax? (Show me someone who isn't!) Are you having trouble making ends meet or saving money? Has there been a major change in your financial life recently? If you answer yes to one or more of these questions, chances are you could use some expert help. In general, people with a financial adviser fare better than those who handle their own affairs. Begin the process of finding a financial adviser to help you get started. You need to find an adviser who hears you.

It Helps to Get Help

What do advisers and planners do? The first thing your money expert should do is give you a check-up: How financially healthy (or unhealthy) are you? The next task is to crystallize your long- and short-term goals and develop a plan of action to help you get there. Then, every year, he or she should carry out a money medical to ensure that your plan is still healthy.

How do you find one? Ask friends and family for referrals. Check out the free seminars offered by many advisers and bankers. Try to interview no fewer than three candidates before making your decision. Look for synergy and chemistry. Is this person listening to you? Does she understand your tolerance for risk? Is he close enough in age to you (usually up to 10 years older) to remember what life is like for you? How long has she been in the business? If you are just starting out, you may have simple needs, so a rookie may be just right (and is likely to have more time to spend with you than a veteran with 500 clients). Look for a professional designation or, at the very least, someone who is working towards one. How stable and well known is the company he works for? One final caution: Consider avoiding friends and family in the business, unless you're certain they can be objective about your needs. It's much easier to fire an arm's-length business associate than it is to fire your sister.

Who's Who in Financial Planning

- **Financial planner** Under current Canadian law, anyone can hang out this shingle. Look for a designation (see below).
- **Financial adviser** Usually a commission-based salesperson with no designation who sells the financial products of one or more companies.

Designations

- **Certified Financial Planner (CFP)** Accredited by the Financial Planners Standards Council of Canada. Usually paid on a combination of fee-for-service and commission basis, though many also sell financial products on a strictly commission basis.
- **Registered Financial Planner (RFP)** Accredited by the Canadian Association of Financial Planners. Compensated with commissions, fees, or a combination of the two.
- **Chartered Financial Consultants (CHFC)** A financial planner for the insurance industry. May be paid by commission or on a fee-for-service basis.

Here is where the Canadian Association of Financial Planners can be of help. If you want a list of names of planners and advisers in your geographic area, call them at 1-800-346-CAFP(2237). They won't recommend specific advisers, but they will tell you who has what designations among those who operate in your neck of the woods.

Sweating the Small Stuff

Okay. By now you realize that running your own show includes handling both ends of the stick and every place in between — the good and the bad, the fun and the boring, and the big and the small. This section, in my opinion, is most certainly about the boring.

Record Keeping

Office manager: "I'm afraid you're ignoring our record keeping and efficiency system."
Employee: "Maybe so, but somebody has to get the work done."

Keeping track of your business transactions, like invoicing, bill payments, deposits, interest charges, parking receipts, and credit card statements, is like having to dust the knick-knacks in your china cabinet. You like the fact that you have them (the transactions and the knick-knacks) but you hate having to maintain them. Wouldn't it be bliss just to make the sale and put the money in the bank? Thankfully, you are running a business in the information age when inexpensive, easy-to-use, and intuitive software abounds. These software packages follow your natural business process from invoicing to deposits and from receiving goods and supplies to paying for them. The accounting is done in the background when you print the invoice, input the bill, and cut the cheque. In your first year, you may not have a huge number of transactions, but you will have some. So get yourself organized from the start.

Paula was predestined to walk the accounting path. Her Jiddou (grandfather in Arabic) was a self-made business owner who taught Paula, at the impressionable age of 12, the essentials of good and accurate record keeping. "Right down to the penny," he would insist. Sometimes that penny would elude her for hours and hours. At the beginning, her grandfather did the actual bookkeeping while Paula copied the numbers from the back of an envelope (as good a piece of paper as any) into the big blue and green ledgers with the little ribbon that marked the page. To this day, Paula advises her clients on and maintains her own records with the simple system that her Jiddou taught her. See if it works for you.

Set up the following files to act as landing places for financial information and documentation in progress:

- A file for bills that come in but that haven't been input to your financial system yet, stamped with the date they are received.
- A file for unpaid bills that have been entered into the system, stamped with the date when they were entered and the words "pending payment."
- A file for paid bills, stamped "paid" and with the date paid and cheque number.
- A file for invoices that have been issued but not paid, stamped with the date sent to the customer because this sometimes varies from the invoice date. This file is optional because your accounting software will keep track of accounts receivable. However, a physical file has a way of compelling you to pick up the phone sooner and you may find it easier to refer to the paper file when making those collection calls.
- A file for deposits made. You could include a hard copy of the invoice stamped "paid" and with the customer's cheque or credit card authorization number.

- And, finally, a monthly file in which you place things like bank statements. There are also the interminable tax filing forms to be filled out and submitted with your remittances of payroll taxes and withholdings and GST and provincial sales tax (if applicable). Staple a calendar inside the front cover of the file folder of when recurring payments and filings are due so that you don't miss them and end up attracting interest and late-payment penalties. Once you actually cut the cheque and send it off (a painful task for us cash-strapped newbies), don't forget to move the copy of the completed form to the paid bills file.

To create some sanity and consistency in your life and to prevent you from ignoring this part of the business, set aside the same day every week, two weeks, or month, depending on your life, to process the stuff in these files (i.e., pay your suppliers, yourself and your staff, make collection calls, fill out your tax forms, and reconcile your bank statement). After your bank statement has been reconciled, clear out those paid files and joy, oh joy, start again.

You can file all of the supporting documents (like suppliers' invoices, your invoices, any purchase orders or cheque remittance stubs or credit card copies) with your bank statement. Attach the bills that you paid during the month to the returned cheque. Put the invoices that have been paid with the deposit slip. Then bundle them all up with the bank statement and file them away by month. The "accountant approved" alternative is to file your paid bills and invoices by vendor and customer name so that you can easily access the supporting documentation if there is a question after the fact.

Who should do all of this? That's an easy one for me. Anyone *but* me. Paula, on the other hand, recommends doing it yourself in the first year so that you fully understand how your business operates. She says that record keeping is like any other job, only more important — and that new business owners are too quick to hand it off to someone else. (Who can blame us?) If you don't understand the process and can't set it up on your own, then get help from someone who can. Use the bookkeeper as a co-pilot but do the work yourself for at least six months to a year. Then once you decide to delegate the responsibility, you will know how to ensure that it is being done correctly and the bookkeeper will understand how the system was set up.

There are service bureaus that will handle specific types of payments. Payroll is the most common one and is often administered for a fee by either a financial institution or an independent service bureau such as ADP, which you can find in your phonebook. In both cases they will set up your employees, calculate what the government remittances should be for both the employee and the employer, call you before every payroll to see if they have done it right or if there are any changes, and cut the cheques to the staff and the government. It seems to me that you are better off doing it yourself — almost all of the affordable accounting software packages include a payroll function, you maintain control over the timing of remittance, and you avoid the fee for the service.

The Truth Behind the Numbers

Imagine having a financial wizard who could answer all of your questions about your business. What would you ask her? What information would you want to help you make the best possible business decisions?

How about, *where is our business coming from?* In our first year, we were so concerned with getting business, we didn't care where it came from and what it looked like just so long as it came. In retrospect, it would have helped us immeasurably to know where stuff was coming from so we could have done more of the right things and less of the marginally right or even wrong things. To get at the answer to that question you need to look at sales from a couple of angles:

- by the lines of business (keynote speeches, training, or book royalties)
- by individual customer or type of customer (bank or insurance company)
- by month or season (pre-RRSP season or Christmas time, for retail)

How about, *where are most of our profits coming from?* If we had known this, you can rest assured that we would have actually, gasp, turned away certain pieces of business. To get at that precious information you need to look at the gross margins on sales broken down into the categories noted above.

It is important to understand not only how you are making your money but how you are spending it. So consider asking, *where is all my money going?* In our first year, we could have answered this question easily — out the bloomin' front door. It would have been challenging but helpful to get more specific than that. To figure out where your money may be going, you need to look at your expenses from a number of vantage points, including:

- plain old total dollars spent in each category such as rent, marketing, payroll
- each expense as a percentage of your revenue to get an idea of how your expenses relate to the volume and type of business
- each expense category in comparison to other similarly sized companies in your line of business.

Then see how well you are sticking to your plan by asking, *are we doing what we said we were going to do?* It was impossible for us to know this. This implies that you had to have a plan or budget in the first place. You can only assess this by looking at how sales, gross margin, and expenses compare to your plan or budget.

And lastly, the most important question of all, *do I have more cash coming in than going out?* Remember cash? The oxygen of any business? Your ability to answer this question in the affirmative will determine whether you can continue your business, live on it, and grow it. This question was the easiest for us to answer. We were suffocating. It served as an early-warning signal that we needed to take action because we didn't have enough of a cash reserve. We had to:

- work hard to collect those receivables faster
- cut back and, in some cases, cut out expenditures entirely (like cellular phones)
- ask for extended payment terms from our suppliers
- renegotiate the timing of certain expenditures (like our rent) and renegotiate the term over which we were paying back some of our debts so that our payments were smaller and more manageable
- postpone making any major purchases
- reduce inventory (in our case, books) by either cutting back on purchases or having a significant sale.

These measures weren't sufficient to bridge the gap entirely, as can often be the case. That's when I had to look to outside sources for the fix, like my own pocketbook and a loan in the form of an operating line of credit from the bank.

Oh, how I wish I had had those magic numbers back then. I know sure as my hair is red that I could have minimized the severity of the crunch when it hit. The next chapter will help you determine what your magic numbers are that will give you an immediate read on how well your business is doing. This is so you can accurately register the pulse of your business and anticipate the financial impact of decisions before you make them.

A Word of Caution — Where Revenue Canada Draws the Line

It's been said that income tax has made liars out of more people than golf. An entrepreneur's self-employed status offers opportunities for a lot of tax deductions and write-offs. But if we begin to stretch the limits of our entrepreneurial imaginations, we can expect a knock on the door from Revenue Canada. Here are a few red flags that will catch the eye of this sleeping dog.

- The first is lots and lots of losses. If I claim to be in business but my expenses exceed revenues year after year, someone is guaranteed to smell a rat. The tax code says you have to have a reasonable expectation of profit.

But if I've had losses 10 years in a row, Revenue Canada is bound to ask why. They might even suggest career counselling.

- Meals and entertainment will also raise an eyebrow if they are unusually high relative to overall expenses. Some entrepreneurs do need to entertain a lot, like lawyers or sales people. But plumbers? I've seen people give lavish birthday parties for their kids and try to write them off because one or two business associates attended. Clown rental fees in this case will be disallowed.

- If you run a sole proprietorship or partnership from your home, you can deduct supplies and other expenses that are strictly for business use, such as a business phone. As well, a portion of the expenses that are shared with the operation of the home, such as utilities, insurance, property taxes, rent, and mortgage interest, is deductible. The portion that you can deduct for business purposes is calculated according to the percentage of the home that you use exclusively as a work space. Kitchen tables need not apply, unless you happen to be a caterer and you always eat out (remember "exclusive"). Your home office must be either your principal place of business or you must meet clients there regularly. What will tell Revenue Canada that you are using a little imagination in your deductions? A home office deduction that is large in relation to what was claimed last year or a deduction that is large relative to your other expenses. In fact, if you claim more than 20 to 25 percent of your home, some tax whiz at Revenue Canada is likely to wonder what your house looks like. While you can also claim depreciation on your home as an expense, don't. You already have a "principal residence exemption" that shields you from all tax on the sale of your home. Talk to your accountant.

Technology Is Your Friend

The computer has revolutionized small business. Without it, it would be months before we'd know we were broke. My dear hubby Michael is in the technology business and spends so much time logged on to his computer that he is at more risk of getting a computer virus than a real one. When he hears the muttering and cursing coming from my office, he pokes his head in and says, "Computers are your friend, dear." He quickly ducks out to avoid whatever object ricochets off the door.

He has the knack. I do not. I am thankful in an overall way for technology, but I find computers frustrating. They have a certain arrogance that is really annoying. To me, the following story sums up the attitude of a computer.

It came to pass that the people of the earth banded together to design and build the ultimate computer. Every technology, discipline, and philosophy was represented. Money was no object. The capacity was reported in ZIPS, zillions of instructions per second. They programmed it with every known fact. Meanwhile, a second team was charged with fashioning the ultimate questions, questions to both test the machine and learn the nature of our existence.

Years later, both teams made their reports. The second team, after many agonizing discussions, agreed on the ultimate question that the computer should be asked. It was simply, "Why?" The question was entered into the computer. The machine blinked and whirred and went into a processing mode that was too rapid to measure. On and on it went for days, weeks, months and finally, the great truth, the answer appeared on the screen. It read: "Because."[8]

Put Your Business Needs First

The toughest questions to answer on the technology front are: What will technology do for me? How do I know what I need? How long will this thing be useful before I have to upgrade again? (Lord, let it be longer than a week!) The best approach to the how and when to use technology is one that helps you first figure out and prioritize your business needs, not your technology needs. Too often we buy technology because it's the latest and greatest. It's kind of like once a new technology rolls over you, if you're not part of the steamroller, you're part of the road. The reality is, however, we've just flushed money down the drain. The proper way is to figure out what role technology plays at the strategic level of your business. Once that is done, then and only then should you decide on your technology tools. I read once that if the human race wants to go to hell in a handbasket, technology can help it get there by jet.

There are many ways to use technology to strengthen and grow your business. Regardless of where you are at in your business cycle, strength and growth are possible if you can do the following: increase profits; improve service; enhance communications, both internal and external; more efficiently manage staff, time, and projects; and source important information more quickly. And because we all live and die by our cash flow, you are sure to grow if you can shorten billing and collection times.

So how do you use technology for business's sake instead of technology for technology's sake? It's so simple. Ask yourself, "What short- and long-term results do I want?" Then ask, "How will technology get me there?" For instance, you may want to expand nationally or internationally, yet you don't want to, nor can you afford to, set up an office in every city in which you do business. Could you use the Internet as a way to reach your customers and do business with them?

Women and Money Inc. is a classic example of a company that needed to use technology for business's sake. In the beginning, we had a unique situation whereby all of us worked from our homes. Communication was of paramount importance, both internally and externally. I travelled a lot and needed a way to stay in the loop. Clients needed a central number to call, and Michelle and Barb needed a central place to pick up calls. The ability to have our computers talk to each other would have been very cool. There was no shortage of technological solutions that we could have chosen that would have dramatically improved our business. Instead, we implemented a short-term, inexpensive solution that cost us more in the long run. We did not realize that our need to work virtually was going to remain for the long haul. I was *always* going to be travelling and would *always* prefer to work from home.

We went with a central phone service that gave everyone, clients and staff, one phone number to call, that was separate from our home numbers. The lines were monitored by the three of us every hour from our home-based locations. The system was transparent to the caller who received a voicemail message when they called in. It wasn't ideal, because there was no way anyone calling in could hope to get a real person. We got around that by giving out our home business numbers to people we spoke with regularly. The central system was primarily for first-time callers inquiring about our company and for a central internal message dump that I could call when on the road. I would call forward my home business line to the phone service while travelling so I would only have one place to pick up messages. Cumbersome? Uh, slightly. But until we moved into a central location, it sufficed.

We all had our own computers and I owned a laptop as well. But we would have benefited greatly from technology that would have let us network virtually or use e-mail. Though our personal need for a virtual solution was greater than most small businesses because of our geographic challenges, when WMI started, e-mail and small networks were available but not particularly prevalent. I didn't seriously consider them as viable options because it seemed like e-mail and virtual networking were still out there on the techno-fringe and only for techno-weenies. Instead, we used computer-based faxing to send documents back and forth. It was great for sharing static information. But when a change had to be made, faxing just didn't cut it. We needed to collaborate on the same document, like a proposal, quite regularly. Sharing content back and forth by fax wasn't good enough because we had to reinput the changes other people made. Fax copy quality wasn't too pristine either, even though we used the computer for faxing. If there was a major proposal to work on, as there often was, Barb and Michelle had to come to my place to use my computer in order to keep the data centralized. That meant my work schedule was thrown out of whack. We wasted a profoundly stupid amount of time.

Maintaining my calendar became a joke. Because we didn't have an integrated system, only I could manage it, which wasn't easy travelling as much as I did. I used a paper system that I had used for years. But no one else had access to it. We did set it up on the computer, but it was simply a word processing document. The only advantage was the system version was easier to read. We would print off copies every day or two and fax it to each other. It got out of date very quickly. Often I would get a call from Barb while in Vancouver to see if I was available for a meeting, just to be on the safe side, meaning many additional long-distance charges.

We got so fed up we did attempt to implement a remote "network" in our first year so that we could access each other's computers without having to actually get in a car. We (or shall I say the technical support people we hired) never got it to work, so we plodded along with our archaic system. In retrospect, I should have sat down with someone in our first year and mapped out how we wanted to run the company. Instead, I fell prey to the "Lord, I have enough to worry about" mantra. As a result, Michelle, Barb, and I drove each other crazy. The good news was our system couldn't work for long. Frustration and sizeable growth in our first year forced us to re-evaluate by the end of that year. We did sit down with a technology expert who helped us map out a plan.

Where we did go high tech in our first year was in the area of my keynote speeches and training programs. We also decided to go leading edge by using a computer-generated presentation with an LCD projector instead of slides. There was one small problem, however. We couldn't afford the $15,000 then charged for the projector so we depended on our clients to provide it when I was hired to speak. What a mistake.

I was giving my very first full-day presentation in Vancouver to a select group of women physicians, lawyers, and journalists. As a newcomer to the big league of the public speaking circuit, I was, as they say, "slide dependent." I was so afraid of forgetting what I had to say that I created a computer-based slide for every important point in my presentation.

I arrived at my favourite hotel in Vancouver the night before and immediately made a beeline for the conference room to check everything out.

After two hours of frustrating guesswork, the techie and I got everything working. The next morning, knowing that everything was in relative order, I showed up 45 minutes before the scheduled 9:00 start. I was really nervous, not only because of the finicky new technology, but also because of the level of sophistication in the room. I flipped on the projector to begin the process of getting ready and was greeted with a sickening blank screen. As I swallowed the rising panic in my throat, the sponsor and I went madly about trying to figure out why nothing was working when everything had functioned fine the evening before.

Well, we never figured it out.

At exactly 9:00 a.m., with a room full of people looking on expectantly, I had to turn to the group and say, "Good morning and thanks for coming. To begin, I'd like to inform you that my presentation has been swallowed by the nasty technology monster and is currently hovering somewhere out there in never-never land. I'm in the enviable position of having to wing it today. How do you like me so far?"

Though I was joking on the outside, I was dying on the inside. Tap-dancing for an hour was possible, but a whole day? This was no way to start out a career as a public speaker. Thankfully, the women were not only sympathetic but blessed with a great sense of humour. We had a ball. The morning turned into a seminar/share your own experience session. The women learned as much from each other as they did from me. The real acid test was watching the good-byes at the end of the event. Everyone hugged each other and me while the sponsor (a man) stood at the back grinning like he had just caught a 15-pound trout. When it was over, I almost wept with relief. To my astonishment, I found I didn't need to be "slide dependent" at all. Technology is, indeed, your friend, but it will talk about you behind your back.

Paula's business is a service business. It wasn't long before she too ran into the brick wall of administrative capacity. She explains, "In our first year, inter-office communications began suffering. We would walk over or call whomever we needed to speak with and they wouldn't be there or they would be on the telephone. We realized we needed a system for internal communications — message pads and voicemail were suggested. My choice was to set up internal e-mail using a package that came with our network software. E-mail allowed for easier tracking and follow-up of messages and it enabled us to include our off-site associates in our communications loop. It was only one system to maintain. But I have to say, it was pretty funny watching three people who sat within a stone's throw of each other using inter-office mail like a big company. Today, it is our lifeline. It has allowed us to continue to grow without continuing to add more administrative staff. The result? Increased profitability."

In Women and Money Inc.'s case, we saw that the easiest short-term approach may not be the best long-term solution for the company. It's important to become aware of this for three reasons:

1. Technology is an investment in both time and money. The decisions you make today should produce the results you expect tomorrow. In our case, they didn't. Even a modest growth in our business the first year crippled our productivity.
2. Technology is changing the way we do business. This is increasingly the case as technology becomes more people-friendly, intuitive, and reliable and less expensive.
3. You must think long term because the priorities of your business will change. What you need in the infant stage will be different from what you needed in the conception or birth stage. What you will need in the toddler years may be different from in your first year, and so on. When we sailed out of our first year and into our second, everything changed. We left behind the baby stage and baby ways. We became toddlers. We had to move into an office and do some serious technology upgrading.

The Strategy Versus the Tool

To use technology for business's sake, you must start with the end in mind. You must integrate technology into your business strategy at the highest level, not just relegate it to being used as a tool, like automating a manual task, for example. Technology doesn't have to be "space-age" to be useful. Ray Kroc built McDonald's with the latest technology for making better hamburgers. Because of technology, he built his fortune in an area, eating out, that was already overcrowded. Using technology as a tool, on the other hand, means using a technological instrument to perform an operational activity. Liken it to typing a letter instead of handwriting one, using an electronic calendar instead of a paper one, or using a spreadsheet instead of a calculator.

Technology is also revolutionizing how we sell and market. One of the best examples of using technology as a strategy is amazon.com. They claim to be the largest bookstore in the world. Amazon.com has chosen to be a virtual organization in the fullest sense: It has no store front, you can't browse through the aisles, you can't walk out with the book, and there is no Starbucks. Instead, they use technology to offer their products for sale over the Internet. The customer can quickly search the book they are looking for by using key words.

You can shop from anywhere at any time, no driving required. Reduced overhead means better pricing. Ongoing customer contact is maintained via e-mail. In most cases, delivery time is within a week. Amazon.com has used technology to differentiate itself from its superstore competitors. Traditional bookstores, where you probably bought this book, also use technology, but as a tool. They have scanners that track inventory and process sales faster. If they are using technology strategically, they may maintain a database with not only their customer's names and addresses but also their buying patterns to better target direct mail promotions. This example illustrates the difference between using technology as a business strategy and using technology as a tool.

It is essential to remember that technology, when properly used, can be the link between people and places that will increase efficiency and smooth the way for ongoing communication. But it does not, however, replace personal relationships and the personal contact that is the cornerstone of all business relationships. Technology will never replace the human being. I know of a teacher who made an inquiry to Revenue Canada and received a reply that did not answer her question. After several futile follow-up inquiries, she wrote a note: "Dear Computer: Please have your mother call me." Within a week, she had received a handwritten note telling her exactly what she wanted to know.

When Do I Start?

From the moment I had that first order, that first contract, that first client, that first anxiety attack, my mandate became providing quality service so that we could retain that customer, get that next order, and get another client. This meant that now things like networking, time management, customer follow-up, timely billing, preparing quotes, tracking orders, comparing the real financial results to our projected ones, and being able to access information while on the road became requirements. As I became busier and busier, my inclination was to hire another set of hands. But as we add more bodies, we also need to store things like information, and establish things like process and systems. Technology enables us to do all that.

In the very beginning, WMI had only one serious customer. The idea that I needed to set up a sophisticated technological system to accommodate a customer base of one could be construed as overkill. But that was clearly going to change. I adopted a technological solution for both database management and invoicing. These were areas where I knew I needed to use technology. I would have ended up spending more money in the long run if I had used an interim non-technological solution, like a manual bookkeeping service. I also knew if I was busy then, it wasn't going to get better later.

Unfortunately, the financial management software that was recommended was prehistoric and needed to be replaced a scant year later. Believe me, take the time to research this stuff thoroughly. Hire someone, if you have to. Ask other entrepreneurs what they use and whether it is working for them. You'll save money and, more importantly, time in the long run.

Saving money and time is a big part of the "why" of technology. Here's the "how." We have narrowed the field down to the essential tools. All of these tools are of particular importance in your first year. Because the ability to integrate these applications is so critical, look for "best of class" technology, the stuff that gets good ratings by the computer magazines and that have captured a lot of shelf space.

Information Management

Once you open the door to your business, you may find time and money hard to come by but there is one resource that will be overwhelmingly abundant — information. If not managed efficiently and effectively from the outset, this landslide of information can suffocate your new business. So let's focus on tools to help you gather, manage, and organize information.

Gathering

There is no better information-gathering tool in existence than the Internet. There are conflicting opinions about whether women are Internet users. Let's put this nonsense to rest, shall we? Of course we use it. Recent statistics indicate that women are leading the charge on the Net.

- 47 percent of women business owners currently subscribe to an online service, compared to 41 percent of men business owners.
- 51 percent of women business owners frequently use the Internet to communicate or send e-mail, compared to 40 percent of men business owners.
- 22 percent of women report frequent usage of the Internet to conduct research compared to 14 percent of men business owners.
- 9 percent of women entrepreneurs use the Internet to review business opportunities or make bids on contracts compared to 3 percent of men entrepreneurs.[9]

This is what the Internet can do for you.

Get Information The Internet (a network of computers around the world linked via phone lines) is a huge source of information, whether you know where to look or you do not. If you have the address of a particular site, like raisingyourbusiness.com, you can use an Internet browser like Netscape or

Internet Explorer to get where you want to go. Type in the address and you are off to the races. If you don't have the address of a Web site but you want information on homeopathic remedies for horses, for example, use one of the Internet search engines like Yahoo or AltaVista. Type in the key words — homeopathic, remedies, and horses — and see where it will take you. This is a great way to identify prospective clients, suppliers, and competitors and to keep up to date on what is important to them and what they offer. Information that you find in articles in popular magazines and newspapers are also online (www.inc.com). Search the archives the same way as you would search for horse remedies.

You can get almost any type of information online. In your business you may need:

- directory assistance for a phone number out of your region
- local public transit routes when travelling to that new customer or supplier site
- restaurant menus before making a reservation to entertain a customer
- theatre tickets as a staff perk
- searchable databases (free and pay as you play) to search for prospects, suppliers, and competitors and to add them to your database without retyping.

Searching for this information online saves you time and money, gives you a better shot at getting the most up-to-date information, is always accessible — seven days a week/24 hours a day — and it's a blast.

Get Help Some sites like IBM's Small Business Advisor Online (www.ibm.can.com) provide tools that help you identify areas in your business that could be leveraged using technology. Some, like *PC Magazine*'s site (www.pcmag.com), provide information on good technology buys after having tested the key players in different areas of technology for functionality, suitability to task, and reliability. Still others provide opportunities to advertise for free like Industry Canada's business information site called Strategis (www.strategis.ic.gc.ca). You can even take courses on technology online. Check out Bell Canada's site (www.learning.bell.ca).

Get Known The World Wide Web (www. — the commercial side of the Internet) should be viewed as simply another communications channel alongside print, radio, television, direct mail, etc. The decision to use the Web or not for this purpose should be based on the question, "What can the Web offer me that other either less expensive or more familiar communication channels cannot?" Most businesses would benefit from having a presence on the Web if only as a way for customers, suppliers, and industry associates to get basic information about the company and a feel for its visual brand. It is now somewhat of a cachet for a company to have a Web site. However, do not get caught up in focusing your marketing program on the Web unless your business model is built around it and/or it will provide you with a real and distinct advantage. This is especially important as many business owners rush to establish a home page or a Web site. The Internet is just another communication channel and a Web site is just another marketing tool. It may not be appropriate for your business, so be very critical. If you think that you would like to establish a site, you can either hire someone to create it (a basic site including a few graphics and up to 10 pages should cost about $1000–$1500), or you can create it in-house using a product like IBM's Home Page Creator or Microsoft's FrontPage. If you are not familiar with digital marketing, be sure you have someone who is to guide you through the process the first time. Bad design and bad information on the Web is worse than no presence at all.

Managing and Organizing

Once you have gathered the information that you want, the next monumental challenge is managing it and getting it to work for you. Contact databases or knowledge bases allow you to keep, track, organize, easily access, and use information about the people and businesses that matter to you — information like their name, address, e-mail address, preferred communication method, kids' names, buying preferences, when you last contacted them or they you. Many of the products such as ACT, Goldmine, Maximizer, Lotus Organizer, and Outlook are terrific because they allow you to integrate information about your contacts into your schedules and with your correspondence.

All of these integrate with all of the popular office suites such as Microsoft Office, Lotus SmartSuite, and Corel, although some are better than others. These suites or bundles of software that are sold and work together integrate with fax software such as Winfax and MSFax. They also integrate with popular e-mail packages that let you send Internet e-mail, such as MS Exchange and Eudora. Some, like Goldmine, have special functions that can track what sales are in the funnel and the possibility and date of closing the sale, all to help you track projections. Goldmine also has a built-in knowledge base and telemarketing scripting function that allows you to store and easily access information, such as price lists, that you access frequently or that you may require prompting on, such as the steps in qualifying a prospective client. Some are easier to use because they offer screens that simulate a paper-based system, such as Lotus Organizer's Daytimer look. Which one you choose depends on the functions that you deem most important to you.

Adding a document-management piece of software such as PaperMaster helps you create a seemingly paperless environment. Software such as this facilitates sharing, reduces administration, and doesn't require an increase in real estate for those extra filing cabinets.

Once you have the information you need and organized in such a way that you can find what you are looking for quickly and easily, planning becomes half the task it used to be. Whether it is planning your day, a product launch, your marketing activities, or a client sales presentation, making use of your contact database in conjunction with project management software or presentation software will help your operation run smoothly and successfully.

Communicating

As well as helping the gathering and managing of information, technology also offers some wonderful tools for communication. For writing letters, proposals, quotations, and for creating presentations, consider using integrated suites to combine words, numbers, and splash; your contact database to track who you sent what piece of correspondence to and when; or voice dictation, like ViaVoice or Dragon Naturally Speaking, if you are a two-finger typist.

For your voice communications consider using call display to see who is calling so that you can better manage your priorities throughout the day. You can get many of the trappings of an expensive phone system, like voice mailboxes, voice messaging, call forward, and call answer services from your telephone service provider. You may even choose to integrate your phone system with your contact database so that inbound calls pop up the caller's contact record as the call reaches your phone or your outbound calls can be timed and logged.

For electronic communications such as faxes, e-mail, and Internet chats, you may consider maximizing your benefits by using your fax software as a scanner or as a secretary to convert printed words into electronic text using the optical character recognition (OCR) function that comes with most fax packages. Just fax to yourself articles you want to keep, click start OCR, and watch your physical documents be translated into electronic documents without having to retype the whole thing. Use e-mail instead of voice to stay in touch with all your customers and prospects and to save on long-distance charges.

Here are a few final tips to make sure things go smoothly.

- Remember to plan, keep current, and backup regularly.

- Ask people who use the software you are considering buying how they are using it. Go to the technical support page of the company's Web site and scan the users' questions posted there before buying any technology so that you can get a feel for what the marketing materials don't really tell you — what doesn't work well.

- Be conscious of the importance of security. As your company grows, you need to have tighter restrictions on files, and if you are going to maintain your own Web site server, make sure you install a firewall (special security software) on your Web site to avoid the possibility of someone getting into your system from the Internet.

The Hard Stuff

The level and extent of hardware you will need to purchase or lease really depends on three main things:

1. What kind of business are you in? Are you a service provider? Are you producing or distributing a product?

2. What are your plans for growth? Do you want to continue to work solo? Have a staff? Offices around the world?

3. Will your operations be centralized or will you require remote access to your information systems?

We recommend that your basic hardware be able to accommodate basic word-processing, spreadsheet, sales database management, scheduling, financial management or bookkeeping, e-mail, and Internet browsing. Today, a good-quality desktop computer with at least 24 megabytes of memory or RAM, 1 gigabyte of storage or hard drive space, a 15-inch colour monitor, and a fax/modem that connects at 28.8 kilobytes per second would handle these tasks without too much ado. If you travel a lot, you may wish to go with a laptop computer with similar specs (an internal modem a must). If you have a number of people that need to access the same information, you will have to substantially increase these criteria when you look for a computer to act as the main server. Finally, a laser printer with a minimum of 300 by 300 dots per inch for high-quality output is a good bet. Maybe even consider a backup colour bubble jet printer to snaz things up a bit. If being accessible no matter what is part of the job description, you'll either need a cellular or PCS phone or pager.

My neighbour, Carolyn Hamill-Best, is an accountant who runs a home-based business that specializes in automating small business financial systems. She has a great tip for technology newbies. The world of computers changes so fast, it's liable to give you the bends. A scant six months from now (or even less), our recommendations will become obsolete. Caroline suggests you take the computer section in your local paper, look at the ads, and see what the common "vital statistics" are. If everyone is advertising a Pentium 333 megahertz processor, with a 4 gigabyte hard drive and 128 Kb of RAM, then that's what has likely become minimum industry standard, and that's what you should be looking for.

The Soft Stuff

Every business should be using the following categories of software:

- Database software or contact management software: ACT, Maximizer, Goldmine, Outlook, FileMaker Pro, ClarisWorks, Access
- Finance software: Entry level — QuickBooks, MYOB, Simply Accounting, Small Business Financial Manager, QuickTax. A step up — ACCPAC
- Word processing software: Microsoft Word, Corel Wordperfect, ClarisWorks
- Spreadsheet software: Microsoft Excel, Lotus 123, ClarisWorks
- Presentation software: Microsoft Powerpoint, Corel Presentations
- Backup software: Retrospect. Most tape backup manufacturers provide the software you will need.
- Virus protection software: McAfee Viruscan, Inoculan, Norton, Virex
- Web browser: Microsoft Internet Explorer, Netscape Navigator/ Communicator
- Other software: MS Exchange/Messaging (e-mail), Eudora (e-mail), Acrobat Reader, Winzip (compresses large files).

Optional Software

- Graphics software: Photoshop, Canvas, Illustrator, Painter, Quark, Pagemaker
- Web site creator: Microsoft FrontPage, IBM's Home Page Creator, BBEdit, Adobe Pagemill, HOTMETAL Pro.

The Important Stuff

Ellie Rubin, entrepreneur and author, and her husband Christopher Strachan, own a media archive and library software firm, The Bulldog Group Inc. It's headquartered in Toronto with offices in Los Angeles, London, and Amsterdam and has 60 employees worldwide.

Since Ellie is one of those classic "techno-weenies" I so fondly refer to, I asked her to share some tips on the best way to protect your investment in technology.

- Make sure you hire the right people when sourcing the equipment and when training people on how to use the technology. Hire people who know how to troubleshoot as many issues as possible. There is no use getting a sophisticated computer system and then not having anyone who can help people get familiar with it and fix problems (because there always are problems) fast. This person might be someone in your organization or someone on contract.
- Remember, you get what you pay for. A customer asks the computer sales-person, "If these computers are as inexpensive as you say they are, how do you make a living?" "Easy," says the salesperson. "We make our money fixing them."
- Make sure your people are well trained and respect the cost of technology. That doesn't mean just the equipment cost, but usage fees and so on.
- If you are in your first year of business, find an expert who can help create a long-term plan. Get someone who can help you map out your projected technology needs to ensure that you are not buying something that will limit you as your company grows. Get the expert to comparison shop for you and ask others what they use. Once you make a decision, make sure that you are comfortable with your choice. Ongoing technical support is essential.
- You need to ask your technology support person questions. Ask for refer-ences from other customers, especially ones who had similar needs to yours. Make sure the person trains you directly on a program to verify their ability to train your employees. Give them a small job and pay them for it as a test for what you will want them to do on a larger scale. Get a per-sonal referral from others you trust, but make sure that they are in your price range. Do not necessarily go to a large company; if your job is rela-tively small, you may not get the attention you need.
- In terms of the technology service provider, there are various plans. Some are based on a flat fee, others on usage. Ellie suggests sticking with a well-known technology provider rather than a small one. She says she knows people who chose the smaller one and their providers eventually closed down shop. Often there are trial periods. Once you determine and assess your needs you can determine what plan works best for you.
- There are tons of books on this topic that will give you a good grounding. Ellie believes that speaking with others in your industry with similar needs

is the best way to get familiar with what kind of technology to use at the various stages in your company's growth. Be careful that you do not buy the very top end or invest in technology that is way beyond what you need and will need in the foreseeable future. This often leads to higher costs and a high level of fear and frustration on your part as you try to wrap your mind around technological capabilities that you don't need and that require a higher level of familiarity and knowledge.

Integrating Spiritual, Emotional, and Physical Health

Your first year is crammed full of decisions about technology, image, hiring, firing, sales, and marketing. This process of raising a business can be so all-consuming, before you know it, it can suck everything out of you. You may not even be aware that it's happening. Before we leave the first year and get too deep into the toddler years, we need to figure out a way not to lose touch with the stuff that makes us *who we are*. Our core self, the very essence of who we are, needs daily acknowledgement of her existence. She needs nurturing and care. After I started WMI, my core person went into deep hiding. I stopped doing the things that kept me aware of her. And I stopped doing the things that gave me deep personal joy. Sure, the business gave me a kind of joy, but not the sustaining kind that you get from inner peace and a balanced lifestyle. I discovered first hand that if I didn't remain centred, I was of little use to myself, let alone anyone else. I discovered how integrated with our emotional selves our bodies really are. To believe that you can ignore your spiritual and physical health for prolonged periods of time with no consequences is dangerous to your overall well-being and performance. It is critical that you care for the primary asset of your business — *you*. After all, you are at least as important as the computer or the photocopier.

For seven years, after I hit the magic age of 30, I took great care of my total person, inside and out. I exercised religiously. I had massages to ease the stresses I put upon my body. I stopped eating red meat, gave up alcohol, and spent time doing things that gave me joy. I travelled a bit. I spent a lot of time with soulmates. I cherished and nourished my relationships with friends and family. I devoured books from spiritual gurus like Scott Peck and Thomas Moore. Along with spiritual reading, communing with nature also helped me understand the higher, natural order of things. I came to recognize the value of time spent on becoming a *human being* instead of a *human doing*. I was as content as it is humanly possible for someone to be.

Now, seven years of dogged practice living a balanced life is a long time. Yet, because I hadn't deeply considered the ramifications of becoming an entrepreneur, the wheels began to wobble when the rubber hit the road. I didn't put any thought into how I would maintain these life-enhancing activities after I began WMI.

Almost the second the company was born, these habits evaporated. It started with exercise, which went from four to five times a week to whenever I could find time. My ability to handle the monumental stress that came with starting a business was dramatically reduced. Massages became a luxury. My diet suffered and my weight crept up. I said no in all the wrong places, like to time with friends and family. Because I feared not being able to pay the bills, I said yes to any form of business, regardless of the consequences to our cash flow and human resources. I ceased to live one day at a time and lived constantly in fear of the future. I spent a lot of time beating myself up for what I perceived to be less than 150 percent effort every single day, since the company was an extension of me. I became so preoccupied that if I were anywhere near a tree, instead of enjoying its presence, I walked into it. Because everything needed my immediate attention, my ability to let go of any kind of control, especially the destructive kind, disappeared.

I let go of the things that gave me personal joy. Why? Because I *thought* I had no time. I believed that time spent on the business would be of far greater value than time spent on maintaining emotional, spiritual, and physical balance. I began the process of shrivelling inside. My world became very small. It was only when I was snake belly low to the grass that I began to see the black hole I was living in.

I finally stopped the downward spiral by slowly introducing those spiritual principles back into my life — exercise, proper eating, becoming more gentle with myself, accepting that I was doing the best I could. To be in the public eye, open to constant scrutiny, is exceptionally tough for a perfectionist. I can't begin to tell you the number of times I laid awake at night, groaning with embarrassment as I relived, blow-by-blow, a nationally broadcast television interview or a filled-to-capacity seminar that, in my estimation, I had blown. I wasted so much vital energy beating myself up for anything that was less than perfect. I eventually had to give it up as a bad habit and began to learn how to cut myself some slack. I had a daily mantra that went, "I am a mere mortal. I do good work and I do bad work. But at all times I am doing the best I can."

I finally learned to say no. Oh yes, and I got pregnant. That did more to set me back on track than just about anything. Kate's well-being depended on it.

Please take the time *now* to rediscover what gives you joy. Figure out a way *now*, when the business is in its infancy, to make it stick. When you get into the full swing of entrepreneurship, self-nurturing gets much, much tougher to sustain. If you can, work into your business plan how you intend to keep your sanity. Whatever it is that gives you joy, *hang on to it for dear life.* Just as important as figuring out financing is figuring out how to be with friends, family or your pet, maintain your exercise program, take long walks, listen to music, read, go to movies, meditate, or dance in a mosh pit. I spoke at a conference in Winnipeg last year and stayed on afterward to participate in a workshop on work/family balance. One of the exercises was to think of the things we do to bring us joy or connection. I was sitting at a table with both white and Aboriginal women. Most of us came up with ideas like candlelit bubble baths and a night out at the movies with the girls. To my dying day, I'll never forget one Native woman's recipe for joy and balance. Very quietly, she said, "I kill a moose."

Everyone at the table stopped speaking and looked at her. "Say what?" I asked.

"My husband and I charter a plane to go up north overnight and we go moose hunting. Usually, he shoots and I clean." She said this as matter-of-factly as I would say "I get a massage."

There was dead silence for about 10 seconds and then we all broke up, including the story-teller herself. There were over 700 women in the room and she won for most original idea, hands down.

Imagine there is a bank that credits your account each morning with $86,400, carries over no balance from day to day, allows you to keep no cash balance, and every evening cancels whatever part of the amount you had failed to use during the day. What would you do? Draw out every cent, of course. Well, everyone has such a bank. Its name is *time.* Every morning, it credits you with 86,400 seconds. Every night it writes off, as lost, whatever of this you have failed to invest to good purpose. It carries over no balance. It allows no overdraft. Each day it opens a new account for you. Each night it burns the records of the day. If you fail to use the day's deposit, the loss is yours. There is no going back. There is no drawing against tomorrow. You must live in the present on today's deposit. Invest it so as to get the utmost in health, happiness, and success. The clock is running. Make the most of today.

The Top 10 Entrepreneurial Traps

You can't do much about the length of your life, but you can do a lot about its depth and width. So, what do you do when you discover, as I did, that your business is running you instead of the other way around? Think long and hard about why. Chances are you've fallen into one of Thomas Leonard's top 10 entrepreneurial traps. Avoid doing any of the following:

1. Getting wedded to an idea and sticking with it too long. Don't marry a single idea. Remember, ideas are the currency of entrepreneurs. Play with many ideas and see which ones bring money and success.

2. Trying to be something other than an entrepreneur. Entrepreneurs are entrepreneurs. You'll give yourself a hernia if you try to act like other people. Your difference is your strength.

3. Believing your own BS. Entrepreneurs are genetically wired to be optimistic. Just don't believe everything you say to others.

4. Ignoring your cash position. The world (a.k.a. customers) doesn't respond to even superior products in the time frame that you think they should. You'll need plenty of cash to sustain yourself in the meantime.

5. Attracting weak staff members. Not that many great employees will put up with a mercurial or childish/immature entrepreneur. If you're attracting weak people, you'll need to mature as a human being.

6. Confusing possibility with reality. The successful entrepreneur lives in a world of possibility but spends money in the world of reality.

7. Selling too hard. If you find yourself selling an idea or product too hard to too many people, perhaps it's time to listen to why they are not buying and learn from that versus trying to become a better salesperson.

8. Not setting up support structures. Hire people and services to handle many of your business and personal needs. Most entrepreneurs do better when they are fully supported, even if transparently. Be responsible enough to arrange this.

9. Overdelegating. Most entrepreneurs overdelegate tasks and accountabilities to others, a.k.a. dumping. Better to learn the skill of knowing when and how much to delegate than to assume/hope/need that others will come up to speed quickly enough on their own. Most people cannot. (Author's note: This is not a problem most women have. *Au contraire.*)

10. Giving up. Some of the most successful entrepreneurs failed several times before doing extremely well. So, if you're failing, fail. And fail fast. And learn. And try again, with this new wisdom. Do NOT give up. Yet, do not suffer, either.[10]

Trying to Run Before You Can Walk

Businesshood, like parenthood, is a gamble. You never know when you are going to be driven out of your mind. The first year is overwhelming and anything but dull. We warned you, 365 days and not one of them the same. It's strange, though. While we are exhausted, we are also euphoric. We've managed to bring to life something that didn't exist a year ago except in our minds and our hearts. It now lives and breathes in the real world. It's an incredible accomplishment.

I remember thinking similar thoughts at Kate's first birthday party. I was standing back, watching her wobble precariously as she tried to chase her cousins, marvelling at the changes over the last year. I thought to myself, "It feels like we have accomplished the impossible. The exhaustion, the patience — thank God the hardest part is over." Just then some wisecrack came along who had obviously been reading my mind. "If you think you're tired now, just wait until they *really* learn to walk and want their independence. Then you'll know what patience, exhaustion, and victory really feel like."

And so we move to a new stage. As I did with Kate, I had to acclimatize myself to my business's toddler phase. I had to learn ways to manage both Kate's and the business's growth. Kate says "No" to everything and "I love you, Mommy" often. I want to hug her and throttle her in the same motion. My heart skips a beat when I see her, even if I have seen her only five minutes ago. She has taught me so much. It's not a big distance from walking to running or, as I discovered, walking behind and running after. In order to keep up with your toddler business you have to be prepared and realistic in your expectations. Now you have rapid growth coupled with independence. More things will happen that are outside your control, but you still have to deal with them. You will experience both good and challenging behaviours. As with all toddlers, your business will attempt to run before it has really mastered walking. In your attempt to be all things to all people and to take advantage of every opportunity that presents itself, you will likely suffer the "ever-expanding value proposition" syndrome and end up taking your business in a thousand directions. Then you'll have to realize that you can't service every request and that you can evolve your concept while keeping your focus on what makes you unique. The stakes will be higher, the learning curve steeper, but the rewards greater.

The 5 Toddler Years

*The more people have studied different
methods of bringing up children the more
they have come to the conclusion that what
good mothers and fathers instinctively feel like
doing for their babies is the best after all.*

Benjamin Spock (1903–1998)

"Has anyone ever died from lack of sleep?" I moaned.

It was 3:00 in the afternoon and I was sitting at my desk, still in the T-shirt that I had slept in the night before. My hair hadn't seen a comb since the morning of the day before. I couldn't tell you if I had eaten that day. My brain was completely befuddled and I was unable to make the simplest decision, like when to take a shower. I was talking to Paula, thankfully on the phone.

"Take heart, Joanne. I suspect it's better to die of exhaustion than boredom. Why so tired, chum?" Paula asked.

Groaning, I said, "It started about three weeks ago. 'Til then, we had been so blessed. Kate had been a model sleeper. She hadn't shown the slightest interest in getting out of her crib and she's two and a half, for Pete's sake. So, Michael and I have been sailing along with a night-time routine that's been a total breeze. It was 4:00 a.m. on a Saturday morning, and I was, naturally, asleep. I remember, however, feeling slightly disturbed, which made me slip from REM sleep into a more conscious state. I became aware of breathing that wasn't my own. I slowly opened my eyes, only to be staring straight into a pair of baby blues no more than a foot away from my face. A surge of adrenalin shot straight through me and my heart leaped right out of my chest. I bolted upright, looking incredulously at Kate, who, for the first time and without a sound, had managed to climb out of her crib. I had no idea how long she had been standing there staring at me. I was so astounded that I started to laugh. Kate stood there, grinning from ear to ear, incredibly proud of herself. From that second on, she cast aside her crib and tried to claim our bed as her own."

"Ah, I see. It's the 'I'm a big girl now' epiphany," Paula laughed.

"Yeah, but something really weird is happening. Because she's now a big girl, she flat out refuses to be in her crib, but she won't stay in her own 'big bed.' I mean, she was totally excited as she helped her dad take the crib apart and put her own big bed together. She chose her blankets and took great pride in lining up every member of her stuffed menagerie, all 893 of them. But she still insisted that she sleep with us, we sleep with her, or hold her hand until she fell asleep. If I don't get some sleep soon, I'm going to die."

"Good Lord," Paula said. "It's like she really wants to be a big girl yet at the same time hold on to her baby status. That must be heart-wrenching to watch."

"That's an understatement. One night I said to her, 'Honey, Mommy and Daddy need to sleep all night in their bed and you need to sleep in your bed. You're a big girl now.' She was sobbing when she said, 'I don't want to be a big girl. I want to be a baby.' This from a kid who if you tried to help her put on a sweater or pour her a drink would become totally indignant because, in her words, 'I can do it all by myself.'"

"What do you think is going on in her mind?" Paula asked.

"Gut response?" I answered. "Parent torture."

"Any other ideas?" Paula asked.

"Actually, yes. She's a toddler. She is growing so fast that I think she is confused by the rapid changes. She wants to be a baby but cast aside baby things at the same time. She wants to be a big girl, but there are things she can't quite do yet. The crib to bed thing is the perfect example. Dust the crib and sleep in a big bed, but only if Mom and Dad stay with her. She's got a mind of her own but the notion of consequences hasn't been fully developed yet. It's kind of like a 'dependent independence.' You know, this child-rearing thing is a little like wrestling a gorilla. You can't quit when you're tired, you can only quit when the gorilla is tired."

"Is it getting any better?" Paula asked hopefully. "Three weeks can be an eternity with no sleep."

"There has been major progress. She's up only once during the night now. But here's the kicker — once I'm awake, I can't fall back to sleep. That's when the committee in my head reconvenes and that's why I'm such a mess."

"Take heart, it doesn't sound like it's going to last much longer," Paula said.

"I know. It's been a torturous but fascinating process helping her come to terms with not being a baby anymore. Watching her trying to let go, test new waters, and then come running back to us, only to venture cautiously out again. I don't want her to grow up and, at the same time, I can't wait. Strangely enough, I have this recurring sense of déjà vu. It's as though I've done this before."

"You have done this before, Joanne," Paula observed. "Think back to a couple of years ago when the company began to grow. Didn't it feel similar?"

"Maybe. I think I became as wingy from lack of sleep then as well," I said.

"Think about it. Companies in the toddler years, like Kate, often get to experience rapid growth. If you think back, when your business went through this stage, it started to have a mind of its own, though not yet fully developed. Its short attention span was constantly being tried by the rapidly increasing number of opportunities. The tough part was that you as the business owner were in the same developmental spot and so confusion naturally reigned. Like your business, you can't hold Kate back or stifle her ability to learn and explore new opportunities on her own. But you have to balance being too permissive with assuming control when you need to protect her. You become the safety net, the watchful eye that knows when to step in before things get dangerous."

"That's so true," I said. "I felt I needed to be all things to all people — staff, family, and especially customers. I took on business and activities that I had no business doing. I lost sight of what made the company unique, albeit temporarily."

"Yeah, I remember only too well," Paula said. "And do you remember how I said there would come a time when you would need to leave your business toddler with babysitters the odd time? You would need to hire out certain functions to independent contractors. Then the time would come, when your business became an older toddler, that you would have to decide upon part-time or full-time care in the form of employees. And all of this would collide with your screaming desire to keep the company safe by making it stay close to home. This is a normal part of the growing process. But businesses in the toddler years often start running without mastering walking. And, as it was with your experience, it means more bumps and bruises along the way. But, like Kate, the business ends up better off in the long run if managed and guided properly."

"That's reassuring," I said. "So, can I come over and sleep at your house tonight?"

Moving Into the Big Bed

This chapter is about managing your first growth spurt so that you don't fall into the trap that most new entrepreneurs do, moving into the big bed too soon. In business parlance, this means your expenses are growing faster than your sales. The result is simple: losses instead of profits. Most entrepreneurs do what I did when I became overwhelmed by rapid growth. I got absorbed with the workload and added overhead expenses to help manage the load. The next thing I knew, I found myself frantically looking everywhere, anywhere, for more money, all the while baffled as to how I got to such a state.

These toddler years are the years when you are trying to be all things to all people. There are a few signals that your business is now moving into the "terrible twos." On the personal side, you may begin to experience overload, staffing issues, and internal strife; on the financial side, no profits and cash flow crunches; and on the customer side, not enough business, focus problems, and poor customer service. You need to ask yourself....

Personal Overload

Are you feeling the weight of the blur among priorities? Are you so overwhelmed with working "in" the business that you don't have any time to work "on" the business? Are you feeling vulnerable because you may not

have all of the skills or experience needed to handle this stage? Are you finding it difficult to keep your personal choices relegated to your personal life and
prevent them from spilling over into your business life? And vice versa?

Tough Staffing Issues

Do you worry about your staff "wearing out"? Or are they just plain not
pulling their weight and taking more from the business than they are giving
to it? Are they sticking with you during the tough times like Michelle did,
or are they bailing out? Do you struggle with keeping the good ones and
finding a way to let the not-so-good ones go?

Internal Strife

Is an internal struggle within the ownership or staff diverting precious time
and energy away from the business? The time and energy that Barb and I
spent trying to fix our problems could have been used to close a lot of additional business. It's important to watch if the personal circumstances of employees or owners are overflowing into and having a negative effect on your
company.

Lots of Business But Still No Profits

Have you lost sight of your profit goal or are you just finding it difficult to determine if you are actually getting there? Are you convinced that you are
running your business with enough profit or any profit at all? I couldn't figure out how a company as busy as ours still struggled to make a profit.

Cash Flow Crunches

You know what a cash flow crunch is; the anxiety around payroll time or
guilt as a result of delaying payments to some suppliers. Are you feeling the
discomfort of constantly calling your clients to get them to pay up? I always
felt that calling the client to get them to pay us made us sound too desperate. We are *so* over that now. Or, are you reluctant to do so because your invoice was so late in being sent?

Not Enough Business

Are you having difficulty making sufficient sales each month to cover your expenses and your profit target? Are you sure that what you are doing to get new
business is paying off? For example, we sent out no fewer than three mass
mailings of *Balancing Act* to our target markets. It was a seriously expensive way

to market and frankly, even to this day, I haven't a clue if it paid off in terms of getting new business. My gut says no, so we don't do this anymore.

Lost Customer Focus

Have you lost your ability to see the ends because you are constantly doing battle with the means? Have you expanded too quickly, in too many, or in the wrong directions? Are you trying to focus on too many business missions and too many types of customers, therefore stretching your resources too thinly? During one particularly intense period in our growth spurt, I had agreed to pilot our program in two different institutions. That meant not one but two complete customizations. Customizing the day-long program was months of work on top of what was already a frenzy. I was completely worn out. I went to the doctor complaining about symptoms of mono. After asking me no more than 10 questions in five short minutes, she diagnosed me as having clinical depression and prescribed Prozac. Shocked and appalled at such a serious diagnosis in such a short time, I called my doctor brother-in-law. He said, "You are a classic burn-out." Instead of the "Take a Prozac and call me in the morning" approach, he said, "Take a holiday and call me in two weeks." I followed his advice and my sanity and equilibrium was restored. We nicknamed those two pilots the "Prozac Projects." That full bottle of Prozac sits prominently on a shelf in my office as a sobering reminder never to be that stupid again.

Poor Customer Service

Is the business fraught with a large number of complaints about your products or service? Is the number of requests for refunds or discounts going up while your number of customers is going down? I witnessed first hand from a customer's perspective what happens when a company is broadsided with a huge growth spurt. One of my suppliers experienced exponential growth when they landed Bell as an account. Consequently, customer service was dramatically affected. There were times when she couldn't get back to me for a couple of weeks. Since we were also in a growth phase, many of my issues required immediate attention. I also found that the poorer service I received, the more demanding I became. In short, I became this supplier's worst-case customer. As we will see later, we had to take drastic action.

Those entrepreneurs who are aware of these potential pitfalls and make the necessary contingency plans will find this stage exciting, adventurous, and extremely fulfilling. But those who do not prepare themselves for the "terrible twos, the trying threes, and the fearsome fours" will ride the wildest rollercoaster in the amusement park as their business rushes head long into a crisis state. This chapter will help orient you around the twos, threes, and fours. In reality, these years in both your biological and business children's lives are not at all terrible, trying, or fearsome. This is when they begin to test their boundaries and go through the wondrous experience of discovering who they really are. These children only tend to become terrible if you try to have absolute control over something you have no business trying to control in the first place. I have found if I guide instead of control, nurture instead of jump in and fix, let go instead of force, the experience of the toddler years, with both Kate and my business, becomes far more pleasant and much more rewarding.

All Things to All People

In my first year, I learned that "I must do something" always solved more problems than "Something must be done." It was the most amazing feeling to turn nothing into something, a vision into reality. If you too have done this, promise us you will take a moment, right now, to consider the magnitude of this accomplishment.

As with every other business stage, advice abounds and is usually divergent. You will hear from the pundits contradictory directives, everything from "Expand your product line" to "Stick to your core business." "Hire before you need to" to "Take on only what you can handle yourself." I was told by one adviser that I'd be foolish to expand into the training business. He told me it wasn't my core business and I should stick to what I knew — keynote speaking and writing. If I had followed that advice, I wouldn't be writing this book. I'd be writing a book on surviving a bankruptcy. Not that fear of bankruptcy is such a bad thing. Frank Borman, former astronaut and now a business executive, says, "Capitalism without bankruptcy is like Christianity without hell."[1]

So many opinions and so little time. Be very clear, however, that because of this, it is perfectly normal to experience a crisis of confidence. Or several, for that matter. Look closely at the poised, confident image you see of Paula and me on the cover of this book. (I'm the cute one.) We got that way by having *and surviving* crises of confidence at every stage of the business. Some days, every 12 minutes. Often, at 3:00 a.m. Oh yes, and remember that 3:00 a.m. witching hour that plagued us at the start-up phase of our business? It's ba-a-ack! Times 100.

So what type of parent do we need to become to guide our toddler business through these next two to three years? Just like with parenting a biological child, our role has to evolve in step — no, strike that — ahead of step with our business. My last thought each night before drifting off is, "Please God, tomorrow, please let me stay just 20 minutes ahead of Kate and the business."

We now have to play the part of fearless leader, inexhaustible cheerleader, and proud mom. This, alongside the rational, reasonable, responsible disciplinarian and counsel called the manager.

Me, Leader

Becoming a leader is often synonymous with regaining yourself. It is precisely that simple, and it is also that difficult. Because of the incredible demands on our time, we need to learn the fine art of establishing boundaries.

Once, at the height of my despair, I told Paula I was going to blow up, that I just couldn't do any more. She said, "You have to do one more thing, Joanne. Do less."

My response? "Easy to say, but how does everything get done that needs to be done?"

Paula replied, "Who decides what needs to be done? Isn't that you? Isn't that one of the main reasons that you started this business in the first place, to be able to control what gets done and how? Well then, it's time to reassume control. As the primary caregiver of a toddler business, get used to it, woman, you have to master the art of *no*."

The truth of this resonated deeply. I was so exhausted and worn out that I started to cry.

Paula passed me a tissue and said, "Now, let's look at how, as an entrepreneur with a growing business, you might be able to get a grip on how you are doing things. You need to become better at setting your boundaries."

Wow, was this hard. Saying no wasn't part of my sterling skill set. It was tough to become an effective leader when I was indeed being pulled in 900 directions by 900 different people. Setting boundaries? I was so clued out, I didn't even know the words to say. Paula shared her practical approach that helped me evolve in my new role as leader and attempt to stay sane as well.

1. Let others know in advance what your boundaries are: "I can't be disturbed between 3:00 and 5:00 on Monday or Wednesday afternoons," or "I'm not available for any appointments before 10:00 a.m. each day."

2. If some people aren't respecting those boundaries, let them know the very minute they have overstepped and ask them to stop. Say, "Sorry, I can't answer your question right this minute. As I mentioned, I'm not available until...."

3. If they are particularly dense and still persist, escalate your reply to insistence: "Please find another time when I am available to discuss this. I can't right now."

I discovered the hardest part was not setting the boundaries, it was respecting them myself. As for other people, I learned that, just like a toddler, boundaries will always be tested before they are respected. It's always easier for people to respect what they clearly understand and what is consistently applied. That's the stuff of effective leadership. Easier said than done? You bet. Dennis R. Tesdell, a business and personal development coach, offers help on how to hold true to your boundaries in a civil way when they are being challenged.

Use "I" Statements Rather Than "You" or "We" Statements

When you start a sentence with "We" or "You," you are speaking for a lot of people or for someone else. Using "I" statements "owns" what you say as speaking for yourself in a direct and clear way. If you want to give a less defensive response, and have clarity and power, start your sentences with "I." It shows you respect yourself and feel fine owning your opinions, feelings, and needs.

Be Willing to Have "Compromise" Boundary Discussions

This is helpful if the situation you are in is not a clear boundary invasion, or black and white. You can state a boundary conditionally and still allow the person to clarify for you or explain their words or actions. An example would be, "I'll go with you to the dinner, but I cannot stay past 10:00 p.m. I have to be up early tomorrow." There you are meeting the person half way and still setting and holding to your boundary and your need for a specific time frame.

If You Are Not Getting Anywhere, Be Willing to Change Topics or Move On

Sometimes, trying several things to communicate your boundaries and how you are feeling doesn't work. If that is the case, and you do not want to or cannot leave the situation, it is helpful to allow for the flexibility of a change in topic. One way to do this is to change from discussing your first topic and express how frustrated you are feeling in trying to resolve things. This is a shift from the original problem to the "process" problem. Some appropriate statements might be, "We're going in circles here, so why don't we just agree to disagree?" or "I don't know about you, but I'm tired of this discussion and I'm wanting to end it. Maybe we can talk about it another time." When it becomes obvious there is nothing but a lose/lose situation, it's usually best to give it up and save your energy and time.

Bring in the Fog

"Fogging" is an assertiveness technique that has been taught for many years. Basically it is used when you are in a touchy situation with a stubborn or agitated person and you want to state your position or boundary without getting into a debate or fight about it. The way to do this is to acknowledge the other person's statement or position without agreeing or disagreeing with them. It is an ambiguous response from you, confusing them (hence the name "fogging"), and it often prevents any form of confrontation. It's like saying, "Yes and no." For example, if someone you work with is telling you they know the "right" way to do what you are doing (some people call them "Know-It-Alls") you reply with, "Maybe you feel that is the best way for me to do this, Madeline. I feel just fine doing it the way it works for me, doing it my way." That usually diffuses things. They may be trying to make you wrong, but in your response you don't resort to making them wrong, which often causes a fight and ill feelings, and is unnecessary.

I discovered the real challenge of becoming a leader is to lead by example. That's a lot of pressure, but done right it's very powerful. Here is one of the best illustrations of this: "Early in life, I decided that I would not be overcome by events. My philosophy has been that regardless of the circumstances, I shall not be vanquished, but will try to be happy. Life is not easy for any of us. But it is a continual challenge, and it is up to us to be cheerful, and to be strong, so that those who depend on us may draw strength from our example."[1] This was said by Rose Kennedy.

Me, Manager

I'll bet you can relate to having "too many" everything. Too many appointments, meetings, things to do, phone calls to make, paper to shuffle, stuff to read, interruptions, unexpected events, unmet needs, crossed lines of communication. I'd also bet that you are tired and feel guilty about having "too much" undone stuff. But as Richard Carlson says in his book, *Don't Sweat the Small Stuff*, your inbox will be full when you die.

While your superhuman entrepreneurial powers have worked extremely well up to this point, it is right about now that it becomes essential to modify your approach to getting things done. There can be no denying that what you have done up to now has resulted in your being able to get a new business off the ground. But you will find that unless you evolve to being able to include and manage others, things will simply cease to work. At this age of your business, you will need to modify your language from "I" to "we" when referring to accomplishments, and from "Go!" to "Let's go!" when needing to get something accomplished. You need to move from knowing how it gets done to showing how it gets done. You need to lead instead of boss, coach instead of drive. A good manager takes a little more than her share of the blame, a little less than her share of the credit.

In our toddler businesses, we have to rewire our sense of accomplishment from being triggered when we do something ourselves to when we have supported others who have made it happen. While micro-management, managing down to the smallest detail, will drive you and your company into the ground, too much of a "hands-off" approach will turn your business into a wild child that will burn itself out.

If you are anything like Paula and me, the only thing we go through more of than water on a hot day is time management secrets, systems, solutions, and software. I have resigned myself to the fact that you can't manage time, only what you or someone else does with it.

Cynthia Calluori, an executive coach for women in corporate Canada, shared with us a couple of pointers on how to work smarter instead of longer:

- ask for what you need instead of what you think the other person can give
- say "no" first and then negotiate to "yes"
- most importantly, stop accepting or tolerating what you don't like.

So now that you are learning to reframe, reposition, and redeploy yourself in your new role in your toddler business, what about the rest of the crew? How do you manage to keep and inspire those who continue to grow with the company and free the business from the burden of those who don't?

Managing and Motivating Employees

Keeping the Good Ones

After you go through the investment of finding, selecting, and training an employee, they will eventually be ready and able to start giving something back to the organization. Now the challenge is to keep them. You need to figure out ways to motivate your employees and help them keep pace with the growing responsibilities of their position as they fill the ever-changing needs of the organization. This was supremely challenging in my early years. I couldn't figure out how to add being a super coach and manager to my already staggering job description. Through personal experience and Paula's help, this is what I learned.

- Share everything.
- Ask for the moon but do so clearly.
- Supporting your staff does not mean doing it all.
- It's the small stuff that really matters.
- Training means growing for tomorrow.

Share Everything

Overcommunicate! More is always better. Though I tried as best I could, with travelling and things whirling about at breakneck speed, this was often a tall order. Paula also struggled with this. We both spend most of our time inside our own heads with our own thoughts. I'm always astounded when Rosa or Michelle react in surprise to something I was absolutely positive I had already told them. Paula's business partner, Debbie, has to constantly beat her over the head with the fact that others do not have mind-reading powers.

So, some advice from two people who have finally learned the hard way about the amazing benefits of sharing information. Please pay close attention.

- Share information, both the good news and the bad.
- Share the results of the work, both the rewards and the disappointments.
- Share the responsibility, not just the tasks.
- And most importantly, share yourself. It fosters open communication and creates trust.

It means being a grown-up. Trust your staff, customers, peers, colleagues, and bankers with the truth. Respect them enough to leave it up to them as to how they handle it.

Ask for the Moon But Do So Clearly

The flip side to the "overcommunication" coin is "high expectations." They go hand in hand. However, many time-pressed, busy-minded entrepreneurs forget the explanation part of the expectation equation. We feel justified in setting high expectations for everyone around us because we live by the same standard. But since we are setting expectations for someone else, we have to be clear about what our expectations are and how they are to be accomplished.

There is something called the Carver model. Its fundamental principle is that you could set the goals for the organization and then tell the staff what they can *not* do in order to achieve those goals. For example, if you need to reduce expenses in a particular area, tell the staff the target needed to be achieved, say five percent. Explain this isn't to include a downgrading in the quality of service to the customer. This simple, non-conventional approach really works because it allows staff to come up with their own ideas, their own means, their own approach to making things happen. It releases you from the shackles of the inevitable ten thousand questions on how something should be done and the equal number of requests for permission.

Willie Shoemaker, the best jockey ever, said that he kept the lightest touch on the horse's reins. "The horse never knows I'm there until he needs me."[2] Today, because of this approach, I have stopped thinking to myself, "If I have to figure it all out myself, what am I paying you for?"

Supporting Your Staff Does Not Mean Doing It All

So the context, the bar, and the boundaries had been set for the staff. Next, I needed to learn to support others' successes — and expect those that I supported to do the same. Here is a lesson on distinctions, however. I learned the hard way that support does not mean *doing* their job. Nor does it mean solving the person's problems for them. Trust me, there is still not likely to be enough time to help them fight all of their fires and keep your own blazes under control. Support simply means giving encouragement, information, and perspective when asked for. The real value of support, I discovered, lay in making it "proactive."

We had a mega-huge project to complete where we had to translate all of our courses into French, find and train a suitable trainer, and roll out and complete the training program in three weeks across the province of Quebec. About six months before this was to happen, I asked Rosa what she was going to need in terms of support to handle her part. (Incidentally, her part constituted 90 percent of the whole project.) Well in advance of the roll-out, Rosa worked through what she was going to need to get the job done and highlighted the potential challenges. She used me as a sounding board along the way so I was able to add a few words of caution or encouragement. If there was a weakness in the planning process, I could alert her and I could also get a sense of where I might be needed down the road. We were quite anxious about this project. It was even bigger than the initial designing of the courses. The results? Spectacular. The project went off flawlessly, with only a minor annoyance or two. I gave Rosa support in the form of encouragement, but she pretty much singlehandedly pulled the whole thing off.

It's the Small Stuff That Really Matters

Communicate, expect, and then? Acknowledge — immediately and regardless of whether your acknowledgment comes in the form of praise or constructive feedback. Immediately after Rosa successfully pulled off the Quebec launch, I gave her a cash bonus. But acknowledgment can take many forms. What's most important is that you do acknowledge, not the size of the acknowledgment. Paying attention comes with a very affordable price tag. Around the time Rosa was to go on holidays, she got hit with a $1000 vet bill for her cat. The day before she left, she found an envelope with a little extra to take with her on vacation. She was speechless. This meant more to her than a $2000 raise. Informal appreciation, spontaneous celebrations, awards, special privileges, and bonuses are all terrific motivators, according to the Entrepreneurial Education Foundation.[3] As an alternative to cash, consider giving a gift certificate to ensure the money is spent on something the employee really wants rather than on paying bills. I've given $100 gift certificates from people's favourite restaurants. Certificates from their favourite clothing boutique is another idea. Incentives should be highly personalized. You might want to consider creating a questionnaire and asking your staff what incentives would be the most meaningful to them. This is a fun area in which to get creative. Change them frequently and tailor your rewards to reflect your company's values. Don't do as I did in the first year and get too busy and stressed to continually recognize exceptional performance. But it also helps to keep the words of economist Al Bauman in mind: "A wage hike is very hard to take away, but bonuses and profit-sharing can disappear very quickly in hard times.... More people are realizing that bonuses look like raises, but really aren't."[4] A balanced approach is always best.

Training Means Growing for Tomorrow

For small companies to grow, the people, including you the owner, need to grow. It is no longer true that you can manage your business growth by adding layers of people. Putting more people on a project to get it done more quickly doesn't necessarily work. You can't create a baby by having nine women pregnant for one month.

You have to keep ahead of the game to stay in it. That means making the absolute best out of your existing resources. Professional development doesn't have to be expensive to be valuable. I've sent Rosa and Michelle to professional development workshops and software training courses and have had a number of day-long in-house professional development days. To save her staff time and to provide "just-in-time" professional development, Paula highlights or summarizes articles of value, cuts and pastes relevant snippets of information from the net into e-mails, and leaves broadcast voicemails of sales techniques or phrases that she has found work well. Remember, growing your business will require that you make professional growth a condition for everyone's continued employment.

They Get Sick, They Leave

You can do all of the above to make sure your employees are happy, fulfilled, and inspired, but they are mere mortals. They get sick, they have family or personal issues, their circumstances change, and, yes, they leave — some with warning, some without. Regardless, you are usually left with a gaping hole in your organization and you find yourself having to dig deep for another incredible whack of time and energy to find, hire, train, and integrate someone new.

The only way to stave off this disaster is to plan. Succession plans are often referred to as what needs to be done when the business owner herself is ready to call it quits. We mean flat-out quits. Not to be confused in any way with the thousand and one everyday, run of the mill "I quits" that we constantly utter. You should create mini-succession plans for each of the people in your fold. So if you don't want to have to fill the gap yourself, what can you do to lessen the blow when key employees (and at this stage, it's likely that they are all key) have to take time off, either temporarily or permanently? You can:

- Cross-train your staff. When they have to cover for each other during vacations, sick days, and days off, have them note what they didn't know how to do or were unaware needed to be done. When Barb left, we scrambled to replace her and repeated the same mistakes again. Finally, we changed our system. Among Michelle, Rosa, and myself, we made it work. I took over the responsibility of sales (which should have been mine all along), Michelle stepped in as sales support, and Rosa did all the administration. Both Michelle and Rosa could do each other's job perfectly.

- Identify an understudy for each position. This person can be either already in the company or currently outside the organization. You need to know in advance what it will take to bring them over, either on a full-time, short-term, or consulting basis, and what it will take to bring them up to speed.

- Set up a reciprocal agreement with another business owner with similar staffing needs. You may even want to swap staff occasionally during non-peak times to get them familiar with each other's operations, systems, products, and services.

- Document as many of the critical processes as possible. We have a documented critical path that we use every time we close a large training contract. Every step and procedure is outlined. It makes any transition in staff more seamless.

- Have each employee do a walk-through of their responsibilities with you on a regular basis so that you are aware of how they have adapted to their ever-changing roles.

- Computerize all that you can afford. Replacing or upgrading hardware and software is often easier than replacing or redeploying employees.

Now, not all people transitions are outside your control. Sometimes you just need to grasp the reins before the horse grabs the bit.

Firing a Used-to-Be-Key Person

When I made the decision to write this book, I had other very tough decisions to make. I would be taking off the better part of a year. This meant that I didn't need two full-time administrators. Next to the breakdown with Barb, my most painful experience was having to let Michelle go. I wrestled with this decision far longer than was prudent. It was finally my business adviser who pushed me into action. "You're going to go broke if you don't cut some of your expenses." But, I reasoned, Michelle had been my trusted sidekick for three years. But, I reasoned again, her skill set was different from what I needed now since I had to narrow the business focus in order to survive. So I was forced to let her go. We both cried a river. But, I kept Michelle on for a period of time on a contractual basis because I couldn't bear to cut the cord completely.

Letting a person go can be one of the most distressing things in business, whether you own your own business or are an employee charged with that responsibility. This charge carries even more weight simply because of the size of the company. In the toddler years, your company's ability to absorb the impact of a poor performer isn't that great. Humorist Doc Blakely says, "Firing someone is healthy. It gets rid of the poor performer and gets the attention of everyone that wasn't fired."[5]

The starting point of an employee's termination actually happens long before the decision to fire. It happens when you give people clear feedback on whether or not they are meeting the standards of their job and what they need to do to continue in that position. Much easier said than done. Providing people with feedback when their performance is lacking is considered to be one of the most difficult tasks by new entrepreneurs.

I find myself often in a position where I have to confront someone in some way, whether it be to correct a mistake or get them more in line with the company mission. I used to detest telling people what to do when they weren't doing it right. I thought it was rude and bossy, no matter how nicely you tried to put it. The process involved in accepting that people may be angry with me was a very tough one. But frankly, it has become one of my most important business and life skills.

Just remember to be specific about the behaviour or issue that you have, ask for their feedback to round out your perception of events, and be clear on the consequences if the problem isn't fixed.

To be defensible in a court of law (and to be safe, just assume that is where you will end up), your feedback to the employee has to be in writing. Don't presume that being considerate will in any way be an adequate substitute for being "lawful" in these matters. Again, be sure to check with your provincial Employment Standards Act and an employment lawyer to ensure that you are within the law.

But let's assume the feedback doesn't work and the employee simply has to go. When you let someone go, it is *always* wise to have a formal exit interview and *always* in the presence of another person. It's in this interview that you advise the employee of your decision to terminate their employment. Give them your reasons for dismissal and tell them whether you want them to work out their notice period or if you intend to pay them in lieu of notice. That means they are free to leave immediately.

There are many reasons why you may choose to fire someone. But, as a new employer, you may be unaware that you don't have to have a reason — unless, of course, your employee belongs to a union. In that case, what you can and can't do is laid out in the union's collective agreement. You can let any employee go as long as you provide them with proper notice. The legal notice period depends on a lot of factors, not the least of which is how long the person has worked for you. It also varies from province to province so consult your provincial Employment Standards Act for the goods. Also, you should be aware that the Act only gives you the minimum notice period. A lawyer will take into consideration all of the variables and advise you as to the proper notice period. In most cases, the minimum notice requirement doesn't apply if people have been with you for less than three months. It also doesn't apply to those hired for a specific term or job, those who have been temporarily laid off, or to those people dismissed for "just cause," such as theft.

If you don't feel comfortable having someone continue to work during the notice period because they have access to your customers or important assets, pay them an equivalent wage for that period and then immediately show them the door. Even though you end up paying for work that isn't done, payment in lieu of notice is almost always the more prudent way to go. It eliminates any possibility for misunderstandings and allows both of you to immediately get on with life.

Whether they leave you or you fire them, you have to provide the person and the government with a Record of Employment. This is one ugly form. It must be completed, filed, and given to the employee within a specified period from their last day of work. That time period is set by your provincial Ministry of Labour. In that same time frame, you have to come up with the wages earned up to the day they left, money received in lieu of notice, severance pay (if applicable), and payment for any vacation time earned but not yet taken. Revenue Canada can provide you with an employer's guide. To give you a sense of how ugly this form is, Revenue Canada has people to help you complete it properly and to help you calculate what you owe the person.

No matter how they leave you, it may be wise to have the employee sign a general release. Get your lawyer to help you determine if a release is appropriate, and if so, help you prepare a document that will protect you from recourse by the outgoing employee. Some people tell the former employee that if they sign a release, they will give them references. Just remember that you're the employer, you can establish any policy that you want. You can decide never to give references or only to confirm the fact and dates of employment. Your lawyer can also advise you on the question of providing references and the appropriate thing to say.

Indispensability Breeds Vulnerability — Insure Yourself and Your Business

As both leader and manager of your toddler business, you are indispensable. Now you have to make a plan for when or if something happens to you. And this isn't all doom and gloom like being injured, getting sick, or, yikes, dying. What about if you decide to have (or not, but end up having) a little bundle of joy? An important W-FACTOR is that entrepreneurs who own more than 40 percent of their incorporated businesses are not permitted to contribute to Employment Insurance (EI) premiums. *All* sole proprietors and partners are not allowed. That is understandable since you have the power to lay yourself off. However, the flaw in all of this is that EI is the primary mechanism by which we are able to support ourselves during maternity leave. I know women entrepreneurs who returned to work a week after giving birth in order to keep the business going. I know the harrowing struggle I went through financially when I had Kate. Since I couldn't insure, I should have planned. More later on becoming a better financial manager.

So what happens if something goes either wrong or right and circumstances force you to be away from the business for an extended period of time? What can you do to mitigate the impact on your business during its very tender toddler years? It's called insurance. It's available to cover the assets of your business, namely you, your key people, your property, your revenue streams, and the well-being of your employees and suppliers.

There are a number of ways that you can replace lost income potential, or even soften the impact of losing a key person through illness or death. There are even ways to protect yourself against a natural disaster, theft, or a lawsuit against the company. Let's start with you.

People Assets

For those people whom you could simply not replace or replace at what you pay them (and that includes ourselves) you can arrange to purchase key-person insurance. This type of life insurance pays a fixed amount to either your bank if you have a loan, your business partner to help them buy your share of the business, or your family so they can close, sell, or buy the business.

You may also suffer an accident or become ill. Disability insurance will cover you by providing you with income if you are unable to work as a result of either. As we discussed in chapter 4, how much your benefit will be and how soon your benefit will begin will be reflected in the amount of the premium. Again there is a certain level of protection through Employment Insurance for those who are allowed to contribute to EI.

Business Assets

Regardless of whether you decide to insure yourself, make sure your business's ability to carry on and earn you an income is protected in case of an emergency, lawsuit, or natural disaster. Property and general liability insurance are the most common types that cover losses caused by physical damage, theft, or loss of use of certain things in your business. It will even cover you if someone gets hurt while visiting your place of business. Don't leave home without this kind of insurance. After all, you wouldn't drive a new car without collision and liability insurance.

Bad things do happen to good people and mistakes do sometimes occur even if you are careful and diligent. That's why there is business interruption and errors and omissions insurance. Business interruption (for example, fire or flood — "El Niño" insurance really) will provide you with money to cover your costs and potentially a loss in income. Errors and omissions insurance will help you with some of the costs of defense and settlement if something that you do or fail to do causes harm to someone else or their business. Both are significantly more expensive and a lot more difficult to get than the property or liability insurance. Do you need this kind of insurance? It depends on the type of business that you run and the risk and the impact of these events on your business.

Most of the premiums for the insurance that we have discussed are tax deductible. Check with your accountant to make sure that they are structured in such a way that you can claim them as business rather than personal expenses. Prepare yourself for how expensive they may be because the policies are often written on only one or two people in a small company. You may be able to reduce your premiums or shorten the waiting period before you are eligible. Use an insurance broker who shops around for you or join a club or a professional association. Many of these insurances are not available until your business has a bit of a track record. That's because many of the payouts are based on the business's income levels and key persons' salaries. That's why it's so important for you to thoroughly understand your business, and especially how your business makes money.

Understanding Your Business From the Inside Out

In my first year, I spent most of my time and energy creating sales, servicing customers, building a team, and paying my bills (when I had the money). If the words "financial management" had been added to this list, I would have run out of the room screaming. However, it got added to the list suddenly one day when I discovered we didn't have enough money to last to the weekend, let alone to payroll.

In the beginning, my business had been run primarily on gut feel and "just in time" crisis management. It became abundantly clear that I needed to be a touch more systematic and proactive. Just like its biological counterpart, my toddler business needed to have intuition and reaction replaced by consistency and discipline — especially when it came to things like adding new products, hiring more staff, figuring out pricing, and buying equipment. Financial management, as I discovered in a heated discussion with Paula, is a lot more than preparing financial statements, signing cheques, and deciding what or what not to spend.

Who Should Be Your Financial Manager?

It was a familiar lament. "Don't make me do this!" I cried.

It was the customary threesome sitting in Paula's office — me, Paula, and Sheila, her dog.

Paula was unrelenting. "Stop whining and get on with it. You need to get a handle on this part of the business. Your instinct has been great so far, but it isn't enough anymore."

"Why can't you do this?" I asked. "You like this financial management stuff. That degree on your wall says you're an accountant, for heaven's sake. Isn't this your job?"

"We've been through this already, Joanne. Your company's primary financial manager needs to be intimate with the whole range of your business. This person needs to understand not only where the business has come from, she needs to know where it is now and where it's going. This manager should also be heavily invested in the company's success."

Resorting to bribery, I offered hopefully, "That could be you. I'll pay you anything, name your price."

Paula rolled her eyes and continued with an exasperated sigh, "I could retire in the Swiss Alps with the money you have been threatening to pay me to do this for you. Listen to me carefully, Joanne. When I say the person needs to be heavily invested in the company's success, that rules out the bookkeeper who only comes in once a week for a day, the financial adviser who goes over your plan with you once a quarter, and your accountant with whom you may touch base once a month."

"But you see my financial statements…"

"Once a year and three months after your year end," Paula interrupted. "Face it, kiddo. The primary financial manager in your business is and always will be you, the owner."

"Yeah, but…"

"If you still want to argue that you can delegate the ultimate responsibility on this one, answer the following questions. They will point to the person who should be wearing this mantle. Who is responsible for determining what business you are in and who you call a customer?"

"I am."

"Who is responsible for establishing the price for your product or service?"

"I am."

"Who does the most worrying when cash is tight?"

"The bank." Paula's stare didn't waver.

"I do."

"Who had to personally guarantee the money borrowed from outside parties?"

"I did."

"Who has put their own unpaid time and money into the company?"

"I did. I don't like where this is going."

"Who figures out what to do when things aren't going as expected?"

"I do." I sighed deeply and began to shift uncomfortably.

"Who has to make the really tough decisions?"

"Yeah, yeah. So what does all this mean?"

"Do we agree, albeit reluctantly, that the primary financial manager of the business is the one with the most to lose and the most to gain?" Paula asked.

"If you expect me to raise my hand and volunteer for the job, you are sadly mistaken. I don't have a clue how to be a financial manager. I'm hard-pressed finding enough time to earn the money, let alone do the financial management thing," I pouted.

"Joanne, you're lumping this job with accounting, ratios, financial statements, and other unsavoury things. But it's not that stuff. It's simply understanding your business from the inside out. Contrary to popular belief, there is a difference between understanding how to read financial statements and understanding how to read your business."

"Read my business? Whaddaya mean, read my business? That doesn't mean calculating ratios, does it? I'll do a swan dive out the window before I'll go down that road," I said.

"I promise you won't have to. Look, I'm an accountant, for Pete's sake, and I discovered there was quite a difference between what I knew professionally and what I learned as an entrepreneur."

"Explain," I said.

"Did I truly understand the difference between reading a financial statement and understanding how my company made profit and generated cash, just because of my training as a chartered accountant?"

"No?"

"No."

"I'm shocked," I said.

"Why? Sure, I could pull together a set of financial statements from any mess that lay in front of me. I could fill pages with this ratio and that ratio. I could create and maintain the most complicated of financial spreadsheets. But just like every other entrepreneur, I had to learn by suffering the consequences of not really understanding until I actually lived through it how my company made and lost money and how long it took to convert my sales into cash. I learned first-hand about the perils of adding overhead to create profit instead of after profit had been created."

My eyes were wide with amazement. "Can it be true? Are you a mere mortal like the rest of us?"

Paula laughed. "What I knew about financial management really amounted to my training and experience with financial record keeping and analysis. While I did start my business with this solid foundation, the real lessons came to me as a result of having to make increasingly tough decisions about my business. And yeah, I was unsure whether those decisions would create the results I wanted. I did, however, feel a growing sense of unease when I made a decision based on gut feel and with only some vague sense of the financial impact. I wanted to really understand what was going to happen if I zigged instead of zagged. I wanted to know how much zigging and zagging I could do and still get the results I wanted."

"You can't tell me, though, that being an accountant didn't give you a decided advantage over an accounting dim-bulb like me?" I scoffed.

"Sure," Paula said, "I knew that an income or profit and loss statement gave me a picture of what income I had over and above, or not, my expenses for a certain period. I knew that it could show me how much my sales, minus directly related sales expenses, were contributing to overhead costs like rent and salaries. But income statements couldn't tell me diddly-squat about whether I would have enough money in the bank by the time the GST or the payroll remittances were due or when suppliers had to or could be paid. What I really needed to learn and understand to run my business was quite different."

"Such as?" I prompted.

"Well, to start with, I needed to know what that sales number and gross margin number had to be in order to ensure that I was not losing money and making a profit. I needed to know who was not generating their share of that sales number or who was running their area at too low a margin to cover their own share of the business's overheads."

"Like their own salaries, I presume," I said.

"Like their salaries. Sometimes I couldn't purchase a new computer or piece of software or hire one more person because there wasn't enough profit."

"I know that one well," I said. "What else couldn't you learn in your textbooks?"

"I needed to have money to make money. And I had to figure out how much in order to make a new sale. That was one of the biggest revelations. I also had to learn how much and what would have to go if we lost a major client account or couldn't collect the money the customer owed us," Paula said.

"Oh yeah, that's my personal favourite. Getting stiffed is a tad annoying," I agreed.

"Any loss is a very bad thing. It requires immediate and serious counteraction on the expense side in order to rectify it," Paula said. "I also learned that I could sell myself further into the hole if I sold things that cost more to produce than I could sell them for. I learned how critical it was to account for *all* of the costs, including marketing, administration, and financing, when deciding what we should sell to whom at what price. I had to learn how to figure out whether or not some of our products were even worth it.

"The same thing applied to a balance sheet. Wearing my accountant's hat, I knew the balance sheet showed me what I owned, including the promises from other people to pay me, also known as receivables. A balance sheet also showed me what cash I had in my bank account as well as what computers, desks, copiers, and printers we had bought. Naturally, it also showed what I owed to suppliers, the bank, employees, and my family. A balance sheet basically showed me how much profit or loss my business has generated from the moment we opened to any particular point in time."

"So how is that different from what you would need to know when you put on your entrepreneur's hat?" I asked.

"I had to make sure that what people owed me and what I could reasonably collect were always at least one and a half to two times greater than what I owed to others. This was so I could make sure that I had enough money at the right time to pay my overheads and suppliers," she said.

"Get out. For real? That's a pretty helpful guideline," I said.

"For real, although the number is a bit different for every business. And like most entrepreneurs, I used our bank balance as our financial bellwether. It wasn't really how much money was in the bank at any given point that was important, but rather the reason for the pattern or direction of that bank balance. If a series of balance sheets showed a growing overdraft, I had to figure out whether it was because of healthy growth or because the business was spending beyond its means."

"I always assume the worst," I said gloomily. "I discovered at one point that the bank was more of an owner of my business than I was."

"It's wise to assume the worst," Paula agreed. "Another thing I had to learn from that balance sheet was what financial return I was managing to reap on my investment of time and money. But frankly, this statement still didn't answer those questions about whether I could make payroll or pay suppliers."

"This is all planning stuff and not at all 'accountanty,'" I said. "What scared me was the thought of getting lost in the forest of financial analysis and never coming out the other side. Instead, it seems you're telling me that all I need to know is what the important numbers are and what they tell me about my business."

"That's right," Paula said.

"It's hard to believe that I can focus on a few numbers to understand everything that matters to me as the owner of a business. It sounds a lot like 'you can't control what you don't understand.' I imagine that understanding instead of guessing makes for a better night's sleep," I conceded.

"Eureka, I'm being blinded by that light bulb over your head," Paula cracked.

"Okay, okay, uncle. I'll be the financial manager. Net it out for me, what do I do now?" I asked grudgingly.

"Presuming that you have come to this place with your arm firmly wrenched behind your back and that your distress is likely being caused by a shortage of cash, your first charge as the financial manager is to find out why you don't have enough money. Is it because there is a profit issue, in other words, not enough money in the bank when the money is there? Or is it because there is a cash flow issue meaning the money is not in the bank when you need it because it's tied up somewhere else like receivables or inventory?"

"This sounds like a serious amount of work," I started.

"Don't panic. It does take some analysis and investigation to figure this out. But you can enlist the aid of your bookkeeper and accountant to help you compile the information. *You*, however, will need to do the analysis."

So, with Paula's help, I took the plunge and donned the hat of financial manager. And, of course, it wasn't nearly as painful as I had imagined. However, sitting on the dock at the cottage reading a good book on a sunny afternoon still wins hands down.

The first thing I had to learn was the meaning of a few key terms:

- **Profit and Loss Statement** A snapshot of how much income you've made minus your expenses over a certain period.
- **Balance Sheet** This shows what a company owns, what it owes, and what it has made since its inception.
- **Gross Sales** The total amount of sales in dollars — hopefully many dollars.
- **Cost of Sales or Cost of Goods Sold** The cost of the labour used to make the sale, the cost of the material, marketing, sales, and administration used to make and deliver each sale.
- **Gross Profit** The dollar difference between gross sales and the cost of sales.
- **Gross Margin** The percentage of the money left over after the cost of sales. Gross profit and gross margin are the same thing. Gross profit is expressed in how many dollars you have left over after you pay for the cost of sales and gross margin is the percentage of dollars you have left over.
- **Retained Earnings** The cumulative net profit that shareholders decide to keep in the company year after year.

The Profit Picture

The difference between a business that is merely surviving and one that is meeting its owner's personal and financial objectives lies, in fact, with the entrepreneur herself. Owners of successful businesses (and do recall that you are the one who defines success) can blend that optimism with healthy realism about their revenue streams — this, of course, while maintaining constant control over the bulging expense belly of the company.

Here is one of the simplest financial management lessons you'll ever get: *Always assume that your current revenue and profit streams will cease to flow at the end of each month and year. Find the costs to be trimmed since there is always expense fat in every company. It is healthy to try to do more with less.* It may be simplistic but it works. Why? Because it ensures that your view is balanced and includes both sides of the profit equation — sales and expenses. But which sales of which products or services to which customers should we keep, add, or delete? And similarly, which expenses? Rather than throw a gazillion financial ratios and calculations at you, we are going to help you to become better business owners, not accountants or financial analysts.

So let's look at the stuff that is most relevant to the decisions that you as business owner have to make every day. These would be the ones that are likely to have the greatest impact on the profitability and viability of your business. We'll start at the top with sales (okay, that's long enough) and move right along to the middle and meat of the matter, gross margin.

It's All in the Margin

Revenue is vanity… margin is sanity… cash is queen. Most entrepreneurs remain steadfast in their refusal to give up the notion that if they aren't making enough money, it's because they are not making enough sales. This probably stems from the fact that most of us have had to take whatever sales came our way when we first started in order to put food on the table. At this toddler stage, we need to take a step back and figure out whether we are making or losing money from the sales we make.

To do this, you need to become intimate with your margins. You have to know your cost of sales, i.e., how much the sale of each type of product or service is costing you. From there it becomes a simple subtraction exercise to find out how much is left over to cover overhead. This is known as your gross profit. The gross margin number is the one you will use the most because it's often easier to work in percentages. For example, if you have two products that you sell for different prices, your profit on each one will likely vary. Product A sells for $10.00 and you generally make $4.00 on every sale. Product B sells for $20.00 and you make $8.00 on every sale. Though the dollars or gross profit are different your gross margin percentage is the same — 40 percent.

Calculating Your Margin

Product/ service	Sales (a)		Cost of Sales (b)		Gross Profit (c=a−b)		Gross Margin % (c/a)		Total Sales % (a/Total a)	
	Mont	YTD*	Month	YTD*	Month	YTD*	Month	YTD*	Month	YTD*
Product A	1,000		500		500 = (1,000 − 500)		50% = (500/1,000)		6.25% = (1,000/16,000)	
Product B	5,000		3,500		1,500 = (5,000 − 3,500)		30% = (1,500/5,000)		31.25% = (5,000/16,000)	
Product C	10,000		8,000		2,000 = (10,000 − 8,000)		20% = (2,000/10,000)		62.5% = (10,000/16,000)	
Subtotal	16,000		12,000		4,000 = (16,000 − 12,000)		25% = (4,000/16,000)			
Commission on All Sales	1,500									
Total	16,000		13,500		2,500 = (16,000 − 13,500)		15.6% =			

*Year to Date

Try using the simple worksheet on the previous page to help *you* with *your* analysis (note the italics). Again, this is not an exercise that takes very long. It will help you decide whether a product or customer is costing you more than it's worth, whether you should accept or decline new business, or even whether you need to increase your prices or decrease your costs.

First, armed with a strong cup of coffee and a good night's sleep, find a comfortable chair. Take this worksheet and begin to list your main products or services down the left-hand side. From your financial system, have on hand the printed report that shows your monthly sales by product (standard fare in most financial computer packages). Slot these into column (a). If you track your cost of sales (i.e., direct labour, material, selling, administration, and promotional costs) by product, use the report from your software that tells you the total cost of sales for each product. Record them in column (b). We use QuickBooks Pro, which allows us to assign a project or job number to each client or program we work on. That way we can track all the expenses relating to a specific job, which makes figuring out whether or not we made any money a lot easier. If you aren't tracking your actual cost of sales by product, start today. In the meantime, you can estimate how much the cost is. Revisit Chapter 3 for a list of what could qualify as a cost of sale. If you are finding it difficult to split some of these expenses between each product, don't fret. Just include them in one lump sum below your subtotal line (as we have done with commissions). It's important that they be included as part of your total cost of sales so that you can get an accurate read on what you are really netting from your sales efforts. The rest, as they say, is just math. How much detail you need to get into with this worksheet really depends on what types of decisions you need to make for your business. You may choose to calculate your margins on the basis of product/service categories. In my case, I use categories like consulting, keynote speeches, book sales, and training courses. You may choose to break these categories down further and into the individual product if there are likely to be significant differences in price or cost. For example, book sales could be broken down into *Balancing Act* and *Raising Your Business*. It is also a good idea to take the widest view of cost of sales as possible.

Once you have completed the worksheet, notice how your products/services rank on the basis of gross margin. As you can see in our example, the product (Product C) that accounted for the most sales contributed the lowest profit margin. "Ah," you might say, "but it generated the most dollars." "All right," we would say back, "let's try it your way. Then we'll try it our way to see which would be the better plan for next month."

Your Scorecard Because Product C makes you the most absolute dollars, next month you want to sell 100% of Product C (let's assume $16,000 worth — the total sales amount for the month). Your results for next month, were you to sell $16,000 of Product C at a gross margin of 20%, would be $3200 ($16,000 × 20%).

Our Scorecard We'd want to put all of our time and money into producing $16,000 of Product A, the highest margin product. We'd end up making a total of $8000 ($16,000 × 50%). We win.

When you go over the above worksheet, you may decide to drop the lower-margin Product C and redirect those resources into promoting product A and/or B. Or you may even replace it with a higher-margin new product. You can also decide to increase the price of Product C while trying to whittle down its cost of sales. Presto, increased margins. Regardless of what you choose to do, you now have the facts and the basis upon which to figure out the following: Do your decisions about your sales focus, production costs, product pricing and mix create the overall results that you want?

How Much Are Your Expenses Really Costing You?

Now that we have figured out *how* to figure out how our business makes its money, let's inch our way down the profit and loss statement and look at how the company spends its money.

As a new entrepreneur, I very quickly realized that I was making a fatal error in how I went about deciding whether or not to add or approve new expenses. In the haste of making decisions, I was only considering whether or not I could make enough sales to cover the actual amount of the expense. I was totally forgetting about how much it cost to make and service the sale itself. So now, margin rules in my little world. Whether the expense is real or contemplated, related to sales or part of overhead, I use this simple calculation to guide my judgement on whether to say yea or nay. It will tell you for every dollar you spend, or intend to spend on the new expense, how much in sales you will need to bring in to cover it, given your current gross margin. (Author's note: Personally, I didn't want to include these ugly old formulas but Paula made me.)

The following formula shows you how many new sales you need to generate to cover any new expense. It does this by dividing how much you sold during the year by how much gross profit you made on those sales.

$$\text{Amount of New Sales Needed} = \frac{\text{Annual Sales}}{\text{Annual Gross Profit}} \times \text{New Expense}$$

Let's see how it works with an example. You may be considering hiring someone to help you in the office at an annual salary of $24,000. Right now your annual sales are $100,000 and your annual gross profit (total sales minus total cost of goods sold) is $60,000.

$$\textbf{Amount of New Sales Needed} = \frac{\$100,000}{\$60,000} \times \$24,000 = \$40,000$$

Therefore, to stay just as profitable, you will have to generate another $40,000 in sales if you authorize this expenditure. If it is realistic that having someone handle administration will now enable you to achieve this kind of sales growth, then it is a good decision.

If you are even a little unsure, consider some alternatives. What if you can only realistically increase your sales by $24,000? Use the formula again to work backwards to what amount you can afford to pay for that help. Rework the equation this way: Divide the amount of new sales that you expect to make given that new resource (expense) by your annual gross sales divided by your annual gross profit.

$$\frac{\textbf{Affordable}}{\textbf{Expense}} = \frac{\$24,000}{(\$100,000/\$60,000)} = \$14,400$$

In our example, the formula shows us that we can only afford to pay $14,400 for new help if we only expect to generate $24,000 in new sales. This now gives us some direction to make our decision in hiring help. Maybe the person will agree to either work part-time or take a lower hourly rate.

We've gone one step further to simplify the application of this principle by helping you arrive at one number you can use to make sure you are making money. Can you imagine how efficient it would be to walk around armed with the fact that for every dollar of expense you add, you have to generate $2.50 (profit multiplier) in sales to cover the existing cost of sales, the new expense, and what you want to end up on the bottom line? Try figuring out your profit multiplier by dividing your total annual sales by your total gross profit. Subtract the total net profit you want to make during the year (your bottom line, so to speak).

$$\textbf{Profit Multiplier} = \frac{\textbf{Annual Sales}}{(\textbf{Annual Gross Profit} - \textbf{Net Profit})}$$

OR

$$\textbf{Profit Multiplier} = \frac{100\%}{(\textbf{Annual Gross Margin\%} - \textbf{Target Annual Net Profit\%})}$$

So, let's say that your business operates with total annual overhead expenses of $120,000 ($10,000 per month). You make a 40% gross margin on your sales. You've decided you'd like to have a bottom line profit of 10% this year. You need to figure out how many sales you need to generate. Using the percentage version of the formula you can determine what multiplier to apply to your total or any expense in order to arrive at how much in sales you need to drive. Divide 100% by your gross margin percentage, reduced by the percentage of profit that you want to appear on the bottom line. In this case, the math looks like this:

$$\textbf{Profit Multiplier} = \frac{100\%}{(40\% - 10\%)} = 3.33$$

What this tells you is that in order for you to cover $120,000 in overhead expenses and make a 10% profit, you will have to make $400,000 in sales ($120,000 × 3.33).

You can also use this formula in reverse to figure out how much you have to reduce expenses if your sales are not living up to your projections. Using the same scenario as above, let's say your sales are falling short of your $400,000 sales projection by 10% or $40,000. So by the end of the financial year you must reduce your expenses by:

$$\textbf{Expense Reduction} = \frac{\$40,000}{3.33} = \$12,000$$

Paula says that, as an accountant, she knew that profit was revenues minus expenses. But as an entrepreneur, she learned (we both did) that you've got to have enough profit. Why? Because you need to:

1. Provide a cushion of comfort (read: cash) to buffer the natural fluctuations caused by business cycles and changes in market conditions.
2. Fuel future growth.
3. Reward the people that made it happen, namely you and the employees.

You need to keep enough of the earned profit in the company (hence the name "retained earnings") to satisfy requirements #1 and #2. It doesn't hurt to include a little extra for margin of error or the inevitable unanticipated catastrophe. The balance you can safely use towards #3. Being able to gauge quickly the impact of any problems that prevent you from making enough profit or that eat into your current profitability is critical. This understanding will afford you enough time to take action that will make a difference.

So now that you are sure that your business is generating "enough" profit, let's see what happens to the cash that is being generated from all that selling and expensing you're doing.

Where Has All the Cash Gone?

As we mentioned in chapter 3, cash can sit in the bank, be tied up in receivables, inventory, and fixed assets, or be repaying those who loaned it to you in the first place. As the owner of a toddler business we have been looking at everything as people and things: staff, office space, coffee makers, photocopy paper, phone lines. Now we have to see them as cash.

We've done well to understand how our business makes money. We've come to also understand how much more money we need to make if we intend to spend more. Now, one of the final steps in your transformation into the financial manager is to be able to understand how much cash is needed to support a new sale. Norm Brodsky is a veteran entrepreneur and a popular *Inc. Magazine* columnist. His suggestions for entrepreneurs struggling to manage the finances of their businesses are terrific. He unlocks the real meaning of financial information by appealing to our entrepreneurial reality. This is his formula to figure out how much cash you need to carry out any number of new sales.

He says, first we take how much the new sales are expected to be, less the gross profit we intend to make. Then add whatever money is needed for additional overhead to support that sale. Divide the whole kit and caboodle by how long it takes to complete the sale. Then multiply by how long it will take to collect the money after we've completed the sale. Add an extra amount for contingency. Doing this analysis will give us a pretty good idea of how much money we need in advance of landing all those new sales so that we can avoid a potential cash flow problem.

Here it is for all you left-brained people:

$$\text{New Cash Needed} = \frac{(\text{New Sales} - \text{Gross Profit}) + \text{Extra Overhead}}{\text{Time Frame in Days for Adding New Sales}}$$

$$\times \text{ (Average Number of Days You Collect Your Receivables} + 20\%^*)$$

(* 20% is added as a safety zone)

Let's use the earlier example to figure out how much cash we need to have on hand to be able to handle an increase in our sales activities. Remember that your business operates with a gross margin of 40% and you needed to generate total annual sales of $400,000 to cover your overhead expenses of $10,000 per month. Suppose the target of $400,000 represents a $75,000 increase in sales and $10,000 per month represents a $1000 per month increase in expenses from the previous year.

Before we tell you what Norm suggests you do, I need to be perfectly honest. There is no way in hell that I would even read, let alone attempt to understand, the next few paragraphs. If you are anything like me, don't despair.

That's why we have accountants. I let Paula explain this to me 400 times in the context of my own business before I finally got it. But for all of you who like numbers, fill your boots.

Start by figuring out your cost of goods sold (COGS) on the new business ($75,000): the amount of money you'll have to lay out to produce or acquire whatever you're selling. Since your gross margin is 40% of sales, your COGS is 60% (100% − 40%), or $45,000 (75,000 × 60%).

Add to that the extra overhead you're going to need — $12,000 (the extra $1000 a month) — and you get $57,000 ($45,000 + $12,000) in new expenses to be incurred to fill $75,000 in new orders.

Divide the total by the number of days in the period covered in your projection — in this case, 365 — and you find out that the new business is costing you $156.16 ($57,000/365) a day. If you then multiply that number by the number of days it takes you to collect your receivables (60 days), you get an idea of your additional cash needs. For safety's sake, increase the collection period by 20%, so in this example, multiply by 72 days instead of 60. The result: 72 days × $156.16 a day = $11,243.52.[6]

So what if you don't have this kind of cash just lying about? Where can you find $11,000 odd dollars to achieve your new sales plan? You do have a few options when trying to wring more cash out of your business.

- See if you can negotiate with your suppliers terms that match your receivable collection period plus your contingency of 20%.
- Pare down the number of days it takes you to collect receivables. Negotiate partial payment of $11,243 or roughly 15% up front.
- As a last resort, you can always borrow the money, if you don't mind increasing your bank debt and adding to your costs.

We had an experience that not only allowed us to shorten our receivable collection period, get partial payment up front, and match payment terms, but also ensured our business was going to survive through my maternity leave, which was in no way a sure thing. The elation we all felt the day we got the word that Royal Bank was moving forward with our training program was, uh, considerable. This contract was significant not only in dollar value but in credibility value as well. But I was growing more aware of the costs around such a sale. I needed to make sure the billing was such that we could handle those costs. We set up the billing in such a way that we charged a 25 percent non-recoverable retainer, with the next three installments spread out over the year. This money was going to help fund my maternity leave and keep the company afloat.

I was sitting in our downtown office going over the plans for the roll-out with Rosa when we got word that our trainer, the one who was going to handle the bank training, had decided at the very last minute to move on to other things. Rosa and I looked at each other, simultaneously gulping down the urge to panic. I was having a baby in three short weeks. The roll-out was in four weeks. With Rosa looking on, I picked up the phone and called my contact, Sherry Fotheringham, who was in charge of the bank's women's market initiative. Unbelievably, I was connected to Sherry right away. With false bravado, I launched into my pitch. "Sherry, I've got a sweet-heart of a deal for you. We've run into a minor glitch with the facilitator for our program. But don't worry, I will do the training for the bank myself. But," I swallowed hard, "we can't start it for at least another 10 months."

It was as if she didn't even hear the second part. "You want to do the training yourself?" Sherry asked in amazement. "We'd love that. My soul, we've waited this long to make it happen, 10 months more won't make much difference."

Massive relief spread through my body. But the worst was by no means over. My mind raced, "How can I ask the bank to pay me the retainer if I'm not going to perform a single service for another 10 months?" Sherry and I had developed a close business relationship so I decided to come clean. Meanwhile, Rosa was sitting across the desk, barely breathing, watching the drama unfold. I grimaced and closed my eyes tight. With a deep breath, I plunged, "Oh yes, and, uh, the financial arrangement was that the retainer and first installment were due sometime around now. I was depending on this to help with my maternity leave. What are the chances of still being paid now but with delivery later?" No one was breathing.

Nonchalantly, Sherry replied, "Oh sure, no problem. Hey, it will be great to have you on board."

My jaw dropped. Rosa's eyes grew wide as she saw the smile spread across my face. She shook her head in disbelief. To this day, Rosa and Michelle talk about the horseshoes that, in their opinion, must have taken up permanent residence in an unmentionable part of my anatomy. The moral of the story? Never be afraid to ask.

Armed with your new financial insights on how your business really makes money, it's time to integrate this new intelligence into each key function within your business — marketing, sales, financing, and technology. Let's start with marketing.

Marketing: A Lesson in Focus

Rosa had an onslaught of people descend on our office one day. As a result, I got booted out of mine. I headed for the boardroom, which boasts beautiful high-beam ceilings and solid brick walls. I was working on updating our marketing plan and was getting seriously bogged down. As the owner of a toddler business, I found myself caught in the vicious cycle of responding to "can I have this" and "can I have that" from my customers and prospects. My mind was constantly "on," devising a new spectacular product, service, or scheme. In short, I felt like an untethered sail in the wind.

Staring at the brick wall, I was unaware that I was actually pounding the table and talking to myself, sounding a bit like a broken record, "Focus, focus, focus."

Weirdly enough, deep in the recesses of my brain, the brick wall spoke back. "On what?" came the response. Even stranger was the fact that the voice sounded a lot like Paula's.

I decided to engage the brick wall. "I haven't a clue what to focus on, wall. Any suggestions?"

"Focus on what makes you different, not just on what you're good at or what you can do. Focus on that best customer, not on every opportunity that crosses your path. Focus on what people pay you well for. Focus on the customer, not the competition." This was a pretty bright wall.

I leaned back and put my feet up on the table, my hands clasped behind my head. Playing devil's advocate, I said, "So what am I supposed to do, just ignore other opportunities, forget the competition, never create another new product or service for as long as I live?"

"Okay," the brick wall said, "it's obviously time for a lesson on distinctions."

I hated walls with attitude.

"Focus is *not* the same as being aware. Focus directs your actions after you become aware. Remember? Narrow your focus to broaden your appeal. Focus has to do with sharpening, seeing more clearly, not ignoring or eliminating things from your viewfinder."

"I thought I had already created my marketing focus," I whined.

"Yes," came back Paula's voice, "but you got so busy that you lost it. And now it's a struggle to get it back on track."

Just then I heard Rosa's voice calling softly from the other side of the boardroom door. Knowing that I was alone, her voice registered alarm. "Joanne? Are you on the phone?"

I started to laugh. "No, my friend," I answered. "Just rapping with the wall. Everything's cool." And with that I got up and opened the door. Rosa just stood there, shaking her head.

Sound vaguely familiar? Of course it does. Just as we had to when we became human resource managers and financial managers, we need to adjust our perspective in order to pick up our marketing manager's hat. Here is where you need to develop a real marketing plan and then work the plan. No more a little bit of this and a little bit of that. No more "I think that worked fairly well." Now it's time to say it worked or didn't work exactly the way it was planned, here is why, and here is how we have to modify it to make it work better.

The Science of Marketing

In previous chapters we talked about the different ways that you could get the word out on your products and service to your target customers. In this chapter, we'll help you figure out which of the myriad ways are best for you — the ones that will provide you with the right return on your investment of time and money. While the science of developing a formal marketing plan is not exact, it's more precise than gut feel and guesswork.

When posed with the question 'How much money do you intend to make this year?' most owners of toddler businesses respond, 'Well, I need to make $150,000 in sales.' Knowing your total annual sales target is a great start. But your projections can be refined by using the tools suggested in the section on financial management. This can boost your confidence that your projected level of sales will actually cover your expenses and make enough to pay you a reasonable salary plus profit.

So, let's assume that you have identified your magic number for the total sales needed next year. The next, much tougher question is: How do you intend to achieve that level of sales? In other words, how many sales of which of your products and services will you have to close and fulfill in order to reach that magic number? How many of your target customers do you need to get excited about what you have to offer in order to get enough sales leads and to then close enough sales? How will you go about actually generating those sales leads? How? How? How?

Figuring out the *what* is always easier than figuring out the *how*. Like we said before, there are a thousand different ways to get from here (standstill) to there ($150,000 total annual sales). Whether one particular way is more right or more wrong depends on you, your business, your customers, and your time and money. As the owner of a toddler business, you simply don't have enough time and money to keep up the "let's try it and see" approach. We are at the point in our business where we have to put our scarce resources to the best use so that we can maximize the return on our investment.

When our budgets of time and money are modest, we need to be choosier about where we invest them. Do we hire someone to help in the office? Or would it be better to join that association, place an ad in the local paper, launch a Web site, contract a bookkeeper, send out a promotional flyer, write an article, or contract a sales person or telemarketer? How do we choose? There is only one way. It's based on calculating the results that we expect to have happen before we start the wheels in motion. Calculating the return on your marketing investment, be that advertising, public relations, promotions, or sales programs, requires that you track certain information.

The Costs

You need to estimate, in advance, your direct costs of researching, designing (the ad, flyer, tradeshow booth, direct mail piece, Web site, sales literature, tele-marketing scripts), producing, distributing, and administering the marketing program. Also, don't forget about the downstream costs to handle the inquiries or responses, like staff, long distance phone charges, and follow-up materials, or to fulfill any special offer you have made, such as a promotional discount or additional incentives like that free cosmetic bonus pack you get when you make a purchase over $50. You need to estimate all costs, every last penny.

The Reach

While it's important to know the number of people or businesses that your communication will actually touch, the more important and often much smaller number is made up of those that are actually touched and fit the definition of your target customer. Both sets of numbers should be available from the seller, broker, provider, or organizer of the communication vehicle that you are using, be it a newspaper, trade show, billboard, or direct mail list. The latter number is critical because any time or money spent on marketing to people who are not your target customer is better spent on that CD player you've been dying to buy.

The Responses

As we start to get down to the nitty gritty, you need to set up a way to connect the dots. You need to connect the response to a particular piece of communication to whoever is doing the responding. A mechanism for doing this might be a special number or extension people can call. You can place a special code on fax or mail-back forms. It can be training staff that take inquiries to ask how the person found out about the company. This information is usually gathered by the people responsible for sales or customer service.

The Leads

Not every inquiry or response you receive is a lead. When I was on *Pamela Wallin Live,* we got 35 responses in a 24-hour period. Ten of the responses were people inquiring about becoming a financial adviser, eight were people calling to try to sell *us* something, another 15 were from individuals who were looking for financial advice, and the remaining two offered real business potential. The next step after identifying the leads is to prioritize them. Put them into a category that identifies their "closeability" so that you can direct your sales attention to the "hottest" or "biggest" first.

The Sales

Here we have to identify the number and the dollars of sales made, over what period of time, and of what product or service. In order for your financial system to be able to provide you with this information, it will also need a way to connect the sales information to the communication program (i.e., a financial code, class, or category). Simply put, it's these numbers that we need to calculate our return on investment. The information on the costs and the sales is there to help you become better at predicting the sales generated from new marketing programs.

The Return

You now have all the numbers you will need to calculate your expected return (that's before you launch the marketing program) and the actual return on your investment (once the program is launched). The math looks like this:

$$\text{ROI} = \frac{\text{Sales Volume} \times \text{Gross Margin \%}}{\text{Total Cost of Your Marketing Program}} - 1$$

So let's walk through the following example:

You have joined an association in which 5000 of its members represent your target customers. You are thinking about sending them a letter introducing your business and offering them a 10% discount. The particular product you have chosen for this promotion retails for $250 and costs you $100 to produce and deliver. Let's expect that 150 people (or 3% of the 5000) will call to get more information and 50 (1/3 of the 150 people inquiring) will actually buy the product at the promotional price.

1. **The Costs**

Association fee	$ 250.00
Design and production of letters, labels, envelopes, stamps (5000 × $0.50/letter package)	$2500.00
Handling inquiry ($15/hour for staff × 10 minutes per response × 150 people)	$ 375.00
Promotional 10% discount ($250 × 10% discount x 50 people)	$1250.00
Contingency of 10% of total costs	$ 437.50
Total program cost	$4812.50

2. **The Sales**
Gross Sales = $250 × 50 people = $12,500

3. **The ROI**

$$\text{ROI} = \frac{\$12{,}500 \times \left[\dfrac{(\$250 - 100)}{250}\right]}{4812.50} - 1 = .5584 \text{ or } 55.84\%$$

A positive ROI indicates that your marketing program made you money. The larger the number, the more money you made. Conversely, a negative ROI means that your program cost you money.

Improving Your Marketing ROI

If this is the case, or you would just like to increase your profitability, there are a number of ways to improve your return on your marketing expenditures:

- Work hard at lowering your program costs, e.g., consider faxing instead of mailing.
- Do some *"what-iffing."* Check to see how sensitive your results are to a change in your program costs, estimated number of responses, leads, and sales. Since most entrepreneurs are ultra-optimistic when it comes to sales projections, force yourself to always run one "disaster" scenario before giving the program the go-ahead. Remember there are many external factors like market trends, shifts in your target market's buying patterns and behaviours, natural disasters, competitive responses, and economic conditions that can impact your results. Look outside to see what those external influences might be.

- Run a small pilot or test of the program with a smaller reach, and therefore lower costs, before pulling out all the stops. Most of us get caught by the fact that it's cheaper when you produce more marketing pieces at one time. Ignore the lure of volume discounts first time through any new program. Consider total dollars at the trial stage. You can always negotiate getting the discount applied on the smaller quantities if and when you decide to bump up the volume after a successful trial.

- Consider, evaluate, and compare some other programs before going ahead. Don't just go with any program, even if it qualifies by providing you with the ROI that you need. Compare it to others to make sure you choose the one that has the largest ROI.

- Go for synergies. Try to co-ordinate your programs to work together, so that some of the costs can be spread over a number of programs. One-offs are always more expensive than programs that complement each other. For example, consider recycling the work that you have done for an article into a press release and onto your Web site.

- Don't promise what you can't deliver. Make sure that you, your staff, and your systems are ready to fulfil those promises that you are publicizing.

- Make sure you are spending money to communicate your unique features and benefits. You should have a very small number of highly focused messages that you are using in your communications. Remember, repetition is a good thing. Remember, repetition is a good thing.

- Compare your expected results with your actual results. You've come this far. Make sure you don't stop short of the real benefit to all this up-front work. Remember that thing about being able to control only what we understand.

- Stay within your budget. Just like a home renovation, decide in advance what you can spend on marketing and what you need to achieve with those dollars and stick to it. It is too easy to get carried away and spend money that you have yet to make. It is a vicious circle that often results in the demise of many businesses. Don't be a marketing casualty.

You can see you need to use a disciplined approach to marketing. If you know the answers to "What products and services should I focus on?" and "How do I best reach my target customer?" your efforts will be translated into cascading sales.

Sales and Customer Service in the Toddler Years

Entrepreneurs need to learn to let go of some of their responsibilities so they can grow. Here's a case in point:

A successful entrepreneur almost single-handedly got her company sales to $100,000 a year. When she sought venture capital to expand, the potential investors asked her, "Who is your president?"

"Me."

"Who is your chief financial officer?"

"Me."

"Who is in charge of sales?"

Again the answer was, "Me."

One of the panelists asked, "How much time do you spend on sales?"

He was told, "About 10 percent."

She was told, "You don't need money to expand. If you spend 100 percent of your time on sales, you should quickly get to the million-dollar mark."

As the owner of a toddler business, spending 100 percent of our time exclusively on sales is not only unlikely but it's also not the most profitable way to run a business. For me, it was way up the impossibility curve because initially, I was the product. Many women entrepreneurs do, in fact, go into business with a special skill set; therefore, they are likely to be the best sales representatives for their businesses. But now that your business is standing on its own two feet, you may be ready to bolster the selling end. In the first year, we cautioned against prematurely handing the privileged position of being "front and centre" with the customer over to someone else. We recommended that you hold firm in that role because you needed to establish, maintain, and learn from your relationship with your customers. But, as a toddler, you now need to change that role. However, before adding salespeople, resellers, agents, or additional distribution channels, there is something else you need to consider. You need to evaluate how to streamline your sales and distribution so you can serve up more sales without incurring an equal amount of cost. As a sales force of one (with probably a couple of other supporting hands), you have to begin to evolve and refine your sales and distribution plan much the same way you focused on the management of your marketing, finance, and human resources plans.

The Channel Options

Let's get acquainted with the options for selling and distributing your product or service and then look at what to consider before selecting what works best for you.

Other People

You can augment your own direct selling and distribution efforts with a variety of people in a variety of ways. You can hire commissioned sales representatives or agents who will sell and/or distribute your product directly to the consumer. These folks can be either full-time, part-time, or on contract. Consider the following ways to configure your sales team:

- Choose reps who have already established a network, spent time with, or served your target customer. Perhaps they worked for a larger company in the same industry, the competition, or even a company selling complementary products and services. Perhaps they're retired and spend their R&R time rubbing elbows with the very people that you want to get to.
- Split the sales effort into "prospecting" and "closing." Hire according to the talent, experience, and knowledge required for each position. Usually you can get people to prospect or telemarket for you at less cost than a seasoned salesperson. Instead, use the experienced salesperson to build the relationship and close the deal.
- Create a team to land the big accounts. When the item you are selling is complex or expensive, this approach often works well to speed up the sales cycle, increase closing rates, and add credibility. On the minus side it does chew up a considerable amount of resources in the short term because you have to drag out the whole team to every practice as well as to every game.

A bit further removed from your control are distributors and resellers. These are the people who have their own businesses that may or may not exclusively sell or distribute your product to their customers. This option may require a lot of up-front time to get them up the learning curve on your product or service. It is often frustrating because, unlike a dedicated sales person, they usually carry other lines. You cannot directly control their actions and priorities. You will also part with anywhere from 35 to 50 percent profit because you are selling the product at a discount. Frankly, this may put this option out of the running for a toddler business. Where you do find this as a common option is in highly competitive industries like the software industry, where you need to get as many people as possible mobilized and selling your product before it becomes obsolete or the competition raises the bar.

Another option that has exploded in the last five years is also in response to the demand for a massive direct selling approach. This is multi-level networking. This approach combines recruitment with sales and distribution. This sales method and channel has received mixed reviews. Some of the upsides include the relatively low investment to get started and the flexibility of a motivated, independent sales force. The minuses are the purported "aggressive" recruitment tactics and sales distribution and commission structures that border on "pyramid" selling, where money is the only product changing hands. Carefully assess this option and expect that only a handful of those that are recruited will actually produce meaningful sales volumes. This is because of the minimal (if any) screening criteria when it comes to recruiting. The hard fact is that selling is a not a skill that everyone can acquire. Be clear on what may appear to be a relatively low cost and expeditious way to get your products into your customers' hands. Make sure that your customer will appreciate the way in which they are being sold.

Lastly, you could simply license the sales and distribution rights for your product or service to another person. You would then receive a royalty on sales either through a formal franchise agreement or by means of a contract. This sales and distribution method is often used when your brand or business concept has become known and has value.

Other Places

Setting up your own retail location is a very capital intensive and often risky option for small businesses. We advise that you either have retail experience within your organization or some means to get it before you go down this path. You may consider sourcing your products through existing retail outlets such as specialty shops, general department stores, or a "big box" retail chain, like Home Depot, as an alternative to setting up your own shop. You will be able to do this faster, with less financial risk. But the trade-off will be lower margins. This is because you now have a commissioned team of sales representatives or you now need to give a significant discount to a middle person known as a distributor. Another creative option to going 100 percent retail is to rent a space for a short but meaningful time frame, like H&R Block does at tax time. Or try participating in a trade show a couple times a year in different locations. It's kind of like travelling retail.

Other Means

Sometimes the right choice for new sales channels is the newer or virtual options. These include direct mail or Internet/online sales. Both types of selling and distribution put the customer in charge. The decision on what to buy and how it should be delivered is unaided by another person. This approach usually requires a significant up-front investment in the design and production of the sales materials such as the catalogue or Web site, but the cost of fulfillment is likely to be more modest. Why? The customer self-administers most of the ordering by way of a standard form or online interface.

You may also choose to outsource the fulfillment aspect of the process to another company whose only business is fulfillment. Often we do special book offers or discount offers to different organizations and associations. For example, through their newsletters, CIBC, Trimark, the Canadian Association of Physiotherapists, and the Canadian Nurses Association, to name a few, offered *Balancing Act* to their clients or membership at a significantly reduced price from the bookstore price. We were able to do this based on volume. Naturally, we didn't have the means to collect all of the requests and cheques. Nor did we have the storage space to store the books. Nor did we have the people power to fill the orders. Nor did we have the ability to take advantage of the cost savings that an outfit who did nothing but mail things for people did. This kind of place is called a fulfillment house. For a very reasonable price, they will handle it all for you, from acting as a mailing address, to storage, to sending the material out. It's a brilliant invention.

Deciding What Channel to Tune Into

Weighing your options carefully before choosing a distribution and sales force alternative may result not only in more sales, but in a more profitable operation. If you decide that more than one channel of sales and distribution suits your business, which is common, you still need to figure out which channel will take precedence in your strategy. You need to figure out how you can use that channel as a starting point to leverage the development and operation of other channels. When assessing which channel strategy to begin with, look at the required investment of time and money first. Which path offers the least resistance? From there, consider which strategy most closely aligns the delivery of your product with your target customer and the image of the product or service. For example, potential purchasers of high-end items such as expensive sports cars or jewellery may be unlikely to buy through a catalogue or online. Suffice it to say, these customers prefer an upscale and exclusive approach where they are treated like VIPs. Other critical factors that will affect your evaluation and eventual selection of the best channel strategy for your business include:

- whether you have the skill and experience to manage that strategy
- what your competitors' strategies are and how they are likely to respond to your approach to the channel
- how much money you have to invest in, manage, and administer the channels and sales force options.

Helen and Tamar Zenith: Their Channel Advantage

Let's look at a mother-and-daughter team who use a dual approach to selling and distribution. They use a *retail outlet* to display the products of the artists for whom they also act as *agents*. Helen and Tamar Zenith are co-owners of Newzones Gallery of Contemporary Art, which opened in Calgary in 1992. The success of the art gallery is largely due to their remarkable ability to sell, market, and distribute a unique product.

Helen explains, "The art gallery dealer operates a gallery that sells art, but as art directors or agents we promote the artists, nurture the artists, educate the public, continue to nurture the artists, and continually educate the public. The general public is intimidated by contemporary art and does not understand the art or the artists, and the artists cannot cope with why they are not understood. Both the public and the artist require a lot of attention and this is a challenge for the art dealer."

Helen describes her unique distribution approach, along with its upsides and downsides. "We chose to be a true contemporary art gallery rather than a store, and we chose our artists very carefully. Unfortunately, these two choices hamper quantity of sales. Sometimes more expensive paintings require a more affluent clientele. We cater to two generations, Tamar's generation and my generation. Some young collectors can afford higher priced paintings but many cannot.

"Unlike in a store, I do not order the product. I invest in the artists and then work with their paintings. Every painting is unique and every painting is different. We could often sell the same painting 10 times over, but we cannot tell our artists what to paint — they are not manufacturers, they are artists, and we are not selling just one painting but a concept of collecting an artist's work."

They opened in the boiler room of a steel plant, no street access, with five artists from Calgary, two from Toronto, and one from Saskatoon. It was very rustic, bohemian, and difficult to find in Calgary's roughest neighbourhood, a charming space but small — no bathrooms, and constant problems with dust and pests. But it was cheap. With no visibility and relatively unknown artists, Helen and Tamar *had* to market. Since their rent and labour were cheap, they used most of their budget for sales and marketing to create a destination shop — a place where people set out to go to when they left their front door step. Newzones' marketing consists of professionally curated exhibitions with beautiful four-colour invitations, catalogues, participation in art fairs, ads in major magazines, television and radio, press releases, and write-ups in critical magazines. They explored all avenues of exposure. Throughout Helen's own artistic career, she had befriended many artists, critics, collectors, and museum curators, and had had first-hand interactions with some excellent art galleries. She brought all of these connections to her business.

Because they are dealing with a luxury product and a sophisticated clientele, the gallery has to reflect the clients it is trying to attract as well as the artists it represents. The gallery was barely a year old when they went to a major international art fair at huge risk and expense. They had no clients in cities such as Seattle, Los Angeles, Vancouver, or Portland; the art fairs they selected included the most prestigious galleries from around the world. Positioning themselves with prominent galleries from New York, Europe, South America, and other countries created powerful opportunities and ultimately an excellent profile.

Their growth during their toddler years was impressive. They grew from 1400 square feet to 6500 square feet and now represent 25 artists. In 1992, they financed the renovation of the space and their marketing program with bank financing. In 1997, they financed the project privately. In 1992, the concept was very straightforward, the variables — rent, labour, equipment — were either non-existent or very cheap. Now the project is more complex. Helen says, "Try to explain the concept of a contemporary art gallery to a banker. We are not a typical retail store. We do not pay for inventory. Inventory is on consignment and of course initially this sounds fantastic. We are a distributor whose money is not tied up in inventory. And we are also an agent, we represent the artist. In essence, we are the artist's business partner. Once we acquire the artist's inventory, the actual selling of the artwork is only one part of the equation. Our job is to promote the artist and his/her genius and creativity. The challenge is to succeed on all fronts for the artist — we are the artist's mentor, parent, therapist, professional adviser, business adviser, and confidante."

As the Zeniths demonstrate, by considering your available resources and management capabilities, the image and positioning of your product, your customers' buying behaviours, and your competitors' approach to sales and distribution, you can ensure competitive advantage, growth, and profitability.

Sometimes Turning Down Business Makes Sense

Not all the sales that come through the channel are keepers. Let's look at what types of sales you should say yes to and which ones should get the proverbial thumbs down.

When should you consider turning away business? Most new entrepreneurs would say, "When I'm cold and in the ground." But remember our discussion in chapter 3 on opportunity costs. When you are overbooked, understaffed, and can't afford to finance the new piece of business, you should consider saying no. Why? Because saying yes may cost you more than you can afford to pay. You may not be able to make good on your promises, or you may have to hire new staff too quickly and before you have time to train them, or you may have to burn the midnight oil and then work at a diminished capacity with the rest of your customers. The risk to your reputation and financial health and well-being may be too great.

Knowing When to Fire the Customer

Just like having to fire an employee, firing a customer is an inevitability in your business. Not all business is good business. Let's face it, we've all been there. On a bad day we think what we dare not say — "How great the business would be if we didn't have to deal with the customers." Naturally, not all fall into this category, just the 20 percent that manage to take up 80 percent of our time, money, and energy. In short, the ones we lose money and precious sleep over.

The customer may always be right but they don't always have to be a customer. No one has said it better than Marilyn Moats-Kennedy of Career Strategies in Wilmette, Illinois: "An unprofitable customer is a misdemeanour. Keeping an unprofitable customer is a felony."

So how do you spot a bad customer and how do you go about firing them? If you can answer yes to more than half of the questions in the following list, you may just have the proverbial bad apple in your customer basket.

- Are they always trying to get a "deal"?
- Do they lack appreciation for the extra mile you go to ensure that their needs are met?
- Do they withhold their expectations from you, even when asked?
- Do they constantly let down their end of the relationship, agreement, bargain, or promise (i.e., payment)?
- Do they hold you to a higher standard than they hold for themselves?
- Is price the only thing that matters to them?
- Does your customer treat your employees and staff with disrespect? Are they in any way abusive?

Customer loyalty cuts both ways. It is a bond built by two, not one. So if you find that you are the only person expending effort to build, nurture, and grow the relationship and that you are losing money doing so — fire them. Nicely, gently, respectfully. The short answer is always the best. Explain that you don't feel that you are able to meet their needs at this price and offer to refer them to another supplier. Or provide them with some feedback on what type of supplier might be more suitable. If you are looking for an easy way out, here are a few other methods to accomplish the same objective:

- Increase your fees the next time an order is placed and stand firm.
- Advise the customer that you are currently operating at full capacity for the type of work that they are needing.
- Just say no to any new business — no reason needed.

When all else fails, check call display before picking up the phone.

Now, it just may be that in order to implement your carefully chosen and configured sales and marketing plans, you need to bolster your own financial resources with money from outside sources. Let's look at what you, as a toddler business, get to choose from.

How to Get Other People's Money — The Banks

Paula and I were guests at the Canadian Woman Entrepreneur of the Year Awards gala one evening. Our table consisted of eight women entrepreneurs, including Paula and me. There was Lindsay, a graphic designer, Zula, an accountant, Roberta, a manufacturer, Delia, a retailer, Sunera, an agricultural specialist, and Hiroko, an exporter. While listening to the winners' speeches, I was struck by the fact that every woman seemed to thank her husband, nanny, and banker, in that order. I began, "What do these women have that gets such a buy-in from their bankers? What are they doing right?"

"Probably a zillion things," Paula answered.

"I wonder what their secret is," I pondered aloud. "I can't tell you how much time I spent pitching the first bank I went to to get an operating line of credit. They just didn't get what I did. Thankfully, the second time around I found someone who not only listened but actually thought what I was doing had merit."

"Consider yourself lucky that you only had to go to two," Zula said. "I got to visit the hallowed halls of all of them. The last one finally gave me a small operating line."

"You know, if you're not clear on what business the banks are actually in, it's real easy to get teed off," Paula said.

"Bankers don't do a good enough job of educating the public. That's part of the reason why so many people crowd on the bank-bashing wagon," I said. "I remember how I really learned about the world of banks. My real lessons didn't come from the contact I had with them through our training programs, though that helped immeasurably. I really learned when I became a customer trying to get a loan. What an eye-opener."

"We want dirt. What happened?" Delia asked.

"It started when I ran into Paula at some function not unlike this one. She made the fatal mistake of asking, 'How's it going?' I burdened her with my sad tale of woe about our cash flow problems. That's when she suggested a solution I wouldn't have considered in a million years."

"What was that?" Hiroko asked between mouthfuls of gravy-laden chicken.

"She said, 'Joanne, now that you have some contracts on the books and the semblance of a track record, you should consider going to the bank.'

"I remember saying, 'The bank? Don't you have to have money before they'll give you money?' That's when I got my lesson on what the bank actually does. Or doesn't do."

Laughing, Paula said, "Joanne, not unlike most other entrepreneurs, you didn't understand that banks aren't in the business of providing capital, which is the type of money you need when you have none at all. Many new businesses begin life without enough capital, and banks aren't in the business of taking on that kind of risk."

"Yeah, but the bank's definition of risk and my definition as a business owner may not be the same," Zula said.

Paula agreed. "True. I understand that as the business owner and person in the driver's seat, you don't feel your business is as risky as the person in the passenger's seat, such as your banker. Face it, we implicitly trust ourselves. But the banker's choice is whether or not or when to get in or out of the car."

"How's that again?" Hiroko asked.

"Banks are in the business to provide money for a specific purpose, like to tide you over until receivables come in or to finance a big asset purchase," Paula answered.

"Like that new sailboat I'm dying for?" Roberta offered.

"As long as it fits in your bath tub," I shot back. "Banks, I discovered, do have a responsibility to protect their shareholders' money. And since chances are that all of us at this table are bank shareholders if we own a mutual fund, we should be somewhat relieved they aren't taking high levels of risk. In order to keep us the shareholders happy, they need to walk a pretty fine line between a good investment and a safe investment."

"It comes down to this: If you want a more willing passenger, one who doesn't mind the perceived risk of you doing the driving, I'm afraid you need to go elsewhere," Paula said. "Check out a private investor or the venture capital folks. But in Joanne's case, a bank was exactly what she needed."

"Yeah," I said, "and I was worried. I have a classic woman-owned business; the only long-term assets I have are the ones that go down the elevator with me at the end of the day. Banks have really struggled with that. In the past, they have been deeply entrenched in 'bricks and mortar' mentality. People like me who own nothing but brilliant ideas, who have significant brain power and creative but intangible products, often find ourselves outside of the loop."

Paula interjected, "It's that control thing again, Joanne. Bankers can't control the assets between your ears. Lord, you have a hard enough time doing that. But they do have more control over the tangible stuff. Still, there is some change in the wind. Banks are regularly getting trashed for not lending to small business and they are intent on changing that perception. In your case, there was value in your being an author and recognized speaker. You also had already packaged your intellectual property in the form of a developed course. Plus you had been in business about a year and had signed and pending speaking contracts, so it was worth giving it a shot."

"So," I said, picking up the cue, "I decided to take me and my brilliant ideas to see if the bank would give me a small $40,000 business operating line of credit to help me through these cash crunches. We were also in dire need of upgrading our technology so I needed a loan for that as well. I adopted an attitude of on-the-job training. I knew it was going to be a learning experience regardless of which way the wind blew, but let me tell you, I couldn't have anticipated what I was soon to learn."

With a captive audience hanging on my every word and a riveting story in my pocket, I forged on. "We had put together a comprehensive business plan. It had everything in it including what I had had for last night's dinner. As well as the financial information, we covered our sales and marketing plans, biographies of each of the players, including the 12-person advisory board, and a rather cheeky bit on our competition. We had a page with the heading, "Competition." The only thing written on the entire page was, 'There is none.' This business plan was so thick, we had to have it bound. The bank needed about one one-hundredth of what we had given them. They were really good-natured about it though, groaning that they had to rent a forklift truck to carry it around.

"What I did is what a lot of people do. I went to the bank that I had dealt with for my personal stuff. It didn't occur to me that I could or should have shopped this thing out. I met with the account manager for the first time. As I followed her into her office, she commented, 'Women and Money. That's an odd name. You know, there really is no difference between women and men when it comes to money or business. I don't subscribe to the notion that there really is a women's market. It's all just marketing hype.'"

"Oh, how very encouraging," Lindsay said. "A sterling example of open-mindedness."

"No kidding," I agreed. "I spent over an hour trying to explain to her that it wasn't about products, it was about process. I told her my work was about getting banks up to speed on the profound changes occurring in the marketplace so their lending and customer service policies would reflect the new economic reality. I told her that women tossing off their aprons and donning business suits was the most significant sociological change of this century. I pointed out that women entrepreneurs were one of the largest growth segments of the market. This reality alone could render the bank's traditional lending, sales, and marketing strategies obsolete.

"Oh, and another thing," I continued. "I said to her that if the bank truly understood the demographics, shouldn't its staff reflect the market it now served? I could tell she thought she had me when she gleefully answered, 'The majority of the bank's employees are women, in fact almost 75 percent.' So I countered, 'How many of them are in traditional administrative jobs?' She had to concede almost all of them. I told her that fewer than 20 percent of the business banking account managers were women and a far smaller number were women of colour. Though banks were making strides in getting women into the executive suites, there was still a considerable distance to travel."

"I never thought of that," Hiroko said. "When I think about it, most companies can name the women and visible minorities in management or on their sales force by name."

"Wow," Zula added. "This is all so unbelievable. And this account manager was a woman!"

"Zula," I answered, "I learned long ago that just because women share the same chromosomes, we in no way share the same ideas. But one thing is for sure, there are powerful common elements that bind women together that are not acknowledged by the bank's traditional approach. And it was this point I was trying to hammer home to the account manager."

"You actually took the time to explain all of this to her?" Roberta asked.
"Yep."
"Did she finally get it?" Lindsay asked.
"Nope."
A sad, quiet laughter rippled through the group.
"Do you think banks discriminate against women, Joanne?" Lindsay asked.
"No," I replied. "I think there are far more occurrences of gender bias that may, in very isolated cases, be linked to discrimination. I think outright *conscious* discrimination is a thing of the past. But the problem is that you can't legislate gender bias. Every person on this planet has some form of bias, gender or cultural, that gets brought into the workplace with them. Women entrepreneurs and bankers still labour under outdated perceptions of each

other. All too often I hear women entrepreneurs described by bankers as 'married-to-professionals, home-based, crafty' kinds of business owners. As well, I hear bankers portrayed as money-grabbing, cigar-smoking greedmongers. The reality is that both stereotypes are inaccurate.

"Here is a perfect example of how gender bias can get in the way of fair financing. I had a banker in my course who was telling the class a story about a woman who wanted to start a construction company. He was concerned for a variety of reasons, not the least of which was her lack of experience in the construction arena. Even though she had successfully run another business, after careful deliberation he determined she was too big a risk and declined her request for financing. Later in the day, this same banker told a second story. Its intent was to be a humorous anecdote about one of his male clients. This client came to him with a request for financing for a new business venture. This guy had 20 years' experience as a purchasing agent with the Canadian Armed Forces. His responsibility had been to buy tanks, guns, and other military hardware. The hilarious part of the story was that he had left the military and now wanted to set up a lingerie shop. The banker was quite taken aback. He said, 'This guy wanted to go from tanks to teddies!' Naturally, everyone laughed. I asked him if he gave the guy the money. He said yes. He went on to say, 'I was concerned about the lack of experience in the bra department, but he proved to me he could handle it.' Something clicked in the back of my mind. Before I could say anything, his branch manager, who was also in the course, blurted out, 'What about the woman and the construction business? You turned her down because of her lack of experience.'

"There was dead silence in the room. I didn't say a word. A good minute ticked by. The banker looked up at the branch manager and said, 'Oh, my God. I have no answer for that.'

"There were 30 bankers in the room who all of a sudden got very thoughtful. In fact, I could have ended the day right there. But in reality, I think this happens only in a few cases. The banks have carefully constructed systems to evaluate credit worthiness, and gut instinct is only a part of it. That being said, however, I know for a fact that women are turned down more than men and pay higher interest rates on their loans than men do. But it's not because they are women. It's because of the types of businesses we open."

Paula added, "The low-to-no hard asset type of business that banks are uncomfortable with."

"That's right. If a man came to the bank with a request for an operating line for a restaurant, or for a business that had no hard assets, he would likely pay higher interest rates too. Or he would be turned down."

"Joanne, can we get back to your account manager? I'm dying to find out what happened," Sunera said.

"Oh yes. Well," I continued, "she remained highly skeptical. And it wasn't just her, but her whole organization. This particular bank didn't support the notion of a 'women's market.' They still hung on to the dated notion that if you treat everyone the same, meaning well, you don't need to segment the market. In a perfect world maybe, but this approach can be naive."

The waiter came by to fill everyone's glasses. I paused only briefly, then went on, "It would be a grave understatement to say things didn't look good. Not only that, one month after giving this woman our proposal, we still didn't have an answer. I decided it was time to try somewhere else. I had been dealing with the Royal Bank who had committed to piloting our *Reaching the Women's Market* program. So I literally crossed the street. I was really surprised at how difficult a move that was. I had been with that other bank for 10 years, and on the personal side, had found them wonderful to deal with. But this new revelation was too disturbing to ignore. I had to strike out and see what lay beyond."

I took a sip of my water. "I was introduced to an account manager who was, in a word, amazing. I immediately took to Kathrine because she was part of a very special group within the sisterhood — a fellow redhead. Her candour and upfront approach were so refreshing. She made absolutely no guarantees and even went so far as to tell us she was going to have to circumvent the system. She was encouraging yet completely realistic at the same time. She worked with us closely to make sure the t's were crossed and the i's were dotted. But the best part was she was already targeting the women's market. I didn't have to convince her of the viability of our business plan or company mission statement. She presented our plan to the credit risk manager."

Lindsay asked, "Pardon my ignorance. What's a credit risk manager?"

Sunera jumped in, "They are the ones behind the scenes who evaluate the risk of a loan proposal."

"Anyway," I said, "we sat back in anxious anticipation and much to our surprise, within 48 hours, our request for a line of credit was approved. It was such a validating experience. A couple of days later I went to see Kathrine to clean up the paperwork. By pure coincidence, the credit risk manager walked by her office, so she called out to him to come in and meet me. I'll call him Chester to protect the guilty."

"'Chester,' Kathrine began. 'This is Joanne Thomas Yaccato, one of the bank's newest customers.'

"Chester stuck out his hand and said, 'Terrific to meet you, Joanne.'

"I said, 'Chester, I'd like to thank you for your vote of confidence in our endeavour. I realize you had to go out on a limb to approve us and I'd like you to know I really appreciate that.'

"Chester didn't miss a beat. He said, 'No problem. You know, that's quite a nice little hobby you got going for yourself there.'"

There was a collective gasp around the table.

"'Hobby?' I thought. That word hung ominously in the air. Kathrine and I both immediately and instinctively knew that had I been a man standing there with the same business and the same plan, the word hobby would never have left Chester's lips. I felt incredibly patronized. So did Kathrine. Her mouth opened and closed like a fish with no sound coming out and I, for the first time in my adult life, was rendered speechless. On his way to another meeting, Chester muttered a quick farewell, turned, and walked out of the office.

"Everything crystallized for me at that moment. I was smack in the middle of witnessing why I do what I do. The issue wasn't discrimination; we had got our operating line. It was gender bias."

"What in heaven's name did you do?" Zula asked.

"Well," I answered, "I needed to talk to Chester and discuss what had happened. It was necessary for a couple of reasons. I wanted him to understand how patronized I felt. You mustn't think for a second Chester intended to insult me. He didn't have a clue that he had. Gender bias isn't some nasty overt prejudice because in the vast majority of cases, it's unconscious. But here was the kicker. Royal Bank's first pilot was going to be in a couple of weeks and was being sponsored by Chester's branch. Chester was going to be there."

I was sure you could hear the laughter from our table in Inuvik. Paula said, "Indeed there is a God."

"When we met, I started off by telling him my perception of the meeting. Was his reaction swift! Chester was astonished and appalled at his choice of words. He shook his head in disbelief and said, 'I have no idea why I would use the word hobby. I have three daughters. I would never want them to feel put down like that.'

"I went on to explain to him that this was exactly why I do what I do for a living. I told him I wanted to educate bankers that this stuff goes on all the time and in 99 percent of the cases it is done unconsciously. To illustrate the point that people don't understand each other's reality, I gave Chester a little quiz.

"I asked him, 'Chester, tell me who said this, a man or a woman: I was wondering if I could possibly get a loan for new computers?'

"With no hesitation, he said, 'A woman.'

"'Why?' I queried.

"'I was wondering,' 'If I could possibly' — those are things a woman would say.'

"I continued, 'What about this: I need an operating line for $50,000.'

"He started to laugh as he said, 'Definitely a man.'

"'Why?' I asked.

"Chester said, 'He's direct and assumes he's going to get the money.'

"So I probed a little further. 'So the first style is indirect?' I asked him.

"'Absolutely,' he said.

"Pushing a little further, I said, 'How does that style sound to you?'

"He thought briefly, then replied, 'To be honest, it sounds hesitant, tentative, not very confident. Actually, it sounds pretty weak.'

"Bingo. I had him. 'Would you agree many women speak in that style?' I asked.

"'For sure,' he said. 'My wife and daughters, to name a few.'

"This was going exactly where I knew it would go. 'Okay, Chester, what percentage of the credit granting process is based on gut feel or subjective evaluation of the person asking for money?'

"He was surprised by my question. 'A lot,' he exclaimed. 'Probably anywhere from 30 to 50 percent of an account manager's decision can be based on gut feel.'

"Feeling a home run just around the corner, I asked him, 'Do you think tentative, hesitant, and lacking in confidence are character traits that bankers look for when deciding to lend someone money?'

"The light went on. Chester smiled. He knew he'd been had. 'Absolutely not.'

"I said, 'Do you think you can put lacking in confidence and entrepreneur in the same sentence?'

"He said, good-naturedly, 'I'm seeing your point.'

"So I went in for the kill. 'Is it possible, Chester, that bankers confuse a conversation style with a character trait?'

"Rather sheepishly, he said yes."

The women at the table cheered.

"I went on to say, 'I invite you to consider that women entrepreneurs do not lack confidence and are in no way tentative. Many have a communication style that is based on *politeness*, not weakness. Chester, did you know that women entrepreneurs report being taken seriously as their greatest challenge as business owners, not access to capital? Would you consider this an unconscious bias and could it have an effect on granting credit if the banker wasn't aware of it?'

"'Quite possibly,'" he said. 'Oh, and Joanne, I'll be the guy sitting front row centre in your class.'

"Not only did Chester attend and become my star pupil, he also gave me permission to tell this story and to name him in the training session so his peers could put a name and face to the behaviour. It was pretty powerful. Chester went from zero to hero in 12 seconds flat. And not just in my books, but to his peers as well who respected his courage and honesty. Today, Chester tells me he is infinitely more aware of the challenges his daughters may face. This makes him a better parent and a better businessperson."

The women at the table just shook their heads. Paula was the first to speak. "You were lucky to have had the awareness to understand what was going on." Turning to the rest of the table she said, "Joanne shared that story with the decision makers at Royal Bank to underline the point of her training."

"How did they react?" Roberta asked.

"They signed a contract to train all 1400 of their account and credit risk managers," I said.

"Paula, you're the business adviser here," Lindsay said. "What advice can you offer us as brand-new baby entrepreneurs with no experience in getting financing." The other women leaned forward in anticipation of picking up some valuable free advice.

"Yikes, that's a pretty big question, Lindsay," Paula said.

"Yeah, Paula," I said. "What could you have told me before I plunged off the cliff the way I did? What should I have done before going out there to get money?"

"Well, to begin with, Joanne, I would have tried to help you figure out what your starting point was. I've discovered that most people are in one of the following stages when the financing dragon rears its head. The first is where you were, Joanne — you have no idea how much money is needed, only that money is needed. Another stage is you know how much money is needed, but don't know how to structure or package your request. For example, you don't know how long a loan term to ask for, how much collateral is needed, and so on. Or, you have developed rudimentary projections as to your cash needs over the next year, but no documented basis as to how these projections came to be. There are no records of your financial or sales and marketing assumptions but some sort of business plan has often been started. Then there is the stage where you have a proposal, have made a pitch, and the banker has reviewed your package and is asking you to fill in some of the gaps. It's hard to figure out how to get where you want to go if you don't know where you are starting from."

"Okay," I said. "Let's assume I actually had a clue of my starting point, what then?"

"You've got to know and understand your financing options," Paula said. "This takes a ton of work."

"Options?" Hiroko asked with a healthy dose of skepticism. "I'm so small what possible options could I have? Surely the bank wouldn't even look at me."

"Research shows that although they don't like doing it, women use love money borrowed from friends and family. Then they go to the banks," Paula said. "But banks aren't the only game in town. Using other people's money in your business comes in a few different forms. There are investors who provide capital in return for a piece of the action. Then of course there are banks who are in the debt business and will loan you money for specific things. But anyone who lets you use their money, products, or services, and lets you pay them over time, is really a potential financier. That includes the leasing company for your photocopier, your suppliers, and even your employees, especially the ones who work on commission. In all these instances, you get the benefit now and pay for it later or over time. Of course, in most cases, you are obliged to pay these folks extra bucks for the privilege of using their money."

"Just think," Delia sighed, "if all your terms of payment to other people matched exactly your terms to your customer, you would never need money from the bank to bridge the gap between the two."

"But how do I know what type of money I should be looking for and who are the right people to go to?" Hiroko asked.

"It pretty much comes down to this," Paula explained. "The major banks offer operating loans, typically referred to as lines of credit. These loans have a fixed limit but no fixed repayment period. We use these to ease the burden caused by having to pay for stuff before we collect from our customers. Then there are term loans that have a fixed length of term, much like a mortgage. They are used for specific purchases like your inventory or expenses relating to an expansion. Banks now offer small business credit cards that you can use for daily expenses and specific purchases. There are small business loans a.k.a. business improvement loans that you can use to do physical upgrades to your office. These loans are also used to buy hard assets like furniture, computers, and other office or factory equipment."

"This stuff gives me such indigestion," Lindsay said. "Next to the number of hours in a day, money is my scarcest resource. Getting some seems so complicated."

"It is hard," Paula said. "Getting the right financing for your business depends on making sure you are aiming at the right target and then on how well you market your company to that prospective financier. Your financing proposal must request the proper mix of financing and correctly match the type of financing with its intended use. For instance, you wouldn't request a two-year loan to help you deal with the cash flow crunch of waiting for your customers to pay you within the usual 35 to 45 days, nor would you request an operating loan to buy equipment.

"And I repeat — it's all in the marketing. A successful entrepreneur understands the supreme importance of marketing. The way to get proper financing is to market your business from this perspective: Instead of customers and clients, your target market is bankers, investors, and creditors. Financial investors are targeted in the same way that you target your traditional customers. You develop a descriptive profile and then go searching. You don't waste your time or your money on people who don't fit the profile. Instead of selling your expertise or product or service, the real product that you are packaging and selling is *your* business and *your* ability to run it."

"So if I'm going to the bank, what type of banker should I go to?" Hiroko asked.

"It really depends on your business and you. Try to focus on three things: First, find a banker who is knowledgeable and has recently done deals in your industry. It's really good to know that they are in the market to do business. Watch out that you don't waste too much time in having to educate them. Joanne would have done well to have figured this out in advance. Secondly, find someone who fits. Even if Joanne's previous bank had agreed to lend her money, I doubt the relationship would have been sustainable. And break-ups get very messy when there is money involved. Finally, look for a point of attraction or common personal interests and values as the spark to light the fire. Do not compromise when choosing a banker."

"How do you find this good banker?" I asked.

"The first thing you do is *don't* do what you did," Paula said. "Don't automatically assume that you will take your business where you personally bank. I would recommend talking to other small business owners who are in the same industry or community as you're in and find out about their experiences."

"Let me tell you, I could save someone a lot of time and trouble if they came to me first," I said.

"You can also try a lawyer or accountant who is familiar with small business needs. There are always your compadres in clubs, associations, and service groups. Don't forget family members and, of course, business consulting firms."

"Of course," I said, grandly gesturing to Paula.

"I don't have to tell Joanne the importance of prescreening a banker or anyone else that you are considering as a financier. You know only too well that your time is at a premium. You need to be realistic about what you have to do, how long it is going to take, and what the result of your efforts will be," Paula said emphatically. "Any significant chasm between your expectations and reality can result in your becoming demoralized and eventually giving up. Guard against this with all your might.

"Many people lose faith or simply run out of steam part way through the process. Rejection, in my experience, is usually a result of one of three things. First, you may be asking for more money from the bank than your business can reasonably carry. You really should spend some time fine-tuning your business so you can lessen your financial need and the expense of using outside money. Or you may have started down the wrong path. Maybe you started with a bank when what you should have been looking for was a private investor to add some capital to the business. You should analyse whether your need for money is because of timing, not the amount of cash flow. Lastly, you may be spending too much time talking about your product instead of how you intend to make money on your product. It's your abilities as a business owner that count in the eyes of a banker. And believe me, your ability to run your company is being judged from the moment you open your mouth. Never underestimate the weight that first impressions carry.

"Just as you have competition in the sales arena, assume that you have substantial competition for your banker's money. You will have to answer why they should choose your business over other businesses. Bankers are just as concerned about your ability to provide ongoing support to your business as your customers are. It is mandatory to show your banker that your business can support the financing requested not just today but over the entire term of your commitment.

"Okay," Paula took a deep breath and continued. "We'll assume Joanne is going to try to do this thing all over again, but with a bit more planning this time. The first thing Joanne should have done was to develop a strategy to market her loan application to the banker. One tactic might have been to reduce the amount of money she asked for up front and agree to have additional funds advanced if certain agreed-upon targets are met, like sales, receivables, or profit of a certain amount. She could have tried restructuring the loan so the money is advanced in smaller amounts over a period of time. She could have asked for a combination type of loan, for example, an overdraft with a credit card or a term loan for some of the loan in place of an overdraft."

"Why would I be doing this? It would make sense if I had been turned down," I asked. "Is it to make it sound like we are asking for less than we really are?"

"Not at all — in fact you should be extremely careful not to accept financing for less than what you really need. It is one sure-fire way to back yourself into a financial corner. No, the point that I am trying to make here is that you may have some wiggle room on the timing and type of financing you arrange. You may consider modifying your plan in order to test out your ability to handle the increased debt-load before pulling out all the stops. The point is to set your strategy so you don't get turned down or it doesn't cost you a small fortune.

"The next step would be to create professional or thorough cash flows. This will substantiate the amount of money you are asking for, using somewhat conservative figures. It's always better if your projections get blown out of the water for being on the light end," Paula said.

"What the heck is a professional cash flow? I trust it's quite different from my amateur status in this department?" I asked.

"It's one of the most important management tools a business owner has. It's really nothing more than a chart that shows the cash ebb and flow of your business. For example, when you expect your cash from sales or from the sale of an old computer to come in and when your cash will go out to pay suppliers, the bank, and your staff. You may track and project your cash flows weekly or monthly to manage day-to-day stuff but quarterly or annual projections are enough for the bank. They just need to see that you will be able to have enough cash around when it comes to paying back what you borrowed. Plus interest.

"The next thing you need to do," Paula continued, "is to write a narrative or business plan that supports your cash flow projections. It has to showcase you as a competent money and operational manager."

"As opposed to that high-spending, free-wheeling flower child of my past," I said. "In other words, no little happy faces in the margins?"

Paula pressed on. "Your ability as a business owner is substantiated or undermined by the strength of your key people. This should be played up or down as the case may be."

"So," Lindsay sighed, "it looks like another epic in the making."

"Not at all," Paula replied. "It doesn't need to be lengthy. Just peer into your crystal ball and answer any questions about the business you think your banker may have. They are interested in how your business makes its money, how you spend it, and whether or not you will be able to pay them back. It's incumbent upon you to demonstrate how little risk the banker will be taking when they say yes."

"Is that it? C'est tout?" I asked.

"Not even close," Paula said. "The laundry list continues. What Joanne did that helped her case was to add copies of signed contracts for upcoming work and a copy of the premises lease so her banker knew where to find her. She even provided quotes for the big ticket items, like computers, that were going to be paid for with the bank's money. You can include supplier quotes, written appraisals, and copies of catalogue pages of the stuff you want to buy."

"I also included client testimonials, lots of them. We had garnered a tremendous amount of attention so I included a media package as well. That went over big," I added.

"Yeah, but what if you aren't a glamorous media starlet like our friend here?" Delia asked.

Paula laughed as she said, "A nice touch can be magazine articles on your industry, product, or service, especially if continued growth is forecast. That will work just fine. Naturally, you will need to have a statement of your personal net worth, and that of any other partners or shareholders in your business."

"That's the part that made me the most nervous," I said. "Other than my RRSP, every cent I had was chewed up in that year's sabbatical and business start-up. When I went to the bank, I was in debt. When I think about it, those bankers took a pretty big chance with me."

"That's why your signed contracts were so critical. And the fact that your debt could be explained away when you put your book in front of them. If there is a good story, they'll listen," Paula said.

"So once I've got this package together, then what?" I asked.

"Now you need to pick the right lending officer and institution," Paula said. "This should be based on research by pre-positioning the loan application through an initial call or visit. This is how you can introduce your business and its needs. Make sure the person reviewing the presentation package is actively involved in the small business loans market. Make sure they understand the typical constraints you have as a small business applicant."

"I sure understand that now," I reflected. "One quick visit with that first account manager could have saved me a lot of trouble."

"So, Paula, what should we expect from a good banker?" Roberta asked.

"Let's compare Joanne's first and second banker. The first is the kind that should send you screaming out of the room. The fact that Joanne's application was still in limbo after a month suggests that there was absolutely no responsiveness or sense of urgency in reviewing and approving her loan application. Look at banker number two — 48 hours later — an answer."

"And the right one, I might add," I said.

"Exactly. Kathrine had respect for your experience, knowledge, and time. Both her and Chester's willingness to think outside the box was tremendous. They both saw possibilities, not roadblocks. Banker number one clearly saw nothing but roadblocks. It's also evident that Kathrine had a long-term vision and focused on the relationship that was going to develop with Joanne. Joanne was nothing but a loan application to the first banker. The fact that Kathrine had a desire to be working with entrepreneurs, in particular the women's market, showed that she understood the importance and growth opportunities in the small business segment.

"Once you have chosen a lender you'd like to work with, give them a copy of the presentation package in advance of the meeting so they can do a preliminary review and analysis," Paula said. "Bankers really like it when you do this. They hate surprises, and this respects their time and their thought processes. It lessens the number of questions so your next meeting can be shorter. You can concentrate on answering the more involved questions like understanding the actual details of your loan request."

"So, have you done everything now?" Delia asked.

"Mostly, yes," Paula said. "But other parts of the process could include getting a copy of your personal credit rating from Equifax Canada in advance. This is so you can reverse any mistakes on your credit record before approaching the banker. Banks place supreme importance on personal credit worthiness. They are particularly interested in not only your ability to support the business but how you would repay the loan if the company couldn't."

"So, if I do all this, does it mean I'm going to get what I ask for?" Lindsay asked.

"No, but there are tactics you can use during the negotiation process to get the best possible deal. For example, volume buying can give you a better loan deal for your business. Banks want all of your banking needs and will be open to discussion about new or, for that matter, lost business that may be tied to the development of a relationship for business purposes."

"When I changed banks," I said, "part of the reason I'm sure my request was approved was because I took everything across the street with me. I had a well-used personal line, but I was now paying *them* interest on it. I moved over my RRSPs and all my personal banking. And that's really paid off for them. Today, my mortgage and Kate's RESP are with them."

"My bank asked me to personally guarantee everything," Lindsay said. "I took that rather hard."

"I did at first as well," I said. "But then I thought, I believe so passionately in what I'm doing, I shouldn't feel too much discomfort putting everything on the line for it. It showed the bank I was very, very serious."

Paula agreed. "Bankers may ask for your personal guarantee when the business has not yet proven that it can stand on its own two feet, meaning that the current financial state is not strong enough to handle more debt. I always recommend that people ask their banker to limit their personal guarantee. Keep it to only the portion of the loan where there is no other type of security or collateral. While your personal guarantee gets reduced as your loan balance decreases, try to get a commitment up front to have the personal guarantee released once you have demonstrated that your business can hold its own. If your own guarantee is not enough to support your request, the bank may ask a family member, business partner, or financial benefactor to lay it on the line for you.

"The last thing you need to remember when looking for outside financing is that financing is not only about getting money when you need it and don't have it. More importantly, it's about the proper balancing of your finances. Different types of financing have different conditions and costs attached. Sometimes mismatching can be easier and faster in the short term but you will pay dearly in the long term. Think of it this way. Let's say instead of saving for the start-up phase of your business, you take out a personal line of credit. That means you start out personally debt-laden. When it comes time to get a small business loan to buy a computer and your personal guarantee is required, it may not be worth much since you are already highly leveraged. It could be that your growth may be stunted."

"Or not," I said. "As Paula knows, that is exactly the route I took. Naturally, if there is a choice between the hard way and the easy way, you can be guaranteed what road I'd choose. But the bank still gave me an operating line."

"Your banker really believes in what you are doing, Joanne. There are no hard and fast rules here. Many of us, myself included, have done this and still continue to use a personal line of credit as a buffer for the business. That's why it's recommended that you try to get the biggest personal line you can while you are employed and before you start your business. It can, in fact, be a good fall-back position if you get stymied trying to arrange financing. While you shouldn't use your personal line as a regular financing mechanism for your business, it's wise to have one as a safety net. Sometimes unforeseen circumstances come up and you can't get the financing for the business reworked fast enough to handle the cash flow."

"I know what you mean," said Delia. "I've often pulled out my credit cards and done the old cash advance thing to get through a particularly rough spot in my business."

I jumped in since I was an expert in the world of credit card abuse. "Credit cards are usually an entrepreneur's first line of credit, but without proper care and feeding, they could end your business life almost before it gets started. Your personal credit rating can significantly affect your ability to borrow money or lease equipment for your business and determine whether or not you can finance your home, car, and other personal purchases. Try renting a car or buying tickets to an awards dinner without a credit card."

"What about getting a partner with a good credit rating if yours isn't pristine? Or a partner whose pockets that haven't been picked quite so clean?" Delia asked.

"I can't tell you how many times I've had to talk Joanne out of finding a partner," Paula replied. "It's not an uncommon thought, but she somehow has it in her bean that bringing someone in with money will solve all her troubles. It won't. Finding out and fixing the root causes of her troubles is necessary if she wants the solution to be permanent instead of just a band-aid."

Lindsay spoke up, "So it really pays to try to look past immediate needs towards those that are to come. Clearly you will be better off in both the short and the long run, but without a crystal ball, how do you do this?"

I jumped in. "You've got to learn to become your own financial manager. Trust me. It's a cake walk."

Paula threw me a withering glance.

The MC called for our attention as the evening's events continued. As we twisted in our chairs to view the stage, Paula said, "Ladies, leave your cards on the table, please. Your bill will come in the mail."

What Do You Do When the Bank Says No?

After the crying jag is over, you have repaired the hole you kicked in the wall, and you have decided against taking a contract out on your banker's life, you sit down, take a deep breath, and try to figure out why they turned you down. Most often when the bank says no to your application, some important piece is missing either *in* your business or *from* your business plan. Or, something has happened somewhere between your words leaving your mouth and getting to the banker's ears. Or there has been a breakdown somewhere between your banker's ears and brain. Something may have been poorly communicated by you or misunderstood by your banker. So your next step is simple. Sit down and ask your banker why the answer was no. Think of it as the kind of no you get from a customer. As we said, often no is the first step in the sales process towards yes. Ask your banker what's needed in order for a yes. Ask if he or she will revisit your financing proposal if you are able to make the required changes.

My banker, Denise Araiche, says declines can happen for a variety of reasons. Sometimes it's a matter of a credit rating getting cleaned up or perhaps you have applied for the wrong type of financing. For instance, if it's a product that's being developed, maybe what the client really needs is venture capital which is not traditional bank financing. But Denise says one thing is for sure, your banker may not always give you what you want, but should be able to provide you with options on how to get there.

It is important not to burn bridges no matter how unjustly you feel you have been treated. Do your homework, get other opinions, then go back (if you care to) and discuss your point of view. If this is the only financial institution that you have shopped your proposal to, *take it to another bank!* Make the adjustments suggested by the declining banker that make sense to you, and see if the new banker agrees with the first's assessment. It's always good to get a second opinion, whether that be from another banker, your accountant, your business adviser, or another trusted entrepreneur. Most banks have an imperative that when they turn you down, they have to give you options. Aside from your banker, a great resource on where to go is our friend Doug Gray's book, *Raising Money: The Canadian Guide to Successful Business Financing*. Take a look at Barbara Orser and Alan Riding's book, *Beyond the Banks: Creative Financing for Canadian Entrepreneurs*. They cover where to get money, from the banks to "angels" and everything in between.

We had an experience during our meltdown in the first year that forced us to get inventive. Kathrine, our first banker before she moved on to other things, was part of our team and was generally the first or second person I called whatever the nature of the news, good or bad. That particular day, her tone was much different from the usual "How's it going?" attitude. She was calling in response to my desperate plea for an extension on our already bursting operating line of credit. There was no money to make payroll.

"That's it, Joanne. You're tapped out. They won't give you any more credit," she stated bluntly. "You're going to have to get money elsewhere."

"Elsewhere?" I asked plaintively. "Please explain this elsewhere? I have to meet payroll in two days, our rent is due, I have no fewer than a dozen suppliers who are demanding to be paid yesterday, I have no salespeople to bring in business, I'm under contract to revise *Balancing Act* so I have no time to sell, I've got a claim against the company, and I have got to start thinking about saving for a kid's education and how to fund a non-existent maternity leave. Any other brainstorms besides elsewhere??!?"

She coughed nervously and admitted that in this situation, she didn't have any brilliant ideas other than the bank of Mom and Dad. It didn't matter that we were expanding into more stable lines of business. The bank agreed we had phenomenal opportunities awaiting us, but it wasn't prepared to put any more money on the line. Though Kathrine believed wholeheartedly in what we were doing, she needed to remind me again that, as Paula had said, banks are not venture capitalists. They fund erratic cash flows, not zero cash flows. I closed my eyes, clenched my fists, and, through gritted teeth, pleaded for a temporary bulge in our credit line. I felt what little self-respect I had evaporate. We got a flat-out no.

I needed to depersonalize this experience to clear the way for proper action. This wasn't about me, it was about the financial state of my company. So, I got creative. As an individual I had total personal credit of around $50,000. It was split between a $10,000 credit card limit and a $40,000 personal line of credit. My personal line of credit was maxed out but I still had $10,000 on my credit cards. Instead of borrowing from my credit card at stratospheric rates, I negotiated with the bank to move $5000 of the credit limit from my card to my personal credit line. I subsequently took the money from my personal credit line and moved it to my business credit line at only one-third the interest rate I would have been charged had I borrowed from my credit card. I made payroll with minutes to spare. Paula joked that maybe I was an accountant deep down. The thought made me shudder.

Bank Initiatives in the Women Entrepreneur Market

There are three banks that have identified women entrepreneurs as a market segment. At the time of writing, the following are the initiatives that have been completed or are underway.

Royal Bank of Canada

Royal Bank has a Women Entrepreneur Advisory Council whose members include leading female entrepreneurs, consultants, and Royal Bank account managers. This group acts as a source and a sounding board for ideas, and helps the bank keep in touch with the views of the women's market.

Training and Education
- Sponsor of an award-winning educational video entitled *Women Entrepreneurs: Making a Difference!* created to inspire young women to develop their entrepreneurial skills.
- Account managers and other staff are sensitized to gender issues and the importance of the women's market through "Reaching the Women's Market" seminars developed by Women and Money Inc.
- Two-day seminars entitled "Your Business Matters" are conducted for women entrepreneurs, with topics such as marketing fundamentals, sources of financing, and components of a business plan.

- ViaSource links small businesses and entrepreneurs to networks of re-sources. Through no-cost, confidential forums with professionals from such areas as accounting, banking, legal affairs, and marketing, small business owners and entrepreneurs can receive direction and insight about business issues.

Mentorship

- Co-sponsor of "Women in Film & Video/Vancouver, Moving Up Mentorship Program," designed to assist mid-level professionals in the industry move into non-traditional careers in film and media.
- One of three corporate sponsors of the Step Ahead program, which teams new women entrepreneurs with experienced female mentors.
- Supporter of Women's World Finance, a new community loan fund program in Atlantic Canada that is designed to fund and support women micro-entrepreneurs through mentorship.

Sponsorships/Conferences

- Founding sponsor, in alliance with Women Entrepreneurs of Canada, of the International Meeting of Les Femmes Chefs D'Entreprises Mondiales (FCEM), a worldwide organization representing women business owners in 33 countries.
- Sponsor of Women Entrepreneurs of Canada, an association of experienced businesswomen with chapters in Toronto and Vancouver.
- Founding sponsor of Women Business Owners of Canada (WBOC), which will act as a virtual channel for information, education, and services for women business owners.
- Sponsor of YMCA's Canada-wide Women of Distinction Award Programs, which honour women who have distinguished themselves in their chosen field.

Women in Trade

- Presenting sponsor of the Team Canada Businesswomen's Trade Mission, November 1997, at the Canadian Embassy in Washington.
- Sponsor of Women's Software and Technology Association (WSTA) which promotes international trade opportunities for software and technology developers.
- Sponsor of the 1999 Canada/USA Trade Summit in an effort to create and promote commercial relationships between Canadian and American businesswomen.
- Major sponsor of the Trade Research Coalition, a Department of Foreign Affairs and International Trade initiative that focuses on women exporters and the obstacles they face.

- Sponsor of a technology-based Virtual Trade Mission beginning July 1998 and supporting Canadian women entrepreneurs with trade from Malaysia and Singapore. This pilot initiative relies on Internet-based business matching and video-conferencing.
- Sponsor of the Alliance of Manufacturers and Exporters Canada and the Canadian International Development Agency (CIDA) Women in Development Award. This award is presented to a company for a project that demonstrates concrete measures taken to incorporate women's challenges into its design and implementation.

Bank of Montreal

- Founding sponsor of The Canadian Woman Entrepreneur of the Year Awards and Conference.
- The Bank's Institute for Small Business sponsored *Myths & Realities: The Economic Power of Women-Led Firms in Canada*, a landmark study that paints the first national portrait of women-led firms as a powerful economic force in the Canadian economy.
- Lead corporate partner in Women and Economic Development Consortium. Eight donors from private, voluntary, and co-operative sectors have committed to spend $2.3 million (1997–2000) to support the best ideas of women's organizations working to help low-income women move forward with viable business initiatives leading to economic self-reliance.
- Teamed with *Woman Newsmagazine* to offer complimentary advertising to small businesses in the start-up stage.
- Sponsored production of *Minding My Own Business*, a three-part women entrepreneur TV series seen across Canada. The series draws on the experiences of businesswomen and maps out a series of steps for establishing a successful business. Available at Bank branches, local public libraries, and through many local school boards.
- Endowed $225,000 to Mount Saint Vincent University for provision of capital and skills training at the University's Centre for Women in Business; $250,000 to the University of Ottawa for their Women's Studies Programs; and $250,000 to McGill University.

Scotiabank

- $300,000 grant to Simon Fraser University to open a resource centre for women entrepreneurs.
- Scotia Professional Plan defers loan principle payments for up to eight months upon birth or adoption of a child.

- Works with consultants to explore ways to best service the woman entrepreneurial market on an ongoing basis.

More Capital — Where to Look

After knocking on the bank's door and being turned away, the next question that most owners of toddler businesses ask, "Should I be looking for an outside investor?" This question is heard most often from those who experience continual cash flow crises in their business. There are a number of different reasons why people ask this question. Some ask because they perceive that it is easier to find a person rather than a bank to lend them money. Some ask because they want to share the management load with another warm body. Others ask because their banker told them that's what they needed in order to get a loan or operating line. And still others ask because their growth plans for the company are ambitious and they require a hefty amount of money to achieve their objectives.

But bringing more capital into your business almost always means parting with some of the ownership and the stuff that goes with it, like control and autonomy. That's the give for the get and they are inextricably tied. Getting equity from outside sources creates a long-term and often complex partnership. You should only be contemplating going this route if you have a long-term need for money or you are seeking a long-term relationship with a person who will assume some ownership responsibilities. As we mentioned in chapter 3, sharing ownership in your company is not wise if your need for another person, set of skills, or money is short term.

Great, you say, but how do I know if my cash need is long or short term? When should I be looking for an investor instead of going to a banker? You need to go through a process of elimination. Have this conversation with yourself:

1. "Is my company operating profitably?" That means that your profit margins are healthy and stable, your expenses are lean, and you are generating enough business to put profit on the bottom line. Investors aren't particularly keen to finance losses. If they decide to give it a go for the challenge of turning the business around, be prepared to give up a significant amount of your share in your company. Your opening position is weak and the investor will expect, and rightly so, that most of the benefits of their investment will come back to them.

2. Once you have dealt with the first question, ask, "Can my cash flow dilemma be solved by reworking the timing of my cash flow? Can I change how I manage my receivables, payables, inventory, or capital investments,

like purchases of equipment or machinery? Can I finance them through debt, like an operating line or term loan?"

3. Now, take a look at your long-term strategic plans. "Do I require significant upfront investments to get my product or service into the hands of my customer?" These investments might include research and development of the product or production process; infrastructure like equipment, locations, machinery, distribution channel, information systems, and staff; and significant and ongoing management expertise that you do not possess.

Dealing with these questions will help you decide whether looking for an investor is the right financing path for you. However, ask anyone who has gone down this road. They will tell you that, at first, they thought the hardest part would be getting the business plan together to present to potential investors. But the truth is, the hardest part is finding the right investor and striking a deal that you can both live with.

So how long do you think this process will take from start to finish? It's rare to see a deal concluded in fewer than 12 months, especially if you have to create the financing or information memorandum — the business plan that you present to potential investors that you first have to find. Success and time lines depend on the quality of your plan and whether or not it's realistic. They also depend on the amount of investment you need, the type of business you're in, what type of investor you are looking for, and whether you already know anyone who fits the bill.

You then need to know what options are out there once you have accepted that you want to share your pie. Remember that one of the advantages of incorporation was the additional options available to you by way of financing. (Not all options are available to unincorporated businesses.) While not an exhaustive list, here are some of the most common equity financing options for small business.

Mergers, Joint Ventures, Acquisitions, and Strategic Alliances

All of these are ways of combining businesses through co-operative arrangements in order to share costs. Sharing costs means reducing the total amount of investment money that you have to come up with on your own. Most of these arrangements are contractual and range from two businesses becoming one (mergers and acquisitions), two businesses becoming three (joint venture), to two businesses staying two businesses and sharing costs, assets, and the expertise needed for research, production, marketing, or distribution (strategic alliances).

Private Investors

This is the most typical route for small businesses bringing in an outside equity partner for the first time. Private investors are often referred to as "angels" because they provide not only money but also a helping hand. Most angels are attracted to a particular type of business investment for a variety of economic and personal reasons. Maybe they have just retired and want to keep active in the business community. Maybe they are a recently laid-off senior manager from a large corporation who has received a severance package and wants to become part of an entrepreneurial venture. They may even be a veteran entrepreneur who has successfully started and sold a number of businesses and now wants the variety of being involved in a few going concerns. They may be employees of your company who want to benefit from the long-term success of the business. These employees may want to make part of their compensation dependent on the overall performance of the company. (A word of caution if you are considering going this route. Make sure that you have considered whether or not you will be able to share control with these employees. Or, for that matter, do you want to have employees hold shares in your business? If they leave or have to be terminated, what effect will their being an owner have on such a situation?)

We often refer to angels as strategic investors, as opposed to financial investors who just provide money. Angels typically act as business adviser as well as financier. Angels are often instrumental in helping with other business connections, like customers, bankers, suppliers, or alliance partners. Most are not interested in controlling the business and have fewer restrictions on the type of business, financing terms, and type of return on investment that they will entertain compared to, for example, venture capital companies.

Sometimes finding these people is like trying to find an unstoned person at Woodstock. Start by asking your accountant, banker, lawyer, business adviser, other entrepreneurs, suppliers, and even a choice customer or two. There are business brokers or angel networks that offer matching services between businesses and angels. But do be careful how you get the word out when looking for an investor. After all, this is your business and your plans should be treated as strictly confidential. Be sure that you have anyone involved in the process sign a confidentiality agreement that has been reviewed by your lawyer.

Venture Capital Companies (and Other Institutional Investors)

These companies are really looking for the next latest and greatest in business. This is the world of high risk for high return. Start-ups are usually not potentials for this type of financing. Typically the entrepreneur has to have a significant market advantage. If this isn't your business (yet), then don't bother going down this road. They rarely make exceptions to their rules when investment opportunities don't fit their formula or strategic direction. Why? Because venture capital firms have their own investors to satisfy, like private individuals in labour-sponsored funds or public companies like the banks. They are out there supplying dollars and expertise to select companies that have a high rapid growth potential and that need large amounts of capital, almost certainly over $500,000. All this for the chance to make a very high rate of return, 20–40 percent; in a very short time, three to seven years; in return for at least a 30–50 percent share in the ownership.

Venture capital firms have a reputation for negotiating tough financing terms and setting high demands on target companies. They can either help you reach the moon or drive you into the ground. So make sure you don't venture into these waters alone. People experienced in negotiating these types of deals will help protect your intellectual property and trade secrets. They will help ensure that the process of negotiating the deal will not break you or your company. One of the best sources for these types of people is the venture capital companies themselves. Call them up and ask them for whom they have done work. Then ask people successful at getting venture capital who they used to help them prepare and negotiate their proposals. It's better to work with people that you know have been successful and are already known to the folks with the money.

Initial Public Offerings (IPO)

While this form of financing is very unlikely for most small businesses who have not already gotten private or institutional investors, you should have a general understanding of what it is. "Going public," as it is often called, is simply the process of offering shares in your business to the public at large. The way you do this is through an initial public offering that is just a special "business plan" called a prospectus. The prospectus must meet the standards set by the security commission that governs the stock exchange where you will be listing your shares. Raising money this way is extremely expensive because of all the initial costs of going public and the regulatory requirements of being a "public" company on an ongoing basis.

If a small business meets certain criteria (the number of people you intend to sell to and the dollar amount of the individual offerings is small), you can then sell shares to a small group of investors (not the general public) without being subject to provincial securities laws. The criteria and restrictions vary from province to province so it is best to consult your lawyer who will help you understand the legalities of soliciting money from the public through the issuing and selling of shares.

Franchising

Franchising your business concept is a cross between a strategic alliance and private investment. An outside person, the franchisee, pays you to use your name and for the right to sell your trademarked product or service using a system that you provide. While the ownership stays with you as the franchisor, you get to license the right for other people to use. You then get to share some of the costs, risks, and rewards of your concept with others. You receive money in the form of an initial franchise fee, service, training, or support fees, equipment sale or lease fees, and royalties. This influx of money along with an expansion strategy will allow you to grow very quickly. You need to control your initial expansion, however, by setting up a couple of other sites that you run yourself. These test sites will ensure that your concept will make a good prototype for a similar business in a different location. If your expansion proves successful and your concept "franchisable," you then face the same daunting task as others seeking other types of equity financing — finding the right person to act as the franchisee.

Lynn Charpentier: Finding Her Franchise Concept

Lynn Charpentier is one such person for whom franchising was the right path to financing and expanding her business. A 45-year-old mother of four and grandmother of two, Lynn opened the first Centre de Langues Internationales Charpentier (CLIC) in 1978 to provide individuals, corporations, and children with a variety of language services through a network of private language schools in the province of Quebec.

Convinced that she would be unable to get financing from any bank (she had no collateral), Lynn agreed to sell her then husband 50 percent of the business for $20,000. All her hard work paid off with very unexpected and rapid growth. After the first year, she opened a school in Jonquière and another in Granby the year after, then one in Drummondville, which further tested the concept.

In order to support her growth both physically and financially, Lynn decided that franchising, which had never been done in her business, was the vehicle she needed. She had the daunting task of developing a system that would provide franchisees with:

- help to set up a CLIC school
- teachers trained according to the CLIC method

- conception, strategic planning, and marketing administration
- tools to train in management, administration, and specialized sales techniques
- quality control
- CLIC's sales products
- clientele evaluation (ratios/statistics)
- access to experts and consultants and the marketing and pedagogic departments.

Eventually, and with a bank's help, she pulled it off. But the most painful aspect for Lynn was letting go of the idea that she could not be everything to everyone. Growing the way she did required a total turnaround in attitude, philosophy, and the way she was used to doing things. Lynn and her staff had to create different companies and different departments. She admits, "I was the slowest and worst one in my outfit to adjust." She held on to the good old "mama" days for a long time. Lynn said, "This change was very hard for me because I had to adjust to the fact that I had to let go, to leave my employees enough room to manage their departments, make their own decisions, and simply to breathe. If you are too much of a mother hen, you can actually strangle initiative out of people. If you don't readjust and wake up quickly, you will lose good people and it will eventually slow down your expansion process because you just can't be everything to everyone, however hard you try.

"Our main objective is, of course, to make sure that the franchisee will offer to the public the high quality standard of CLIC's products and that they will be assured of a good revenue stream in the very first year of operation. For this opportunity, a franchisee would pay an initial franchise fee of $30,000 cash plus allow for an additional $20,000 in working capital to ensure a good business launch. For this initial fee, the franchisee is assured of a protected territory of approximately 100,000 inhabitants where they can carry on business."

Lynn says that survival and success require staying on top of things, especially if you intend to lead the pack. This simple philosophy has sure paid off. Lynn owns the largest network of private language schools in Quebec. Looking to the future, Lynn says, "In a franchise structure, you have to put your finger on what your clients will need from you down the road." They went from their original formula (private language lessons), to small then bigger group tutoring, all the way to discussion clubs and immersion programs. They were able to offer services to clients before they even realized they needed them.

Lynn told us, "Well, we are still expanding and still going strong 20 years and 20 schools later. Cash flow is not an issue anymore. My mother taught me that the past is a good indication of what the future will hold for you, meaning learn from your past, it will guide you in the future. Also, remember who your friends were when you needed them. When you become a success or are recognized as such, everyone wants a piece of you. I have an excellent memory. I remember who did what for me and this memory dictates a lot of my choices."

Whether you decide that you need more capital, a loan, or more sales and profits to finance your dream, chances are good you will also need to do more with less and faster. It is at the toddler stage that technology has to become an essential partner in your business.

Technology — Where Has All the Productivity Gone?

Sometimes I believe technology and productivity are incompatible. Yes, technology is great. But only when it works. I often question the promises made by the software vendors (let's not even travel down that road), technology service providers (the bane of my existence), my techno-weenie kid brother, and my engineer partner. I haven't reaped the life-altering benefits touted by those who see technology as another religion. But deep in my heart I know that I have to use it to stay alive.

As baby entrepreneurs in our first year, we managed to get the pieces in place when it came to marketing, sales, finance, human resources, and technology. Now we need to tie them all together in some meaningful fashion to wring more return out of that sometimes annoying investment.

Let's take an inventory of some of the basic techno-bits and pieces that you may be using:

- a desktop computer with either a laser or colour bubble-jet printer,
- a "suite" of some sort that includes a wordprocessor and spreadsheet,
- fax software and/or a fax machine,
- e-mail software,
- a database to house your contacts and maybe your calendar and to-do lists,
- financial software to keep track of your bookkeeping information,
- a hands-free telephone with call display and voicemail, and
- a cellular phone and/or pager.

If you have managed to assemble this basic list, you have laid an excellent foundation for your business operations. But you may still find that either it is falling short or, because of time and cost, you've put off getting your technology to an adequate working level. There may be a couple of missing pieces to your incomplete productivity puzzle.

Completing the Productivity Puzzle

I was issuing the standard stream of curses when, through call display, I noticed Paula was calling. It was the third time that day that my computer had crashed and I was under the most intense of deadlines. The keyboard was actually in my hands as I seriously deliberated whether to toss the thing out the window. "Ah, perfect timing," I thought. "The techno-queen."

I put down the keyboard and picked up the phone. Without so much as a "top of the morning," I launched into a steaming diatribe. "Rarely, if ever, have I seen a conspiracy as elaborate as this one to sabotage my last remaining nerve. This computer is going to make a marvelous bird feeder in the back yard."

"Is there a more appropriate time to call you back, perhaps during your mid-life crisis?" Paula asked.

"Please explain to me why this technology seems to do something and nothing at the same time?" I asked. "We've got all these technology bits and pieces and we spend what seems like half our working lives fine-tuning our systems only to get half of what we need out of them. And that's on a good day."

I took a deep breath. "Thanks. I'm over it now."

After Paula helped me through what amounted to the 762nd technological meltdown, she said, "Joanne, to get a good return on your technology investment, you have to invest time and money to integrate all of the applications that you use. You aren't going to want to hear this, but you may even have to replace some of what you are using now. It may be the only productive solution."

"What a wild sense of humour you've got," I retorted. "As bad as this system is, it's ours and I know how to use it. You're suggesting that I learn new scheduling and database management software? I'd rather stick needles in my eyes, thank you very much."

"Your needs have obviously grown with your business and my guess is that some of what you are currently using may not be doing what you need. What do you need, by the way?"

"Well, things have changed a lot since we first started, though mostly what I'm after is peace of mind," I answered. "A lot of the same requirements still exist from our first year but our so-called solutions still aren't working that well. I'm still constantly on the road so I need to access information on the 300 projects we have underway that need my immediate attention. And, naturally, all of our customers want everything yesterday. It would be amazing to be able to make and approve decisions not only while on the road but also from my home office, where I am 90 percent of the time. Another huge problem is the size of the presentation files we now work with. We have one- and two-day training courses, complete with hundreds of complex cartoons and graphics, stored on Rosa's computer. The time it takes to make even the most minor change to any of these files is downright obscene. Managing my schedule is still a world-class pain in the butt. And rather than lug my dumb laptop everywhere, I still use an archaic paper-based system because it's so much easier and quicker to write stuff down. I feel out of touch since all the important information is either at the office with Rosa or locked in my desktop computer in my home office."

I stopped to catch my breath but only for a brief instant. I carried on with my litany of complaints. "I do all my own writing and research for magazines and television. My office has completely disappeared under a ton of newspaper and magazine articles that I have collected for research. I have to get a handle on this paper monster or I'm going to have to move into another office just to have space to swivel in my chair."

Paula laughed. "Have faith. You're already a good piece of the way there, Joanne. You do use a database program to keep track of all your contacts. You are used to using scheduling software, just not the right one. You need one that integrates with your database and with Rosa."

"You make it sound easy. That means you're lying to me again," I said.

Brushing my comment aside, Paula said, "You know, with the database management software you are already using, you can synchronize your copy of the database with the changes that Rosa makes and vice versa. It's great because you can both work simultaneously on one master database without worrying about having to re-enter the same information into the other person's copy. It keeps track of all your changes, additions, and deletions to your contacts and your calendar to boot."

"My calendar? It will handle my schedule as well?" I asked, hoping I had heard her right.

"Yes, ma'am. And it will pack up all your changes neatly in an e-mail and deliver them to Rosa via the Internet. It will then automatically update her copy of the database with a click of a button. And if you want to avoid shlepping that relic you call a laptop across the country or shelve the paper-based system you are using, get yourself a personal data assistant like the PalmPilot. I have one and I call it my pocket brain."

"Probably works better than the real thing," I said.

Paula ignored me and continued, "The new breed of PDAs allows you to take and modify the most important information from your desktop computer, like your address book, your calendar, small documents, and even spreadsheets that you are working on. You can then synchronize these with your desktop when you get back to your office or fax and even e-mail them directly from your PDA. The best part is that you don't have to squish your fingers to fit those puny keyboards any longer. Most allow you to hand-write notes using a pen-like stylus. Some even translate your handwriting into text so that there is no need to retype the information that you want to keep or incorporate into a document, fax, or e-mail. Talk about saving time and money."

Skeptical, I said, "This sounds too good to be true. Frankly, I wouldn't know what to do with myself if I became that efficient. So what about the junk yard I call an office? How do I tame the paper beast?"

"Use the Internet, Joanne. Almost every article that's sitting on your floor or in mammoth piles on your desk is sitting in paperless form right in your computer."

"Why do I feel like such a technological Luddite?" I asked, sighing deeply.

"This stuff is all relatively new. You've got to give yourself a bit of time to acclimatize to the changes. Look what you've done with your banking," Paula said.

"This is one place, Paula, where technology has had a wonderful impact," I agreed. "Before we used electronic banking, I never knew what was in our account until a month after the fact. Even though Rosa uses QuickBooks to keep track of all our accounting, the reports were never right. Internet banking is amazing. Now, Rosa and I can log in any time, any day, from any city, to our bank's Web site and review our account. I can even transfer money between accounts if necessary. Rosa pays our credit card and telephone bills on the date they're due without having to physically go to the bank. With an automated bank machine card, she makes deposits on her way home instead of taking time out of her busy day. All of these services finally released us from banking jail."

"It sounds like you're not as much of a technology grump as you make yourself out to be," Paula observed.

"Don't you ever have technology meltdowns, Paula?"

"Are you kidding?" Paula said. "When my business moved into its toddler stage, we had the same problems as you've experienced. We were having trouble retrieving the right file, record, and piece of information. Our hard drives were crammed with files containing who knows what and we were swimming in paper. The right information was either going to the wrong people, evaporating, or clogging up the communication channel. Our system was fine in the first year but it fast became too narrow to handle our current volume of communications."

"Sounds vaguely familiar," I said.

"Our associates needed to be integrated into our company's administrative life like they were already integrated into our clients' lives. But I didn't have enough time to communicate with all of them on everything they needed to know. We also needed to maximize the value of the information that we processed in order to maintain our value to our clients. We were using the Internet as a communication channel for customers and prospects and as a research vehicle. So we decided to apply the same technology to help us with our communication with and management of employees, associates, and suppliers. We created an Intranet."

I groaned at the prospect of learning about more technology that could potentially screw up.

"It's kind of like having a dynamic electronic bulletin board that everyone in and outside of the office can go to for information. Our sea of paper is down to a puddle because we now have our associates enter their notes from their client sessions into a secure online form. Our associates love it because they can access the form any time. I love it because we are getting consistent, current, and complete information from everyone."

"Sounds great but expensive, complicated, and profoundly time-consuming," I said.

"Creating the Intranet is one of the best moves we have made. The information is available to all who need it, and it's easy and cheap to maintain."

"And who did you hire to do all this for you? Some brilliant MIT graduate, a teenager, or did you do it yourself?" I asked.

"I wasn't about to add Web master to my title," Paula replied. "We hired someone whose dedicated focus, responsibility, expertise, and business is to develop, maintain and host Web sites. It just so happened that he was also my brother."

I sighed. Still extremely skeptical, I said, "Give me strength. It makes you wonder how we ever survived before this onslaught of technology. All right, tell me the first thing I need to do."

Today, you wouldn't recognize our company. My personal data assistant (PalmPilot) has my entire life stored in something that fits in the palm of my hand. I can get phone numbers and book appointments at the drop of a hat. Rosa and I synchronize our database and schedule every day, no matter where

I am in the country. Even our phone systems have gone high-tech. I have voice recognition on both my home office and cellular phones. All I do is pick up the receiver or use hands-free, say the name of the person I want to call, and that's it. I must admit, though, that I do get really weird looks from people as I drive along, appearing to have a rather animated discussion with no one but myself. We upgraded our hardware so now Rosa waits mere seconds to save one of her huge graphics files instead of an hour or more. The process of inputting customization changes to our training programs went from two days to an hour. Rosa, Cynthia, and I e-mail everything back and forth so there is absolutely no duplication of effort. In fact, while writing this book, Paula and I e-mailed this manuscript back and forth every day so we were both always working off the most current version. It saved an incalculable amount of time. You'd be hard pressed to find a scrap of paper anywhere in my office. I use the Internet for all my research. It really is "the mother of all distribution channels" for anyone who is in the business of moving, managing, or selling information. That's practically anyone in business.

The Internet Is the Best Employee I Ever Had

I have this great employee called the Internet. Without it, this book would never have gotten written. The Internet delivers and picks up my mail, does my banking, hosts meetings, sells my products, supports my customers, orders my airline tickets, takes orders from customers, trains me and my staff, and brings me my newspaper and magazines. It couriers information immediately to and from all of my people — customers and suppliers. A low-cost Web site gives me, at an absolute minimum, a dynamic, cost-effective information source where I can direct people immediately. This bridges the wait time when they ask, "Do you have any information on your company that you can send me?" I can strike while the iron is hot.

It always knows something about absolutely everything and it even remembers where I've been and helps me figure out where to go next. It works seven days a week and 24 hours a day for peanuts and never complains.

Whether you use the Internet to receive information or provide it, it has fast become an intricate part of business life. Many companies are using the Internet for all sorts of practical purposes including recruiting employees, advertising product features and benefits, automating order taking, maintaining supplier relations, and even posting articles and press releases. The Internet gives you access to monumental amounts of information on your prospective customer (what do they really want or need), your competition (who else is in the game), potential suppliers, new employees (résumé posting boards), technical support (to keep your technology working for you instead of the other way around), and the trends influencing your market (market statistics and research, new product and service announcements).

Women have especially embraced the opportunity to add the Internet to their payroll. It's worth noting that IBM in particular has acknowledged the power of the women's market and women's use of technology. They have someone in an organizational position entitled "Segment Manager: Women in Business — Worldwide Marketing," with people in the Asia-Pacific, Latin America, and North America regions reporting to her. IBM is committed to women business owners in Canada through several relationship marketing initiatives:

- partnership with Women Business Owners of Canada (WBOC)
- partner with Women Entrepreneurs of Canada Association (WEC)
- sponsor of International Conference FCEM/WEC
- contributor to the film *Women Entrepreneurs — Making a Difference*
- sponsor of the Canadian Woman Entrepreneur of the Year Award
- involvement in the Women Leaders Network and the Canadian Women's International Business Initiative (CWIBI) Trade Mission
- various education seminars created specifically for women business owners.

None of this should be surprising. Women and the Internet work on the same principle: connection.

Busting at the Seams — Growing Up and Moving Out

With all this activity, all this management, all this technology, it may be likely that your home office has overtaken the home and that mission control has become more of a three-ring circus. While technology can help you work with more people without necessarily needing more space, there comes a time in the lives of most owners of toddler businesses when they need or prefer to find an office outside the home. The new office can either augment or replace your "starter" home office.

When it comes to venturing outside your home, the options for your first leased office space will raise a thousand questions. "How do I find the right place? Will I be able to afford lease payments? How long do I have to commit to? What are all the things the new space has to have? Where should it be located? How big should it be?"

It is important to take the time to figure out precisely what your wants are, how your needs stack up against your wants, and lastly, the deal breaker —

what you can afford. You need to go "office-shopping," looking at a number of places (and more than once) before signing the lease. If the sound of this makes your already eye-popping blood pressure scream skyward, hire a shopping buddy. Get a real estate agent to do most of the legwork for you. They can narrow down your search and even help you with negotiating your lease. But keep your eyes open. Real estate agents undeniably save you time and money, but many of them work on behalf of both the landlord and the tenant. Watch out for conflict of interest and be sure to work out how they get paid in advance.

It doesn't matter if you are looking for a spot to house your office, a retail store, a distribution centre, or someplace to store inventory or extra equipment; before you or your agent start roaming around town, you first need to narrow down what type of space you are looking for. Naturally you'll start with what you want but eventually you'll have to settle on what you need. Here's some guidance on how to do both.

What You Want ...

Close your eyes and imagine what your office will look like. Once you wake up from your desperately needed nap, notice if the office is within walking distance or a short drive from your home. Is it modern architecture or in a part of the town that has recently been rejuvenated? Do the windows open? Is the boardroom formal or casual? (Does it have brick walls you can converse with?) Is it in a hustle-bustle or quaint-and-quiet part of town? How is it decorated? Open concept or individual offices? Consider what you need in the way of a location to make the business successful. I envisioned something almost palatial. Then reality in the form of what I really needed hit me square between the eyes.

What You Need ...

What I needed was a touch shy of palatial. I needed a centralized location for all the activity and all the staff. We were in sore need of more space. We were getting requests for meetings at our location from our bank and brokerage clients. They were used to mahogany-filled boardrooms and silver tea sets. My kitchen table and cracked teapot just wouldn't do. We needed a downtown address to enhance our image as a player. We found a perfect spot that gave us all of the above (minus the silver tea set) for an extremely good price. It gave the staff a sense of working for "a real company" with a "real address" and I could still afford to work from home. We went the shared office route.

Shared office arrangements are a little like living in a house with a bunch of roommates. Our situation works extremely well. There are four or five small businesses sharing a whole floor in a funky renovated brewery. We have an office, access to a fully functional kitchen, a really nice boardroom, state of the art voicemail system, and a photocopier when we need it. Everything else we own. And the price is unbelievable. In downtown Toronto, we pay $400 a month.

But be aware that sometimes privacy and identity can be diminished at best and lost at worst. Luckily that's not been our experience. Shared office arrangements range from informal to formal sharing of commercial space and from permanent to when-you-need-it. But it is important to remember to balance out the obvious savings of sharing overhead and not having to rent more space than you need. Be aware of the following drawbacks:

- You have to pay your share for things you don't need, like a full-time receptionist who can only greet and direct traffic, a prime location that doesn't have an adequate supply of parking, a bigger and faster photocopier and other extraneous office equipment, a spacious reception area, and extended hours of staffed operation.
- You might have to fight for resources when you really need them, like fax lines that are tied up when one of your roomies puts an ad for an administrative assistant in the local paper.
- You won't be able to control the behaviour and actions of others you share the space with.

If the shared office concept makes you nervous, take the standard road. Because you have likely already been operating for a while, the following questions will be fairly easy to answer. They will help you determine and prioritize your needs: Do you need a particular location that you, your staff, your customers, and your suppliers can easily access? Do you need to be closer to your customers, suppliers, or employees? Do you need to locate close to or away from your competition? What about other businesses that attract the same type of customer as your target market? Do you require high visibility or heavy consumer traffic to draw business? Do you need special facilities or features, like parking, docking, or 24-hour security (an important consideration for women entrepreneurs who tend to work long hours)? Does the nature of your business require that your address and location make a particular statement about your company and its image? Do you require your space to be flexible and open for collaborations and presentations or do you need privacy? Will the location let you expand? Once you have decided what you need (and don't be surprised if you have disguised a few of your wants as needs), the next step is to come up against the cold, hard truth. Money.

What You Can Afford ...

Before you sign on the dotted line, are you sure that you have figured out how to keep your leasing costs to a minimum? Here are some ideas to keep your overhead costs down: Use technology to extend the use of the space that you already have available. Think about having your employees use a part of their home as a home office. We did this for the longest time. Do what I did. Keep your home office and only lease the additional space needed to run your business. All I did was rent additional storage space, an office for employees, and a central place for suppliers and customers to visit. It really minimized the amount of space I needed to pay for.

In the toddler stage it is important that your business have what it needs to operate effectively but be careful not to get caught up in the excitement. You need to figure out, before you go out on that first date, how much you can afford to spend.

- **Step One.** Calculate how much money you have to spend on your new office. The rent is only one aspect of the cash you'll need to dole out in this process. There are also moving expenses, places to sit and desks to put your feet up on, signage, decorating, leasehold improvements, telephone and security systems, parking, coffee makers, cups, and microwaves.

- **Step Two.** What is your current level of profit? Most of us believe that spending money will make us money. However, go back and do the calculation in the section entitled "How Much Are Your Expenses Really Costing You" to determine exactly how much in new sales you will need to be able to afford this new expense. Then jump into the bad-news scenario by asking yourself, What will I do if I can only bring in half that amount in sales? Will I still be able to pay the rent and everything else or will someone have to go without a paycheque? (That usually means you.)

- **Step Three.** Consider the timing, pattern, and predictability of your cash flow. As we are only too aware, cash flow tends to be a little erratic in the early years. As you did when you *"what-iffed"* a dry spell in sales, think about how you would handle your new obligation if you were to experience a prolonged cash flow crunch. If you are at all uncertain of your future cash flow, here is where less is more. Take less both in terms of office size and length of lease in order to keep some of the risk at bay. It's often easier to add than take away.

What's in a Lease?

Once you have settled on an affordable office site, everything now has to be put on paper. Negotiating a commercial lease is often a bit daunting if you haven't done so before. It is significantly more complicated than a rental or mortgage agreement for an apartment, home, or condominium. A commercial lease is a legal contract that binds you and your business for possibly long periods of time. It can have a significant financial impact on your business, so get it reviewed and negotiated by a lawyer who is familiar with commercial leases. We have demystified the ordeal by providing you with some of the basic terms and provisions of a commercial lease. This is what you may want to look out for:

- **Gross rent** refers to the amount that you are paying for the rental of the space excluding taxes, insurance, and maintenance. The gross rent amount can either be fixed throughout the term of the lease or escalate as the years go by. Sometimes the landlord even shares in your business fortunes or misfortunes by tying part of the rent to your sales levels. This is common in retail situations. Make sure that you are comparing apples to apples when evaluating different rental payment arrangements. If you have to do significant modifications to the space or you agree to a longer lease term, you may even be able to negotiate a certain period up front where you don't have to pay rent. If your business is seasonal, you may want to pay more rent when you have more cash and less or none during your off season. Don't hesitate to ask for what you need. You'd be surprised at how negotiable landlords can be.

- **Net rent** is just the gross rent plus all of the other expenses that you have to pay as a tenant, like the above-mentioned property taxes, maintenance and property management costs, and insurance. These expenses are usually divvied up to each tenant on the basis of the total square feet of space they lease. It is common that these expenses are estimated at the beginning of the year and adjusted towards the end of the year once the landlord has calculated the actual costs. You will likely be responsible to pay your share of any shortfall between the estimated and actual assessment or you will get a credit if the landlord has overshot the mark.

- **Lease term** identifies how long your lease will be in effect. If it's important to be able to stay at the same location past the initial term, try negotiating a renewal option that entitles you to renew the lease with additional time for a specified period for a set rent amount. This may get you a more attractive gross rent or protect you against significant rent increases when your lease term expires.

- **Maintenance** will tell you who maintains what part of the premises, both inside and out. Because of security issues, if you are responsible for cleaning and maintenance, your landlord may want to approve who you use. If your landlord provides these services, make sure the rates are competitive.
- **Subletting** will either be prohibited or permitted under certain conditions and to certain types of sublessees. Your landlord may want to reserve the right to approve the sublessee you have chosen. Or, they may wish to be notified only if you choose to do so since subletting does not release you from your obligations to the landlord. If you want to be able to sublet, make sure that the lease entitles you to assign your rights to someone else.
- The **improvements and modifications** section will tell you whether or not and what type of changes you can make. The landlord will want to approve your plans and maybe even your choice of contractor before you begin tearing down or putting up walls. It is important to make sure that your lease does not say that you have to restore the space to its original state when the lease expires.
- **Insurance and liability** says who is responsible for paying for the casualty and liability insurance for your space and how much coverage you have to have. You may also run into a bit of a snag if both your landlord and your banker want to be identified as beneficiaries on your policy. Your lawyer can go a long way to reconciling these two points of view.
- **Competition** is something else to consider, especially if you are in a shared retail or office space where location is likely to be a competitive advantage. Consider including a clause to restrict your landlord's ability to lease other space in your location to businesses similar to yours.

I remember that the day we got our own office was the closest I had ever felt to being a grownup. But in true toddler fashion, I still wanted to stay close to home and operate virtually. But what a difference it has made to others', as well as to our own, perception of ourselves. We began to think of ourselves a lot more in terms of being "a real business with a real address." That view has changed now with the explosive growth of home-based businesses. There is much less, and in many cases, no stigma attached to people working from their homes. Today, people get to feel professionally grown up in their very own homes in their very own bathrobes and fuzzy slippers. You've got to love it.

Have the Courage to Move On

Paula and I chose to share this story because of the incalculable value of its lesson. It's likely going to shock and amaze you. In an earlier section, I mentioned having a supplier who was in her own toddler years and suffering the crippling effects of rapid growth. She was engulfed in a wave so huge that she was being pulled underwater before she even had a chance to don a life jacket. In my own toddler business, I was dealing with rapid cycles of growth, decline, then huge growth again, so I needed a lot of immediate attention from this service provider just to stay on track. The problem was timing. This supplier had landed a large and lucrative contract and her time evaporated right at the time I needed her most. And the supplier was Paula.

I was faced with having to make a heartwrenching decision. My business was in intensive care and needed help. Paula tried to be there but was going to have a nervous breakdown if she didn't quickly tame her own wild beast. A couple of years earlier, I had sat on a panel at a function for the Canadian Women's Foundation. Leslie Slater was the requisite accountant/business adviser along with a lawyer, a stock broker, and myself as the personal finance expert and comic relief. I had been quite impressed with Leslie so I gave her a call. After several long chats, and not without huge guilt, I came to the conclusion that she would fit well into our group. But I was extremely reluctant and afraid to tell Paula. Again, I agonized over this decision for far too long. Instead of framing it as a business decision, I internalized it as a personal one. "I'll hurt her feelings." "She's been with me since the beginning." "Her work is great when I can get her." "She's a friend, for heaven's sake!"

But there came a time when I couldn't put it off any longer. With my pulse pounding and my heart breaking, I told her we were moving on and why. Just when I thought I knew all I could about her, she astounded me again by her reaction. "I understand, Joanne. Just know that I am working very hard to address all of your concerns. And listen, my friend. It is perfectly normal to outgrow someone's services and want to move on if they can't give you what you need. It's suicide for your business if you hang on to something or someone out of misplaced loyalty. You're a grownup now and that means grownup decisions. It's best for both of us that you find someone you're happy with." We continued to use her company for technological support, and sales- and marketing-related projects, but for the more time-sensitive stuff like business advisory, we moved on.

We were just sailing into our fifth year when Leslie became our business adviser, and she's been a great asset. Paula managed to get her growth issues under control and leaped into her fifth year with gusto. The purpose of telling you this story is to address one of the most difficult issues for women in business. It's a classic W-FACTOR. Many of us feel the need to like those we do business with, whether that be staff, suppliers, or clients. Men don't do this. They can get the job done without a need to like or be liked. It would be terrific if we all liked each other and got along all the time. We don't and we can't. That's perfectly normal. It is important to respect and have faith in the work of the person you are dealing with, but liking is way down the continuum. Why? Because it means we hang on to people longer than we should and become afraid to hurt feelings if the relationship no longer works. Just remember that people don't die from hurt feelings. The collaboration on this book is absolute proof.

For us, the toddler years were fraught with growth fallout; they were the time for serious maturing. There were far too many days when I was convinced we were going to have to lock the doors for the last time. Then there were others when I thought we were going to live forever. The benefit of coming through the toddler years is discovering that somewhere down the middle is the real truth.

I've lost valuable staff and gained others. I've made incredible friends and an enemy or two. Business losses or disasters that used to devastate me are now taken in stride. Business life is more on the organized as opposed to the disorganized side of the ledger. I have finally created a company that doesn't need to be 100 percent me. Our senior trainer, Cynthia Caron Thorburn, and our French trainer, Lynn Charpentier, are brilliant additions to our fold. They do all the training, leaving me to do what I do best — sell, write, and talk. We finally have proper technology, which has increased our productivity a hundredfold. And, I have finally mastered the art of setting boundaries and letting go to let people do what they do best.

When I think about it in retrospect, it's what we collectively as women entrepreneurs have managed to do, both well and not so well, that has contributed to our evolution and our perspectives. Today, when we ask ourselves the question that we've asked untold times, "Would I do it all again?" we find ourselves reflecting on everything that we have done.

Take a few moments and consider how your own thinking, behaviour, and decision making as an individual, in each aspect of your business, have evolved or may evolve over those four or five years, from conception to birth to having it stand and run on its own two legs.

As a business creator and leader, you have translated a business vision into a real live business. You have created a culture you can be proud of because it reflects your values and makes a difference in the lives of others. Whether your big idea was a spontaneous Aha!, surfacing from a mire of adversity, chaos, and confusion, or the result of a more methodical culling from a full deck of ideas, you discovered we all go through the same growing pains. You loved the buzz of the idea stage. You then breathed life into your ideas and made them into viable and tangible components of your business strategy: the customer, the product or service, the staff, the finances, the sales and marketing efforts, the administration, and the technology. It was like working in a vacuum because you didn't really know what you didn't know. Yet you somehow managed to sketch out what you were going to have to do in the short, medium, and long term.

Take your products and services. You were the one who distilled a really good idea and perception of what the market needed into a saleable product, with features and benefits and a price tag. You were the one who figured out why it sold or didn't sell and whether or not you made money. You were the one who balanced your desire to respond to every customer request with staying focused on what you did best and most profitably. By winning that struggle, you were the one to reap the benefits of getting the best possible return on the investment of your energy, time, and money.

The same holds true in the evolution of your management of your customer. From conception through the toddler stage, you were the one who figured out who would buy what you were selling. You determined whether or not there were enough of the right customers that you could reach. After experimenting with ways of getting the word and your product out to those customers, you figured out the most profitable way to do it. From your business name, to your business card, to your business brochure, it was you who created an image of your business that would compel people to buy. You anticipated how many sales you needed to make. You were the one who finally realized that the distance between needing sales and the effort to reach 10 people to get one on the books was vast. You were the one who learned that managing profitability had little to do with accounting and everything to do with learning to read your business. It was you who sweated over how long your cash and energy reserves could last. And when you finally became a "big girl," it was you who figured out when not to sell, who not to sell to, and how to turf a bad customer from the flock.

As you grew from a baby entrepreneur to one ready to run full tilt, this same evolution took place in your relationship with others, be they your staff, your associates, your suppliers, or your business partners. It was you who determined what other people would play a role in your business, what role that would be, and how to best make yourself heard. You assembled all the individual components of the administration of your business and wound them together with technology to create your business's true nervous system. You also learned to be an electrician when the system needed rewiring, shorted out, or the wires got crossed. You figured out how your business needed to be structured and where it needed to live and when it was time to move away from home.

It is imperative that you return to the genesis of your business to relive that high of creation. Go back to the place where the world stood at your feet and anything was possible. Think about where you have come from. Nobody else made that happen. You breathed life into your creation through sweat and tears, your unconditional belief — unwavering even in the face of a thousand critics — some false starts, and that irritating little voice that's always asking if we've made the right choice. You are the one who had to constantly remind yourself that owning and running a business is a perpetual journey, one that doesn't have an end unless you decide on one. You will have succeeded in raising your business when your life starts becoming a bit more your own, just like when the kids start going to school.

As Women and Money Inc. leaves the toddler phase and prepares to enter the next stage, we are struck by the fact that the business does not keep us awake at night any longer. Our big thing now is, "What's next? What do we want to be now that we are almost grown up?" There is so much to ponder. Entrepreneur and writer Norm Brodsky says it best:

> "I prefer chaos. Deep down, I like having problems. It's hard to admit, but I enjoy the excitement of working in a crisis atmosphere. That's one of the reasons I get so much pleasure out of starting businesses. You have nothing but problems when you're starting out. You're always on the firing line. You're juggling a dozen balls, and you can't afford to let any of them drop. Everybody is counting on you. No one questions your decision-making process. You're almost like a god in that situation, and you run on pure adrenalin. It's exciting, stimulating, and challenging, and I love every minute of it. But that stage doesn't last. If your business is viable, it eventually reaches the point at which it can sustain itself on its own internally generated cash flow. When it gets there, it moves off the danger list and begins to develop a whole new set of needs."[7]

We are finally off the danger list.

Epilogue

What Now?

My father has been an entrepreneur for most of his life and the highs and the lows have been plentiful. The day Paula and I finished writing this book, he suffered a heart attack. A nasty 50-year smoking habit coupled with the stress of his entrepreneurial life sent him into the hospital's emergency room at the tender age of 65. It's only been 24 hours since it happened and the prognosis looks good. Still, I can't seem to be rid of this terrible ache. Kate and her grandfather are very close and I am so fearful she will grow up not having known him. It's been a wake-up call for all of us.

I know I would have written this epilogue very differently yesterday. Kierkegaard said life can only be understood backwards. My dad's heart attack has made me think long and hard about this life that both of us have chosen. I marvel at the similarities and the stark differences between us. He chose to be an entrepreneur for the autonomy and control of making his own business choices. I wanted autonomy and control so I could make my own life choices. And though it's often been a struggle and the choices always difficult, I can say with great pride that my life is successful.

Both Paula and I have managed to accomplish everything we set out to, from conception right up to the end of the toddler years — no doubt with our fair share of the requisite bumps, bruises, and wrong turns. What happened to my dad cemented the importance of staying connected to the reasons I chose to become an entrepreneur in the first place, especially now that I am entering the next stage of my business life. The question of what's in store for me over the next five years fills me with a sense of wonder and, yes, worry.

Naturally, I have concerns over whether or not I have what it takes to grow this business. A friend of mine, Barbara Orser, a professor at Ryerson Polytechnic University, did a study with Sandra Hogarth-Scott and Peter Wright of Bradford University in England. The study, called "The Role of Intentions and Experience," looks at the growth of small businesses. What makes this study unique and relevant is that it focuses on small business owners' growth intentions. It confirms what Paula and I have suspected all along.

There are three things that affect the growth of people's businesses. To quote directly from the study, "The growth of the firms was strongly correlated with the owners' objectives with respect to growth, with the breadth of the owner's managerial experience, and with an effect associated with the owner's gender." In other words, women don't grow their business the same way men do.

It's very easy to explain this. It has nothing to do with being afraid to succeed. Women's recent entry into the workforce has put us in a catch-up position when it comes to acquiring broad-based managerial experience. Couple that with career interruptions to have children and our own unique vision of what constitutes a successful business and the result, for the moment anyway, is that our businesses, are and stay on average smaller than men's. And that may be fine, thank you very much. Or, for you, it may not.

That's one of the reasons I wanted to write this book. Paula and I decided that women could get technical help anywhere, but what women really needed was some insight into the experiential side. Though this book was intended to help those who are thinking of starting or who are in the early stages of starting a business, we also wanted to be sure it gave women enough substance to decide for themselves whether or not and how they wanted to grow their business. It comes back to planning. How can you plan if you don't have some sense of what the future may hold?

And it's this very thing I find myself facing today. The conversations with Leslie and Paula are very different now from what they were in the beginning. They centre mostly on "What now? Should I maintain the status quo or get bigger? Do I want to give up the intimate working relationship I have with my clients or go mass market? Should I expand out of the financial services field into other areas?" One client in the technology industry, for example, wants to do a pilot for their resellers on how to reach the women's market. That means a whole new market and a whole new product line. What would the time needed to develop this mean to my business and personal life? I've done work in the U.S., the Caribbean, with The Bank of Ireland, and with the Australian bank, WestPac. This has whetted my appetite for possible international opportunities, like exporting my expertise and developing strategic alliances. Thinking back to the very beginning when my biggest concern was whether or not I'd have enough money to pay for letterhead, the idea that I could even be entertaining thoughts of global expansion is surreal. But, what would this kind of travel mean to my personal and business life? If I go international, it then becomes a question of speed. Do I do it incrementally or go whole hog through acquisition? How much time and money am I willing to invest? What will the ramifications be to my personal and business life?

The answers to these questions are life altering. And it's a classic W-FAC-TOR. My family will be the major factor in my decisions. Kate's only three. It's my choice not to go international right now. But there are a million other things that I can do as an entrepreneur that allow me to stay balanced and feed my passion. I will expand into other industries and I'll get bigger in the one that I'm in. I'll hire more people to do the things that I no longer have to. This will allow me to be a sane mom, wife, daughter, friend, boss, and business owner.

And I have now decided this is the time to write it all down. Reacting got me this far. I can only imagine how far I might have gone if I had actually planned and directed. As I mature, I realize I want to determine my company's destiny. I want to be in the driver's seat. I no longer want to feel like an untethered sail. Writing a plan will help me get to the next level. I now understand how my business works and how it doesn't. A physical commitment of my business plan to paper feels like a psychological commitment to its success. At this point, writing a business plan is no longer the mechanical exercise it was in the beginning, but an intimate one based on real experience. The last five years contribute to making the plan real and tangible. It can be shared with others on my team so they will know how they can contribute to making it happen.

I also need to constantly remind myself that it is not a race, that I am not competing with anyone. What happened to my father reminded me powerfully of this. People may take three or four years to evolve their toddler business or they may need or choose to take 10 years. When I go back to the place where it all began, I remember that a clear benefit of being the ship's captain was that I, and only I, set the pace. Now that I have passed through the toddler years, I'm choosing to replace "should" and "shouldn't" with "will" and "won't."

The process of writing this book has changed both mine and Paula's lives, and I do not say this lightly. It brought a sense of wholeness to our lives as entrepreneurs that had previously been a set of fractured and fragmented experiences, somehow haphazardly connected. It is this spirit that we have attempted to pass over to you. The words printed here are, for the most part, concepts. And though much has been said about my own and others' personal experiences, you must write your own story. Pamela Wallin couldn't have said it better. You will shed both tears and your fears in the process.

Endnotes

Chapter 1

1. Armand Eisen, ed., *A Woman's Journey: Reflections on Life, Love, and Happiness* (Kansas City: Andrews and McMeel, 1995), page 222.

Chapter 2

1. "Paths to Entrepreneurship: New Directions for Women in Business," *Report of National Foundation for Women Business Owners and Catalyst* (New York: February, 1998).

Chapter 4

1. Joe Griffith, ed., *Speaker's Library of Business Stories, Anecdotes and Humor*, (New Jersey: Prentice Hall, 1990), page 65.
2. Rob Gilbert, Ph.D., ed., *More of the Best of Bits and Pieces*, (New Jersey: The Economic Press, 1997), page 220.
3. Joe Griffith, ed., *Speaker's Library*, page 36.
4. Special thanks to Karen Wright, Toronto-based marketing consultant, for her input to this section.
5. Thomas Leonard, www.thomasleonard.com
6. *On Hire Ground: a Study of Job Creation in Canada's Small- and Medium-sized Business Sector*, (Canadian Federation of Independent Business, 1996).
7. "Job Survey, Part 1," (Canadian Federation of Independent Business, April 1996).
8. Joe Griffith, ed., *Speaker's Library*, page 90.
9. "Embracing the Information Age: A Comparison of Women and Men Business Owners," *Report of the National Foundation for Women Business Owners*, (September 30, 1997).
10. Thomas Leonard, www.thomasleonard.com

Chapter 5

1. Joe Griffith, ed., *Speaker's Library of Business Stories, Anecdotes and Humor* (New Jersey: Prentice Hall, 1990), page 191.

2. Joe Griffith, ed., *Speaker's Library*, page 189.

3. "Small Business Briefs," *The Globe and Mail Report on Business*, (*The Globe and Mail*, Monday, July 13, 1998).

4. Joe Griffith, ed., *Speaker's Library*.

5. Joe Griffith, ed., *Speaker's Library*, page 120.

6. Norm Brodsky, "Paying for Growth," *Inc. Magazine*, (October 1996), page 29.

7. Norm Brodsky, "Paying for Growth."

Fast Forward
A Resource About Women and Entrepreneurship in Canada

The organizations listed here offer programs and resources designed to help women entrepreneurs or women who wish to become entrepreneurs. It is not an exhaustive list, but it is as representative as possible of initiatives and resources across the country.

In some cases, programs open to men as well as women have been listed, but only if the program offers something special to women. If no mention is made, it is understood to be open to women only.

As well, both non-profit and profit-making organizations are listed. If known, the status of the organization is stated in the description. Although the emphasis is on programs and activities provided at no cost or nominal cost by non-profit organizations, profit-making companies are listed if they are taking unusual approaches or providing services of special interest or use to women entrepreneurs.

Each listing gives as many contact options as possible — telephone and fax number, as well as an Internet address, if one exists.

In the program descriptions, the emphasis is on summarizing key information about organizations' mandates and programs designed for or appropriate for women entrepreneurs or women who wish to become entrepreneurs. The objective is to give ideas and information that may be helpful, interesting or thought-provoking.

The information about the organizations listed here was gathered between June 1997 and January 1998. Since then, there may have been changes in organizations' mandates, programs or contact information. In some cases, for example, programs were being piloted or secure, long-term funding was being sought. As a result, some of the programs referred to in *Fast Forward* may no longer be available, may have different requirements or may now charge fees. Although some programs may no longer be available or have changed considerably, the descriptions still offer valid ideas for programs or activities that women entrepreneurs or organizations concerned with women entrepreneurs could organize in their own communities.

From *Fast Forward,* reprinted here courtesy of the Honourable Dianne Cunningham, Ontario Minister Responsible for Women's Issues.

Alberta Women's Enterprise Initiative Association

Toll Free 1-800-713-3558 (within Alberta)

Edmonton Office
10237 - 104 Street
Edmonton AB T5J 1B1
Tel 403-422-7784
Fax 403-422-0756

Calgary Office
800 - 6th Avenue S.W., Suite 260
Calgary AB T2P 3G3
Toll Free 1-888-411-2934 (within Alberta)
Tel 403-777-4250
Fax 403-777-4258
e-mail aweia@compusmart.ab.ca
Website http://www.compusmart.ab.ca/aweia
Contact: Corinne Tessier, Executive Director

The Alberta Women's Enterprise Initiative Association (AWEIA) is a non-profit organization committed to helping Alberta women succeed at starting and expanding businesses. Funded by Western Economic Diversification (a federal government department), AWEIA provides workshops, networking opportunities, links to information and resources, business advice and support and business loans (from $250 to $100,000) at competitive market rates. Women's Enterprise Circles (information exchange and networking) are held every month in Edmonton, Calgary, Red Deer, Lethbridge, Grande Prairie and Fort McMurray.

Assiniboine Credit Union

200 Main Street
Winnipeg MN R3C 2G1
Tel 204-958-8550
Fax 204-958-3549
e-mail rothne@assiniboine.mb.ca
Contact: Russ Rothney, Community Development Co-ordinator

The Assiniboine Credit Union provides up to $100,000 funding per year for the Winnipeg Community Economic Development Resource Group's Credit Circle Program. These lending circles are made up largely of women who run their own small home-based businesses. Participants must attend 12 business training sessions, develop business plans, evaluate and approve the business plans developed by other members of the lending circle and sign for each other's loans. Individual loans start at up to $1,000. Ten per cent of the amount of the loan must be placed in a group emergency fund. All loans within a lending circle, which is usually made up of four to seven participants, must be in good standing before new loans will be granted. Second loans may be up to twice the amount of the first loan.

Association communautaire d'emprunt de Montréal

15, boulevard Mont-Royal Ouest, bureau 112
Montréal (Québec) H2T 2R9
Tel 514-844-9882
Fax 514-844-7650
e-mail acem@accent.net
Website http://www.total.net/~acem/
Contact: Ranko Djogo, Co-ordinator, Technical Support

The mandate of the Association communautaire d'emprunt de Montréal (ACEM) is to give financial support to economically viable small businesses to start up or expand. Founded in 1990, this not-for-profit organization community loan fund gives preference to socially disadvantaged women and men who propose projects related to the co-operative, environment, recycling, reprocessing or training sectors.

All loan requests are assessed by a committee of five volunteers from various fields. Requests for loans of more than $8,000 are reviewed by the Board of Directors. The maximum loan amount is about $20,000 per project and the maximum term is four years. The interest rate varies according to risk.

Private foundations interested in supporting community economic development provide most of the loan funds and get a small return on their investments. Some funds come from private individuals and Human Resources Development Canada. The ACEM contracts with each investor group to pay interest, usually at the rate equal to the rate of inflation, twice a year on the amount invested.

In its first seven years of operation, this Montreal community loan association granted more than 60 loans, most of which have been repaid.

Association de la Main-d'oeuvre Autochtone de Montréal

31, rue St-Jacques, bureau 500
Montréal (Québec) H2Y 1K9
Tel 514-848-0040
Fax 514-848-0256
e-mail awam@mlink.net
Contact: France Lamarre, Economic Development Agent

The mission of Association de la Main-d'oeuvre Autochtone de Montréal (AMAM) is to improve the quality of life for the Native community of Montreal. This includes liaison with Service d'Aide aux Jeunes Entrepreneurs, an organization that helps young entrepreneurs start small businesses. Founded in 1992, AMAM is financed by Human Resources Development Canada. It serves both women and men. At present, about 60 per cent of its clients are women.

Association of Atlantic Women Business Owners

PO Box 4
Truro, NS B2N 5B6
Toll Free 1-800-858-6461
Tel 902-895-4495
Fax 902-893-8881
e-mail aawbo@ns.sympatico.ca
Website http://www.bizbureau.com
Contact: Executive Director

The Association of Atlantic Women Business Owners (AAWBO) is a non-profit organization formed in 1985 to address the needs and concerns of women business owners in New Brunswick, Newfoundland, Nova Scotia and Prince Edward Island. The AAWBO's mandate is to foster networking with a goal to raise the profile of women business owners and become a voice for them. Members are committed to sharing information and supporting and encouraging each other.

B

Black Business Initiative

Canada/Nova Scotia Business Service Centre
1575 Brunswick Street, Suite 601
Halifax NS B3J 2G1
Toll Free 1-800-668-1010 (within Nova Scotia)
Tel 902-426-2224 or 902-426-2881
Fax 902-426-6530
e-mail bbi@cbsc.ic.gc.ca
Website http://www.bbi.ns.ca
Contact: Rustum Southwell, Executive Director

The Black Business Initiative (BBI) is a non-profit organization formed to support the development of business and job opportunities for Black Nova Scotians. Open to women and men, BBI's mission is to foster a dynamic and vibrant Black presence within Nova Scotia's business community. Its goals include furthering entrepreneurial development, education and training and creating and improving access to private and public sector business support. BBI programs emphasize hands-on support for entrepreneurs. BBI's services include business start-up and assistance with developing business and marketing plans, doing research and accessing funding. Activities include workshops, seminars, networking, mentoring and counselling.

Business Inter>Connect

135 Third Street
Duncan BC V9L 1R9
Tel 250-746-1004
Fax 250-746-8819
e-mail cfdc@cowichan.com
Website http://cowichan.com/comfut/comfut.htm
Contact: Joanna Rotherham, Executive Director, CFDC - Cowichan, Region; Wendy Klyne, Facilitator, Business Inter>Connect (Tel 250-416-0404).

Business Inter>Connect (BIN) offers established women business owners the opportunity to network with other established business owners, talk about common issues and arrive at creative solutions to business issues faced by participants.

The Business Inter>Connect Team meets every second week with a facilitator, exchanges information, solves problems and discusses goals. Every third meeting, guest speakers address topics chosen by participants, such as developing strategies for business directions, maintaining and expanding the business, being an effective business owner and managing time to ensure the business does not take over one's life.

Administrated by the Community Futures Development Corporation - Cowichan Region, Business Inter>Connect is a non-profit corporation funded by the federal government and user fees.

Business Success Teams

601 West Broadway, Suite 400
Vancouver BC V5Z 4C2
Tel 604-713-8606
Fax 604-713-8601
e-mail info@BusinessSuccessTeams.com
Website http://www.BusinessSuccessTeams.com
Contact: Rachel Duboff, Program Administrator

The purpose of Business Success Teams (BST) is to create a forum for entrepreneurs in the Vancouver area. The goal is to inspire, inform, advise and support women's efforts to generate ideas, build wealth and lead balanced, fulfilled lives. BST's program focus is to assist businesses in accelerating growth, increasing sales and developing new business relationships. Sponsored by Bank of Montreal, Ernst & Young, Russell & DuMoulin and the Vancouver Board of Trade, BST puts together round tables of 15 to 25 entrepreneurs from non-competing businesses, a facilitator, an accountant, a banker and a lawyer. Participants meet twice a month for a minimum of three months to share ideas and information, explore issues, discuss problems and make contacts. BST also provides an Internet business solutions service, telephone information exchange and business development resources. While BST programs are open to both women and men, it offers women-only round tables if the demand is sufficient.

C

Calmeadow

365 Bay Street, Suite 600
Toronto ON M5H 2V1
Tel 416-362-9125, ext. 228
Fax 416-362-0769
e-mail calmead@inforamp.net
Contact: Vida Dhaniram, Director of Canadian Operations
5670 Spring Garden Road, Suite 300
Halifax NS B3J 1H6
Tel 902-492-3585
Fax 902-422-8955

Calmeadow was the first organization to run a North American loan fund based on the peer group lending model. Under this system, clients form borrowers' groups and vouch for each other's loans. This replaces the need for the collateral required by conventional lenders.

Outside Canada, Calmeadow works in developing countries. Its focus is supporting the creation of formal financial institutions to serve the micro-enterprise sector.

In Canada, Calmeadow operates in Toronto (Calmeadow Metrofund) and Nova Scotia (Calmeadow Nova Scotia). The focus is offering business loans and other support (such as networking, sharing expertise and a loans fund directory) to individuals who wish to invest in their own home-based or small-scale businesses. Conventional collateral and extensive credit histories are not required.

The lending circle format Calmeadow uses in Canada is a business credit group of at least four individuals. All must have their own businesses. Loans are issued when all members of the group support the business concept and when all members are up-to-date with their own loan payments. First-time loans are limited to $1,000 per person. Subsequently, loans for up to $15,000 may be granted. Getting more credit depends on the group's repayment record.

Calmeadow is a Canadian-based, non-profit organization founded in 1983. It is supported by the Canadian International Development Agency, Royal Bank, TD Bank, Bank of Montreal, United Way, individual donors and private foundations.

Canadian Association of Women Executives and Entrepreneurs

2175 Sheppard Avenue East, Suite 310
North York ON M2J 1W8
Tel 416-756-0000
Fax 416-491-1670
e-mail taylor@interlog.com
Contact: Mary Catalfo, Administrator

The Canadian Association of Women Executives and Entrepreneurs (CAWEE) is a not-for-profit organization founded in 1976. CAWEE's mandate is to provide an environment for women to grow and to increase the visibility of women executives and business owners. CAWEE's program is designed to provide a forum for women to develop and expand their businesses and professions while increasing the overall visibility of women in executive, professional and entrepreneurial roles. CAWEE's activities include monthly meetings featuring guest speakers, networking events, trade shows, workshops and conferences. CAWEE is affiliated with the Metropolitan Toronto Board of Trade.

Canadian Women's Foundation

133 Richmond Street West, Suite 504
Toronto ON M5H 2L3
Tel 416-365-1444
Fax 416-365-1745
e-mail info@cdnwomen.org

The Canadian Women's Foundation (CWF) is a public charitable foundation that raises and grants money to charitable organizations that help women and girls across Canada achieve greater economic independence, self-reliance and safety. CWF gives grants to groups committed to working for social and systemic change on behalf of girls and women. One area of interest for CWF is imaginative, results-oriented projects that promote economic development, including micro-enterprise development strategies for women (defined as self-employment or small business).

Founded in 1989, CWF is accessible to grassroots' women's groups. The projects funded in 1997 include a thrift store feasibility study in Victoria, a feasibility study to determine the viability of operating a small business selling healthy frozen casseroles in

Calgary and an aboriginal women's home business training program in Sioux Lookout, Ontario. CWF does not review unsolicited grant applications. Instead, twice each year, CWF issues Requests for Proposals (RFPs) that state which organizations may apply, the types of projects that will be considered, CWF's priorities, the size of grants and other information.

Carrefour de relance de l'économie et de l'emploi du centre de Québec

210, boulevard Charest Est, bureau 600
Québec (Québec) G1K 3H1
Tel 418-525-5526
Fax 418-525-4965
Contact: Guylaine Mongrain, Project Officer

The mandate of the Carrefour de relance de l'économie et de l'emploi du centre de Québec (CRÉECQ) is to support the economic recovery of central Quebec City. A not-for-profit community economic development corporation, CRÉECQ is funded by federal, provincial, regional and municipal government grants.

In 1995, CRÉECQ launched a lending circle program targeted at low-income women and men with business ideas and who live in selected economically disadvantaged districts of central Quebec City (Saint-Roch, Saint-Sauveur and Saint-Jean-Baptiste and Limoilou). The program provides training, coaching and financing. Participants join lending circles of five to seven members. The first loan is limited to $1,000 but subsequent loans may be for any amount.

In its first two years of operation, the lending circle program helped 52 participants create 20 businesses. About 35 per cent of the participants are women.

Centre des femmes de Montréal

3585, rue Saint-Urbain
Montréal (Québec) H2X 2N6
Tel 514-842-6652
Fax 514-842-6376
Contact: Claudette Dion, Counsellor and Co-ordinator

The overall mandate of Centre des femmes de Montréal is to offer professional, educational counselling and orientation services to help women help themselves. Founded in 1973, the Centre is a not-for-profit organization financed mainly through grants from Centraide, the provincial Ministère de l'Emploi et de la Solidarité and Human Resources Development Canada.

In March 1998, the Centre launched a new program designed to help women on social welfare become economically self-sufficient by starting their own businesses. The program begins with six individual counselling sessions to help participants become aware of their entrepreneurial potential. This is followed by a two-week group training session focussing on business start-up issues, such as advice on how to draft a business plan. After completing the Centre's program, participants are referred to other organizations with resources to help them get their businesses started. The Centre's role is to follow up and track progress.

Centre des femmes de Ville-Marie

28, Notre-Dame-de-Lourdes
Case postale 1349
Ville-Marie (Québec) J0Z 3W0
Tel 819-622-0777
Fax 819-622-2377 or 819-622-0777
Contact: Danielle Labrie, Community Worker

The mandate of Centre des femmes de Ville-Marie is to improve living conditions of women in the Témiscamingue region of northwestern Quebec (near the Ontario border). The Centre's activities are designed to alleviate poverty among women and include lending circles and a mini-centre for business start-up.

The Centre is a not-for-profit organization run by staff and volunteers. It is financed through grants from the provincial Ministère de la Santé et des Services sociaux, community donations and sponsorships. Since its foundation in 1982, the Centre has helped more than 30 women entrepreneurs. In 1997, the Centre served 83 members, including participants in its lending circle program.

The Centre offers a mini-centre for business start-up where women can use computers, a fax machine and telephones. They also receive some financial support for baby-sitting and transportation costs.

Centre for Women in Business

c/o Mount Saint Vincent University
Halifax NS B3M 2J6
Tel 902-457-6271
Fax 902-443-1352
e-mail gerry.martin@msvu.ca
Website http://www.msvu.ca/cwb
Contact: Gerry Martin, Business Counsellor

The Centre for Women in Business (CWB) was established in 1992 as a not-for-profit organization to supply information and referral, facilitate networking, promote women in business, provide access to training and manage research activities. Since then, its services have evolved to include one-to-one counselling, networking, workshops, training programs, mentoring and public presentations. Its mission is to create and nurture more successful entrepreneurs.

The CWB's Business Circle program provides supportive, informative sharing experiences that help women entrepreneurs' personal and professional development. Each group consists of about 12 women who operate non-competing businesses. Members sign a confidentiality agreement and pay an annual fee. Once formed, participants decide on rules of conduct, meeting formalities, delegation of responsibilities and meeting time, location, format and agenda. Each circle selects its own focus and objectives, for example, identifying stumbling blocks and devising strategies to overcome them or developing networking opportunities.

Cercles d'emprunt de la Vallée-du-Richelieu

230, rue Brébeuf, bureau 101
Beoloeil (Québec) J3G 5P3
Tel 514-446-8279
Fax 514-446-3806
Contact: Claudine Duval, Co-ordinator

The mandate of Cercles d'emprunt de la Vallée-du-Richelieu is to help women in the Richelieu Valley start their own small businesses by offering training, support and access to financing. Founded in 1996, Cercles is a not-for-profit organization financed by federal, provincial and municipal government grants.

Cercles's training consists of workshops dealing with such topics as self-assessment, market research, marketing and business plans, financial forecasts and detailed planning. It will also provide access to working capital through lending circles. The maximum amount of credit is $2,000 per year.

In its first 18 months of operation, 97 women took the training workshops and nine started their own businesses. (All got financing through conventional channels rather than lending circles).

Cercles d'emprunt de Montréal

15, Mont-Royal Ouest, bureau 112
Montréal (Québec) H2T 2R9
Tel 514-849-3271
Fax 514-284-9502
Contacts: Denise Audet and Danyka Morissette, Facilitators

The mandate for Cercles d'emprunt de Montréal is to support women of the Centre-Sud and Plateau Mont-Royal districts of Montreal who want to start micro-businesses. Founded in 1990, Cercles is a not-for-profit organization financed through grants of the provincial government's labour assistance fund and the Conseil régional de développement de l'île de Montréal.

Cercles forms lending circles of four to seven women, helps them assess and clarify their business ideas and then provides access to very small loans of from $200 to $2,000, depending on their circumstances. The money itself is advanced by Caisse d'économie to Cercles. All members of a circle must co-sign loans given to members of the circle.

Cercles is part of the lending circle program of Quebec, which has associates in Abitibi-Témiscamingue, Eastern Townships, other organizations in Montreal, the Ottawa River, Quebec City, Richelieu Valley and Laval.

Communicating Power Inc.

Toll Free 1-888-406-7152
Edmonton Office
Suite 305, AUPE Building
10451 - 170 Street
Edmonton AB T5P 4T2

Tel 403-444-1940

Fax 403-483-5378

e-mail mail@communicatingpower.com

Contact: Shawn Jorgensen, Managing Director

Calgary Office

Suite 218, 6715 - 8th Street NE

Calgary AB T2E 7H7

Tel 403-730-0166

Fax 403-274-4969

e-mail calgary@communicatingpower.com

Contact: Helen Webster, Managing Director

Montreal Office

1010, rue Sherbrooke Ouest, bureau 1800

Montréal (Québec) H3A 2R7

Tel 514-286-6601

Fax 514-641-9345

e-mail andree@communicatingpower.com

Contact: Andrée Crevier, Managing Director

Communicating Power Inc. (CPI) is a full-service marketing firm that provides industry-specific facilitators to help entrepreneurs develop business plans. Founding in 1993, CPI provides one-on-one and small group coaching. It is funded by user fees and government funding (from Human Resources Development Canada and Alberta Advanced Education and Career Development).

Two CPI programs are designed specifically for women. The Smart Women[TM] Entrepreneurs Program is designed for low-income women who wish to become self-employed but who need to develop management skills in order to turn their business ideas into viable enterprises. The Young Women's Entrepreneurial Program is for women aged 18 to 30. It is designed to help younger women assess their abilities, match them to entrepreneurial opportunities, write a strategic business or personal plan and support them through the first year of business start-up.

communi-K

21 Water Street, Suite 302

Vancouver BC V6B 1A1

Tel 604-688-7050

Fax 604-688-7052
e-mail communik@vancity.com
Contact: Patti Malone, Loans Officer/Administrator

communi-K is a peer group lending service provided by VanCity Credit Union to micro-business owners in Greater Vancouver and the Fraser Valley. Formerly known as Calmeadow West, communi-K offers loans ranging from $1,000 to $5,000 to help micro-businesses acquire assets, establish a credit rating or expand. Traditional collateral is not required. Loans are advanced to members of peer lending groups.

Each group has between four and seven members who are interested in borrowing for their own businesses. Group members must disclose their credit histories. Loan approval is based on the group's commitment, resourcefulness and ability to repay. If one group member defaults, the other members of the group must pay back the loan in order to be eligible for future financing. Further loans are available only to members of groups with an excellent repayment history.

Comox Valley Women's Resource Centre

780 Grant Avenue, Suite 103
Box 3292
Courtenay BC V9N 5N4
Tel 250-338-1133
Fax 250-334-9251
e-mail niwss@mars.ark.com
Website http://mars.ark.com/~niwss
Contact: Emma Payton, Program Co-ordinator

The North Island Women's Services Society (NIWSS) was founded in 1980. In 1984, NIWSS sponsored the Comox Valley Women's Resource Centre, which is also supported by B.C. Ministry of Women's Equality, Secretary of State Canada and the United Way.

The Centre acts as a drop-in facility and information and referral service for women. Business-related programs and activities include workshops on starting a small business, informal coffee mornings for women in business, speakers and special events. In 1996, the Centre piloted the Comox Valley Credit Circle Program, an alternative form of financing for women entrepreneurs.

Corporation de développement de l'Est

4435, rue de Rouen
Montréal (Québec) H1V 1H1
Tel 514-256-6825
Fax 514-256-0669
e-mail lrcdest@total.net
Contact: Gilberte Plourde, Lending Circle Counsellor

Corporation de développement de l'Est (CDEST) is a not-for-profit organization formed to revitalize the Mercier/Hochelaga-Maisonneuve area of Montreal. It is financed through grants from provincial, regional and federal circles.

In 1993, CDEST launched a lending circle program. Before joining a circle, candidates take an eight-week training session. A member's first loan may be for up to $1,000; subsequent loans may be up to $2,000. In its first four years, the CDEST's lending circle program granted 50 loans through 20 lending circles. Both women and men are eligible.

COSTI
Yes I Can Start My Own Business

700 Caledonia Street
Toronto ON M6B 4H9
Tel 416-789-7925
Fax 416-789-3499
e-mail Bulhan@costi.org
Website http://www.costi.org
Contact: Safia Bulhan or Priti Ramjee

COSTI's mandate is to provide services to newcomers to Canada and their families. Founded in 1962, COSTI is a charitable organization that offers services in more than 30 languages. Its programs include English-language training, skills re-training for injured workers, employment and training centres, family counselling and a refugee reception centre.

Yes I Can Start My Own Business is a program designed to support women of all ages who have a business idea. It consists of small business workshops dealing with such topics as self-assessment, selling, negotiating, marketing, developing a business plan, financial planning and legal issues.

E

Économie Communautaire de Francheville

763, rue Saint-Maurice, bureau 3
Trois-Rivières (Québec) G9A 3P5
Tel 819-373-1473
Fax 819-378-0628
e-mail ecodefra@tr.cgocable.ca
Contacts: Caroline Lachance, Economic Development Agent; Jean-François Aubin, Co-ordinator

The mission of Économie Communautaire de Francheville (ÉCOF) is to improve living conditions for low-income residents of the Francheville area. It focuses on improving employment and access to jobs for low-income persons with little schooling and those who may be marginalized by society.

ÉCOF supports the creation of micro-businesses. It is also a business incubator. About 100 individuals used the organization's services during its first two years of operation. All were women, although the organization's services are also open to men.

A not-for-profit organization operating since 1995, ÉCOF is financed by government grants (federal, provincial and municipal) and income generated from fees from contracts with various organizations and a work co-operative.

Edmonton Community Loan Fund

10211 - 105 Street
Edmonton AB T5J 1E3
Tel 403-944-1558
Fax 403-425-3876
e-mail abubel@connect.ab.ca
Contact: Anna Bubel

Edmonton Community Loan Fund is a non-profit organization established to provide small business loans of up to $5,000 and advisory support to socially responsible businesses that benefit low-income individuals and groups in the Edmonton area. It operates by borrowing money from individuals and institutions and then lending this money to low-income individuals and groups at favourable rates of interest. The loans are supplemented with technical assistance and mentoring programs. Applicants must demonstrate managerial competence, show fiscal soundness, be credit worthy and provide a viable business plan. The program is open to both women and men.

Enterprise Legal Services

84 Queen's Park
Toronto ON M5S 2C5
Tel 416-978-0590
Fax 416-978-0589
e-mail els.clinic@utoronto.ca/els
Website http://www.law.utoronto.ca/els

Enterprise Legal Services (ELS) is a student-run legal clinic, supervised by qualified lawyers, which supports people's efforts to achieve economic independence through self-employment. Women and men starting or running small businesses can get help with partnership agreements, incorporations (including shareholders' agreements and bylaws, articles of incorporation and directors' resolutions), contracts (such as confidentiality, non-competition, sales and employee waivers) and other legal issues related to small business. Services are free subject to financial eligibility and approval by supervising lawyers.

F

Femmes Autochtones du Québec Inc.

460, rue Sainte-Catherine Ouest, bureau 503
Montréal (Québec) H3B 1A7
Tel 514-954-9991
Fax 514-954-1899
e-mail qnwafaq@micropec.net
Contact: Manon Lamontagne, Co-ordinator, Employment Initiative

The mission of Femmes Autochtones du Québec Inc. is to improve living conditions of all Native women in Quebec, regardless of where they live in the province. Often referred to as QNWA (the initials of its name in English, Quebec Native Women Inc.), the organization provides financial support to women who have the potential and desire to become self-employed or to start their own small businesses. Participants receive $200 per week for 26 weeks. They may use the funds to get training or upgrade their employability through existing resources. Founded in 1974, QNWA is a not-for-profit organization funded by the federal government (Native Affairs Secretariat, Health Canada and Human Resources Development Canada) and the provincial government. QNWA operates from 63 locations (60 located on Reserves and offices in Montréal, Québec City and Hull) and serves about 2,000 women.

La Fondation du Maire de Montréal pour la Jeunesse

275, rue Notre-Dame Est, bureau 4.126
Montréal (Québec) H2Y 1C6
Tel 514-872-8401
Fax 514-872-8433
Contact: Marguerite Blais, General Manager

The mission of La Fondation du Marie de Montréal pour la Jeunesse is to help disadvantaged young Montrealers enter the labour market. Founded in 1995 as a non-profit charitable and educational organization, the Foundation is supported by public funds and corporate donations.

The Fondation's Entrepreneurship Program is designed for low-income youth between the ages of 18 and 35 who wish to create businesses and jobs. The Fondation offers seed money for business start-ups and follow-up support. The size of the grants depends on the needs of the businesses. Priority goes to creative, profitable projects that create jobs and have a positive social impact. As a rule, the maximum is $20,000 or 25 per cent of the total investment required.

Young entrepreneurs must be residents of Montreal and provide a viable business plan, background information and letters of reference. They must also find their own mentors and receive entrepreneurship training through other organizations, such as the Montreal Community Loan Association and the Service d'Aide aux Jeunes Entrepreneurs.

In its first two years, the Fondation helped launch 39 businesses, about 60 per cent of which were started by women.

Fonds d'emprunt économique communautaire (Québec)

210, boulevard Charest Est, bureau 600
Québec (Québec) G1K 3H1
Tel 418-525-5526
Fax 418-525-4965
Contact: Linda Maziade, Project Officer

Fonds d'emprunt économique communautaire (Québec) is a not-for-profit organization founded in 1997 to develop the economic and human potential of Quebec City. FEÉCQ's community economic loan fund gives credit of up to $20,000 and technical support to low-income individuals, not-for-profit organizations and co-operatives with viable business ideas that will have a positive effect on the social and economic environment. It also consolidates micro-businesses launched through the lending circle program of the Carrefour de relance de l'économie et de l'emploi du centre de Québec (CRÉECQ).

FEÉCQ is funded by provincial, federal, regional and municipal government grants and serves women and men. Women account for about 20 per cent of its clientele.

G

Grassroots Economic Opportunity Development and Evaluation

450 Morin Street
Sudbury ON P3C 5H6
Tel 705-674-5587
Fax 705-674-5732
e-mail geode@tyenet.com
Contact: Katrina O'Neill-Major, Program Co-ordinator

Grassroots Economic Opportunity Development and Evaluation (GEODE) is a community-based non-profit organization, founded in 1992, which seeks to produce sustainable economic development for persons living in the Regional Municipality of Sudbury. One program, based on a peer-lending model, develops micro-enterprise credit for very small home-based businesses and part-time economic activities. Other programs include a barter exchange, community kitchens, good food boxes and bulk-buying circles, child care circles and community shared agriculture. GEODE programs are open to women and men; many programs, however, are developed with the needs of low-income women and youth in mind.

Groupe Conseil Saint-Denis Inc.

1453, rue Beaubien Est, bureau 302
Montréal (Québec) H2G 3C6
Tel 514-278-7211
Fax 514-278-2493
Contact: Catherine Ferembach, Youth Module Co-ordinator

The priority of Groupe Conseil Saint-Denis Inc. is economically disadvantaged young people between the ages of 18 and 35 who live in the Rosemont—Petite-Patrie district of Montreal to enter the labour force as entrepreneurs or independent workers.

The Groupe has two programs for entrepreneurs. Introduction to New Work Models assesses the entrepreneurial potential of participants and the feasibility of their business plans and develops strategic action plans for their integration into the labour force. Intended primarily for women, this new program attracted 100 participants in its first 18 months of operation.

The Groupe's second program for entrepreneurs, Strategic Circles, creates support groups of future entrepreneurs and independent workers and provides access to micro-credit using the lending circle format. This program was introduced in December 1997 on a pilot basis.

Founded in 1984, this not-for-profit organization is financed by the provincial anti-poverty fund (Fonds de lutte contre la pauvreté) and the innovation and experimentation support fund (Fonds régional d'aide à l'innovation et à l'expérimentation), Human Resources Development Canada and the City of Montreal. It serves its clients (women and men) free of charge.

I

Imagine That!

231 Craig Street
Duncan BC V9L 1W2
Tel 250-748-6776
Contact: Elaine Kerr

Imagine That! is a non-profit co-operative founded in 1994 by women artisans to market and sell their own creations and those of other local artists. Members volunteer their time to staff the Imagine That! retail store and handle sales, display, business management and shop maintenance. Imagine That! carries a wide range of original works, such as home furnishings, accessories, artwork and gifts. The co-operative also sponsors activities such as retail seminars, an annual bird house show and an annual members' art show.

Imagine That! also sells a comprehensive "how they did it" information package for $40.00. The package includes sample governance documents, operational policies, copyright guidelines, business forms, contracts, inventory sheets and many other items used in the store.

Impact Communications Limited
HB Communications Group, Inc.
Uniquely Creative Arts Show Program

2949 Ash Street
Abbotsford BC V2S 4G5
Tel 604-854-5530
Fax 604-854-3087
e-mail icl@bc.sympatico.ca
Contact: Barbara Mowat or Paula Mowat

Impact Communications Limited (ICL) offers a business development and training model designed to help small producers of arts, crafts, gifts and speciality foods to develop, compete and market their products globally at a critical stage of business development. Called the Uniquely Creative Arts Show Program, it is divided into two parts.

The Adjudication Process helps micro-business owners assess whether they have reached the professional standard needed to reach a wider marketplace. Products are evaluated by merchandising, marketing and sector specialists. Producers pay a nominal fee and receive detailed written reports.

The Wholesale Trade Show Process provides an opportunity to display and sell their products at an international trade show mounted with the assistance of Southex Exhibitions, the largest trade show producer in the world. Participants pay a nominal fee and are coached on taking orders, producing schedules, marketing, selling, exporting, after-show follow-up and booth display.

At present, ICI offers Uniquely Creative in three provinces (British Columbia, Alberta and Ontario). It is funded by user fees, corporate donations and government sponsorship. ICI is planning to expand the Uniquely Creative development model to include micro-enterprise in other parts of Canada and to countries belonging to APEC.

Initiation au développement entrepreneurial de l'Estrie

31, rue King Ouest, bureau 324
Sherbrooke (Québec) J1H 4N5
Tel 819-829-5111
Fax 819-829-5143
e-mail idee@abacom.com
Contact: Martin Maltais, Training Counsellor and Lending Circle IC

Initiation au développement entrepreneurial de l'Estrie (I.D.E.E.) offers services to both women and men who want to turn to a new career, become self-employed or start their own small businesses.

I.D.E.E. is financed through grants from Human Resources Development Canada. It is a not-for-profit organization which adds about 300 clients every year to its existing client base of 60 to 100 members. Since it was founded in December 1991, I.D.E.E. has helped about 1,500 clients, including about 600 women. Overall, its membership consists of about 60 per cent men and 40 per cent women. In the category of inventors' support services, the proportion is about 80 per cent men and 20 per cent women. I.D.E.E. is exploring the possibility of creating much-needed lending circles for single mothers in 1998.

Inter-Cercles de l'île de Montréal

1453, rue Beaubien Est, bureau 302
Montréal (Québec) H2G 3C6
Tel 514-272-1777
Fax 514-278-2493
e-mail cercles@hotmail.com
Contact: Nicole Houde, Co-ordinator

Inter-Cercles de l'île de Montréal acts as a research and development resource and launching centre for lending circles on the island of Montreal. Founded in 1997, Inter-Cercles is a not-for-profit organization financed mainly by the provincial Fonds de lutte contre la pauvreté and by fees paid by its seven member organizations. Inter-Cercles' role is liaison, trainer and facilitator. It does field work for its member organizations and for others interested in launching lending circle programs.

L

Life★Spin

P.O. Box 2801
360 Queens Avenue
London ON N6A 4H4
Tel 519-438-8676
Fax 519-438-7983
e-mail life@execulink.com
Website http://www.execulink.com/~life/index.html
Contact: Katherine Turner, Program Director

Life★Spin, which stands for Low Income Family Empowerment★Sole Support Parent Information Network, was founded in 1991. Its mandate is mediation, advocacy and community economic development for low-income people in the London area. A non-profit organization, Life★Spin's programs include a peer lending circle for women, a program for Métis women, a community loan fund, a school student gardens program, a green market basket program and mediation and advocacy resources and advocates.

M

Motivaction Centre de Formation et de Consultation Inc.

405, Place Chaumont
Saint-Lambert (Québec) J4S 1S5
Tel 514-923-3279
Fax 514-923-5488
e-mail germaing@minet.ca
Contact: Georges Germain, President

Motivaction Centre de Formation et de Consultation Inc. is a training and counselling centre serving the South Shore of Montreal. It helps individuals and small groups with business ideas assess their entrepreneurial potential and the profitability of their projects. It also provides start-up and guidance services for small businesses. This includes support in drafting business plans and obtaining credit from traditional sources (financial institutions) and non-traditional sources (lending circles and community loans).

Participants are referred to Motivaction by government agencies such as school boards, Human Resource Centres, Société québécoise de développement de la main-d'oeuvre, Centres travail-Québec and Société locale d'investissement dans le développement de l'emploi. These agencies pay the training and counselling fees for the participants they refer.

Motivaction serves both men and women. At present, about 60 per cent of its clients are women.

N

Newfoundland and Labrador Organization for Women Entrepreneurs

240 Water Street, Suite 301
St. John's NF A1C 1B7
Tel 709-754-5555
Fax 709-754-0079
e-mail mwall@nfld.com
Contact: Mona Wall, Executive Director

The Newfoundland and Labrador Organization for Women Entrepreneurs (NLOWE) is a not-for-profit organization aimed at promoting and fostering women's success in business in Newfoundland and Labrador. The organization's focus is women entrepreneurs in the start-up phase. NLOWE helps women business owners get small loans, build credit ratings and network. NLOWE's activities for members include networking, mentoring, seminars and consulting.

NLOWE offers most services on a cost-shared basis. The services include regional facilitators who link women in rural locations to regional economic zones (in Labrador, Northern/Labrador Straits, Western/Central, Central/East and Avalon), entrepreneurship and business development and policy development. In 1997, NLOWE piloted a micro-lending program in conjunction with the Newfoundland & Labrador Federation of Co-operatives and the Bank of Montreal. The organization is also committed to investigating and promoting other financial support options for women entrepreneurs.

The Niagara Women's Enterprise Centre

178 King Street, 3rd floor
Welland ON L3B 3J5
Tel 905-788-0166
Fax 905-788-9105 and 905-788-0928
Contact: Betty Ann Baker, Executive Director

The Niagara Women's Enterprise Centre was founded by Niagara Peninsula Homes Inc., a non-profit organization partnered with Ontario's Women and Rural Economic Development (WRED) network. The Centre's mandate is to offer support and training for small business development. The Centre's focus is working with unemployed, low-income women to create access to markets for their specialty products. This includes training and support in product development, market research and manufacturing, creating a *Niagara Presents...* label for local value-added products, developing other innovative marketing techniques and developing a model for flexible food manufacturing that can be used elsewhere in Canada. In 1998, with the support of The Welland Business and Community Development Corporation, the Centre will launch a micro-loan program ($250 to $3,000) for businesses owned by low-income women with the potential to sell products and services regionally, nationally and internationally.

Ontario Council of Alternative Businesses

Inspirations
761 Queen Street West, Room 307
Toronto ON M6J 1G1
Tel 416-504-1693
Fax 416-504-8063
e-mail ocab@interlog.com
Contact: Diana Copponi, Co-ordinator

The Ontario Council of Alternative Businesses (OCAB) supports the development of economic literacy and independence for psychiatric survivors in Ontario. Founded in 1993, OCAB actively promotes the idea of "real work for real money" by creating viable economic opportunities. One program, Inspirations, is designed specifically for women artisans with entrepreneurial aspirations.

Inspirations provides workshops on craft-making, marketing, sales techniques and display skills. Participants are encouraged to make arts and crafts, which are then sold at the Inspirations gift boutique and elsewhere. They are also encouraged to develop and share business skills, such as writing business plans, identifying target markets, record-keeping and calculating profit margins.

Option Femmes Emploi

430, boulevard de l'Hôpital, bureau 202
Gatineau (Québec) J8V 1T7
Tel 819-246-1725
Fax 819-246-3884
Contact: Marie-Claude Desjardins, Director

Option Femmes Emploi (OFE) is a not-for-profit organization devoted exclusively to women. Its mission is to improve living conditions for women through their professional development. Its services include employment orientation, job searching, training and entrepreneurship support.

OFE is financed through grants from the provincial ministère de l'Emploi et de la Solidarité, the Société québécoise de développement de la main-d'oeuvre, Human Resources Development Canada and school boards.

A new project for OFE is lending circles for women, which it plans to launch in 1998. The purpose of the project is to introduce the lending circle model, assess participants' potential, assist groups and individuals and provide access to micro-credit. Each lending circle will have five to six members. Participants co-guarantee the loans granted. Contact OFE for details.

P

PARO: A Northwestern Ontario Women's Community Loan Fund

105 May Street North, Suite 110
Thunder Bay ON P7C 3N9
Tel 807-625-0328
Fax 807-625-0317
e-mail rlockyer@microage-tb.com
Contact: Rosalind Lockyer, Loan Fund Co-ordinator

Founded in 1995, PARO: A Northwestern Ontario Women's Community Loan Fund is a grassroots charitable peer-lending organization that aims to increase the economic independence and self-sufficiency of women and their families through initiatives that help them develop their micro-enterprises. Its programs include small business loans, business development training, networking and mentoring, access to information, opportunity to market and enhanced counselling to women starting businesses. The small business loans program uses a peer-lending model. Lending circles have from four to seven women who vouch for each other's character. Loans range from $500 to $3,000 and may be used for start-up or expanding micro-enterprises or home-based businesses. Circle members must also create an emergency fund to cover defaults.

Penticton Entrepreneurial Women's Alumnae

113 - 437 Martin Street, Suite #136
Penticton BC V2A 5L1
Tel 250-490-0644
Fax 250-493-0099
Contact: Daryl Meyers

The Penticton Entrepreneurial Women's Alumnae offers networking and support to women who are in business or interested in starting a business. The Alumnae provides a forum for continuous learning with guest speakers at monthly meetings. It also sponsors and co-ordinates business training and an annual Women in Business Trade Show, giving women in business an occasion to showcase their businesses to the public. The long-term goal of this registered society is to provide an annual scholarship for a female graduate to pursue studies in business.

Projet de relance économique et sociale de quartier

585, rue James, bureau 201
Buckingham (Québec) J8L 2R7
Tel 819-281-5579
Fax 819-281-5522
Contact: Christiane Cloutier, Collective Entrepreneurship Development Agent

Projet de relance économique et sociale de quartier (PRESQ) is a neighbourhood economic and social renewal project that grew out of a partnership with Corporation de développement communautaire Rond Point, the Société d'aide au développement des collectivités of Papineau and the City of Buckingham.

A not-for-profit organization formed in 1997, PRESQ focuses primarily on socio-economic revitalization and the development of entrepreneurship. It supports business enterprises proposed by women and men who face disadvantages in obtaining employment and on young school drop-outs. It is financed by public funds from the City of Buckingham and the provincial Conseil régional and the federal Office of Regional Development in Quebec) and by corporate donations.

In January 1998, PRESQ expanded its area of service to the rural communities and the regional county municipality of Papineau.

Q

Quint Development Corporation

Room 202, 230 Avenue R South
Saskatoon SK S7M 0Z9
Tel 306-978-4041
Fax 306-683-1957
e-mail quint@link.ca
Contact: Gary Wilson

The Quint Development Corporation (QDC) is a non-profit community economic development corporation founded in 1995 by residents to build on the capacities of inner-city Saskatoon neighbourhoods. One objective is to create job opportunities by investing in new businesses and supporting viable existing businesses. The Small Business Loans program provides financial assistance and technical support to individuals who are unable to secure it through traditional lending systems. To qualify for a loan, applicants must be credit worthy, have a viable business plan and show that the business will have a positive impact on the community. Applicants may borrow up to $5,000 to start, expand or upgrade a business. The program is financed by user fees, loan interests, corporate donations, government funding and volunteer support.

R

Regina Economic Development Co-operative for Women

2732 - 13th Avenue
Regina SK S4T 1N3
Tel 306-565-2380

The Regina Economic Development Co-operative for Women is a small business loans association. It makes loans of up to $5,000 to Regina businesswomen who have difficulty getting funding through traditional financial institutions.

Regina Women's Construction Co-operative

P.O. Box 33084
Regina SK S4T 7X2
Tel 306-565-0556
Fax 306-565-3484
Contact: Denise Needham

The mandate of the Regina's Women's Construction Co-operative is to provide women with carpentry apprenticeship experience. It trains Level 2 apprentice carpenters through the Women's Work Training Program under the supervision of qualified journey carpenters. The Co-operative specializes in barrier-free renovations. It also handles general renovations.

Regroupement des femmes La Sentin'elle

218, chemin Gros-Cap
C.P. 862, Cap-aux-Meules
Iles de la Madeleine (Québec) G0B 1B0
Tel 418-986-4334
Fax 418-986-6448
Contact: Linda Déry, Co-ordinator

Founded in 1982, the mandate of Regroupement des femmes La Sentin'elle is to promote the well-being of women living in the Îles de la Madeleine. One of its priorities is to address the issue of poverty among women. It is a not-for-profit organization devoted exclusively to women and is funded through grants from the provincial and federal governments.

For women who wish to develop as entrepreneurs, La Sentin'elle offers support in assessing entrepreneurial potential and helping participants prepare their business plans. The organization is also helping create a soon-to-be-launched businesswomen's association in the Îles de la Madeleine.

Regroupement pour la relance économique et sociale du sud-ouest

1751, rue Richardson, bureau 6509
Montréal (Québec) H3K 1G6
Tel 514-931-5737
Fax 514-931-4317
Website http://www.resol@iq.ca
Contact: Jean-Marie Pressé, Business Support Co-ordinator

The mandate of Regroupement pour la relance économique et sociale du sud-ouest (RESO) is to support the economic and social recovery of Montreal's southwest. Created in 1990, RESO is a community development organization that works with individuals, corporations and unions to develop and implement training programs, create jobs and support entrepreneurs who wish to start businesses. The organization is active in the districts of Saint-Henri, Petite-Bourgogne, Pointe Saint-Charles, Ville Émard, Côte Saint-Paul and Griffintown.

RESO's support for entrepreneurs includes basic training in business start-up, market research, preparing business plans, finding locations and helping the entrepreneur find start-up funds.

Renaissance Montréal

7250, boulevard Saint-Laurent
Montréal (Québec) H2R 2X9
Tel 514-276-3626
Fax 514-276-5899
e-mail renmont@generation.net
Contact: Houcine Mouloudi, Manager, Business Guidance Centre

The mission of Renaissance Montréal is to help individuals and groups participate in the economic life of the community by supporting their efforts to start small businesses. The businesses may be privately owned, not-for-profit or co-operative.

Renaissance Montréal runs a business guidance centre specializing in helping co-operative and not-for-profit organizations get off the ground and eventually become self-financing. The centre offers three-hour training workshops every month on topics such as entrepreneurship awareness, business planning, financial forecasting, marketing and accounting. The training is given by employees of the centre and by mentors from the business community.

Renaissance Montréal also plans to create a business incubator centre where very new businesses may share premises and technical services and have access to mentors.

Founded in 1995, Renaissance Montréal is a not-for-profit organization financed through private donations, grants and income generated by its four second-hand clothing shops. It serves both women and men. At present, more than 60 per cent of its clients are women.

Réseau des femmes d'affaires du Québec

1350, rue Sherbrooke Ouest, bureau 900
Montréal (Québec) H3G 1J1
Toll Free 1-800-332-2683
Tel 514-845-8256
Fax 514-845-3365
Contact: Chantal Chagnon, Market Development Manager, ext. 123

The mandate of this Quebec businesswomen's network is to contribute to the success of businesswomen (entrepreneurs, managers and professionals) by promoting contacts, self-help and a dynamic business network. Founded in 1981 under the name of Association des femmes d'affaires du Québec, Réseau des femmes d'affaires du Québec is a profit-making organization financed through membership fees. Its Montreal head office is run by staff while its regional offices are run by volunteers. It has about 3,000 members. Most are in Quebec, but there are a few in other parts of Canada and it Europe.

Réseau's core activity is running mini-networks called self-help cells. Each cell consists of 15 women who meet once a month to exchange information and give advice based on their fields of expertise. Each cell must have at least one lawyer, one banker and one accountant and usually has about five entrepreneurs. Two-thirds of the 47 cells are in the Greater Montreal region. The rest are located in smaller towns throughout the province.

Réseau also offers advice for beginning or expanding businesses, promotes inter-member buying, operates Step Up®, a Business Development Bank of Canada training and mentoring program, provides speakers and works with its members to develop positions and action plans on issues relevant to women in business.

S

Saskatchewan Women's Institutes

337 Kirk Hall
117 Science Place
University of Saskatchewan
Saskatoon SK S7N 5C8
Tel 306-966-5566

The goals of the Saskatchewan Women's Institutes (S.W.I.) are to provide networking and learning opportunities to rural women through training, workshops and information sharing. The largest rural women's organization in the province, the S.W.I. is working with the Women Entrepreneurs of Saskatchewan to provide workshops throughout the province.

Self-Employment Development Initiatives

130 Spadina Avenue, Suite 405
Toronto ON M5V 2L4
Tel 416-504-8730
Fax 416-504-8738
e-mail info@sedi.org
Website http://www.sedi.org
Contact: Kelly McCormick

Self-Employment Development Initiatives (SEDI) is a non-profit organization formed to promote self-employment as a viable road to self-sufficiency and employment for the unemployed and underemployed. It specializes in helping local agencies and organizations set up programs and deliver services to special needs groups in the community, such as low income or unemployed women. Formed in 1986 and funded primarily by Human Resources Development Canada and corporate donations, SEDI's programs include training in micro-credit, organizational development, self-employment and micro-enterprise. SEDI provides research, policy development, conferences and workshops.

Society for Canadian Women in Science and Technology

535 Hornby Street, Suite 417
Vancouver BC V6C 2E8
Tel 604-895-5814
Fax 604-684-9171
e-mail SCWIST@sfu.ca
Website http://www.harbour.sfu.ca/scwist
Contact: Mary Watt

The Society for Canadian Women in Science and Technology (SCWIST) promotes science and technology careers for women, including starting science-based businesses. Programs and activities include networking events, entrepreneurial training workshops, mentoring matches and labour market surveys.

Step Ahead

7305 Woodbine Avenue, Suite 648
Markham ON L3R 3V7
Tel 416-410-5802
Fax 905-731-9691
e-mail c.klein@utoronto.ca
Contact: Chips Klein, Director

Step Ahead is an association offering one-on-one mentoring for women business owners seeking to expand. Funded by corporate sponsors, such as Coopers & Lybrand, Royal Bank, Fasken Campbell Godfrey and *Profit* magazine, Step Ahead facilitates networking of women business owners, arranges mentor/protégée relationships among members, provides business information and supports the perspective of women business owners to government and business groups. Programs and services include mentoring workshops, monthly meetings with guest speakers, networking sessions, financial resource contacts, a business help hot-line and access to products, services and events for women business owners.

T

Third Thursday Network

c/o Lynn McMinniman
KPMG
Frederick Square
77 Westmoreland Street, Suite 700
Fredericton NB E3B 6Z3
Tel 506-452-8000
Fax 506-450-0072
Contact: Lynn McMinniman, Chair, Core Committee

The Third Thursday Network (TTN) is an organization of Fredericton-area women from various backgrounds and careers who meet to exchange information and increase their circle of social and business contacts. The monthly luncheon meetings are held on the third Thursday in different locations. Most meetings feature a guest speaker and networking. TTN members are encouraged to market themselves and their services. Membership fees are modest.

V

Victoria Women Work! Society

513 - 620 View Street
Victoria BC V8W 1J6
Tel 250-381-7784
Fax 250-381-7734
e-mail wwork@islandnet.com
Contact: Laura Grootveld, Executive Director

The mission of the Victoria Women Work! Society is to help low-income women gain financial independence by helping them turn their skills and talents into opportunities for self-employment.

Founded in 1996, this non-profit charitable organization provides economic, emotional and training resources. These include self-employment assessment workshops, a 16-week entrepreneurial training program and a mentorship program.

Single-parent graduates of Women Work! are eligible for the Women Work! micro-loans. Repayment is tied to their ability to generate income. During the first year of operating their business, graduates also have access to one-on-one and group follow-up support.

West Coast WomenFutures Community Economic Development Society

956 West Broadway, #217
Vancouver BC V6J 1Z2
Tel 604-737-1338
Fax 604-737-4901
Contact: Melanie Caun

West Coast WomenFutures Community Economic Development Society is a non-profit organization that promotes the participation of women in community economic development. Founded in 1985, WomenFutures' programs include education, research and a Loan Guarantee Fund. The Loan Guarantee Fund provides limited financing designed to enable women to participate in community economic development. The purpose is to ensure loan repayment in the event that the women or group can no longer do so.

Women and Rural Economic Development

379 Huron Street
Stratford ON N5A 5T6
Toll Free 1-800-790-9949 (within Ontario)
Tel 519-273-5017
Fax 519-273-4826
e-mail wred@sentex.net
Website http://www.sentex.net/~wred
Contact: Charlene Gordon, Project Manager

Women and Rural Economic Development (WRED) is a non-profit organization dedicated to providing rural women in Ontario with increased participation in rural economic development. Founded in 1993, WRED's programs and services include self-employment training, skills workshops, business women's networks, farm ventures, rural enterprise micro-loans, business consulting, small business seminars, mentorship and business development training. WRED's Business Basics program is a 42-week program designed to help participants aged 18 to 30 develop business plans and find the information and knowledge they need for business start-up. The program uses a combination of lectures, group activities, individual projects, videos, guest speakers and a workbook. WRED's Rural Enterprise Loan Fund offers micro-loans of up to $3,000 to WRED members. Funded by a combination of government and private sector support, WRED also supports community development through information services and promotional activities, such as affiliated networks and enterprise alliances.

Women Business Owners of Canada Inc.

1243 Islington Avenue, Suite 911
Toronto ON M8X 1Y9
Toll Free 1-888-822-WBOC (9262)
Tel 416-236-2000
Fax 416-236-1099
e-mail bsegal@wboc.ca
Website http://www.wboc.ca
Contact: Bunny Segal, Executive Director

The mission of the Women Business Owners of Canada Inc. (WBOC) is to increase business opportunities for women-owned businesses in Canada by providing information, services and support through a strong network of peers. The intent is to act as a catalyst in the success of Canadian women-owned businesses. WBOC is a non-profit organization. Membership is open to associations, women business owners, partners and corporate owners.

Women Entrepreneurs of Canada

3 Church Street, Suite 604
Toronto ON M5E 1M2
Tel 416-361-7036
Fax 416-862-0315
e-mail wec@wec.ca
Website: http://www.wec.ca
Contact: Marilyn Ryder, Administrator

Women Entrepreneurs of Canada (WEC) was founded in 1992 to bring together women who own or control a company to encourage and foster exchange, promote communication and trade in

Canada and abroad, to represent WEC members to media and government and to provide advocacy and support for women entrepreneurs. WEC is the Canadian representative of Les Femmes Chefs d'Enterprises Mondiale (FCEM), the largest organization of women business owners in the world. WEC's program includes guest speakers, meetings, workshops, seminars, promotional events, conferences, trade shows and exhibits. To be eligible for membership, a woman must have been a business owner for a minimum of four years. WEC has chapters in Toronto and Vancouver.

Women Entrepreneurs of Saskatchewan Inc.

Toll Free 1-800-879-6331 (within Saskatchewan)

Saskatoon Office
2100 Eighth Street East, Suite 112
Saskatoon SK S7H 0V1
Tel 306-477-7173
Fax 306-477-7175

Regina Office
2124B Robinson Street
Regina SK S4T 2P7
Tel 306-359-9732
Fax 306-359-9739
e-mail women@the.link.ca
Contact: Laura Small, Executive Director

Women Entrepreneurs of Saskatchewan (W.E.) is a non-profit organization for women planning, starting or operating a business. Funded by Western Economic Diversification (a federal government department), W.E.'s priority is to help women in Saskatchewan reach their entrepreneurial goals. W.E.'s programs and services include seminars, resource kits, networking, mentoring and access to a loan fund. W.E. also operates chapters for women in rural areas and programs for young women, including girls.

Women's Business Network

P.O. Box 3941
Whitehorse YK Y1A 5M6
Tel 867-668-3600
Fax 867-668-6489
Website http://www.yukonweb.com/business/wbn/

Founded in 1989, the Women's Business Network (WBN) is a non-political, voluntary organization formed to provide opportunities for women in Yukon to establish business and personal relationships. WBN encourages the exchange of education and business-related ideas and information and promotes the development of leadership, communication and management skills. Activities include meetings, workshops and a quarterly newsletter.

Women's Business Network Association of Ottawa

1200E Prince of Wales Drive
Ottawa ON K2C 1M9
Tel 613-723-7233
fax 613-723-8792
Contact: Lynn Anderson, Administrator

The purpose of the Women's Business Network Association of Ottawa (WBN) is to provide opportunities for established businesswomen in the Ottawa/Carleton region to network, share expertise and knowledge and promote the business interests of its members. Founded in 1982, WBN is a non-profit association with a membership mix of women who have owned their own businesses for at least two years, who earn a significant portion of their income from commissioned sales and who hold senior private sector management positions.

The WBN's programs include a Mentorship Program aimed at assessing and grooming potential new members. To qualify, a woman must be sponsored by a WBN member, willing to serve on a WBN committee and willing to become a full member when eligible. The Mentorship member and her mentor meet for approximately two hours per month. Other WBN activities include an annual Businesswoman's Achievement Award, an Ottawa-area businesswomen's directory (updated annually), meetings, workshops and social events.

Women's Enterprise Centre

240 Graham Avenue, Suite 130
Winnipeg MB R3C 0J7
Toll Free 1-800-203-2343 (within Manitoba)
Tel 204-988-1860
Fax 204-988-1871

TTY 204-988-1870

Website http:/www.mbnet.mb.ca/wec/

The objective of the Women's Enterprise Centre is to offer a range of services to encourage and assist women to start or expand businesses. Funded by Western Economic Diversification (a federal government department), the Centre offers business workshops and seminars, an on-site resource centre, access to business advisors, networking, mentoring and counselling services and loans of up to $100,000. It has offices in Winnipeg, Brandon, The Pas and Thompson.

Women's Enterprise Society of B.C.

2070 Harvey Avenue, Unit 14
Kelowna BC V1Y 8P8
Tel 250-868-3454
Fax 250-868-2709
e-mail wesbc@silk.net
Website http://www.wes.bc.ca
Contact: Diana Groffen, Executive Director

The Women's Enterprise Society of B.C. (WES) was formed to encourage the establishment and growth of women-owned and -controlled businesses in British Columbia. Funded by Western Economic Diversification (a federal government department), WES's mission is based on the principle that encouraging women-directed businesses will strengthen and diversify the B.C. economy, encourage job creation through self-employment and business development and promote economic equality between men and women.

The Women's Information and Support Centre of Halton

Hopedale Mall
1515 Rebecca Street, Suite 301
Oakville ON L6L 5G8
Tel 905-847-5520
Fax 905-847-7413
e-mail netwomen@globalserve.net
Contact: Mary Koster, Director

The Women's Information and Support Centre of Halton (known as The Women's Centre) is a charitable organization that offers a safe, caring haven for women in Halton Region. Programs and services include workshops, courses, a library and peer counsellors. In 1997, the Centre launched Smart Start, a three-month self-employment training program for women who wish to become entrepreneurs. The Centre also sells the *Eight Steps to Self-Employment: A Practical Guide for Women* and *Smart Start: Ten Steps to Running a Self-Employment Training Program for Women*. The Centre is funded by the Ontario Women's Directorate, program and membership fees and the United Way.

Women's World Finance/Cape Breton Association (WWF/CBA)

P.O. Box 1142, 54 Prince Street
Sydney NS B1P 6J7
Tel 902-562-8845
Fax 902-562-4273
e-mail bace@auracom.com
Website http:/www.bizbureau.com/wwf

Women's World Financing/Cape Breton Association (WWF/CBA) is the only Canadian affiliate of Women's World Banking, a global not-for-profit financial institution. WWF/CBA was incorporated in 1989 as a not-for-profit organization concerned with women entrepreneurs in Cape Breton. In 1996 WWF/CBA expanded its mandate to cover women entrepreneurs throughout Atlantic Canada and launched a program to build a stronger network in the region. One project was a study, *Measure the Economic Impact of Women Business Owners in Atlantic Canada*, published in July 1997.

YMCA Small Business Development Centre

42 Charles Street East, 9th floor
Toronto ON M4Y 1T4
Tel 416-928-3362
Fax 416-928-3325
Contact: Sally Wilkie, ext. 4057

The Young Women's Entrepreneurship Program is a project funded by the Government of Canada and run by The YMCA of Greater Toronto at its Small Business Development Centre. The program is similar to the 1996 pilot, which was designed for women aged 18 to 29 who were highly motivated to start their own businesses. Participants were required to have a specific business idea and the drive and determination to develop the idea into a viable business. The 10-month program was divided into two segments. Segment 1 (four months) consisted of intensive workshops, seminars and assignments designed to provide the women with all the information they needed to write and present a business plan. Segment 2 (six months) consisted of consulting services to help participants implement their business plans. Participants received child care and training allowances, were partnered with banker-mentors, were given access to business equipment and were given opportunities to display their products and services at trade shows.

YMCA Notre-Dame-de-Grâce

Aurora Business Project
4335, avenue Hampton
Montréal (Québec) H4A 2L3
Tel 514-486-2640, extension 238
Fax 514-486-6574
Contact: Debbie Harrison, Director, Community Economic Development

The YMCA is a charitable association run by staff and volunteers. Its mandate is to offer programs and services that contribute to personal growth and service to others.

In 1994, the Notre-Dame-de-Grâce YMCA launched the Aurora Business Project for low-income English-speaking women with business ideas. The purpose of the project is to provide training, access to micro-credit and follow-up meetings and technical support.

The training deals with introduction to entrepreneurship, business and personal skills development and making the lending circle work. Lending circles are made up of four to seven members. Credit is provided by the Royal Bank. Each member may borrow up to $1,000 at first and up to $2,000 for each subsequent loan. The members of each circle have follow-up meetings twice a month.

The Aurora Business Project is financed by the provincial Fonds de lutte contre la pauvreté. In its first three years, it has helped 76 women. In 1997, there were four active lending circles.

YWCA of Calgary

Women's Trades Centre
320-5 Avenue S.E.
Calgary AB T2G 0E5
Tel 403-750-2501
Fax 403-262-0494
e-mail ywwecs@freenet.calgary.ab.ca
Website http://freenet.calgary.ab.ca/wecs/main.html
Contact: Jacquie Kelly, Administrative Assistant (Tel 403-294-7332)

The mandate of the Women's Trade Centre (WTC) is to promote women into and support women in the building industry in both working and entrepreneurial roles. WTC programs include a pre-apprenticeship trades program, mentoring, networking and guest speakers. A new initiative is the WTC home renovation business project. A 1996 feasibility study indicated a market strong enough to support a home renovation business operated by women. The WTC developed a five-year business plan with the goal of starting the business, making it profitable and using the profits to subsidize other WTC initiatives. The YWCA of Calgary's WTC partners include Women and Economic Development Consortium, Human Resources Development Canada, Southern Alberta Institute of Technology, Wild Rose WITT and Habitat for Humanity.

Additional Resources

Government Offices Responsible for Women's Issues

The following government offices worked with the Ontario Women's Directorate and The Women Entrepreneurs of Canada Foundation to develop *Fast Forward*. They are a good source of information about government or government-related programs and resources for women, including women entrepreneurs, in their jurisdictions.

For example, the Ontario Women's Directorate published *Opening Doors: A Woman's Guide to Ontario Government Programs and Services*. This booklet overviews services and programs to open doors to women and economic self-sufficiency as well as education and training, health and social programs, justice related services, communities and volunteer opportunities.

In Manitoba, the Women's Initiative Program of the Manitoba Business Resource Centre published *Entrepreneur's Resource Guide for Manitoba Women*. This booklet lists business programs and services, economic development organizations, non-government women's groups and contact numbers for more information about what's going on in the province.

Alberta

Human Rights and Citizenship Branch Alberta Community Development

Standard Life Centre, Room 800
10405 Jasper Avenue
Edmonton AB T5J 4R7
Tel 403-427-3116
Fax 403-422-3563
Website http://www.gov.ab.ca/~mcd/mcd.htm

British Columbia

Ministry of Women's Equality

712 Yates Street, 5th floor
Victoria BC V8V 1X4
Tel 250-387-0413
Fax 250-356-9377
Mailing Address
P.O. Box 9899, Stn. Prov. Govt.
Victoria BC V8W 9T9
Website http://www.weq.gov.bc.ca

Canada

Status of Women Canada

Constitution Square
350 Albert Street, 5th floor
Ottawa ON K1A 1C3
Mailing Address
700 - 360 Albert Street
Ottawa ON K1A 1C3
Tel 613-995-7835
Fax 613-947-0530
Website http://www.swc-cfc.gc.ca

Manitoba

Manitoba Women's Directorate

100 - 175 Carlton Street
Winnipeg MB R3C 3H9
Tel 204-945-3476
Fax 204-945-0013

New Brunswick

Status of Women

Executive Council Office
670 King Street
Fredericton NB E3B 5H1
Mailing Address
P.O. Box 6000

Fredericton NB E3B 5H1
Tel 506-453-2071
Fax 506-453-2266
Website http://www.gov.nb.ca/sw_cf/index.htm

Newfoundland and Labrador

Women's Policy Office

4th floor, West Block, Confederation Building
St. John's NF A1B 4J6
Mailing Address
P.O. Box 8700
St. John's NF A1B 4J6
Tel 709-729-5098
Fax 709-729-2331
Website http://www.gov.nf.ca

Northwest Territories

Status of Women Council of N.W.T.

5017 49th Street
Yellowknife NWT X1A 2L9
Mailing Address
P.O. Box 1320
Yellowknife NWT X1A 2L9
Tel 867-920-6177
Fax 867-873-0285
Website http://users.internorth.com/~swcnwt

Nova Scotia

Nova Scotia Advisory Council on the Status of Women

6169 Quinpool Road, Suite 202
Halifax NS B3J 4P8
Mailing Address
P.O. Box 745
Halifax NS B3J 2T3
Tel 902-424-8664
Fax 902-424-0573
Website http://www.gov.ns.ca/staw/

Ontario

Ontario Women's Directorate

Mowat Block, 6th floor
900 Bay Street
Toronto ON M7A 1L2
Tel 416-314-0300
Fax 416-314-0256
Website http://www.gov.on.ca/owd

Prince Edward Island

Interministerial Women's Secretariat

Shaw Building, 3rd floor
95 Rochford Street
Charlottetown PEI C1A 7N8
Mailing Address
P.O. Box 2000
Charlottetown PEI C1A 7N8
Tel 902-368-6494
Fax 902-368-6144
Website http://www.gov.pe.ca/pt/index.asp

Québec

Le Secrétariat à la Condition féminine

1050, des Parlementaires, 3e étage
Québec (Québec) G1R 5Y9
Tel 418-643-9052
Fax 418-643-4991

Saskatchewan

Saskatchewan Women's Secretariat

1855 Victoria Avenue, 7th floor
Regina SK S4P 3V5
Tel 306-787-2329
Fax 306-787-2058
Website http://www.gov.sk.ca/womsec

Yukon

Yukon Women's Directorate

204 Lambert Street, 4th floor
Whitehorse YK Y1A 3T2
Mailing Address
P.O. Box 2703
Whitehorse YK Y1A 2C6
Tel 867-667-3030
Fax 867-393-6270
Website http://www.yukonweb.com/government/womensdir/

Other Sources of Information and Resources

There are many other places to get help with entrepreneurship. Governments — federal, provincial and local — provide a broad range of programs and resources in addition to the local organizations listed here. For example, both Human Resources Development Canada and Industry Canada offer programs in partnership with provincial/territorial governments and the private sector.

Educational institutions (such as universities, community colleges and school boards), business associations (such as The Board of Trade and the Chamber of Commerce), financial institutions (banks, trust companies and credit unions) and corporations offer seminars, workshops, courses, mentoring programs and other opportunities for entrepreneurs. Often, these opportunities are offered free-of-charge or at a nominal cost.

While some programs and resources are developed specifically for women entrepreneurs, there are many from which both women and men can benefit. With Internet access, it is possible to not only reach the websites listed in this directory, but also link to other programs or organizations where resources and supports are available, especially through provincial government home pages. If Internet access is not available, contacts to government offices can be found in the blue pages of local telephone directories.

Here are some examples of programs and services across the country.

Federal Government

Industry Canada

Strategis is Industry Canada's website that provides expertise and information resources on entrepreneurship. Industry Canada also operates such programs as Aboriginal Business Canada, which provides business services and support to Canadian status and non-status Indians, Inuit and Métis individuals and to associations and organizations owned or controlled by Aboriginal people on or off reserve.

Website http://www.strategis.ic.gc.ca

Human Resources Development Canada (HRDC)

HRDC funds such programs as Self-Employment Development Initiatives (SEDI) programs for women, Aboriginal peoples, persons with disabilities and members of visible minorities. The programs themselves are run by community partners, such as community colleges and charitable organizations.

HRDC also funds the Youth Entrepreneurship Program for young people aged 18 to 30. It is designed to help them start their own businesses and succeed by providing entrepreneurial training, business plan development, business counselling, mentorship and aftercare.

Website http://www.hrdc-drhc.gc.ca

Atlantic Canada Opportunities Agency (ACOA)

The ACOA is a federal government agency that provides support to entrepreneurs in Atlantic Canada. The support includes financing for capital projects, feasibility studies, innovations development, marketing development, human resource development, supplier development and business support. ACOA has offices in Moncton, Fredericton, Charlottetown, Halifax, Sydney and St John's as well as in Ottawa. The mail toll-free number is 1-800-561-7862.

Website http://www.acoa.ca

Federal-Provincial Initiatives

Canadian Business Service Centres

All provinces have joint venture federal-provincial Canadian Business Service Centres (CBSC). Entrepreneurs can get answers to questions on supports available to them.

Website http://www.cbsc.org

Here is a list of the CBSCs across the country.

Alberta

The Business Link Business Service Centre
Ste. 100, 10237-104 Street
Edmonton AB T5J 1B1
Tel 403-422-7722
Toll Free 1-800-272-9675
Fax 403-422-0055
Website http://www.cbsc.org/alberta/index.html
e-mail buslink@cbsc.ic.gc.ca

British Columbia

Canada/British Columbia Business Service Centre

601 West Cordova Street
Vancouver BC V6B 1G1
Tel 604-775-5525
Toll Free 1-800-667-2272 (within British Columbia)
Fax 604-775-5520
Website http://www.sb.gov.bc.ca/smallbus/sbhome.html
e-mail (to the bookstore) dixon.glen@cbsc.ic.gc.ca

Manitoba

Canada/Manitoba Business Service Centre

250-240 Graham Avenue
P.O. Box 2609
Winnipeg MB R3C 4B3
Tel 204-984-2272
Toll Free 1-800-665-2019 (within Manitoba)
Fax 204-983-3852
Website http://www.cbsc.org/manitoba/index.html
e-mail manitoba@cbsc.ic.gc.ca

New Brunswick

Canada/New Brunswick Business Service Centre

570 Queen Street
Fredericton NB E3B 6Z6
Tel 506-444-6140
Toll Free 1-800-668-1010 (within New Brunswick)
Fax 506-444-6172
TTY 800-887-6550
Website http://www.cbsc.org/nb/index.html
e-mail cbscnb@cbsc.ic.gc.ca

Newfoundland and Labrador

Canada Business Service Centre

90 O'Leary Avenue
P.O. Box 8687
St. John's NF A1B 3T1

Tel 709-772-6022
Toll Free 1-800-668-1010 (within Newfoundland and Labrador)
Fax 709-772-6090
Website http://www.cbsc.org/nfld/index.html
e-mail st.johns@cbsc.ic.gc.ca

Northwest Territories

Canada/Northwest Territories Business Service Centre

P.O. Box 1320
8th Floor Scotia Centre
Yellowknife NWT X1A 2L9
Tel 867-873-7958
Toll Free 1-800-661-0599
Fax 867-873-0101
Website http://www.cbsc.org/nwt/index.html
e-mail yel@cbsc.ic.gc.ca

Nova Scotia

Canada/Nova Scotia Business Service Centre

1575 Brunswick Street
Halifax NS B3J 2G1
Tel 902-426-8604
Toll Free 1-800-668-1010 (within Nova Scotia)
Fax 902-426-6530
TTY 800-797-4188
Website http://www.cbsc.org/ns/index.html
e-mail halifax@cbsc.ic.gc.ca

Ontario

Canada – Ontario Business Call Centre

151 Yonge Street, 9th floor
Toronto ON M5C 2W7
Tel 416-954-INFO (4636)
Toll Free 1-800-567-2345 (within Ontario)
Fax 416-954-8597
Website http://www.cbsc.org/ontario/index.html
e-mail cobec@cbsc.ic.gc.ca

Prince Edward Island

Canada/Prince Edward Island Business Service Centre

75 Fitzroy Street
P.O. Box 40
Charlottetown PEI C1A 7K2
Tel 902-368-0771
Toll Free 1-800-668-1010 (within Prince Edward Island)
Fax 902-566-7377
TTY 902-368-0724
Website http://www.cbsc.org/pei/index.html
e-mail pei@cbsc.ic.gc.ca

Québec

Info entrepreneurs

5, Place Ville Marie
Suite 12500, Plaza Level
Montreal (Québec) H3B 4Y2
Tel 514-496-INFO (4636)
Toll Free 1-800-322-INFO (4636)
Fax 514-496-5934
Website http://www.infoentrepreneurs.org
e-mail infoentrepreneurs@cbsc.ic.gc.ca

Saskatchewan

Canada/Saskatchewan Business Service Centre

122 - 3rd Avenue North
Saskatoon SK S7K 2H6
Tel 306-956-2323
Toll Free 1-800-667-4374
Fax 306-956-2328
Website http://www.cbsc.org/sask/index.html
e-mail saskatooncbsc@cbsc.ic.gc.ca

Yukon

Canada/Yukon Business Service Centre

201-208 Main Street
Whitehorse YK Y1A 2A9

Tel 867–633–6257
Toll Free 1–800–661–0543
Fax 867–667–2001
Website http://www.cbsc.org/yukon/index.html
e-mail perry.debbie@cbsc.ic.gc.ca

Provinces/Territories

Every province has programs and services designed to support self-employment and entrepreneurship initiatives.

Ontario, like the other provinces, has a department responsible for small business development. The Ontario Ministry of Economic Development, Trade and Tourism offers a number of different programs and services for entrepreneurs. Here are some examples.

Business Self-Help Offices

Ontario has self-directed resource centres, called Business Self-Help Offices, where entrepreneurs can get information on starting a small business and attend entrepreneurship skill development seminars. They are managed by the Ministry of Economic Development, Trade and Tourism in co-operation with the local municipalities in which they are located.
Website http://www.ontario-canada.com

Ontario Business Connects

Entrepreneurs can access business registration and licence information, conduct business name searches and apply for permits at 61 Ontario Business Connect work stations located throughout the province.
Website http://www.ccr.gov.on.ca.obscon/welcome.htm

On-Line-Only Resources

Some very interesting and helpful information and resources are available only via the Internet. These are just a few of the many that can be found.

The Canadian Business Women's Network

This on-line network serves as an access point for more than 30 related websites, such as the American Express Small Business Exchange, the Canadian Youth Foundation, Developing a Co-Operative, Franchise Handbook, TD Bank's How to Succeed in

Your Home Based Business and the Marketing Tools Directory. Website http://www.cdnbizwomen.com/resources/bizdev.shtm.

The Canadian Youth Business Foundation

This non-profit, private-sector initiative is designed to provide mentoring, business support and lending to young Canadian entrepreneurs (women and men) who are creating new businesses. Youth Business was formed by the Canadian Youth Foundation in partnership with CIBC and Royal Bank. The Foundation's programs and services are designed to complement existing programs for young entrepreneurs. Most Youth Business programs provide support from start-up through to the first three years of operation.

Website http://www.cybf.ca/frames/index/htm

Financial Institutions

Financial institutions are an excellent source of information and resources. Nearly all the major chartered banks, trust companies and credit unions provide information or other support for owners and operators of small and medium-size businesses.

Business Development Bank of Canada (BDC)

BDC offers training, mentoring and counselling programs designed specifically for women and micro-entrepreneurs.

Toll Free 1-800-INFO-BDC
Website http://www.bdc.ca/

Canadian Bankers Association

The Canadian Bankers Association provides small and medium-sized businesses with publications tailored to their banking and financial needs.

Toll Free 1-800-263-0231
Website http://www.cba.ca

Consulting Firms

Entrepreneurs themselves have been quick to see opportunities in providing programs, services and materials to other entrepreneurs. Here are some examples.

Mentor Information Systems

Mentor Information Systems,
2453 Currie Road, Victoria BC V8S 3B6
Tel 250-592-1071, Fax 250-592-1021
e-mail deanna@enviroenterprise.com

Mentor Information Systems sells a Canadian entrepreneurial training program developed by a team of self-employed men and women to self-employment training agencies, such as Community Futures Corporations and Economic Development Commissions. Designed to be used by self-employed individuals during the first year of business start-up, Mentor pays special attention to women entrepreneurs. A 500-page binder covers a comprehensive list of topics related to starting and running a micro-enterprise. It also includes 13 training course outlines (with overhead slides for trainers) and the Entrepreneurial Assets Test. A youth edition designed for entrepreneurs aged 15 to 25 is designed for use by educators with students.

Service d'Aide aux Jeunes Entrepreneurs

Service d'Aide aux Jeunes Entrepreneurs (SAJE), 6774, rue Sherbrooke Est, bureau 101, Montréal (Québec) H1N 1E1
Tel 514-253-1774, Fax 514-253-0328

SAJE is a not-for-profit management consulting firm which acts as a catalyst for economic development by transferring the knowledge and tools needed for good management by young entrepreneurs and by encouraging their independence. Founded in 1985, SAJE works with governments, financial institutions, colleges and universities. It is part of a national network assisting entrepreneurs.

Women and Money Inc.

Women and Money Inc., 468 Queen Street East, 5th floor, Toronto ON M5A 1T7
Tel 416-367-3677, Fax 416-367-1591

This Toronto-based consulting firm specializes in education and entrepreneurship. Women and Money Inc.'s mandate is to educate women about money and educate financial institutions about women. Founder and President Joanne Thomas Yaccato also writes financial advice columns for magazines, speaks on financial issues at conferences, seminars and workshops and is the author of *Balancing Act: A Canadian Woman's Financial Success Guide.*

Publications

Women Like Me, The Entrepreneurial Networking Directory

Women Like Me Inc., 53 Mallory Crescent, Toronto ON M4G 3L6
Tel 416-696-7621, Fax 416-429-1081
e-mail kfraser@mailexcite.com

Women Like Me Inc. publishes a networking directory that lists women who own or operate their own business. The directory, *Women Like Me, The Entrepreneurial Networking Directory*, lists individuals by type of business (for example, business and professional services, communications and information technology, image and personal development) and organizations (professional associations, networks, support services). The directory is published annually and is distributed through bookstores, by mail order and at *Women Like Me* events.

Women: Toronto Women's Quarterly Newsmagazine

WOMAN newsmagazine, 422 Parliament Street, P.O. Box 82510 Toronto ON M5A 3A0
Tel 416-920-6849
Toll Free 1-800-775-1238
Fax 416-920-8548
e-mail woman@web.net
Website http://www.web.net/~woman

Publisher Elizabeth Scott created this newsmagazine as an information resource for women. It deals with issues common to women in categories such as Profiles, News, Finances & Business, Technology and Arts & Creativity. Published quarterly in September, November, February and May, it is available by subscription and in bookstores and on news stands in many parts of Canada.

Index

Educating women about money and educating financial institutions about women.

Raising Your Business and *Balancing Act* are available in bookstores across Canada. Women and Money Inc. offers corporate rates on offers of 10 or more. To book training and consulting services, hire Joanne as a keynote speaker or to order books in volume, please call or email us at:

Women and Money Inc.
468 Queen St. E.
5th Floor
Toronto, ON
M5A 1T7
Tel: (416) 367-3677
Fax: (416) 367-1591
women@womenandmoneyinc.com

Joanne Thomas Yaccato is the president and founder of the Toronto-based consulting firm Women and Money Inc. Her company specializes in education and research in the area of women as consumers, investors and entrepreneurs. The company's flagship course, *Reaching the Women's Market*, was cited as a "best practice" at the 1998 international APEC conference on Gender and Lifelong Learning held in Taipei.

Joanne's personal experience and hilarious misadventures as a financial reprobate are well documented in her best-selling book *Balancing Act: A Canadian Woman's Financial Success Guide* (Revised Edition), which has sold an impressive 50,000 copies. In the spirit of *Balancing Act*, she continues her journey with *Raising Your Business: A Canadian Woman's Guide to Entrepreneurship*, with Paula Jubinville.

Joanne is a sought-after lecturer on the national speaking circuit and has chaired and spoken at several international conferences from New York to the Caribbean, covering topics that range from women and wealth management to selling and marketing financial services to women.

For more information about Women and Money Inc., visit our website at www.womenandmoneyinc.com. For pricing and ordering information on *Raising Your Business*, you can also visit us at www.raisingyourbusiness.com.

AQUEOUS Advisory Group Inc. has pioneered providing comprehensive, real-life business advice and support to Canadian entrepreneurs and is acknowledged for its unique and special focus on women business owners.

So whether you are:

- thinking about becoming an entrepreneur
- just starting up or now wanting to take your business to the next level, or
- are responsible for helping your organization or association provide proven programs that offer advice and support to this dynamic and fast growing market segment

AQUEOUS Advisory Group offers a unique combination of business expertise, advisory experience and entrepreneurial perspective through a suite of business advisory services.

TeleAdvisor Business Series
Emerging Entrepreneurs Program
Entrepreneurs Support Line

Our innovative business coaching and entrepreneurial outplacement programs are specifically designed to help you achieve your business and personal objectives.

For detailed information about our services and programs for entrepreneurs and corporations targeting the entrepreneurial market, or if you would like to hire Paula Jubinville as a speaker for your next event or seminar, contact us at:

AQUEOUS Advisory Group Inc.
478 Queen Street East, Suite 300
Toronto, ON Canada M5A 1T7
t: (416) 366-9669 or 1-888-228-5518
f: (416) 366-9663
e: info@aqueous.ca

Real-life, real-time business advice & support for Canadian entrepreneurs starting, running & growing their businesses

Visit our website @
www.aqueous.ca

To order Raising Your Business in volume, either contact AQUEOUS or visit www.raisingyourbusiness.com for pricing and order information.